Critical Management Ethics

Also by Thomas Klikauer

COMMUNICATION AND MANAGEMENT AT WORK

MANAGEMENT COMMUNICATION: Communicative Action and Ethics

Critical Management Ethics

Thomas Klikauer

palgrave
macmillan

First published 2010 by
PALGRAVE MACMILLAN

Palgrave Macmillan in the UK is an imprint of Macmillan Publishers Limited, registered in England, company number 785998, of Houndmills, Basingstoke, Hampshire RG21 6XS.

Palgrave Macmillan in the US is a division of St Martin's Press LLC, 175 Fifth Avenue, New York, NY 10010.

Palgrave Macmillan is the global academic imprint of the above companies and has companies and representatives throughout the world.

Palgrave® and Macmillan® are registered trademarks in the United States, the United Kingdom, Europe and other countries

ISBN 978-0-230-23825-1 hardback

This book is printed on paper suitable for recycling and made from fully managed and sustained forest sources. Logging, pulping and manufacturing processes are expected to conform to the environmental regulations of the country of origin.

A catalogue record for this book is available from the British Library.

A catalog record for this book is available from the Library of Congress.

10   9   8   7   6   5   4   3   2   1
19 18 17 16 15 14 13 12 11 10

Printed and bound in Great Britain by
CPI Antony Rowe, Chippenham and Eastbourne

This book is dedicated to

Josef Klikauer

1st *October 1895 to 20th October 1944; born in Konstantynów, Poland; executed at the Nazi Concentration Camp Gross Rosen, Rogoźnicy (http://www.gross-rosen.pl). All royalties from the sale of this book will be donated to the Gross Rosen Museum at Rogoźnicy.*

Contents

Acknowledgements

I would like to acknowledge the assistance, critique, and help on the initial idea for this book: Peter Singer, Gary Weaver, and Robert Phillips. I would also like to acknowledge the proofreading and editorial assistance support of, firstly, my adored wife, Katja and my friend Khalida Malik without whom this book would not have been possible. This book has received no administrative, technical, and editorial support or funding from UWS. I am grateful for IT support by my friend Mark Evans who assembled a computer for me out of old parts and eventually updated it to a workable level and to Louise Ingersoll and others at UWS' IR teaching-group who provided a fountain of administrative knowledge to me shielding me from the worst excesses of Managerialism.

List of Tables

1
Introducing Critical Management Ethics

Many books in the area of management ethics are written under the premise that ethics relates positively, if not affirmatively, to management, business, and corporations. Inside this most common approach to management ethics, ethics is subsumed under the domineering ideas of management. Rather than outlining the relationship between management *and* ethics, ethics is constructed as the management *of* ethics. Rather than viewing management ethics as part of philosophy or applied philosophy, management ethics is seen as part of management. Hence, management ethics is not a branch of management philosophy but a branch of management studies. The emphasis in management ethics is on management, not on ethics. Therefore, management ethics is not viewed as a philosophical study of morals but a study of management morality – minus philosophy which takes the backseat. Management ethics has been turned into a departmental issue like operations, marketing, sales, Human Resource Management (HRM), etc. that needs to be managed.[1] This tends to set tight parameters for the role ethics can play inside the framework of management and its ideological outgrowth of *Managerialism*.[2]

Anchored so deeply inside corporations and society, Managerialism has become the all encompassing ideology of everyday life as *we all learn to think like managers* and accept that *society always has managers* (according to the *Harvard Business Review* Editor Magretta, 2002). With the mass-acceptance of this, Managerialism can even be portrayed as the *end of ideology* because it has been successfully merged with everyday life.[3] Not uncommon for any ideology, however, remains the fact that the exact opposite is usually the case. The reality of everyday life and management can never be converted into pure ideology. Still, selected parts of almost any ethics from Aristotle's *virtue ethics*

1

(384–322 BC) to Kant's *means-ends imperatives* (1724–1804) are used to support management. This process converts ethics into pure ideology. Ethics has been adjusted to the managerial orbit without impacting on managerial practice. Consequently, it has been degraded from being a philosophy to being merely *knowledge in the service of power*.

Under such an imperative, the role of ethics is often reduced to a supportive function of management. It services as an auxiliary to *value creation* which is the managerial codeword for shareholder values and profit maximisation. In sharp contrast to management's use of the term *value*, philosophy applies the same term to something totally different.[4] For ethics, *values* are linked to the philosophy of values. For management only the hard values such as *shareholder values* count. Only when something – marketing, sales, operations, HRM, and even ethics – adds to shareholder value, it is of value to management.

Therefore, in the mind of a manager, ethics and morality are often seen as '*Oh, well, it's all just a matter of opinion, anyway*'. For many managers morality is an issue of a specific *situation* that relates to ethics rather than an overall, basic, and essential part of what they do. In other cases, ethics is reduced to the ten ethical misconceptions one of which is: *some see it that way, others see it differently*.[5] In sum, when the operation of management and *The Real Bottom Line* is not concerned, many managers suffer – sometimes rather conveniently – from *moral attention deficit disorder* (MADD), moral silence, moral deafness, moral blindness, and moral amnesia (Jacoby 1977; Bird 1996).

If ethics is being considered by managers at all, it has to add value to their organisational goals, another codeword of management's bottom line of profits. Management always has to come first and ethics, if it is of value to management, comes later. Ethics is simply a somewhat distant *add-on* to management like *milk in a coffee*, if needed at all.[6] Such *use* of ethics also appears to be the guiding imperative for almost all textbooks in the area of management. In sum, the philosophy of ethics is reduced to operate under the simple and thought limiting equation of: *management + ethics = management ethics* (M+E=ME). This however is nothing but *The Banality of Evil* (Arendt 1994).[7]

In contrast to this formula, one can never simply subsume ethics under management. For one, Kant's *categorical imperative* demands that this has to be done the other way around. For perhaps the greatest ethical philosopher ever – *Immanuel Kant* (1724–1804), the sage of Königsberg – ethics sets *determinants*, *imperatives*, and *musts*. Everything has to measure up to ethics. Ethics cannot be used to supply legitimacy to anything, at the least to management. Kantian ethics is the total negation of the standard M+E=ME approach metered out in almost all textbooks on management ethics. Most commonly, and most wrongly, textbook writers who follow the M+E=ME formula are part of an entourage of affirmative writers on management ethics. They have turned the philosophy of ethics into a pure ideology misusing ethical knowledge to serve managerial power (Baritz 1960; Jacoby 1977). Such uncritical, affirmative, and highly accommodating textbook writers are left with Hirschman's (1970) famous three options of *loyalty, exit, and voice*. They can be: a) uncritically positive (loyalty); b) critically negative (exit); or c) problematic (voice).

a.   The uncritically positive

For affirmative management writers, ethics that is deemed to be positive (M+E=ME) is extended, used, applied, and highlighted through invented cases about so-called managerial reality. Often this is done by compiling real ethics from semi-proper philosophy books and applying those selected versions of ethics to a made-up version of textbook-style management. It is positive because it uses ethics as a plus (+) to management, thus avoiding critical discussion by *negating the negative*. Anything that conflicts management's idea is left out. This is the approach of indifference. Philosopher Hegel (1770–1832) noted that truth lies in the *point of difference* (+/–). One has to see both sides instead of adding one to the other as done in the M+E=ME approach.

Hegel thought that everything has positives and negatives. Once these two different phenomena – one being positive and one being negative – are brought into a relationship with each other, truth will emerge. The core problem of positive management ethics is, however, that it is not directed towards truth but towards the support and legitimacy of management in a very positive way. As a result, most management ethics is not even Hegelian in character. Every version of ethics that is deemed beneficial, positive, non-contradictory, and *indifferent* to management is phrased as non-controversial and good. Hegelian negatives and contradictions are framed as bad. They are to be denied and their representatives to be isolated and marginalised.

Not surprisingly, the entourage of positive, supportive, and accommodating management ethics writers fulfils what 20th century German philosopher Marcuse (1966) described as: *the intellectual and emotional refusal 'to go along' appears neurotic and impotent.* In order not to be labelled *neurotic and impotent* non-critical and affirmative management ethics writers cannot write *philosophical* ethics but reduce their writing to so-called *management ethics* in the M+E=ME style. *The Servants of Power* (Baritz 1960) do this in order to fit ethics into the prevailing managerial paradigm under the formula: *management ethics = ethics that does not contradict management*. But in some cases proper philosophical ethics cannot be *(mis)*-used to support management. In those cases, ethics is deemed to be unsupportive, contradictory, controversial, and a negation of management.

b.   The critical negative

Negatives or the negation of management through ethics occurs where ethics and management are in conflict. This happens when there are tensions and contradictions between ethics and management.[8] For affirmative writers on management ethics, however, this is most unproblematic. In their version of management ethics, ethics presents an easy option that can be diminished and rendered unmentioned. Proper philosophical ethics is often isolated, excluded, marginalised, segregated, and detached from management.[9] This fulfils Hirschman's (1970) *exit option* because contradictory ethics which, in the eyes of affirmative management writers, fails to support management is quietly exited through the backdoor of textbooks on management ethics. All that remains in such textbooks is a small number of cases of *bad apples* showcasing a few wrongs of management to implicitly support and legitimise the majority of so-called morally good management.[10]

Today's management students are largely kept in blissful ignorance to the enlightening potentials of *critical philosophy* that some have argued started with the founder of modern ethics, Immanuel Kant. To circumvent Kantian critique, selected extracts of philo-sophical ethics are mentioned as stand alone statements without any further discussion so that management students are disallowed to make a link between philosophical ethics and management. Simultaneously, however, the servants of power can claim to have mentioned it. There is next to no critical application of ethics to management.[11] However, there is a middle-ground between total positivism and the negation of critical philosophical ethics. In the middle between total negatives (–) on the one hand and the sheer positivism (+) on the other resides the grey area of problematic ethics.

c.   The problematic

The area of problematic ethics sets the real task for affirmative man-agement writers because here they have to twist, turn, deceive, re-interpret, manipulate, stage-manage, and distort those versions of ethics that, in reality, do not fit the dominant paradigm of management. In short, the infamous method of *torture the data until they confess* is applied. The option to re-interpret ethics to suit management, Managerialism, and business interest demands the best academics money, career, and promotions can buy. Jones et al. (2005:43ff.) named affirmative *business ethics* writer and so-called Kant expert N. E. Bowie as the perfect example. In his *Business Ethics* Kant is subsumed under business and management. Kant's *Trilogy of Critical Philosophy* has been expressed in his three core works of *The Critique of Pure Reason* (1781), *Critique of Judgement* (1790), and *The Critique of Practical Reason* (1788). Despite this however, the so-called Kant expert in management ethics appears to deliberately exterminate Kantian *critical philosophy*. The Kantian term *critique* is totally absent from Bowie's books on *Business Ethics – A Kantian Perspective* (1999) and *Management Ethics* (2005). Kant's idea that *under modernity everything has to submit to critique* is nonexistent. In sharp contrast to Bowie's work, a truly Kantian book would have been *A Critique of Business Ethics* and *A Critique of Management Ethics*. The so-called Kant expert appears to be nothing more than the near total negation of Kantian philosophy that took *critique* as a fundamental principle.

That the conflict between philosophical ethics and management ethics is not just a question of labels on a book is illustrated in a second case on the philosophy of Kant. A selective version of Kant's ethics is depicted in Boatright's 6th edition of *Ethics and the Conduct of Business* (2009:66). Here, Kant's famous *means-ends* dictum has been mentioned however it denotes something totally different. For management, means-ends rationalisations diminish ethics by moving managerial decisions onto so-called rational grounds that constitute what Kant called *pure rationality*. Kant's predecessor Hegel labelled this *Zweckrationalität* or rational necessity. For ethics, it is the moral end that constitutes an *end in itself* superseding all *means*-rationalities. Hence, the concept of *means-ends* can never be avoided. It is a central point in Kantian ethics and is also central to management.[12]

The philosophy of Kant demands to treat others *always as an end and never as a means only*. This is carefully re-interpreted by stating *these words are unusually interpreted to mean we should respect other people (and ourselves!) as human beings*.[13] '*Usually interpreted*' stands for trust us experts and textbook writers. Secondly, it also pretends that this is the majority opinion on Kant. The infamous '*we*' creates the illusion of inclusiveness, the idea that it is something *we all do*. Even though Kant does not mention *respect* at all in his categorical imperative – not even in the German original – the invention of '*respect other people*' is being used as it has two functions. Firstly, it diverts Kant's means-ends ethics to merely respect. Secondly, it creates the highly agreeable notion of '*don't we all respect other people*'. This is reinforced through the insertion of '*and ourselves!*' to create the personal feeling of '*well, of course I respect myself*'.

The final touch in the reinterpretation of Kant is delivered through '*as human beings*'. Of course we are all *human beings*. The core question however is why is all this done? Because it is a crucial point at which management and Kantian ethics depart like heaven from hell. Kant demands the *Kingdom of Ends*. Significantly, one of the real experts on Kantian philosophy and ethics, Korsgaard (1996) remains unmentioned in Boatright's textbook. Kant reinforces his point of never treating people as means through his *Kingdom of Ends*. Boatright's textbook avoids this, well aware that management represents *The Kingdom of Means* and not *The Kingdom of Ends*. A critical discussion on Kant's *Kingdom of Ends* versus management's *Kingdom of Means* has to be prevented by the *Servants of Power*.

Despite such *re-interpretations*, the standard case in management ethics is to present ethics in a linear, logical, sequential, and step-by-step fashion so that it can be used *for* management. In most writings on management ethics, moral philosophy is downsized just enough for many managers and management writers to understand it, to follow it, and to apply it. It is not ethics *in itself*, to use a Kantian term, but the value it provides '*to*' management that makes it valuable. Again, not ethics manages management but management manages ethics. As such, standard management ethics often provides *handy hints* formulated as a short number of steps to follow, preferably in bullet points, and accompanied by a short PowerPoint presentation.[14]

The bullet point tactic to ethics provides practical guidelines on how to *improve your business* and to *make your management ethical* so that it appears ethical. In a final step such *useful* publications provide strategies on how to avoid being unethical. This is portrayed as *all what ethical managers need*. It tells them what ethics is by outlining a few necessary buzzwords called *key concepts* and *essential themes*. These can even be presented as *The 5-Minutes Ethics MBA*. *Speed read* sections are skilfully attached to lighten up such publications. As a result, they look more like *Cosmopolitan* than real books and make for easy consumption – not critical study – of ethics by students and managers. They tell the reader how to apply ethics to 'your' business and 'your' management practice. In short, readers are made to believe that they know two crucial things – what management ethics is and how to apply it. They are aware of *the ethics of management* and *the management of ethics*.

In sharp contrast to that, any non-textbook and non-M+E=ME version of a *critical, self-reflective, and self-determining* (Kant), *mündige and self-actual* (Hegel) examination of *critical management ethics* needs to be constructed under a quite different enterprise. It can only ever be worked out if one does not seek to provide yet another handy book for managers under the M+E=ME formula. Therefore, *Critical Management Ethics* is not another work which asks simple management supportive questions that textbook writers on management ethics have already formulated and answered. Neither is it about questions that people think they already know.

Instead, Kantian, and even more so Hegelian, philosophy demands that one cannot subsume ethics under management and Managerialism.[15] It rejects the task of selecting certain ethical themes that support management as well as any deselecting, rejecting, isolating, diminishing, marginalising, and negating of those ethical philosophies that do not support management. Instead, the formula M+E=ME is reverted to an E→M approach. Here it is not management's needs that build the corner stone but ethics itself is central. A more truthful representation of ethics requires that management is tested on ethics rather than the other way around. To achieve this any discussion on *critical management ethics* faces four options:

1.   A critique of the M+E=ME method

The option to follow the standard M+E=ME method and produce yet another book that is affirmative to management has already been chosen and is visible in the endless array of managerial textbooks on ethics; managerial ethics conferences; academic, semi-academic or non-academic journals; management ethics seminars; business school lectures; experts; and consultants.[16] M+E=ME is one of the core favourites of business ethics writers when a skilful diversion of attention away from moral philosophy is required. In some cases, this is done by starting with none other than *Harry Potter* quickly framing ethics as a problem. In other cases, ethics, so we are told, is not a problem of management but of *Chinese students cheating at Duke University, employees who tend to rationalise unethical conduct,* and *personal values, the Dalai Lama, whistle blowing.* Textbooks like that deflect almost all serious ethical questions by providing a *Manager's Toolkit* on how to make ethics *useful for their business* because it delivers *an array of benefits for the organisation.* Such textbooks close the usual student exercise on: *Do you believe that values drive behaviour?* In sum, ethics has only value to management when it provides benefits. Those benefits are reflected in the marginalisation that ethics receives in standard management textbooks. *Critical Management Ethics* does not follow the M+E=ME approach because it does not adjust ethics to management. It does the exact opposite by reflecting on Kant's *Trilogy of Critiques* (1781, 1788, 1790). This approach examines ethics and critically relates it to management.

2.   Brute facts versus social facts

Rejecting yet another M+E=ME (cook)-book, *Critical Management Ethics* does not want to focus our attention on *facts* and compare them to other *facts*. Such a *facts vs. facts* approach can be seen as comparing *the sun is red* with *the sun is green*. Two issues are relevant for that. There are two kinds of facts in the non-managerial and the managerial world. Humans have to deal with natural or *brute facts* and with *socially constructed facts*. These two sets of facts demand two different forms of analyses and discussions. While one needs to be based on *natural science*, the other is based on *social science*. Since management, ethics, and therefore *management ethics* are socially constructed, they belong to the realm of social science. All three – a) management, b) ethics, and c) management ethics – are not based on *natural theory* but on *social theory*. Hence to understand management ethics, the tools of natural science – the production of brute facts – are ineffective and the tools of social science – critical reflections – have to be used instead.[17]

For many in management studies and adjacent fields the core problem of *facts vs. facts* is the uncritical assumption that theories of natural science can be used in social science.[18] The proponents of this assumption – called positivism – often all too gullibly convert theories developed by natural science into the area of a humanly constructed reality without ever discussing them. They subconsciously assume that humans do circle the sun as a physical and mathematical entity and therefore can be analysed, studied, and measured through the means of natural science. Obviously, this is not so. Management ethics is not a natural *brute fact* and can never be understood by collecting more facts (cf. *Journal of Business Ethics*). Neither management nor ethics exist independent from us but are created by us. Both are socially constructed and can only be understood by applying critical social theory. Social theory is nothing more than a sub-division of philosophy. Therefore to understand management and the ethics of it, one needs the norms of social theory and philosophy to come to terms with it. If the distinction between facts and norms makes sense at all in our socially constructed world, then it is *social-facts vs. social-facts*. But social facts are always related to social norms and those who created the so-called facts. These are *the facts behind the facts!*

3. Philosophical norms versus managerial facts

A third approach highlights tensions and contradictions between management and ethics by relating *norms to facts*. This is the *norm vs. fact* method.[19] Such an analysis compares *norms*, such as an *ethical norm*, to *empirically* testable *facts* such as those to be found in the corporate reality of the likes of the following:

Table 1.1   A Few Examples of Unethical Corporate Behaviour

Agent Orange and Dow Chemical-Monsanto-Diamond-Shamrock, Amato-Barilla-DeCecco-Divella-Garofalo Italian pasta cartel, American International Group; American Shipping, Arthur Anderson's auditing of Enron, Arthur D. Little's waste disposal, Australia's HIH-insurance, BAE's corruption, Baster *vs.* Ford Motor Co., Bath Iron Works, BCCI, Beech-Nut's Bogus Apple Juice, Bernie Madoff's Ponzi scheme fraud, Big Brother at Procter and Gamble, Bre-X Minerals, British-American Tobacco hidden lobbying activities, hiding the truth on addiction and cancer, Charles Keating in Lincoln Savings and Loans, Chevron in the Amazon, Chrysler's Odometer Controversy, DC-10 Crash in Paris and McDonnell-Douglas, Drexel, Burnham and Lambert's insider trading, Dow Corning's breast implants, Enron, Exxon Valdez, Film Recovery Systems Inc., Ford's Pinto, Ford's-Firestone Brawl, Four Seasons Nursing Centres of America Inc., Fraud at WorldCom, GAP's Sweatshops, GAP and child labour, Goodrich Brake scandal, Google in China, Goldman Sachs' CEO's $US68 million pay during the Global Financial Crisis (2007), Guinesty – the Guinness Affair, Heavy Electrical Equipment Anti-Trust Case, Hooker Chemicals' and Love Canal, ITT and Pinochet, Jacksonville Shipyard, James Hardy Industries, Japan's Minamata, Japan's Nitrogen Ltd., Jewish Prison Labour for Germany's Nazi-Industry, Johnson and Johnson's Tylenol, KPMG and tax shelter fraud scandal, KPMG for Enron, Lavish Pay at Harvard, Leeson and Barings, Lehman Brothers, MacPherson *vs.* Buick Motor Co., Malden Mills, Martha Stewart's insider trading, Mattel's massive recall of toys, McDonald's McLibel-Trial, Merck and Aids in South Africa, Mitsubishi Motor Ltd., Morton-Thiokol, Nestle's Baby Formula, Nike in Southeast Asian Sweatshops, Nike's misleading advertising, Parmalat, Procter and Gamble's Rely tampons, race discrimination at Texaco, Revco Medicaid and the State of Ohio, RSV débâcle (NL), S & L débâcle, Sears Auto Centre, Seveso, sex discrimination at Wal-Mart, Shell Oil in Nigeria, Shell Oil's sinking of Brent Spar, Siemens, Solomon Brothers Treasury Bond Scandal, Standard Fruit Company and Banana Republics, Starbucks and Fair Trade Coffee and exploitation, Stauffer Chemical fraud (1982), Subprime mortgage lending (2007–2010), The Arms Industry, Toys "R" Us and Child World, Weapons and Land-Mine Industry, Zeebrugge ferry disaster, Thalidomide: the Drug that Deformed, Three Miles Island Nuclear Accident, UNR Industries Inc.'s asbestos pipe insulation, Union Carbide's Bhopal, US Car-Maker CEO's private-jet begging trip to Washington DC, Visy-Amcor cartel (Australia).[20]

Here, facts of corporate behaviours are related to the norms of morality, often resulting in findings that detect immoral corporate behaviours. Of course, this is a non-exclusive and incomplete list of corporations that behaved unethically. As almost any textbook on business ethics testifies, there are plenty of case studies on corporate immorality. Taken together they deliver a large volume of *facts* on the immoral behaviours of corporations and management. On the basis of these facts, the illusion of isolated cases, the famous *few bad apples*, and just some exceptions are maintained. This implies that the *usually-they-behave-ethically* view of management, managers, CEOs, and businesses is correct. It suggests there is no deeper and no structural problem between management and ethics. As convincing as these *facts* of the immorality of corporations are, adding more to this list would not prove anything beyond what has already been proven and documented. In sum, comparing ethical theory with the facts of corporate misbehaviour has been done to an exhaustive extent. Therefore, it is neither repeated nor continued here.

4.   The norm versus the essence method

After having exhausted the previous three methods, *Critical Management Ethics* needs to be based on the *norm vs. norm* method.[21] Here, an ethical norm is brought into a relationship with the norms of management resulting in two normative contents facing each other. This goes to the core, the heart, the centre, and the *essence of a thing*. It is close to ontology – the philosophy of being – and to Kant's *thing in itself* (*das Ding an sich*). It is also close to Hegel's essence and represents the negation of a rather simplistic application of ethics to management. Unlike *fact vs. fact* and *norm vs. fact*, the *norm vs. norm* method demands that an understanding of the essence of management and ethics is sought by relating them to one another dialectically.[22]

In that way their positives and negatives as well as their accords and contradictions are highlighted. It is not a simple 1+1=2 or M+E=ME operation. Thinking in *pros and cons* does not avoid examining two sides of a coin. Nor does it avoid operating like a legal court that always examines evidence presented by two sides through prosecution and defence. To examine not just the positives but also the negatives means to contribute to the truth about management ethics. The task of negatives and positives is not, however, to simply negate everything. Nor is it to deconstruct and to destroy. It is the exact opposite because only by bringing two concepts – management and ethics – into a relationship that examines positives and negatives (+/–), the true state of management ethics can be highlighted. Only this process can deliver what Hegel called *actual knowledge of what truly is.*

The philosophy of negation drills beyond the *surface structure* down into the *deep structure* to fully grasp the essence.[23] At a first glance, the essence of management rests in its understanding of management as the *construction, maintenance, and improvement of an administrative system which co-ordinates, plans, allocates, and transforms human and material resources into profit-making operations.*[24] The essence of management becomes even clearer when it is seen as *management creates performance through others* and that *management operates through people.*[25] On the essence of ethics, Singer (1994:4) writes on *'what is ethics?'* that it *stands for systematic studying of reasoning about how we ought to act.*

Ethics can be seen as a guide to action while asking the question *'what shall we do?'.* This question has concerned humans for a very long time. The field of ethics stretches back to ancient Greece when philosophy replaced mythology.[26] Today, philosophy, moral philosophy, and ethics represent a development of more than 2,000 years. Almost all forms of ethics contain moral guidance and codes of conduct developed by moral and ethical philosophers.[27] Virtually the whole history of moral philosophy shows an attempt to find an answer to the question of *'what shall I do?'.* In sharp contrast to traditional philosophy the philosopher Hegel thought that there are better ways of developing ethics. He developed the concept of *Sittlichkeit* as a critique on Kant's rigid *formalism. Formalism* expresses ethics in *categorical imperatives.* They represent *'moral musts'* articulated in law-like forms. Hegel thought that those to whom ethical rules apply should also be the ones who make those rules. According to Hegel, they should be involved in the process of creating moral rules. He advocated a social version of ethics using the German term *Sittlichkeit* which indicates a socially based form of an ethical life. Rather than locating a philosopher at the centre, Hegel thought that society itself should be at the centre. Society should create moral codes of behaviour where questions of ethics are concerned. Socially constructed versions of ethics can only be established when people communicate with one another. But even the process of communication has to be seen as a process to which ethics applies. In short, one should never communicate about ethics without engaging in a dialogue that is based on morality. The link between ethics and communication creates *communicative ethics.* Probably the most far-reaching concept of *communicative ethics* has been developed by German philosopher *Jürgen Habermas* (1986, 1990, 1997). The advancement of traditional ethics to Hegel's concept of

Sittlichkeit, and finally Habermas' concept of *communicative ethics*, is shown below:

Table 1.2   From Traditional Ethics to Communicative Ethics

a) Traditional Ethics:	b) *Sittlichkeit*:	c) Communicative Ethics:
Core Ethical Question: What shall I do and How shall I live?	**Core Ethical Question:** How shall we life ethically in society?	**Core Ethical Question:** How can we communicate ethically?
Meta-Ethical Perspective: Philosophy *about* ethics and moral behaviour	**Meta-Ethical Perspective:** Philosophy about socially constructed ethics and moral behaviour (Hegel)	**Meta-Ethical Perspective:** Ethics of a communicatively established dialogue (Habermas)
Normative Viewpoint: Norms, values, rules, standards and principles that guide actions	**Normative Viewpoint:** Ethical institutions organised and run by morally conscious actors (*Mündigkeit*)	**Normative Viewpoint:** Ethical communication organised by participants in discourse ethics
Forms of Ethics: Universalism, Moral Relativism, Irrationalism, Subjectivism, Intuitionism, Act and Rule Utilitarianism, Greek and Modern Virtue Ethics, Social Contract Theory, Kant's Universalism and Morality, Nihilism and Egoism	**Forms of Ethics:** End of master-slave relationship, serving a purpose → having a purpose end of alienation and deception, *Mündigkeit*, autonomy, self-reflection, self-determination, self-actualisation, social development of ethical standards and moral institutions	**Forms of Ethics:** Overcoming distorted communication, end of colonisation and manipulation of speech, symmetrical relations, domination-free dialogue, establishing ideal speech and communicative action, moral dialogue → moral action

Table 1.2 shows three distinctive columns entitled: a) traditional ethics, b) *Sittlichkeit*, and c) communicative ethics. These are developmental stages to be seen as a→b→c. The core difference between a) and b) is that the latter is no longer based on formulas, categorical imperatives, rules, principles, etc. that are developed by a philosopher. Instead, those to whom ethics is applied become the very foundation

of ethics which moves ethics from being constructed by an individual philosopher or a small group of philosophers towards socially constructed ethics developed by society. To achieve this, human beings are no longer seen as atomised individuals but as moral actors inside an ethical society engaged in ethical life. This is what Hegel calls *Sittlichkeit*. At the next stage (b→c) the need for communication becomes highly relevant. Moral actors need to communicate when creating their own ethical rules, principles, and codes of conduct. This needs to happen under ethical principles that are developed inside a particular framework called *communicative ethics*. This establishes the transition from (a) to (b), and eventually to (c).

All three versions of ethics (a→b→c) operate at four levels. These range from i) the core ethical question, ii) the meta-perspective (about ethics), iii) the normative viewpoint, and iv) the form, shape, and *Gestalt* that ethics takes. At the first level, the core question changes from *what shall I do?* to *how can we live ethically in society?* to *how can we communicate ethically?*. The level of meta-ethical perspectives shows the three different versions of how we see ethics. The normative viewpoint demonstrates the development from traditional *formulism* of ethical principles to socially constructed principles of ethics which need to be developed into *communicative ethics*. Lastly, these principles have been expressed in three forms of ethics. The traditional type a) includes all non-socially constructed forms of ethics. In the model of *Sittlichkeit* b), traditional forms of ethics are advanced to a socially constructed version of ethics that includes society, ethical life, and *Sittlichkeit*. Finally, the last row in the last column (the lower right hand corner) shows the form of ethics that is operative when *communicative ethics* is applied to the process of socially constructing ethics. Overall however, the three versions of ethics – a) traditional, b) *Sittlichkeit*, and c) *communicative ethics* – have three questions at their core which they all answer somewhat differently. Common to all of them, however, is that all three seek to establish an ethical framework for i) *what shall I do?*, ii) *how shall we live in an ethical society (Sittlichkeit)?*, and *how can we communicate ethically?* In sharp contrast to these three ethical questions, management's core questions are radically different. First of all, management sees the world from a viewpoint that is different to that of ethics and it asks a different set of questions. The core of management's own existence is represented in a general enquiry into:

- *what is profitable?*;
- *what is relevant to improve shareholder values?*;

- *how can my company be profitable?;*
- *do I have the right cost-benefit strategy?;*
- *do I allocate labour and capital in the best way?;*
- *am I efficient in what I do?;* and later maybe
- *why should I act ethically?*

Moral issues such as *every human being thinks about how to live a good life* are simply no issues for management.[28] Instead, in the non-textbook version of management *business can look like a seemingly mindless game of changes at which any donkey could win provided only that he be ruthless* (Magretta 2002:1). From this it follows that ethics and management have not only two different sets of questions but also use two different methodologies to answer these.

Management and ethics follow two different sets of epistemological – knowledge creating – philosophical questions. *Ethical knowledge* is predominantly concerned with human subjects, while managerial knowledge is foremost concerned with objects, facts and figures, and numbers directed towards profit-making.[29] This is not to say that ethics does not seek objective ethics and management has nothing to say about human subjects, but one creates knowledge on quantifiable matters – *The Real Bottom Line* – while the other creates knowledge about *the quality of life*. In sum, the quest for knowledge in the world of ethics is fundamentally different from the role knowledge plays in the world of management.[30]

It is not by far the first time that philosophy had to deal with two seemingly opposing or contradictory sets of ideas – the idea of management and the idea of ethics. Already one of the godfathers of philosophy and morality, Aristotle, dealt with such issues more than 2,000 years ago. To understand a world that is apparently contradictory and full of tensions – as are the managerial and the ethical world – concepts such as substance, contradictions, essence, affirmation and negation, thesis and anti-thesis, synthesis, unity, plurality, and so on are of vital importance. Greek philosophy originally developed a mode of philosophical discussion that was directed towards finding the truth by contrasting a positive (+) with a negative (–) to come to some sort of conclusion or synthesis.[31] The dialectical model of philosophical truth seeking, thinking, and dialogue has been used by Hegel who transformed it into a full system in his *Philosophy of Mind* and *Science of Logic*.[32] For Hegel it is not so much the immediate that is of interest but what lies behind it; what constitutes the world; and in that positives and negatives are relevant. Hence, Hegel argued that everything has two sides to its existence, a positive(+) and a negative(–).[33] This means if one seeks the truth one needs to understand both sides as there is always (+) and (–). For Hegel, the problem is not only that everything has two sides but that they are often in contradiction with each other. This, so Hegel, is the only way to understand the world.

The aim of affirmative writers on management ethics has all too often been the exact opposite. They sought to create a *comfortable certitude* for management. The aim of Hegel's *critical dialectics is not (to) reaffirm familiar knowledge but to destroy the comfortable certitudes* (Smith 1987:106). The destruction of certitude and Kant's dictum that *Enlightenment means everything must be exposed to critique* severely challenges positive-affirmative management writers and their entourage. Hegel's method of dialectics unmasks and demystifies various forms of self-deception, delusions, and distortions put forward by those who seek to use ethics to legitimate managerial actions. To a certain extent, the philosophy of *pros and cons* carries destructive elements as it does not add one to another. But it includes, and in fact encourages, negations, confrontations, and contradictions from which management all too often seeks to isolate itself. Such obvious philosophical truths are declared as problems and controversial *by The Servants of Power* (Baritz 1960). Management itself as well as *The Servants of Power* seek to confine them into the margins of management thinking.[34]

This is by no means a new process; there have always been conservative forces to hinder the progressive development of science and philosophy. In the history of science and philosophy this has occurred from *Galileo Galilei* (1564–1642) and *Charles Darwin* (1809–1882) to *Albert Einstein* (1878–1955). They have radically altered our thinking by negating (*aufheben*) older explanations. What Hegel meant by his famous term *Aufhebung* has occurred and less adequate forms of scientific and philosophical knowledge have been annulled. At the same time knowledge has been preserved into higher forms of knowledge. This is what is commonly called scientific progress. Einstein may have replaced many of Galileo's and Newton's physics. Their work, however, lives on in Einstein. Without them Einstein might have never been much more than a low level *patent officer* in a Swiss office.

Even the powerful Roman Catholic Church eventually failed to prevent Galileo's knowledge as much as the much more powerful racist war-machine of Nazi Germany failed to prevent Einstein's knowledge and his emancipatory philosophy to flourish. The same applies to the current gatekeepers of Managerialism. Eventually, managerial knowledge will be annulled and replaced by higher forms of knowledge. This will occur even though at present Managerialism has created an aura of mystification and management has been made to appear as God-given that will be with us for all time to come. Hegelian philosophy shows that this can never be so.

But Hegel also goes beyond the simple *pros and cons* and declares that everything is changing, altering, and *becoming* in contrast to Kant's being *in itself*. For Hegel, becoming and relating positives to negatives has also a forward driving force. Hence, the idea behind *thesis→anti-thesis→synthesis* is that the end result of this process – a synthesis – leads to the next level of arguments. This process ends when all contradictions are solved and all negatives are negated, i.e. have become positives. It also means all contradictions between ethics and management have to be solved so that management is truly ethical. In order to fully comprehend Hegel's idea eight forms of negatives or negations need to be highlighted because these elements constitute *critical management ethics*:

1.   Critical management ethics as a negation of early business administration

The first of Hegel's negatives relates to the fact that *things do not exist in their truth*. Things do not exist in themselves but have a history and a future. They always have been something else before they became what they are to us and they always need to *negate* what they have been before. Hence, things are always on the way to becoming something else. They are in the mode of *becoming*.[35] For example, the human invention, or social construction, of management had business administration as its predecessor. Hence, modern management is the negation of what was once known as *business administration* (BA) with business administration's only remnants left in the MBA as *master of business administration*. Today, most MBAs would find it hard to accept that their degree is in administration strongly favouring management. Since the process of developing management is not finished, it may become something else in the future. Hence, management does not exist in itself but is actually no more than negative business administration. Simultaneously, it is on the way to become something else by ongoing reshaping and development. In short, to understand management ethics, one needs to know the negation and history of what it is today.

2.   Critical management ethics as negation of management's non-development

The second negation lies in the fact that every particular existence is different from what it could be if its potentials were realised. For example, if all potentials of management were realised, it would look quite different from what we know it to be. Hence, every thing has its *positive* appearance to us but at the same time it also contains a hidden and somewhat unfinished project inside. Because socially constructed institutions – such as management – do not realise their full potentials, there is always, in everything, also a *negation* of unrealised potentials. The development towards realising its full potentials is, according to Hegel, not a *finite* but a *infinite* process. Hence, the social construction of management is exposed to an ending process of social alteration and changes. In Hegel's terms, *if something or someone ceases to change, the object or person ceases to exist*. Management can never be a thing *in itself*. According to Hegel it is always a thing *in absolute unrest*. Management is constantly converting unrealised potentials (its inherent negatives) into positives in the process of self realisation. In order to understand management ethics we need to know that it is part of a finite process directed towards becoming. It is the negation of a static, so-called *hard facts* view.[36]

3.   Critical management ethics as negation of non-discursive linearity

The third negation lies in the fact that the process of realising potentials is not a conflict free conversion of (–) into (+). It encounters contradictions and tensions. The way management realises its full potentials is a way that is plastered with problems, contradicting view points, and pressures. Inside this development different interests meet in a process of dialogue among human actors. This process turns the illusion of so-called *hard facts of management science* into the reality of common agreement among the human actors on what management is. Accordingly, management, just like any socially constructed institution, is constantly moving. The invented *hard-facts-of-management* view is in reality a never ending process to which even those contribute who claim to have the hard scientific facts on management. Management exists inside a dialogue rather than inside a mindset that asphyxiates management's hard facts.

In other words, the dialogue on management directed towards realising its potentials encounters management's very own tensions and contradictions. It is a process that follows dialectic (–/+) rather than the simplistic and additive logic (2+2=4) of standard-affirmative literature on management ethics. Management ethics can never be a process that simply adds ethics to management in the textbook style of M+E=ME. According to Hegel, this is impossible. Consequently, the only option open for standard textbook writers on management ethics would be dialectics (+/–), not linearity (■→■). Despite this M+E=ME textbooks tend to ignore this. They present ethics as being linear. This creates a nice, easy, handy, non-controversial, consumable, and saleable text-book but it is not a truthful representation of ethics.

4.   Critical management ethics as negation of a non-relationship view

Hegel's fourth negation rests on the fact that dialectical thinking does not only create problems for *The Servants of Power* but also for management itself. Management is a social issue that exemplifies *a mode of existence of man and things made up of contradictory relations* (Marcuse 1941). Despite all the pretence by almost all textbook writers on management, manage-ment does not exist *in itself*. It exists inside contradictory relations. If one seeks to understand management, one needs to examine its positives and its negatives as management is always both at the same time. Once linked to the Hegelian process of *becoming,* management turns out to be a moving target rather than a scientific fact. Management, just as manage-ment ethics, is not a fact but a relationship inside which contradictory forces play itself out. It is not, and can never be, static.[37]

There is a second, and perhaps even more problematic, issue of man-agement ethics in regard to non-existing relationships. It is often pre-tended that management does not function inside relationships to others. For Hegel, *the pursuit of philosophical truth requires effort, a desire to recognise relationships.*[38] In spite of the occasionally mentioned stake-holder theme, management continues to pretend that it acts largely inside the boundaries of corporations and disconnected from politics, society, and history, as well as from social, legal, and ethical forces. It views itself very much as a technical-engineering project inside a scientific management framework. It pretends that it uses scientific, meas-urable, and instrumental-rational ways independent of politics and ideologies. Such a pretended *self-contained-ness* creates a false comfortable existence inside an artificially secured space. Management pretends to exist inside an ethical space that is largely disconnected from social forms of ethics and from nearly all forms of current and 20th century ethics. Management falsely seeks to negate these relationships.

5.   Critical management ethics as negation of *what is* through *what ought to be*

The fifth negation lies in Hegel's adaptation of Kant's separation of *what is* from what *ought to be*. All socially constructed issues are not just what they are but they always contain an element of what they *ought to be*, a progressive element that moves them towards an ideal concept that is an inherent *telos* of everything that is.[39] Everything that is always contains an element of utopian and speculative thinking. For a long time, for example, management's role was seen as one of organising, allocating, controlling, etc. until someone thought that management also ought to have a strategic element and that management *ought to be* strategic.

Today, there is virtually no managerial textbook, management school, and actual management that does not have strategy as part of its *what is*. Strategy used to be in the *ought to be* box. Now it is an established part of management. Therefore, if one seeks to understand management, one needs to view what it *ought to be*. To think of management purely in terms of '*What is management*' (Magretta 2002) negates its internal '*what ought to be*' character. One cannot exist without the other and this applies to management as well as to ethics.

6.   Critical management ethics as negation of what management is not

The sixth negation rests on the issue that everything that is, is at the same time something that it is not. Everything, just like management, can be negatively defined. Here, definitions are not still, asphyxiated, numb, and frozen *facts*. They are created between a sender and a receiver when both have reached common agreement on a certain definition.[40] Hence, any understanding of anything needs Hegel's *Other* and needs to have some sort of relationship with *the Other* in order to understand it. One needs to understand something by understanding what it is not. For example, day is day because we know what night is. Day is a negated night. Light is light because we know darkness. Light is a negative form of darkness. Hence, we only know what management is because we have something else against which we can contrast it. We need Hegel's *the Other*. We need something that is not management to understand management. For example, we have managerial staff and non-managerial staff to distinguish one from the other. And we need both to understand both. Only in a relationship they become constitutes of reality to us.

Hence, everything that is, like management, always and simultaneously contains something that it is not. For most textbooks on management, for example, management is seen as managing six core aspects: *planning, allocating resources, controlling, leading, organising, and performing.*

It appears that management is those six things. It also tells us what management is not. None of the six elements that tell us what management is names ethics as important or relevant. It appears management is six things but it is not ethics. This is not to say that management is unethical but for most management textbooks, ethics is just not a core activity of management. Hegel would say that ethics is not in the essence of management. For management, ethics is *the Other*. In Hegelian terms, management negates ethics. In order to understand management ethics, we need to know what management is not. It does not appear to be predominantly occupied with ethics but with six other aspects. Therefore we need to understand why the essence of management does not include ethics. Why is there a negation of ethics?

7.   Critical management ethics as negation of completeness

Hegel says that everything that exists has positives and negatives and that these together constitute what is. But things that are cannot simply reject the negatives and retain only the positives. Both are always present in whatever is. Hence, subjects must find a way to deal with the negatives as they cannot simply be rejected or annihilated because they are constitutive parts of the whole. Socially constructed institutions such as management are forced to constantly mediate between the negatives and the positives that constitute them. This is a never ending process until all contradictions are solved. Until then, it turns everything that is into a dynamic entity that constantly mediates (+) and (–). In order to be, management must seek to mediate between both and seek to *sublate (aufheben) the negative* (Marcuse 1941). Until all contradictions are solved, an institution like management needs to work hard towards the overcoming (*aufheben*) of all negatives in order to be.

In sum, the idea of management is never complete until all contradictions are solved. It is a constant struggle that sets positives against negatives. Management constantly needs to suppress *what it is not* in order *to be what it is*. But it also needs *the Other* in the form of the negative to distinguish itself from what it is not. Management must struggle not to dissolve into thin air (the negative wins). It can never be fully complete (the positive wins) until all contradictions are solved (*aufgehoben*). Management can never exist without the *Other* (the negative). Therefore it always contains inside itself categories of negations of the negative. In sum, management cannot become management that realises its potentials by pretending ethics is outside of it or by contradicting and negating ethics. Only when all contradictions are solved and management has become a truly ethical actor can it become management.

8. Critical management ethics as negation of repulsion

For Hegel all things are in constant struggle over positives and negatives. This produces a dynamic activity rather than a static and stale non-process. Everything, including management, has these two parts – positives and negatives – as constitutive categories. They are mutually exclusive, if not strongly opposed to each other. Hence, everything is in a constant stage of attraction and repulsion. It is never just one element, (+) or (–), that makes up management. There are several elements attracted to each other on the positive side + ↔ + ↔ + as well as on the negative side – ↔ – ↔ –. But they also contain negative or repulsive energies that drive them apart (+) ▶◀(–). Hence, management is in constant motion to avoid the creation of a coalition of negatives inside it. Simultaneously, it seeks to foster the attraction of positives.

Management needs to create strong positives in order to constitute itself. It is also forced to constantly struggle with the negative elements that are also part of its constituting self. It has inside itself a relentless struggle between attraction and affirmation to management and the repulsion and rejection of the negatives set against management. Hence management is the negation of the negative repulsion that endangers its existence. It also means that management needs to face up to the challenge of negativity as outlined by Hegel. It cannot pretend it is a monolithic bloc that exists apart from *the Other*. In Hegelian philosophy, one of the various *Others* is represented by ethics.

In conclusion, when one seeks to understand what management ethics is one cannot just add ethics to management to create management ethics but needs to encounter all eight Hegelian categories of negativity. These categories of a philosophical understanding of socially constructed ideas such as management and ethics include not only the positives but – necessarily, as Hegel insisted – also the negatives. For one, management is always a negation of what it has been in the past. Secondly, management and management ethics are in a constant state of development. They constitute the negations of the assumption that it is static. It is impossible to define once and for all what management is. Thirdly, neither management nor ethics are founded on linearity. Instead both are only to be understood in a dialectical relationship which negates the linearity of M+E=ME. Fourthly, the falseness of the M+E=ME idea leads to the understanding that management and ethics are in a complex relationship that cannot be understood by simply adding one to the other. Their relationship is positive and negative at the same time. It represents thesis and anti-thesis. It is the negation of linearity.

Fifthly, Kant says everything contains *what is* and *what ought to be*. Seeking to understand one without the other fails to understand ethics and management. Management represents a one sided representation of *what is* while simultaneously negating what *ought to be*. Sixthly, everything defines itself through *what it is not* and therefore needs *the Other* to develop an identity. We know what management is because we also know what it is not. Management ethics is only possible through the negation of *what it is not*. Seventhly, since the inside of everything contains positives and negatives and they are in constant motion nothing is complete. Everything is constituted by an endless struggle between both until all contradictions are solved. Management is constituted through a negation of the idea of completeness. According to Hegel, it can never be Kant's *thing in itself (Ding an sich)* unless all contradictions are solved. Finally, everything is also in a constant state of attraction and repulsion. There are elements inside management that are attractive to ethics as well as those that are repulsive to it. Both are in a constant struggle with each other. In conclusion, having examined management through the philosophy of Kant and Hegel, the relationship between management and ethics turned out to be more complex than many standard books on management ethics suggest. This can be carried forward by bringing core concepts of moral philosophy critically into a relationship with management.

The following chapters will use the eight critiques and Hegel's concept of essence to highlight contradictions between management and ethics. Proceeding from the introduction, Chapter 2 starts with the very origin of philosophical ethics. It outlines the virtue ethics of Greek antiquity. The chapter also highlights more recent philosophies such as Adorno's three virtues. This is followed by an application of utilitarian ethics to management that outlines core concepts of classical and modern utilitarianism (Chapter 3). Since the ideas of utilitarianism greatly influenced what is most likely the principal moral philosopher of modernity, the adjacent chapter is about *Kantian ethics* (Chapter 4). Inside the traditions of 19th century philosophy, Kant's concept of Moralität (morality) has been followed up by Hegel's ethics of *Sittlichkeit*. This is a socially constructed version of morality culminating in *ethical life*. Hence, Chapter 5 is about Hegel's ethical concept of an *ethical life* based on social rather than on individual morality. This is followed by Hegel's second most important ethical concept, the famous *master-slave dialectics* (Chapter 6) which concludes the debate on traditional ethical thinking in philosophy.

Because there are many other forms of ethical debates, concepts, ideas, and philosophies, Chapters 7 and 8 cover many of them inside one of the most comprehensive frameworks for ethics ever developed. The strength of this approach is manifested in its unique ability to cover *all* forms of ethics. On the lower end, one can find the morality of a *German Nazi concentration camp* (Milgram 1974 and Bauman 1989). On the upper level, concepts such as Singer's *Animal Liberation* (1990) are located. In contrast to virtually all other moral philosophers, the American philosopher and psychologist Kohlberg has produced an ascending scale of morality based on developmental psychology and moral philosophy. It includes moral stages that range from zero (amoral) to seven (holistic ethics). Because of the comprehensiveness of Kohlberg's concept, Chapter 7 introduces his model and presents the first two stages of morality. Chapter 8 discusses Kohlberg's moral stages two to seven. Chapters 7 and 8 provide a scale on which practically all other ethical concepts and socially constructed institutions – like management – can be measured.

Kohlberg's comprehensive model of morality is followed by several great challenges to standard philosophies on ethics. Despite the fact that these are somewhat minority views they are highly relevant to present day ethics. These are the ethical philosophies of intuitionism, subjectivism, moral egoism, ethical relativism, nihilism, as well as the ethics of Hobbes and Nietzsche. These philosophies are summed up in the final chapter (Chapter 9) on *Positive Management Ethics*. While all previous chapters often represent tensions, frictions, and contradictions between ethics and management, the final chapter provides almost tension-free examples of management ethics. They unambiguously support management.

The conclusion (Chapter 10) highlights the positive but also some negative forms of management ethics. Inside each chapter, almost all paragraphs are written to adhere to Hegel's idea of positives and negatives. Here, two different ideas are brought into a relationship so that the truth can be examined. Therefore, almost all paragraphs in the main body of the book provide three parts. In the first part they discuss a *thesis* on ethics; the second part applies ethics to management creating supportive evidence for managerial practises or negations of it as an *anti-thesis*. The final section highlights that there are unsolvable contradictions between the essence of management and almost all of what ethics has to offer. But the conclusion is not all about unsolvable dilemmas and contradictions between management and ethics. Given the apparent dilemma of an almost impenetrable contradiction between management and many variants of standard ethics, a positive solution to this problem can still be found. Despite many versions of ethics that appear to negate management, a solution – Hegel's synthesis – in the form of *practical ethics* is also provided. It honours Karl Marx' dictum that *philosophers have only ever interpreted the world, the point, however, is to change it.*

Hence, the only workable solution for solving the contradictions between management and ethics can be found in a proposal for the introduction of *ethics councils* as a step towards practical ethics. Such *ethics councils* need to be constructed in the light of Kantian *autonomy* and *self-determination*, Hegelian *Sittlichkeit, Mündigkeit, self-actualisation*, and *self-articulation*, as well as Habermas' concept of *communicative action*. Such *ethics councils* are to be established at company level. Simultaneously, they also need to be independent of management. As *moral institutions* of Hegel's *Sittlichkeit* they need to have a level of Hegelian *self-articulation* on moral issues. This is what Hegel's of *self-articulation* demands. Therefore, members of such *ethics councils* need to communicate through the establishment of communicative ethics, communicative action and ideal speech as outlined by Habermas (1990 and 1997; Klikauer 2008). This is the task of the final chapter.

2
Critical Virtue Ethics: From Aristotle to Adorno

The ethics of virtues is one of the oldest forms of morality. It is still in use and discussed aiding the impression that virtue ethics – unlike natural science – has not much improved beyond what was said more than 2,000 years ago. Ethics started with a man who lived in way that expressed the very opposite of the smartly dressed, highly paid and employed managers and their entourage of affirmative writers of today's management ethics. He was a poor, unemployed, modestly dressed, and barefooted man with the name *Socrates* (469–399). He lived an ethical life and also thought that an *unexamined life is not worth living*. Today, management and managers represent all too often such an *unexamined life*. They engage in day-to-day affairs – called managing – without even taking the time to reflect, to examine, and to self-examine. They live a double life between what they do at work (profit-maximising, outsourcing, and downsizing) and how they behave at home (family-oriented, caring, and compassionate). In line with their day-to-day performance this leaves scarcely any time for any examination in an ethical sense.

Socrates believed that *nothing can harm the good and just person, while the wrongdoer courts unhappiness and misery*. According to him *wrongdoing harms the soul* and *acting immoral harms the soul of the person who engages in wrongdoing*. Most managers today – even on *Harvard's decision-making tree* (Bagley 2003:19) – do not even ask about the ethical rights or wrongs of their decisions. In general managers are not *happy people* but people who perform, *who make things work* (Magretta 2002). Because of the relentless demands of a self-created and daily reinforced system of competition, the world of management often produces misery and outright unhappiness. Managers are confined in the tough demands of their own system and restricted to the never ending competition with other managers for power, influence, and status. Market and company-internal competition forces them into a constant rat-race as outlined in Schrijvers' *The Way of the Rat – A Survival Guide to Office Politics* (2004). In short, managers accept, enforce, and have internalised the power and money code.⁴¹

Socrates also believed that *to know the good is to seek it*. This might be one of the reasons why management ethics suffers a somewhat marginalised existence in the standard curricula of today's management schools. The core of management and management schools is not to be found in *seeking what is good* (Socrates) but in seeking shareholder value. Similarly, the Socratic ethics of *what is good* has been confined to a marginal chapter in the occasional management textbook. It suffers a *fig-leaf* existence used to claim one has covered the issue while simultaneously making sure that managers are not to be bothered by knowing *what is ethically good* thus preventing them from seeking *what is ethical*. After all, the real essence of management is to *transform human and material resources into profit-making operations* (Magretta 2002), not ethics.⁴²

Not surprisingly, modern management and its management schools also present no more than a Hegelian negation of what Socrates' philosophical successor, Aristotle, demanded. He thought that *a moral life involves developing and manifesting virtue dispositions of character*.⁴³ For virtue ethics, character is the foremost essential concept. In virtue ethics, a virtuous character is the sheer embodiment of humanity. Hence the prime emphasis of virtue ethics rests on building a virtuous character rather than teaching so-called *neutral and objective facts*. However, the development of a virtuous character is almost totally absent from the curricula of most management schools. Instead, they teach everything from instrumental knowledge to the latest MBA buzzwords.

Consequently, Aristotle's ethics also demands that *moral education is absolutely central to the moral life*. Management schools totally negate this by keeping their teachings inside of the confinement of largely four subjects: *marketing, finance, operations management, and HRM*. Ethics and virtue ethics are often not taught at all and are almost never *central* to their teachings. However ethics is always added to the curricula. Often the teaching of ethics is assigned a niche position in the teaching timetable. Its sole purpose is that of an alibi to avoid being accused of not teaching ethics. Hence it is taught – just as a little side-issue that one *has to* (!) cover. In that way management and management schools circumvent Socrates', Plato's, and Aristotle's issue of *akrasia – know what is good for us* – as they teach what is good for business and management.

Similarly, in *The Republic* (written in the 5th century BC), Plato's suggestion that *men and women are* [to be] *equally educated* is negated by management through the predominantly male occupation of management
and through the fact that so-called in-house *managerial education*, training, seminars, etc. are asymmetrically distributed between male and
female employees. Rather than supporting Plato's virtue of *equal education*, management strongly favours the exact opposite and thereby
negates Plato's ethics.

Socrates, meanwhile, saw *personal honour* as one of the highest values.
One might suspect that given the choice between honour and a 20%
increase in shareholder value (plus a 20% rise in one's personal bonus)
many managers would gladly take the latter.[44] Finally, Greek virtue
ethics also thought that *being loved* is a human value to strive for. Here
again, at best one can say that some managers are respected. Most
managers, and an even greater number of non-managerial staff, do not
express *love* towards their managers. The attribute *being loved* is generally not associated with management. Finally, the value ethics of
Socrates identifies five virtues (*aretē*): *temperance, piety, courage, justice,
and wisdom*. Apart from courage, none of the other four are to be found
in management.

From the Ford-Pinto case to British-American Tobacco (BAT), management's essence is not found in *piety* as death, misery, cancer, illness,
etc. are carefully calculated and if any costs are enforced by courts then
these are reluctantly paid. *Justice* is not shown but denied to victims
even when this requires years, if not decades, of deliberately hiding
the truth and falsifying test-results (BAT). Finally, *wisdom* can only be
shown if it contributes to *The Real Bottom Line*. Other than that, it is
not a useful function for management. *Temperance, piety, courage, justice, and wisdom* are what Aristotle called the *highest form of happiness*.
These are not to be found in management. What is found however is
what Magretta (2002) called *The Real Bottom Line*.

But Socrates also advocated the *prudential paradox* claiming that *we
never willingly pursue something that is bad* and *we are often mistaken
about our own true interests*. The Ford Pinto case exemplifies management's relationship to Socrates' *prudential paradox*. Ford's managers did
not willingly pursue the death of a few Ford customers who would die
from lacking safety features but it came cheaper than making the car
safe. In management's cost-benefit dictum, those deaths contributed to
The Real Bottom Line which is, after all, the task of management. They
were merely a calculated side-effect of their *cost-cutting* effort. Managers
are aware of the prime essence of their action in relation to cost: there

are *costs that go into a product (the labour, the raw materials) before they can sell it and recover their costs* (Magretta 2002). Hence, managers *need to recover their costs and make a profit*. That is what *drove* Ford's managers even when it meant incurring *civilian casualties* (Magretta 2002). Finally, managers too are *often mistaken about our own true interests* because they are trapped in the *money and power code* (Habermas 1997) which they believe supersedes all virtue ethics.

Similar to Socrates, Aristotle (384–322 BC) noted that *the life of money-making is in a way forced on a person and not a life chosen for itself*. Aristotle also thought that *making money didn't count for him as a proper activity because we didn't have any point at which we knew when it was over*. And that it was *all right to sell goods if they were excess from your household consumption. But to actually deliberately produce goods with the intention of making money on them, was to corrupt the activity itself* strongly advocating that he was *opposed to producing things for money*.[45]

Aristotle's thinking also denotes that it is not part of the free will to engage in *money-making*. However, making money is the core activity of management. Hence, Aristotle might have supported the idea that it is market capitalism and competition that *in a way* was *forced on a person*. This negates the *free will* which Aristotle thought was needed for virtue ethics. He also contemplated that virtuous activities should have an end to it. But money-making, as very modern managers know, has no end. It presents a never-ending treadmill on a quest for money. Money-making has not *any point at which we knew when it was over* and therefore has no virtue. Rather than avoiding and negating money-making, management does the exact opposite of what ethical philosophy determines as virtuous behaviour.

Furthermore, one should only engage in money-making when one *sells household leftovers* (Aristotle). One should never engage in the purposeful *production of goods* and services *with the* sole *intention for making money*. In sharp contrast to Aristotle, this represents the exact essence of management. As a consequence, management exists in stark contradiction to Aristotle's virtues and is therefore fundamentally unethical, according to his belief. For Aristotle, money-making is not only a *corrupt activity itself* but also corrupts the character of those engaged in it. Not too many would deny that. Consequently, it is rather self-evident that Aristotle was *opposed to producing things for money* and called the quest for it unethical. Hence, management's unethical behaviour may be explained by its ignorance of such ethical demands. In Aristotelian ethics however, ignorance constitutes the opposite of virtue ethics.

Socrates believed that *we should never willingly pursue something that is bad.* On that, Aristotle noted, an *act is involuntary if it is done out of ignorance of particulars.* Under these conditions it is *involuntary only if* management, *on learning of what they have done, come to regret the act or* are *pained at having done it.*[46] The inability to regret management's acts has been demonstrated by management itself with their claim that they only use numbers to decide. With this approach management seeks to shield itself from the ethics of its own decisions. It pretends that by founding decisions purely on numbers, it can relieve itself from ethics. This is not so. *Allocation by number eliminates the politics and numbs the pain* (Magretta 2002). *But it also eliminates the thinking and judgement, and rules out choices that could better match resources to opportunities.* Management tries to rule out self-reflection and judgement by relying on numbers but for ethics judgement is strongly linked to morality which nobody can escape from, not even when pretending this can be done through the use of numbers. In sum, management negates the core principles of virtue ethics.

In Greek ethics it is not so much Plato (428–348 BC) but Aristotle (382–322 BC) who is often seen as the quintessential philosopher of virtues.[47] He developed two forms of virtues, *intellectual* and *moral virtue* and linked intellectual existence to morality for which he saw *theoretical* and *practical* wisdom as essential. Management negates both ideas by not having its prime *telos* directed towards either *intellectual being* or *moral existence.* Rather than being *intellectual* or live a life of morality, management lives towards creating shareholder values (profits). Managers are hardly ever intellectuals and intellectuals are hardly ever managers. The same applies to management versus *moral existence,* nor is management directed towards *theoretical wisdom.* Most managerial texts provide hands-on practical and, above all, non-theoretical instruments, often expressed in simple models using 1-2-3-4-5-6-7-etc-steps to be taken to *turn your business into profits.*

On Aristotle's final concept of *practical wisdom,* management relates more to the word *practical* than to *wisdom.* It does not seek *wisdom* but *practical solutions* to philosophically trivial problems. The predominant use of the *Harvard Business School Case Study Method* in management schools does not teach *wisdom* but simple practicalities. The foremost task of management is to set up a *business model so that an enterprise works* (Magretta 2002). In short, management represents the negation of Aristotle's forms of intellectual and moral virtue and of theoretical and practical wisdom.

In Aristotle's expression of theoretical wisdom, he did see action and a contemplation for ethical judgements about *'what shall I do?'* as the prime idea.[48] Management ranks contemplation secondary to action. *Managers will go about their business of making things work* (Magretta 2002). In addition, the question *'what shall I do?'* is not an ethical one for management but one that is driven by *quantifying methods, finance, decision-science, and negotiation* because they *provide a systematic way to deal with the unknown* (Magretta 2002). Neither quantifying methods, nor finance, nor decisions-science are related to ethics. They have been invented to divert attention away from ethics. It *numbs the pain* as it numbs ethical considerations. In short, management bypasses the core ethical question *'what shall I do?'* by negating the ethical sphere of decision-making. It quickly shifts decision-making into the realm of so-called scientific methods that carry strong connotations to an engineering ideology.[49] Hence, management has developed an internal apparatus that seeks to avoid ethical decision-making negating any deeper contemplation. Both are favoured by Aristotle's ethics.

One of Aristotle's key concepts says *it is a good virtue to have friends.* In Greek antiquity, the concept of friendship was considered important because having friends was seen as related to having a good character. Aristotle developed three forms of *friendship, a shared friendship, the choice to live together,* and *friendship* leading to *a happy and honourable life.* He rejected the idea of solitude. Instead, Greek philosophy favoured social relationships with others as being essential for a moral life. In sharp contrast, friendship is not a virtue fostered by management. Rather than being created out of virtues, friendships for management are established out of a perceived necessity and strategic usefulness. They are only formed as a temporary alliance when competition is of no direct advantage to management. On the whole, however, the virtue of friendship has no value *in-itself* (Kant) for management. It only features as a momentary means to achieve a competitive advantage.

The demand of competition hardly allows management to share anything, least of all friendship. Managerialism often means to see the world in *friend and foe terms.* Competitiveness favours the viewing of others as *foes* rather than *friends.* Rather than *freely living together* as friends, the *Organisation Men* (Whyte 1961) are put together by management at corporate level. This assembling of people – converted into human material or resources – is not based on friendship but on what is useful to management.[50] Schrijvers (2004) even argues that *you can give or deny power to your employees by the place you allocated them in your company*. It is managerial usefulness and managerial power-play, not Aristotelian friendship, that allocates human material/resources.

Finally, Aristotle's ethical concept of *friendship* is also related to *a happy and honourable life* neither of which constitutes anything useful for management. Living a happy and honourable life can never be an *end in-itself* (Kant) for management. It can only ever be a means to a managerial end as it does not constitute a *telos* for management. Management has simply no use for *a happy and honourable life*.[51] In sum, management represents a near total annihilation of the core elements of Aristotle's ethical concept of friendship.

For Aristotle, friendship could be based on i) utility, ii) pleasure, and iii) virtue.[52] On friendship out of utility, he emphasised utility as related to *helpfulness and convenience* rather than *efficacy and advantage*. The latter two are related to management however they are not ethical motives for friendship. For management the idea of friendship has been related to a *business community*. But the illusory claim of a so-called *business community* is negated by the fact that that is not quite a community of friends at all. Inside the *Moral Maze* (Jackall 1988) of management that is governed by competition one might have the occasional functional *friendship* that delivers efficiency and business advantages. But these are more often based on temporary alliances, agreements, and so-called *business partnerships* than true friendships in the sense of Aristotle. Aristotle's first two reasons for friendship – *pleasure and virtue* – are hardly ever found among business partnerships. They are forged out of competitive necessity rather than pleasure and virtue. Predominantly management operates out of self-created and market-driven inevitabilities. Occasionally, this forges alliances, joint-ventures, cartels, and the like. These are established when they are advantageous to management. The driving force behind them is to *sustain a competitive advantage* or better to *eliminate competition* (Magretta 2002), but never the creation of Aristotelian friendships.

In short, only the motive of utility relates somewhat to management. *Pleasure and virtue* are contradictory to the managerial interest of *sustaining a competitive advantage*. Aristotelian friendship only appeals to management when it is of assistance to *competitive advantage*. Other than that, it has no value for management.[53] In sum, Aristotle's ethics does not offer management much to go on. Management represents a negation of Aristotle's ethics on friendship.

Even Aristotle's concept of *sōphrosunē* – *nothing in excess and nothing in deficiency* – does not offer too much for management. Remunerations for CEOs and top-management are often *excessive*. On the other side those *who make things* (Aristotle) – generally the workers – are suffering from a range of *deficiencies*. These span from low wages – to *keep the cost down* (Magretta 2002) – to the much claimed but rather non-existent so-called *work-life balance*. Managerial excesses and workers' deficiencies are not only a contradiction in-themselves but also contradict Aristotelian virtues. According to Offe and Wiesenthal (1980), those *who do* (management) and those *who make things* (Aristotle) operate in accordance with two different sets of organisational logics that reflect two different sets of interests. This results in *excesses* on the one hand and *deficiencies* on the other. The excesses and deficiencies are only a reflection of a general pattern of unethical behaviour in Aristotelian terms. This is shown through two different sets of virtues that compare Aristotle's virtue ethics with the non-textbook reality of management:[54]

Table 2.1   Management and Employees in the Light of Aristotle's Virtue Ethics

	Those Who Do – Management	Those Who Make – Employees
i) Wages/Income Resulting Virtues	cost factor – to be reduced (↓) **parsimonious, penny-pinching**	livelihood, family, existence, life (↑) **caring, justice, compassion, happiness**
(ii) Working Time Resulting Virtues	long – to be extended (↑) **exploitative, unfairness, unequal**	short – to be reduced (↓) **equality, fairness, egalitarian, sharing**
(iii) Working Conditions Resulting Virtues	impediment on the right to manage (↓) **authoritarian, controlling, dictatorial**	autonomy, involvement, democracy (↑) **open, liberal, participative, democratic**

Table 2.1 shows some of the differences in virtues between two groups that Aristotle saw as *those who do* (management) and *those who make things* (labour).[55] In the table, Aristotle's two groups are related to Offe and Wiesenthal's (1980) three core interests that separate management from employees. These interests – *income, working time, working conditions* – have led to stark contradictions between both sides. Wages are a cost factor for management that is to be reduced. On the other side of the coin, for employees wage is the sole means of sustaining their livelihood. Similarly, management often seeks to extend working time, cuts annual leave, and denies or reduces maternity leave while employees seek the exact opposite. Finally, the betterment of general

working conditions often incurs a cost to management while for employees improved working conditions are an element of *organisational happiness*.[56] For Aristotle, as for most other ethical philosophers, happiness is an essential category. This is not so for management. In sum, the table above shows that management negates two fundamental ethical principles, the *ethics of happiness* and all ethical virtues as outlined by Aristotle.

It is telling that management, management ethics, and *The Servants of Power* (Baritz 1960) who write *for* management never mention *organisational happiness*. There is a raft of 'O's (OB – organisational behaviour, OS – organisational studies, OD – organisational development, etc.) but no OH (organisational happiness). In addition, the literature on management *has much less to say of and for those who are managed* (Marsden and Townley 1996; Klikauer 2007:138). Despite the appearance that *those who are managed* and *organisational happiness* are of relevance to management, they are often denigrated to no more than *others*. Magretta (2002) defines management as *management creates performance through others*. For management employees are a mere cost factor. For those un-stated, excluded, and marginalised *others* – or *personas non grata* – however, wages represent the Aristotelian virtues of caring, justice, compassion, and happiness.[57] They allow that those unmentioned *others* care for their families in a compassionate way so that happiness is created.[58]

For management, the opposite virtues are relevant due to the structural need for cost-cutting: parsimony and penny-pinching. Management's virtue rests on *ungenerosity* while employees' virtues seek *generosity*. Aristotle has a critical relationship to money that is the all important driving force behind management but he extends the morally deficient virtue of penny-pinching to loans and interests in general.

According to utilitarian ethicist, Singer (1994:4), *Aristotle claims that it is wrong and unnatural to earn interest on financial loans*. For many managers, charging interest is a vital part of their business, as it is for banks, insurances, financial services, mortgage funds, hedge funds, underwriters, stock exchanges, etc. Aristotle declares all this as morally wrong. On the other end there are those who have to service loans and pay interest. Being on the receiving end is not an excuse for moral wrongdoing. But for Aristotle it is the earning of interest on financial loans that is wrong not the act of servicing them.

Secondly, it is also *unnatural* under Aristotelian ethics to earn interest because moral virtues *come about as a result of habit...none of the moral virtues arises in us by nature*. When management engages in the immorality of charging interest then it acts not only against Aristotelian ethics but also against nature. Charging interest is socially constructed. Consequently, and according to Aristotle, it derives from a morally deficient habit. It is a failure of virtues. On the issues of working time Table 2.1 also shows two structural interest contradictions. These are expressed in two sets of virtues. For one, working time needs to be long. For the other side it should be short. For one this leads to the virtues of exploitation, unfairness, and inequality. For the other it is represented in the virtues of equality, fairness, equalitarianism, and sharing.

Equality, fairness, egalitarianism, and sharing carry close connotations to altruism. Altruism can be seen as an ethical behaviour that benefits others by sharing and helping one another. Usually, we find the greatest altruism within our immediate family and less among those to whom we are not so closely related. Finally, there is *distant altruism*. This is the humanity we feel towards strangers. Overall, altruism has been with us since we became humans. It may originate in food sharing that has been an important step to further the evolution of humanity. It was not competition but altruism and the act of sharing that made us human. Even in primitive societies the key lies in sharing. Marshall (1976:311) writes on this *we give to one another always. We give what we have. This is the way we live together.* In primitive societies, a man who owns a thing is naturally expected to share it, to distribute it, to be its trustee and dispenser. Management represents the total negation of this. It is non-altruistic and does not believe in sharing. Management does not give to another and is not naturally expected to share. It is competition that counts for management. The ethical virtue of altruism, the very origin of humanity, has no use for management.

General working conditions are another area in which one side needs to insist on its *right to manage* – which leads to the virtues of authoritarianism, controlling, and non-democratic top-down or semidictatorial relations – and the other side demands autonomy (Kant), involvement, self-determination (Hegel) and democracy, leading to virtues such as openness, liberalism, participation, and democracy. For employees these virtues apply to both work and society. It is the virtue of democracy that *makes us essentially who we are* as Aristotle believed. For management, the issue of democratic virtues artificially separates the managerial world from the societal world. For them liberal democracy is a moral virtue whilst industrial democracy is immoral. While democracy makes us what we are – a democratic society – for management it challenges their dictatorial right to manage.

Moral life for Aristotle aims to bring to *realisation those things that make us essentially who we are*. German philosopher Hegel (1770–1832) saw ethics in self-realisation. Management negates this by making profits, efficiency, and shareholder values their essentials. For management as seen in Harvard's *decision-making tree* it is foremost the question of *'Does it maximise shareholder values?'* that determines what is right or wrong. Not a moral life – Hegel called this *Sittlichkeit* – but the maximisation of shareholder values *makes* management what it is. Hence the essence of management and even its crypto-ethical *decision-making tree* negates Aristotle's ethics.

Similar to Aristotle's ethics, Protagoras' ethics in his writing *'On Truth'* demands that *man is the measure of all things*. Firstly, management is not about truth but about efficiency, profits, and *The Real Bottom Line*. There is no philosophical truth in a BMW, only saleability. Secondly, for management *man is not the measure of all things*. Man is degraded to an unspoken *other*. Management represents the exact opposite of Protagoras' ethics. For management, it is *things are the measure of all* where things are profitability, output, sales, etc. *Man* is constantly measured against Key Performance Indicators (KPIs), scorecards, output, and productivity.[59] Outside the company, s/he is not measured as man (or woman) but as customer.

Protagoras' *man* is only of use to management as a quantifiable measurement, not as *man in-itself* (Kant). Management is about numbers, not about Protagoras' *man*.[60] Inside managerial ethics, Protagoras' *man* (Aristotle's *those who make things*) is no more than a *cost factor* that needs to be reduced as part of management's endless need for cost-cutting, efficiency, and *The Real Bottom Line*. The idea that *man is the measure of all things* has been continued by Epictetus who wrote in 100 AD that *signs of one who is making progress are: he censures no one, praises no one, blames no one, finds fault with no one, says nothing about himself as though he were somebody or knew something*. Modern management represents the total negation of Epictetus' virtue ethics because firstly, management censures people and their censure ranges from trade union access to workplaces, e-mails, web-access, authoritarian forms of managerial meetings (Klikauer 2008), restrictions of union material, and so on and, as cases have shown, it reaches even into the public domain as liability, defamation, compensation, etc. (Parker 2002).

Secondly, management's negation of *praise no one* is manifested in the very existence of the managerial performance *appraisal*. It is also to be found in public praise for some and not for others. This is used in management meetings so that employees are made to appear *promotable*. Thirdly, the negation of *blame no one* rests on the managerial tendency to *blame others* ranging from other managers to the market, to government, trade unions, and the weather. Anything bad is usually not management's fault unless courts can prove otherwise. The famous buck only stops with management when it is forced upon them. The managerial prerogative of the *right-to-manage* includes the *right-to-blame* others. Fourthly, the same goes for Epictetus' virtue of *finding fault with no one*. In the blame game it is often management's *blame the victim* approach that carries the day. Finally, the virtue of *says nothing about himself as though he were somebody or knew something* is negated by *impression management*. It is also manifested in the millions of articles, journals, magazines, textbooks, conferences, business schools, etc. that praise management (Magretta 2002:1–244). Management is not just a *Narcissistic Process* (Schwartz 1990) but shows all the signs of a narcissistic pathology. In sum, management negates every single virtue outlined by Epictetus.[61] As a consequence, management negates almost everything Greek philosophy on virtue ethics had to offer.

Modern virtue ethics

The foremost moral philosopher of modernity who discussed virtue ethics was David Hume (1711–1776). He thought adults should not be *slaves of their passions* but live a virtuous life. He also believed that reason has only a limited role in ethics because the determination of good and evil cannot be achieved through reasoning. According to Hume, *reason exerts itself without producing any sensible emotion*. Instead, we arrive at good and evil through our inner feelings, our character, and our virtues. For Hume, *vice and virtue are not discoverable merely by reason. Morality therefore is more properly felt than judged.* Hume saw ethics as a question of virtues when *we combat passion and reason*.

Hume, like many others favoured a universal approach when saying that ethics consists of *principles of humanity in which every man, in some degree, concurs*. Claiming that only an ethic that is *common to all men can alone be the foundation of morals...the humanity of one man is the humanity of every one*. Hume's virtue ethics is highly problematic for management because it seeks exactly the opposite of management's beliefs. Management does not treat people according to the dictum *the humanity of one man is the humanity of every one*. For management, every one is different and every difference is used to separate one from the other. It starts with so-called *individual employment contracts* and extends to KPIs, performance related pay, performance management, and individual job descriptions.[62] Management treats every one different, with different privileges, different statutes, different job titles, different positions inside the managerial hierarchy, different payments, different bonuses, different rewards, different benefits, etc. Apart from that, management is not about Hume's ethics of humanity. In short management is the near total negation of Hume's idea of *the humanity of one man is the humanity of every one.*

To achieve such a level of ethical humanity the utilitarian philosopher John Stuart Mill (1806–1873) believed that *utilitarianism, therefore, could only attain its end by the general cultivation of nobleness of character.* Management however does not cultivate a *noble character* but the opposite as the non-textbook reality of the *Moral Maze* (Jackall 1988), *Dirty Business* (Punch 1996), and *Narcissistic Process and Corporate Decay* (Schwartz 1990) depicts. Management schools and MBA programmes do not cultivate Hume's virtues of nobleness, dignity, decency, and courtesy but rather the opposite as management thrives on rivalry, schism, factions, fiefdoms, back-stabbing, dirty politics, manipulation, facades and charades, collusions between various actors, bribery, creative and exotic accounting, benefiting from rule-bending, and corruption. In sum, management exists on virtues that represent the near total opposite of ever single virtue thought important to virtue ethics.

For virtue ethics, the *nobleness of character* constitutes an inalienable right of life where the term *life* signifies every aspect of vitality. The idea of *vita-equals-life* is essential for the *self-determination* of human beings. Management seriously challenges the argument of *life = all aspects of vita = self-determination.* Top-management does not grant other managers and those *who make things* (Aristotle) the right to self-determination and self-organisation. According to Magretta (2002), *self-organisation* which sounds *seductive* is no more than *wishful thinking.* As a *concept of management self-organisation is fundamentally flawed.* Management represents a negation of self-organisation and self-determination. Therefore, it negates the very essence of the ethics of *'life-equals-vita'.* It denies the virtues of self-organisation and self-determination that are essential to an ethical life.

The same applies to a life that sees *knowledge as desirable for its own sake,* being part of a virtuous human being and *not merely* an *instrument.* For management the human virtue of knowledge *in-itself* (Kant) has no use-value. Rather the exact opposite is the case. Knowledge only becomes a value for management if it is deprived of its virtues and of being something *in-itself* and turned into *merely an instrument for management.* In short, the relationship between ethics, knowledge, virtues, and management represents the reverse of what virtue ethics intended it to be. Management does not value *knowledge for its own sake* as it is the opposite of what it wants and needs. It does not even try to avoid it becoming an instrument. For management, knowledge is only useful as an instrument that can be used. In conclusion, management does not support the virtues of knowledge as outlined by virtue ethics.

Very much like *knowledge for its own sake* management also differs on what moral philosophy considers ethical in regard to the virtue of *friendship*. Originating from Aristotle, Hume's ethics saw *friendship as involving acting for the sake of one's friend's purpose and one's friend's well-being*. In the real, non-textbook world of management, a manager *will pose as friend yet operate as spy* to gather *human intelligence. We can spy on managers, colleagues, customers and suppliers and dig up the dirt about them. Don't forget that the organisation is full of people who, because of jealousy or revenge, are eager to leak information to us. The secret is to pose as a friend* (Schrijvers 2004). In a world governed by jealousy, hate, competition, and struggle that runs on the *money and power code*, Hume's virtue ethics of friendship is annihilated.

Managerial *friendships*, or better temporary alliances, are purpose driven under the maxim of *how can I use this for my advantage*. Managerial relationships represent the opposite of Hume's virtue of *having friends for the well-being of these friends*. Managerial friendships, if they exist at all, are targeted, network based, functional, and operate in hierarchical top-down relations. These simulated friendships carry connotations of Baudrillard's *Simulacra and Simulation* (1994) representing mere instrumentalism but not morality. According to Hume's virtue ethics, friendships are important when they benefit *a friend's well-being*. In the competitive world of management, the benefit and well-being of other others is hardly enshrined in the essence of management. On the contrary, grief and misery are more likely to be determining factors inside the *Moral Maze* of management. But ethics also emphasises the importance of *bringing one's emotions and dispositions into the harmony of an inner peace of mind*. Inner harmony and peace are seen as inherent virtues. However, the non-textbook world of management is radically different from what moral philosophy demands.[63]

Inside the managerial world, managers do what the organisation asks them to with the self-pacifying and invented excuse of *'it's my job'*. If management would bring their *emotions and dispositions into the harmony of an inner peace of mind*, it would most likely cease to exist in its current form. *Harmony and inner peace of mind* totally contradict the managerial essentials of competition, cut-throat business, deceiving plans of strategic management, and a *battlefield that incurs human casualties*. Managers, if they want to be successful in management, cannot afford to bring their *emotions and dispositions into the harmony of an inner peace of mind*. The essence of management represents diametrical poles to the essence of virtue ethics. The virtues of *harmony* and *inner peace of mind* can never become part of the essence of management without ending management itself.

To find an *inner peace of mind*, Catholic philosopher Thomas Aquinas (1225–1274) wrote in his *Summa Theological* in 1266 that *in men there is first of all an inclination to good in accordance with the nature*. This creates two problems for management. Firstly, for Aquinas the essence of humans is *to be good, to do good*, and this is a *natural inclination*. For management, Aquinas' truth of a *natural inclination to be good* has to be managerially reconstructed. This is done through conditioning institutions such as business schools but principally through the conversion of human *beings* into human *resources* during the labour process that converts humans into labour through HRM's induction programmes and secondary socialisation (Klikauer 2007:183–204). As a result of such conditioning, processing, and conversion, the sole inclination of managers becomes the money and power code. Aquinas' virtue of having an *inclination to be good* is of no use to management.

The second problem for management is Aquinas' demand to be *good in accordance with the nature* which is hardly possible. Management is based on the exploitation, the use, and, if required, the destruction of nature, the natural environment, the nature of animals, and humans. Management exists in *opposition to* nature, not *in accordance with* it as Aquinas' virtue ethics demands.[64] Management only values whatever can be used and measured in monetary terms.

Commonly, management's *Real Bottom Line* is often articulated in monetary terms because it *is expressed in numbers that matter* (Magretta 2002). Money often features as the measure of all things in management thinking. On this, the Catholic philosopher Aquinas' bible has been very clear. *Jesus Christ threw the moneylenders out of the temple*. Similarly, taking interest (usury) is prohibited in Islam. Buddhism warns that if you harm another person when doing business you will inevitably bring harm to yourself. Almost all *commandments* issued by religions such as Christianity, Islam, and Buddhism are negated by management. Money-lending is the core part of its operation, either in the form of banking and investment or in the form of corporate accounting. Charging financial interest is essential to managerial operations and they do bring harm to others by strictly enforcing conditions from lenders onto receivers. But they also violate the receiver's ethical right to self-determination through the issuing of specific provisions attached to the lending process. In short, management negates Christian, Islamic, and Buddhist value ethics when money is concerned. Hence it can neither be virtuous in a Christian, Islamic, or Buddhist understanding of ethics.

The violation of these principles is strongly related to the issue of *trust and sincerity*. Both are important aspects of all virtue ethics. In his authorised biography, *The Man Who Owns The News – News Limited CEO Rupert Murdoch*, Michael Wolff notes that *he* (Murdoch) *has never made a secret out of not being trustworthy, therefore... you can trust him not to be trustworthy* (Munro 2008:46). But it is not only the Chairman of the world's largest corporate media empire that cannot be trusted. Almost by definition, strategic management is based on war and *general-ship* with the key idea of *deceiving the enemy*. As such it can never be geared towards trust which represents the complete opposite to *deceiving the enemy* (Klikauer 2007:129–134). The militarist thinking of strategy demands not to trust your business enemies. Therefore the essence of management demands that it violates the virtue ethics of trust. Management only trusts itself and even this self-trust is limited. In the words of managers, trust is distorted, deformed, and converted from something ethical into something that can be used, usually in one's own favour and/or against others. In other words, the virtue of trustworthiness is negated by an artificial and instrumental use that exterminates the meaning of trust as well as the ethics of trust.[65]

Being truthful and having trustworthiness is also a virtue that relates strongly to *The Self*. One of the world's foremost ethical philosophers, *Emmanuel Levinas* (1906–1995), noted that *ethics is not a question of 'being' someone, but a question of understanding differences and calling one's self into question*. The virtue of *calling one's self into question* or *living a self-examined life* (Socrates 469–399 and German philosopher Adorno, 1903–1969) is a virtue not conducted and practiced by management. Management's primary task is to examine, to analyse, and to question others but hardly itself. It questions other managers, other corporations, the market, stock prices, market shares, employees, trade unions, government regulations and so on. Rather than applying Levinas' ethics of *calling one's self into question*, management operates the exact opposite. It *calls others into question*. In that way, management shifts blame onto others and absconds itself in a process called *externalisation* (Bakan 2004). It negates Levinas' ethics and thereby fulfils Adorno's dictum that *failing to live a self-examined life means living a false life*.

Avoiding self-examination not only easily leads to a false but also to a selfish life. In his work on *Utilitarianism* (1861) ethics philosopher John Stuart Mill (1806–1873) noted that a selfish person is someone who is *a selfish egoist, devoid of every feeling or care but those which centre in his own miserable individuality.*[66] Such a *selfish person* represents the very opposite of virtue ethics. This is precisely what Magretta (2002) advises management to do when arguing that *allocation by number eliminates the politics and numbs the pain. But it also eliminates the thinking and judgement.* Management is well advised to eliminate thinking, self-examination, and *moral judgement* – Kant's *Critique of Moral Judgement* (1790) – by presenting their decisions in numbers as it makes them appear depersonalised, neutralised, and naturalised (Klikauer 2007).

It also eclipses the managerial anti-virtue of being *a selfish egoist devoid of every feeling for others* (Mill). When a manager cuts 10% of the workforce in '*his*' (sic!) department to receive a six-figure bonus by the end of the year then Mill's selfishness has been achieved as this manager can rest *in his own miserable individuality and moral indifference* (Schwarz 1990; Schrijvers 2004). Inside the morally indifferent world of management, managers also have to negate virtues such as *every feeling or care for others* (Mill 1861), a *willingness to care for others, to trust others,* and the creation of a *feeling of good will.* Neither one of these three virtues is of any use to management. Management cannot afford to care for others as shown in cases from Ford's Pinto to Bhopal and from AIG-Insurance to General Motors as shown during the global financial crisis of 2007–2010. Instead, it cares for itself by bonus- and share-price driven outsourcing and downsizing. Above all, management specifically does not need to *care of others.* This has been perfectly expressed by Noble Prize Winner Milton Friedman (1970): *it is the social responsibility of business to increase its profits.*

Mills' virtue of trust can even be dangerous to management. Managers can never become too trusting of others, especially managers of other corporations. For management, trust is only good when it operates inside a cartel, a *trust* (!), or a monopoly. Lastly, the virtue of a *feeling of good will* has no value for management either unless it can be converted into a will towards power and profits. The virtue of a *feeling of good will* can never be expressed towards other competitors in the marketplace. The managerially supported idea of competition and markets, almost by definition, excludes the ethical concept of a *feeling of good will* towards others. As Magretta (2002) outlined, *in a competitive world, doing a good job of creating value is only the necessary first step toward superior performance.* One also needs to *outperform the competitors* which can hardly be achieved through a *feeling of good will*. Management has to negate the morality of a *feeling of good will* if it is to achieve *superior performance* to *outperform* its *competitors*.

In sum, Mill's three virtues have to be negated by management. If they cannot openly annihilate them, management at least needs to pretend to live up to them (cf. Baudrillard's *Simulacra and Simulation*, 1994). This has been noticed by moral philosopher Levinas who emphasised that *in the modern world, we do not display anything like the openness to Others that he* [Aristotle] *understands as ethics. Instead, we mostly live a pale narrow vision of ethics, and ethics as codes and rules, an ethics that is useful for our business* (Jones et al. 2005:78).

Such a narrow view on ethics disallows for the virtue of *empathy*. Empathy is generally considered to be the ability and willingness to sense a situation from someone else's point of view. Management in general, however, sees the world from its own point of view. It does not even *acknowledge* or *recognise* the view of, for example, their workers. The very few pages on workers, employees, trade unions, and labour in almost every management textbook testify to management's deliberate avoidance to see the world *from someone else's point of view*. Through the avoidance to recognise *Others* (Hegel) – *those who make things* (Aristotle) – management eradicates the ethics of empathy (Honneth 1995).

Because of its own *Narcissistic Organisational Ideal* (Schwartz 1990) management does not need to see the world from someone else's point of view, least of all from the worker's. In addition, in many cases the consequences of managerial decision can be offloaded onto others who are not directly connected to management. These range from customers (faulty products or minor quality), workers (downsizing, retrenchment, cost-cutting), society in general (social and health costs, etc.), and nature (animal cruelty, and environmental destruction). The ability to offload many negative consequences of managerial action does not encourage empathy because in the vision of management these are *externalised costs* that management does not have to cover. Hence, there is no need for the ethics of empathy.

Such an offloading or *cost-externalisation* (Orwell's Newspeak) also relieves management from *the importance of unity and cohesion in an ethical community of friends*. Virtue ethics creates a number of problems for management. For one, and as already established, management is not based on friendship but on competition and *the battlefield with human casualties*. Secondly, management is not an ethical community. It is not even an *organic community* that has grown together. It is rather an artificially composed mixture of different personalities. There is nothing natural or organic in the way corporations are set up by management. Finally, where virtue ethics emphasises *unity and cohesion* management emphasises competition, market forces, and *battlegrounds*. Despite the wishful thinking and pretences of the textbooks' version of management, the reality is not the fabricated place of harmony, invented unity, illusory cohesion, and *community of friends* it is made out to be.

Management always includes Hegel's *Other* which is represented through non-managerial staff. Ever since Taylor's *Division of Labour* (1911) the world of management has been divided into *those who manage* and those *who are managed*. These two groups have also been labelled as *managerial* and *non-managerial staff*. The idea of *unity* between both is more of a textbook illusion than organisational reality. In many cases, the relationship between both groups is defined by an inherent conflict with management on the one side and employees and their trade unions on the other. If their relationship was based on *unity and cohesion* as demanded by virtue ethics, then standard management textbooks such as Kreitner (2009:442–556) might not include whole chapters on *Managing Conflict*.[67] The fact that the relationship between management and non-managerial staff is not based on the ethics of *unity and cohesion* but on conflict has been highlighted by in Offe and Wiesenthal's *Two Logics of Collective Action* (1980). They have outlined the two logics of interests and the resulting collective action. In the arena of *negotiating* (Kreitner 2009:447ff.) three core interests meet: a) *wages* are a cost to management while they are the livelihood for workers; b) *working conditions* and *job security* are also a cost and hindrance to management's right to manage while for workers they reflect decency at work and protection from unreasonable and dangerous workloads; c) finally, management wants working time to be expanded whilst workers want it shortened.

Together with Taylor's *Division of Labour* (1911) these conflicting interests severely impair any hope to artificially create *unity and cohesion* between management and non-managerial staff. They render virtue ethics unachievable for management just as the idea of *organisational culture* is rendered nonsensical (cf. Alvesson 2002). When looking at the deep-structure of management reality rather than the surface-structure of management textbooks, the structural setting of the management–employee/union relationship disallows management the pretence of *unity and cohesion*. If management's reality would be constituted by *unity and cohesion* then rafts of books on organisational behaviour would never have been written and organisational psychology might not even exist (cf. Ackroyd and Thompson 1999). Instead both are established and vital to the managerial process, laying evidence that management is not a natural place of *unity and cohesion*.

While traditional virtue ethics is based on *friendship, unity, and cohesion* among others, German philosopher Adorno's virtue ethics relies on basic human characteristics that enable ethics to flourish. Adorno sees *Mündigkeit*, humility, and affection as core elements of virtue ethics. The ethical idea of *Mündigkeit* originates in Kantian and Hegelian ethics. Kant used *Mündigkeit* as a capacity to use one's own understanding while for Adorno it carries connotations of *taking a stand, refusing to capitulate, adjust to or otherwise play along with institutional forms of domination.*[68] If one identifies an *ethical life* (Hegel's *Sittlichkeit)* with *Mündigkeit* then management demands the exact opposite of what *Mündigkeit* is in the sense of Kant, Hegel, and Adorno. Rather than seeking and fostering employees who *take a stand, refuse to capitulate,* and *play along with* managerial *forms of domination*, management seeks *Organisation Men*.

Throughout its existence, management has always fostered the creation of conforming, passive, submissive, and compliant *Organisation Men*. In addition, almost everything ever written by the *Servants of Power* in the field of management communication, organisational psychology, and organisational behaviour indicates nothing but the complete opposite of *Mündigkeit* whether in Kant's, Hegel's or Adorno's understanding. The task of converting, and thereby deforming, *human* behaviour to *organisational* behaviour creates the very opposite of *Mündigkeit*. Instead of supporting *people who take a stand* (Adorno), management needs people who fall in line and surrender themselves to managerial power.[69] Instead of people who *refuse to play along* (Adorno), management needs good team players under the FIFO maxim – fit in or f**k off!

In the interest of creating *Organisation Men*, management can never support people who refuse to submit to *institutional forms of domination*. Management's instruments range from pre-work educational facilities to induction programmes at work and performance management installed to create *Organisation Men*. Without these instruments management cannot *exercise executive prerogatives at will with subordinates* (Jackall 1988:97). In sum, management has no use for people who have developed *Mündigkeit* as a *capacity to take a critical stand* and to continuously show *vigilance and self-criticism* and therefore has to negate the ethics of *Mündigkeit*.

For Kant, Hegel, and Adorno, it is humility that keeps moral autonomy in check. According to Adorno, humility (*Bescheidenheit*) is the cardinal virtue of today. By this, he means *to do justice won from reflection on one's own limitations*. Not many observers of management would affirm the ability of critical reflection to management. Most of management's actions are the day-to-day activities of running a corporation which excludes time for reflection through self-created pressures and an '*I am busy*' culture. In this process time for reflection and examination is exchanged with being busy. This violates Plato's concept that *an unexamined life is a wasted life*. The '*I am busy-culture*' is deeply ingrained into the managerial process. Management's essence is manifested in *management makes organisations work...it gets the job done* (Magretta 2002) rather than taking time for reflection.

Being prevented from self-reflection, management generally shows no virtues of humility. Instead, corporate excesses, management misbehaviours, and decades of stratospheric CEO remunerations show everything but humility.[70] Adorno also alerted us to the human virtue of *affection* which is not exactly a managerial virtue either. By *affection*, Adorno means *the human capacity to be moved by, not to be indifferent or cold towards, the fate of others* and the *outpouring of warmth and affection*. It is *the very opposite of coldness and indifference* and testifies to a *sensitivity to the vulnerability of others* and the *feeling of solidarity* with them. Management negates all of this. Managerial methods such as *management by numbers, management by objective*, the *allocation of material and human resources*, and *achieving organisational goals through others* (Magretta 2002) lead to anything but *affection*. It negates Adorno's ethical goal of sensitivity, the outpouring of warmth, and the feeling of solidarity.

Inside the *Moral Maze* of management, the exact opposite to sensitivity, warmth, and solidarity are fostered as any sign of weakness, vulnerability, warmth, and affection is ruthlessly exploited by the competitor. As Schrijvers (2004:11) has noted, there *is excitement about dirty tricks at corporate level*. He concludes, the managerial battlefield methods that come into use are *dirty tricks, sedition, coups, blackmail, and emotional cruelty* all of which constitute the very opposite of affection. Adorno noted on his three ethical virtues that *they are personal qualities that individuals must possess if they are to be in a position to perform ethical acts*. In short, management represents the very negation of these *three constitutive characteristics of an ethos*, rendering ethical acts by management unachievable.

The overall conclusion of virtue ethics is that management negates almost everything that virtue ethics has to offer. The brief overview of virtue ethics from Greek antiquity to today (Adorno), covering also the Middle Ages (Aquinas) and the beginning of modernity (Hume), shows the following: rather than representing virtue ethics or working towards it, the essence of management determines that management does the exact opposite. Consequently, management and virtue ethics exist in Hegelian contradiction to each other that represent nothing but an unsolvable dilemma for management. Living up to the demands of virtue ethics would mean that management has to alter its essence so severely that it would cease to be management.

3
A Utilitarian Critique on Management Ethics

The ethics of utilitarianism spans from Jeremy Bentham (1748–1832), John Stuart Mill (1806–1873), Henry Sidgwick (1838–1900), and G. E. Moore (1873–1958) to contemporary ethicist Peter Singer. Utilitarianism is a philosophy which holds that an action, a law, or a rule is right only if it produces the best outcomes which is manifested in the *Happiness Principle*. It states that ethics must bring about *the greatest good for the greatest number of people*.[71] This creates a number of problems for management. Principally, management is not concerned with whether or not an action, a law, or a rule is right but with whether it delivers profitable outcomes for the company.

Secondly, management's best outcome is not geared towards *the greatest good for the greatest number* of people but towards products delivering on ROI (return of investment). Managerial action inside companies tends to focus on the very opposite of the *Happiness Principle* as management seeks to give – or withhold – a limited number of goods (e.g. promotions, wage increases, bonuses, etc.) to relatively small groups or the smallest number possible. For example, there is no use in a 5% pay increase across the board for everyone. It would only increase costs to management – and reduce profits inside management's zero-sum game – without any tangible benefits for management. It is by far better to use the 5% as incentives (receiving) for some and as punishment (not receiving) for others. In managerial terms, *5%-for-all* is a rather nonsensical proposition and that is exactly why it almost never occurs.

Utilitarianism as a moral theory holds that the only thing relevant to determine whether an action is right or wrong is to be found in the outcome of such action. The consequences of an action are important. Hence this version of ethics is called *consequentialism* (Arrington 1998:379ff.). On this, Mill (1861) noted *he who saves a fellow creature from drowning does what is morally right, whether his motives be duty or the hope of being paid for his trouble.* In other words, the utilitarian concept of consequentialism focuses exclusively on the outcome and consequences. If an action produces a good outcome then it is morally right and ethical.[72] The best one can hope for is that management's action has, as a by-product, a positive consequence that management can frame as ethical. Hence, the creation of an action that has good, moral, and ethical consequences is *accidental*, not *essential* for management (Hegel).

The philosophy of *essentialism* sees an act as *essential* if it is not *accidental* but a determining part of an action. Management's accidental action that produces a positive outcome in respect of the *Happiness Principle* is not essential to management. When measured under the condition of *consequentialism*, management is not an ethical actor as it does not engage in actions that produce good, moral, and ethical outcomes. Occasionally such ethical outcomes do happen as a spin-off from managerial actions however the fact that they occur as spin-offs renders them accidental. The essence of *consequentialism* and *essentialism* therefore determines that management is not an ethical actor in the sense of both ethical principles.

Utilitarianism's strong connotation to *consequentialism* results in side-tracking the motives of an action by focusing on the outcome. In that sense, management is much closer to consequentialism and more distant to utilitarianism. Just as consequentialism management measures outcomes, not intentions and moral motives (Kant). But managerial measurements such as ROI cannot be positively linked to the *Happiness Principle*. Therefore, most management ethics does not fall within the parameters of *consequentialism* or *utilitarianism*.

Utilitarianism in general is also a version of ethics that is geared towards the *well-being of all persons*.[73] Management is not geared towards *well-being* but towards *shareholders* which *always must come first* (Magretta 2002). Management might relate human well-being to those *who make things* (Aristotle) when it seeks *satisfied employees because they are productive* (Magretta 2002). However, here well-being is a means to an end and not a Kantian *end in-itself*. The essence of management's action is to create a productive employee and if the *satisfied employee* is a cost-neutral by-product of this action, then management will have *satisfied employees because they are productive*. However, this does not imply that management is generally interested in well-being as an outcome of their action. It is interested in productive employees.

For utilitarianism the *Happiness Principle* also means to prevent harm to others.[74] The *Harm Principle* says *the only purpose for which power can be rightfully exercised over any member* of a *civilised community – i.e. against his will – is to prevent harm to others*. Management exercises power over employees who are not members of a *civilised community* but of a managerially arranged work regime that neither constitutes a civic structure nor an organic community. The essence of management is not to create *civilised communities* but to establish a *company that gets the job done* (Magretta 2002). For that it constructs an artificial so-called *corporate community* that is managerially engineered for the sole purpose of delivering shareholder values. The term *community* is only of value to management when one can sell something to it (Klikauer 2007:140).

In contrast, a real *civilised community* tends to grow organically out of itself without the narrow managerial goal of creating shareholder values. Civilised communities set forth human, not monetary values formulated in a managerial ROI. Finally, managers are foremost interested in preventing *harm to themselves* rather than *to others* as demanded by utilitarianism. Harm is usually offloaded to others as numerous cases of downsizing, outsourcing, false advertising, and environmental destruction have shown. It is mostly *the Other* – not management – that is outsourced or downsized. In the managerial world preventing *harm to others* operates in reverse gear. Harm is also offloaded to nature – through environmental devastation – and to society, the *battleground* that incurs *civilian casualties* (Magretta 2002). In sum, rather than adhering to the utilitarian *harm principle*, management deliberately offloads moral responsibilities to others even when it means *civilian casualties* as in the cases of Bhopal and Ford Pinto.[75] The essence of management demands that it operates on a '*profit-over-people*' formula rather than with the '*people-over-profit*' maxim (Chomsky 1999; Bakan 2004). Based on this imperative, management can only ever represent the extreme opposite of what utilitarianism calls ethical behaviour.

One of the key philosophers who delivered crucial thoughts on the *harm principle* has been John Locke (1633–1704). In his *Second Trace* (1690) Locke emphasises *no one ought to harm another in his life, health, liberty, or possession...and that all men may be restrained from invading others' rights*. This creates two challenges for management. Firstly, management does harm to others' lives (Pinto, Zeebrugge, Bhopal), others' *health* (OHS, Nestle baby food), and others' *liberty* (*managerial prerogative* and the *right to manage*). It often occurs that managerial action, in the pursuit of profit, results in harm to others (people, environment, society, cf. Table 1.1).

Locke also emphasised that *men may be restrained from invading others' rights*. For management it is a case of where their rights and the rights of the corporation start and where individual rights, human rights, civil rights, and environmental rights end. The managerial *right to manage* does, almost by definition, curtail the rights of others. Management cannot respect the rights of others and has to invade them because they would otherwise create a severe hindrance for management.

Utilitarianism formulates two *chief hindrances to human improvement*. The first is seen in not living up to the *principle of perfect equality*, the second in not avoiding *power or privilege*. The essence of management represents the exact opposite of both. It is not based on the principle of *perfect equality* since the sole purpose of management is to create inequality between those *who manage* and those *who are managed*. If management would create *perfect equality*, the present wage structure would collapse and so would company hierarchies, managerial bonuses, the separation between management and non-managerial staff, and finally management itself. In addition, management represents hierarchy based on power. It lives for and with managerial power which it misuses, abuses, and uses to make others do what it wants them to, irrespective of the utilitarian demand for *equality*. Management's essence is manifested in *having power over others*. It also uses, possesses, shows, and even enjoys privileges. Management is not even a reflection but the mere opposite of Bentham's utilitarian idea of *each to count for one and no one for more than one* because the managerial division between management and those *who make things* (Aristotle) results in authority, asymmetric power, hierarchies, and inequalities. This is depicted by almost all forms of management as seen in almost any company. Furthermore, while utilitarianism criticises *power and privilege*, it is one of management's core organising principles that support managerial hierarchies and authority. Managerial hierarchies (*that come with ownership*), the *always important lines of authority*, and *command-and-control structures* (Magretta 2002) are based on the *power and money code*.[76] Without money and power management would not exist. In sum, management represents a near total negation of the three utilitarian principles of *avoidance of power, avoidance of privileges*, and striving towards *perfect equality*.

The utilitarian *Happiness Principle*

Perfect equality is closely linked to the utilitarian obligations that seek to increase *the total happiness levels of existing persons...to improve their lives as much as possible.*[77] This is in stark contrast to management's task of *the real mission which is the bottom line*. Management is also not dedicated to the utilitarian principle that demands to *improve their lives as much as possible*. Instead management and companies are *not serving customers who are unprofitable* (Magretta 2002). Utilitarianism's *telos* is to create happiness for all existing people while management's *telos* is set towards serving those customers who are profitable to support the bottom line. In short, rather than being geared towards *improving their lives as much as possible* management is geared towards *selling them as much as possible*.

For utilitarianism the *Happiness Principle* can be achieved in two ways: *consequential* and *non-consequential*. The former is seen as *act-utilitarianism* that seeks to choose an act which creates the best consequences, the latter as *rule-utilitarianism* in which acts are performed according to rules. Inside both versions of utilitarianism negative consequences are accepted but only in cases where the greatest amount of good occurs as a result. For example, it would be possible to increase wages for all non-managerial staff even if it means not to increase remuneration for top-management. This would also serve the utilitarian *principle of perfect equality* as outlined above. But management's practice of widening the wage gap is the very opposite that, according to utilitarianism, rather represents immorality.

The ethics of reversing the wage-gap, for example, carries connotations to the utilitarian principle that sees people as equals. Management however not only sees people as unequal but has to make them unequal in order to sustain hierarchies and power. For Sidgwick *whatever action any of us judges to be right for himself, be implicitly judged to be right for all similar persons in similar circumstances*. Throughout its existence management has worked hard to ensure that people are not judged similarly. Management's primary drive has always been directed towards the idea that an *action is judged right* when it serves management and *The Real Bottom Line*. But utilitarian ethics demands that *what is right for one person has to be also right for another person*. Management distinguishes between itself and others which are *dissimilar* entities. Therefore others – those *who make things* (Aristotle), for example – do not need to be judged similarly as demanded by ethics philosopher Sidgwick. The managerial dictum ranges from unequal pay for similar work to pay differences between men and women for similar and even for exactly the same jobs. The very existence and structure of promotion and hierarchies negates the ethics of Sidgwick. Management holds the exclusive right to promote or privilege one but not the other, even in similar cases. In conclusion, management can never make an ethical judgement in cases of similar circumstances. If management was to act ethically, it would negate itself. If it acts managerially, it negates Sidgwick's ethics. It appears as if Sidgwick's ethics and management are in an unsolvable dilemma.

The *Golden Rule* of Sidgwick's ethics is: *do to others as you would have them do to you.* For management however this is not so. As an example, management still uses sweatshop and child labour which has been hidden behind elaborate structures of sub-contracts setting up a semi-distance between management and sweatshop and child labour. It is not likely that these managers want *what they do to others* to be done neither to them nor to their children. Managers are also seeking wage reduction that includes reducing bonuses, working conditions, and benefits as a cost-cutting measure for those *who make things* (Aristotle) but are highly reluctant to apply its cost-cutting ideology to themselves. Management operates on the exact opposite of Sidgwick's *Golden Rule* because a pay cut for those *who make things* (Aristotle) and a reduction in their working conditions such as atypical work arrangements and the casualisation of employment for example, often means the exact opposite for management, i.e. bonuses and promotions.

Furthermore, Sidgwick formulates that *it cannot be right for A to treat B in a manner in which it would be wrong for B to treat A, merely on the ground that they are two different individuals.* Again, the reverse constitutes the very essence of management otherwise individual pay, individual contracts, and the systematic individualisation of employees would not exist. That it does, testifies to the fact that management represents a fundamental reversal of Sidgwick's ethics. It treats two individuals differently just because they are different individuals. Playing one off against the other is the fundamental essence of management while Sidgwick demands that *individuals in similar condition should be treated similarly.* For management it reads *individuals in similar condition should be treated differently.* To cover up their immoral behaviour, management is at pains to find even the most microscopic reason to justify that individuals are being treated in different ways. They employ rafts of people such as HR managers and corporate lawyers to find reasons and invent explanations as to why individuals are not to be treated the same. These reasons can be illusive as power rests on managerial power, not on the power of the better argument. Management has hardly ever employed anyone in order to seek reasons to justify why individuals are similar and conditions should be similar.[78]

Sidgwick also believed that *consciousness can be intrinsically good.*[79] That explains why managers do not bring their consciousness into work. Despite being highly moral in their private lives, they *leave their conscience at home* when they enter the corporate world (Schrijvers 2004; 2005). For moral philosophers such as Sidgwick, a moral consciousness is intrinsic to humans. For management however moral consciousness is secondary to their work and best left a home. Management is about *making things work* (Magretta 2002), not about moral contemplations. As Harvard's *ethical decision-making tree* tells us, when it comes to a conflict between the profit-maxim and moral consciousness, the latter loses hands down. For management such a conflict is decided like flipping a coin: *heads = I win; tails = you lose.*

The ethics of pleasure, swine and marmalade

Sedgwick's *intrinsically good consciousness* also carries references to John Stuart Mill's *Higher and Lower Pleasures* (1861). Mill states, *the creed which accepts as the foundation of morals, Utility, or the Greatest Happiness Principle, holds that actions are right in proportion as they tend to promote happiness, wrong as they tend to produce the reverse of happiness.*[80] This is a creed that cannot be accepted by management whose credo rests on shareholder value, profitability, and the rational application of resources to achieve profitable goals. Management can never see the rightness or wrongness of decision-making in the light of *promoting happiness*. The essence of management does not manifest itself in promoting or hindering happiness but in promoting or hindering profits, shareholder value, and resource allocation. It is based on *achieving performance through others* as outlined by Magretta (2002).[81]

Mill's happiness relates to pleasure and he outlined that it is wrong to suppose that *human beings are capable of no pleasures except those of which swine are capable. Human beings have faculties more elevated than the animal appetites* – which is called the *Swine-Principle.*[82] It nominates Aristotle's intellectual pleasures as the pinnacle of ethics. But neither swine nor management finds pleasure in intellectual endeavours. Instead, just as swine have an insatiable appetite for swill, management has an insatiable appetite for shareholder-value, profits, cost-cutting, and *The Real Bottom Line*. For Mill ethics is *the superiority of mental over bodily pleasures*. For management it is the superiority of monetary rewards over mental and intellectual pleasures. Management's essence simply does not contain mental, intellectual, and scholarly virtues.[83]

Mill continues with *it is better to be a human being dissatisfied than a pig satisfied; better to be Socrates dissatisfied than a fool satisfied*. For management, the exact reverse is the case. One of the US' most prolific management-gurus and the world's most widely read writer on management, Peter F. Drucker wrote management first of all appears to be *like a mindless game of chances at which any donkey could win provided only that he be ruthless* (quoted in: Magretta 2002). If management is no more than *a mindless game for donkeys* (Drucker) then it satisfies a *pig* but not a *human* (Mill). It satisfies *a fool* but not *Socrates* (Mill). In conclusion, either the world's foremost management writer and Mill's ethics are wrong or management is indeed satisfying to fools and pigs.

Management however likes to see employees as *satisfied fools* (Mill) because *satisfied employees will be productive employees* (Magretta 2002). For management, the utilitarian concepts of happiness and satisfaction only appear as a Kantian *means* to a managerial *end* which is defined as managerial goals manifested in shareholder values and profits. If however, management is at all interested in employees' happiness and satisfaction, it is management that defines what happiness and satisfaction means. It is the authority of management that allocates – or revokes – elements that create happiness and satisfaction to those it single-handedly deems worthy of it.

On this Schwartz (1990:16) noted that one can define totalitarianism *as the process of defining people's happiness for them. This is the fundamental psychodynamic of totalitarianism. It alienates people from themselves and gives them over to others.* Giving people power over to others is what Bauman (1989) called converting people into *objects of power*. In the managerial process, the unmentioned workers – those *who make things* (Aristotle) – are often only named as *others* (Magretta 2002) and turned into objects of power by the objective power of management.[84] And it is management that has the power to define happiness *for them*. That management excludes democracy from this definition is almost self-evident and never mentioned in affirmative textbooks – a fact which fulfils Schwartz's (1990:16) definition of totalitarianism.[85] The psychodynamic of totalitarianism is completed when management locks itself inside the self-reinforcing managerial fantasy of knowing what is best for those *who make things* (Aristotle) in terms of happiness and satisfaction.[86] Such an illusion is aided by the huge entourage of *Servants of Power* (Baritz 1960).[87]

In sum, employee satisfaction has no intrinsic value in-itself (Kant) for management. It is only pursued if it leads to a *productive employee*, which renders it an instrument to achieve a certain goal. Secondly, management reverses Mill's ethics. For management it is better to have a *satisfied fool* and *a pig* rather than a *dissatisfied Socrates*.[88] A satisfied fool is a productive fool but any philosopher – least of all Socrates – whether satisfied or not, might not be all that productive for management. Mill thought *to be human means to be an intelligent human.* He also stated that people *lose their high aspirations as they lose their intellectual taste.* For management, an intellectual employee is not the prime objective. A productive employee, however, is. Management seeks neither intellectualism nor intellectuality. What is sought, however, is functional knowledge that serves narrowly and managerially defined tasks. Whether an employee has intellectual taste or not is largely irrelevant to management.[89]

For utilitarianism, as for almost any other ethical philosophy, it is the brain and the intellect that turns humans into what they are. Management represents the near total opposite of philosophy. It is the brain in action that is relevant for utilitarianism but not for management. For Mill, the human *being, according to the utilitarian opinion,* [builds] *the end of human action,* [and] *is necessarily also the standard of morality. The end of human action* for management is not utilitarianism but the profit motive as much as the necessary standard for morality is not the *Greatest Happiness Principle* but shareholder-value.

According to Henry Sidgwick's *The Method of Ethics* (1874), the *Greatest Happiness Principle requires the individual to sacrifice his own happiness to the greater happiness of others.* For management, however, it is the other way around. As an example, in cases of denied wages and rejected wage increases for employees, downsizing, cuts in benefits, reductions in working conditions, retrenchments and so on, management has never sacrificed its own happiness for the *greater happiness of others.* In some cases, it is even the direct opposite. A mass-retrenchment of workers often leads to increases in shareholder-value and in bonuses for management. In the non-textbook reality of management this means increased competitiveness for companies and a favourable treatment of managers by top-management. Simultaneously, for those *who make things* (Aristotle) sacrifice and unhappiness become corporate reality. There are hardly any cases when CEOs sacrifice their stratospheric salaries, share options, and other benefits beyond tokenism for the *happiness of others.* In general, the *happiness of others* is sacrificed for management and CEOs. In sum, management reverses Sidgwick's ethics as it *sacrifices the greater happiness of others* in favour of its own.

For utilitarianism the *Greatest Happiness Principle* also means what Locke expressed as *all the fruits it naturally produces, and beasts it feeds, belong to mankind in common (Second Traces,* 1690). For management, however, such fruits and animals cannot belong to *mankind in common* as management has to extract surplus value from them. They become a means to engineer profits. Commodification converts anything into a commodity. The commodification of everything has reached as far as entire forests (including everything in it from frogs to shrubs) having been patented so that management and corporations have the exclusive right to exploit them. For management, there cannot be anything that belongs to *mankind in common.* It is the total opposite that makes management possible. Management therefore has to contradict Locke's ethical position.

According to Sidgwick (1889:478) the *Greatest Happiness Principle* is designed to create happiness and *happiness, whether private or general* [is also] *the ultimate end of action.* Management does not engage much in private affairs other than turning humans into customers. The management of marketing and advertising enters even the bedrooms of consumers through commercial TV and makes consumers believe that happiness is to be found in the accumulation of consumptive goods under the unspoken maxim of *one TV makes you happy; two TVs make you twice as happy!*

Management does, however, engage in *general action.* Here, Sidgwick's ethics nominates happiness as the *ultimate end* agreeing with Kantian ethics that happiness is an end *in-itself.* This establishes Kant's *Kingdom of Ends.* However, management cannot function by directing action towards happiness. Nor can it accept happiness as the ultimate *telos* of their action. For management, the *ultimate end of action* has always been *profits whether private or general* but never happiness, except a pretended happiness shown on TV by happy drivers, happy junk-food eaters, and happy Happy-Meal children. Hence, inside the *Moral Maze* (Jackall 1988) of management happiness has to be negated for management's ultimate ends: *The Real Bottom Line.* In short, management must divert its action away from true happiness as the ultimate end and therefore has to act unethical according to Sidgwick's ethical *principle of happiness* as *the ultimate end of action.*

The ultimate ethical end is to be found in the utilitarian concept of being *veracious, faithful to promises, obedient to law, disposes to satisfy the normal expectations of others, having their malevolent impulses and their sensual appetites under strict control.* These utilitarian ideas appear to be a list of ideas that management cannot deliver on. For example, in his study on *The Morally Decent HR Manager*, Macklin (2007:266) quotes a manager who said *the important thing is to have a good memory so that you don't contradict the lies you have already told*. The CEO of Sun Microsystems has been equally forthcoming. *'Promises'*, he made clear, *'are still promises until somebody delivers the goods'*. But these are not the only occasions where management contradicts utilitarian ethics. Strategic management, almost by definition – as *general-ship that deceives an enemy* (Klikauer 2007:130ff) – cannot afford to be faithful to promises. Deception can never depend on being faithful to promises otherwise strategic management would hardly exist. Strategic management is often seen as the queen of management. Even more than day-to-day management (tactics), the deceptive character of strategic management eliminates utilitarian ethics.

Management can, however, afford to be *obedient to law* except in cases of so-called *creative accounting*, costly OHS regulations, and consumer safety (Ford's Pinto). It generally operates under the maxim *all is fine as long as you can get a way with it.*[90] Management does however not *dispose* itself *to satisfy the normal expectations of others* unless this contributes to *The Real Bottom Line* or when such satisfaction delivers a welcoming by-product. Their intentions and motives are not ethical (Kant) but managerial. Under the ethics of *consequentialism* this might be justifiable. Consequentialism only looks at the outcome or consequences of an action and not at its intentions. Under the ethics of utilitarianism, however this is ethically not justifiable. Management also needs to keep its *malevolent impulses and their sensual appetites under strict control* which hardly seems to be the order of the day when corporate excesses in pay, remuneration, female escort services, *lavish executive perks* (Sage 2007), and the infamous $8,000 shower curtain of an Enron CEO are considered. The corporate world depicts rather the exact opposite.

Utilitarianism also *prohibits falsehoods* based on four reasons: because of the harm it does to others by misleading them; because of the mutual confidence that men ought to have in one another; because falsehood tends to produce a general mistrust of all assertions; and because it violates the general rule of respect in truth. The falsehood of doing harm to others is contradicted by management as it is generally seen as management's task to do harm to others in various ways – *Management must...keep costs down* (Magretta 2002). It ranges from cost and wage cutting for those *who make things* (Aristotle) to the total annihilation of a competitor. Competition on the so-called free market almost in itself demands that management does harm to others.[91] In strategic management, the total annihilation of competitors is achieved by misleading them. It comes as no surprise that *Sage's Encyclopedia of Business Ethics and Society* (2007) states *the ethics of business is more like the ethics of poker than the ethics of ordinary morality*. One of the core principles of poker has always been to bluff and mislead the opponents.

In this spirit it is not management's task to create *mutual confidence that men ought to have in one another* but rather the opposite. If a competitor has confidence in a business, this competitor cannot only predict but also anticipate the business' next move which can be lethal to that business. According to everything strategic management concepts tell managers, this is to be avoided if a business is to be successful. In the reality of industrial relations, for example, the very last thing management wants are trade unions who know how far they can go in wage bargaining. Management has no confidence in trade unions (cf. Kreitner's *Threat of Unionisation*, 2009:42). They may not be lethal for the company but can be very costly for management that *must keep costs down* (Magretta 2002). Finally, management does three things in relation to Sage's (2007) *poker game* analogy. For one, it seeks to separate itself from so-called *ordinary ethics* which is not possible. Secondly, management sees ethics like any other issue inside the *Moral Maze*. Thirdly, management's main actions are games in which one can win or lose, issues of bluffing, deception, and the destruction of mutual trust – the very opposite of what utilitarian ethics considers to be moral.

Almost as an inbred consequence, management has to create *general mistrust* by telling lies and deceiving people.[92] As an example, this is evident in the fact that many companies produce two annual business reports, one for the tax office and the other for shareholders. Another example is the secretive character of management that is enshrined in so-called confidential documents and paralleled by a corporate PR machine installed to eclipse management's true intentions. Management in general do not trust their competitors. Trust is also very low when unfriendly take-overs are on the cards (cf. Sage's *poker analogy*).

Management is not about truth but about success and *The Real Bottom Line*. *The general rule of a respect in truth* is nice to have when it comes along free of charge but it is also something to be disposed of when it hurts *The Real Bottom Line*.[93] In conclusion, it is a structural imperative that management violates all four principles as outlined by the utilitarian *prohibition of falsehoods*. Thereby management needs to be unethical when measured against these principles that together create utilitarian ethics. According to the ethics of utilitarianism, these four aspects are not a menu-like affair from which management can select one while negating others. It needs to live up to all four. Management's inability to do so shows its unethical character.

Utilitarian ethics also includes the principle that a moral action is right when it *produces more good than could have been produced by any other action open to the agent*. Management falls within this principle as it can select from a range of options open to them. Generally, this is the area of decision-making or *instrumental rationality*.[94] Management's decisions are usually made on cost-benefit rationalities (*instrumental rationality*), not on ethics. They impact on day-to-day management and on strategic planning of a corporation.[95] The principle of *producing more good than any other action* is defined managerially (for profit), not under utilitarian ethics (greatest happiness). This is done in adherence to the past and present management ideology of Managerialism rather than as an understanding and the application of utilitarian ethics. In conclusion, whilst management can select from a range of options as the ethics of utilitarianism defines – and therefore falls within the parameters of utilitarianism – it cannot select the options of utilitarian ethics and has to divert from utilitarianism in order to fulfil its own essence of instrumental rationality (cost-benefit). Utilitarianism also demands that things be achieved for the largest number of people. Inside any company, management is usually the smaller number of people, hence, the self-serving small group (management) at the expense of a larger one (employees) contradicts utilitarian ethics. The essence of utilitarianism (the *Happiness Principle*) and the essence of management (instrumental rationality) differ harshly when it comes to decision-making. Restricting ethical options to a small number of people is like piling up marmalade in one corner of your toast.

For *Jeremy Bentham* ethics was simple because the ethics of happiness, so he thought, is like English marmalade.[96] It should be evenly spread around. If one follows Bentham's analogy of *marmalade-ethics*, happiness in the managerial world should also be spread around evenly. Management negates this. Firstly, not happiness but *The Real Bottom Line* is management's essential *telos*. Secondly, managerial power, hierarchies, authoritarianism, managerial privileges, pay structures, bonuses, etc. indicate that management is not at all about spreading things around evenly. The opposite is the case. If management does create happiness it is usually an accidental by-product of managerial actions. Privileges and power are reserved for management. Thirdly, management has reduced happiness to industrially engineered marketing-happiness

that uses the quasi-scientific marketing formula of: 1 TV = happiness
→ 2 TVs = twice the happiness.

Ever since Taylor's *(Un-)Scientific Management* (1911; Klikauer 2007:
143–159), management believes that *management science* is possible. In
contrast to this managerial self-belief, Bentham thought that science
should be *moral science* and scientific advances should be used to enhance
morality and ethics. Management however uses science and scientific
advances to enhance their power and authority, largely *through* management science, organisational behaviour, and HRM. These are management's *'Servants of Power'*. The use of science by management is also
seen as a way to enhance the saleability of commercial goods. For
ethics, science can only be seen as *moral science* with the inherent *telos*
of improving morality. For management, science in the service of management is seen as functional science that leads to improvements of
the money and power code and commercial activity. For one, science
and morality are equal and *moral science* merges with *moral actions*. For
the other, science is subservient to management and supports managerial actions. In sum, the *moral science* of ethical philosophy contradicts
the submissive role science plays inside the managerial framework. But
science in the service of management can even incur *civilian casualties*
(Magretta 2002).

John Stewart Mill's *rule-utilitarianism* demands to obey rules such as
don't lie, keep promises, and avoid hurting people. Mill's version of utilitarianism offers management two choices. They can either act ethically
when they place emphasis on an ethical act or on an ethical rule or
they can avoid doing so and thereby act unethically. Mill essentially
offers routes towards utilitarianism that are directed towards the *Greatest Happiness Principle*. Management negates *rule-utilitarianism* by not
adhering to its rules. Management, as Schrijvers (2004) has outlined,
does lie. It also has problems with keeping promises.[97] Management is
also never, at least not primarily, geared towards avoiding hurting
people.

The utilitarian *Greatest Happiness* principle also includes the concept
of the multiplication of happiness. On this, Mill (1861:391) emphasised *the multiplication of happiness is, according to the utilitarian ethics,
the object of virtue: the occasions in which any person (except one in a thousand) has it in his power to do this on an extended scale – in other words, to
be a public benefactor – are but exceptional; and on these occasions alone
is he called on to consider public utility* (Sample et al. 2004). In sharp
contrast to this, management's essence does not manifest itself in the
creation of a single happiness and even less so in the creation of a

multiplication of happiness. It lacks the ethics of standard utilitarian ethics but also the ethics of the *multiplication of happiness* which negates Mill's *object of virtue.* Not to provide a *multiplication of happiness* if one is able to do so is a clear violation of Mill's core principle of the utilitarian *object of virtue.* It is an ethical demand if *a person has the power to do so.* Management clearly has this power but it chooses not to multiply happiness. Roughly 100 years have passed since the invention of *Scientific Management* (Taylor 1911; Wren 2005). During this time management had the option to multiply happiness but has consistently chosen not to. It testifies to the fact that management is not an ethical actor who has the creation of a *multiplication of happiness* as its essence. This is especially true when considering that management is in the somewhat unique position of being able to use its *power to do this on an extended scale* (Mill). In sum, this is not a failure of management but a clear indication that it is not part of its essence. Management simply does not have the *multiplication of happiness* as an ethical goal.

Finally Mills' ethics also demands that an actor shows that *on these occasions...he is called on to consider public utility.* Hence management would need to consider *public utility* if it wants to be an ethical actor. However, management exists inside the confinements of firms, companies, and corporations and as such argues that these boundaries do not concern *public utilities.* For management, the ethical concept of *public utilities* is negated under the headline of externalisation. The utilitarian ethical concepts of *public utility, public helpfulness, public value, and public service* are not part of management and its ideology Managerialism that both treat *public utility* as an external factor that only needs to be engaged when enforced by regulation. Through the success of the managerial ideologies of *de-regulation* and the so-called *industry self-regulation* management has been able to abscond from many *ethical duties* (Kant) enshrined in public utility. As a consequence, it seeks to insulate itself from managerially unwanted societal consequences of their actions.[98]

In general, management's relations to public utility can be described in two ways. The public is to be used when needed and otherwise kept off limits when management acts. Hence, the corporate-public interchange is not seen by management as a sphere in which happiness can be fostered. It is neither seen as an area in which the utilitarian principle of *the multiplication of happiness* can take place. In short, management's relationship to public utility is rather defined by *taking* and off-loading than by *giving* and servicing.

Bentham and Mill have created an ethical philosophy that raises severe questions for management and forces management into an unethical position. Their philosophy also creates another problem for management. Mill thought that one should *defend a minority against a majority* view because a majority view can easily become a *tyranny of the majority*. Similarly, Bentham thought that *obedience to a majority opinion would actually lead to social stagnation since there would no longer be organised resistance to a decision-making authority*. Both concepts are challenging for management. Firstly, management and its ideological expression of Managerialism are anchored deep inside the majority opinion of today's society.[99] It is also moored inside today's teaching institutions, textbooks, conferences, journals, etc. One of the prime ideologies of Managerialism is *The Privatisation of Everything* (Mandell 2002) that reaches even into private primary schools and down to for-profit kindergartens. The majority opinion on Managerialism remains fundamentally unchallenged and any critique on management's TINA (there is no alternative) is made to appear pathological (Marcuse 1966). Management and its entourage of affirmative writers and *servants of power* have truly established a *tyranny of majority*.

This has not led to stagnation inside management thinking and Managerialism but surely changed the thinking inside today's society. The success of Managerialism has made society unconditionally accept the rules of Managerialism. This has been achieved largely through modern corporate mass media. Today's society is constructed in a way that it functions purely as a support mechanism for managerial capitalism. The original idea of managerial capitalism that supports society has been turned upside down. The whole of society works exclusively towards the support of Managerialism. This is most visible in the reversal of a core utilitarian principle: *fair treatment of all is a higher good than majority rule*. Virtually all advanced capitalist societies show that the *majority rule* of Managerialism has been made a *higher good* than *the fair treatment of all*. Today's global society is departing ever more from *fair treatment of all* but is moving ever closer to a world governed by Managerialism (cf. WTO, GATT, G7, G8, G20, IMF, World Bank, OECD, etc).

According to Mill (1861) another higher good is manifested in *the utilitarian morality* [that] *does recognise in human beings the power of sacrificing their own greatest good for the good of others*. Again, management's core task is to reverse this. It has *the power of sacrificing their own greatest good* because of its position as the sole guardian of the *right to manage*. However, management's power and the *right to manage* is also the very managerial essence that determines the reversal of Mills' concept. Given its power it can never sacrifice its *own greatest good for the good of others*. Nor can it equalise itself with those *who make things* (Aristotle) without damaging the sole source of its own power: hierarchy and control over others.

It appears to be one of the core rules of Managerialism that management excludes itself whenever sacrifices are engineered. Usually, these sacrifices are presented by management in passive terms such as *sacrifices have to be made* (Klikauer 2007 and 2008). Management excludes itself by immediately shifting the burden onto those who have been designed to make the sacrifices that have been invented by management. The *greater good of others* always has to rank below the greater good of management. Those *who 'make' things* (Aristotle) are disposable from management's point of view but not those who '*do*' things (Aristotle) – management itself.   Equality

In sum, utilitarianism's concept of sacrificing *one's own greater good for the greater good of others* (Mill 1861) has to be negated by management. This has happened ever since Taylor (1911) constructed workers as expendable and modern management as non-expendable. The essence of management even disallows the recognition of workers as workers. It denigrates them to '*performance achieving others*' (Magretta 2002). These unnamed and unrecognised others have been constructed as being on the receiving end of managerial decisions (Klikauer 2007:152). Consequently, management negates the complete set of Mills' ethics that has been enshrined in *utilitarian morality*.

Mill also saw what Hegel called *the Other* as equal to oneself rather than on the receiving end. He emphasised *to do as one would be done by, and to love one's neighbour as oneself, constitutes the ideal perfection of utilitarian morality*. This Biblical statement is negated by management at two levels. Management's neighbours are its competitors in the market place. They are the objects of strategic management in an attempt to use military means to win in the battlefield of market shares.[100] Hence, management can hardly ever see their competitors as neighbours and definitely not love them as prescribed by the Bible and by utilitarianism. No textbook on *Strategic Management* will ever advocate the love of one's competitor. Rather the extreme opposite is often the case. In short, strategic management is about winning, not about loving.[101]

If the ultimate utilitarian principle is the Biblical idea that demands *to love one's neighbour as oneself* then Mill's next concept creates even more problems for management. In *Utilitarianism* (1861) Mill notes *the proposition that happiness is the end and aim of morality does not mean that no road ought to be laid down to the goal, or that persons...should not be advised to take one direction rather than another.* In utilitarian ethics, happiness is the end and aim of morality. This is not so in management because its ends and aims are shareholder values, *The Real Bottom Line*, and profit-maximisation. During the 19th century management started to form itself. At the same time Mill's work on utilitarianism appeared.[102] He opened up a road towards *the goal* of the utilitarian *Happiness Principle*. During the late 19th and the 20th century, management could have travelled this road to become an ethical actor under the conditions of utilitarianism however it did not.

It is irrelevant whether managers, management, and management educators knew utilitarian ethics in 1861 or not. What is relevant is management's consistency in negating utilitarian ethics ever since management's self-invention. It did so when it converted itself from management to *Scientific Management* and during the 21st century when it added semi-academic disciplines and its ideology of Managerialism to its portfolio (Baritz 1960; Chandler 1962). Throughout decades of management writing, management education, management seminars, management books, management journals, management conferences, management conventions, management schools, management studies, management theories, and so on, management never took the road that was opened by Mill. It did not become an ethical actor in the utilitarian understanding. Instead management took the road laid out by *instrumental rationality*.[103]

Finally, Mill's ethics also engages in management's *means-ends* calculation. He emphasised that *the utilitarian doctrine is that happiness is desirable, and the only thing desirable, as an end; all other things being only desirable as means to that end.* In other words, if management had taken Mill's road towards utilitarian ethics, it would have happiness as its essence and management's essence of shareholder value, profit maximisation, and *The Real Bottom Line* would have to be negated. Management would have been constituted as an institution directed towards happiness which would have been a severe shift in management's paradigm. All managerial functions would have to serve the ethical goal of happiness rather than the managerial goal of profits and Magretta's statement would have sounded completely different.

> *The job of a CEO is to put the best people on the biggest opportunities and the best allocation of dollars in the right places...performance depends on doing a few things really well. It ensures growth in profitability.*

Instead of the above, an ethical statement would have read something like:

> *together with all others inside a company, an elected spokesperson would ensure that the best people would be put on those opportunities that create the most happiness for them and for others. Their task would be to allocate dollars in those places that create the most happiness for the most people. Creating happiness depends on doing all things in the spirit of happiness. It ensures growth in happiness.*

The fact that none of this ever happened in the last 150 years of management testifies to the fact that management is not concerned with the ethics of utilitarianism. It does not see happiness as an end under which all other activities are seen as means that serve this end. In conclusion, management represents the negation of Mill's ethics of utilitarianism.

The ethics of friendship and aesthetic enjoyment

According to utilitarian philosopher E. G. Moore (1873–1958) ethics entails not only the greatest happiness principle but also *three obvious intrinsic goods* which are *pleasure, friendship, and aesthetic enjoyment* (Moore 1922; Rachels 2003:105). In contrast to Moore's ethics, management's three *obvious intrinsic goods* are shareholder value, profit-maximisation, and *The Real Bottom Line*. Moore's concept of pleasure is annulled by management's essence of not being about pleasure for the greatest number of people. Some managers, however, might gain pleasure from achieving *The Real Bottom Line*, from reducing the workforce in *their(!)* department by 10% to receive an end-of-the-year bonus, or by rejecting wage claims. These managerial actions, however, are not conducted out of an ethical (or unethical) motive. Neither do they result in a good, ethical, and moral consequence for a great number of people.

Moore's ethical concept of friendship has never been part of management. In the non-textbook version of management, Schrijvers (2004) noted *don't tell your colleagues and managers too much. You must sharpen your talent for measuring and exposing others.* Given this, one is hardly inclined to view the *Moral Maze* of management as a place of friendship. Hiring people, for example, is not about friendship but about integrity, intelligence, and energy.[104]

Moore's third concept is that of *aesthetic enjoyment*. Inside management, next to nobody has ever been hired for showing *aesthetic enjoyment*. Employees who engage in *aesthetic enjoyment* are all but useless to management. Nor does the history of management testify to Moore's concept of *aesthetic enjoyment* when it comes to workplaces. The early cotton mills and blacksmith workshops in 19th century England, underground coal mining, fragmented workplaces of Taylor's task-divided factories in the early 20th century, Ford's assembly line of the mid-20th century, modern sweatshops, child-labour places, and not even today's standard office or cubicles have ever depicted *aesthetic enjoyment*.

In the 21st century, neon-lit offices furnished with cheap laminated standard desks, uncomfortable office-chairs, grey computers with non-ergonomic but equally grey keyboards, a bleak joyless plant in the office corner, and a standard poster on the wall of any standard office are not exactly depictions of *aesthetic enjoyment*. Moore's *three obvious intrinsic goods* of *pleasure, friendship, and aesthetic enjoyment* build utilitarian ethics but management has never engaged itself with even one of them. Instead, it relies on the *three qualities of integrity, intelligence, and energy*. Rather than living up to utilitarian ethical values, management demands its own values that represent a near total negation of Moore's concept of utilitarian ethics.

Utilitarianism also entails that in *the real world when people lie, others are hurt, and their own reputations are damaged*. This concept is continued with the line *when people break their promises, and fail to return favours, they lose their friends*. In the real world of management it is not people as such but managers who lie. Workers are converted from human *beings* into human *resources*, they are exposed to being *objects of power* (Bauman 1989), and they show obedience to organisational authority (cf. Milgram 1974). However *The Organization Man* (Whyte 1961) are those who hurt others.[105] Management's own reputation is hardly damaged when blame can be shifted onto others such as employees, an enemy manager, trade unions, and so on.

The reputation of managers can even be enhanced by a lie or a broken promise. What counts for management is *The Real Bottom Line*. Managers contribute significantly to *The Real Bottom Line*, even when lying. They do so when their own power base supports their action as Milgram (1974) has comprehensively shown. Managers are even more willing to operate with untruths when these can be offloaded onto those positioned downstream in the managerial hierarchy. This is especially the case when those downstream are so powerless that repercussions for management can be minimised or annulled altogether.

In the eyes of other managers and top-management these sorts of managers have often achieved the unachievable. They are deemed promotable. Lying and deceiving the enemy are the classical tools of strategic management used on the battlefield in which one has to win. For Peter F. Drucker to win means to *be ruthless*. In other words, ruthlessness, lies, broken promises, and deceptions are part of the managerial game. It is the negation of Moore's ethics of *not lying, not hurting others, not damaging reputations, not breaking promises, returning favours, and not to lose friends*.

The core assumption of Moore's version of utilitarianism is that in the *real world* people *lose their friends* if they engage in actions such as *lying, breaking promises, and hurting others*. In the artificially created *unreal* world of management, things are different. These three unethical elements are all part of the daily routine inside the *Moral Maze* of management. The world of management is not based on *friendship* and therefore losing friends is not an issue. The trick however is, according to Schrijvers (2004), *not to lie to the people who have power over you and not to break promises that one makes towards management*. Loyalty is an issue of the upstream, not the downstream position in the managerial hierarchy. In short, *loyalty is a one-way street*.

Finally, *hurting others* is an idea that can be fully supported by management. Hurting employees that are to be dismissed (cost-cutting and downsizing), customers who die (Ford Pinto), damaging the public (Bhopal), animals (lab-testing), and the environment (Exxon Valdez and Brent Spa) are all part of management (Taylor 1981; Singer 1990; cf. tab. 1.1). In sum, rather than working actively against the unethical behaviour of *lying, breaking promises, and hurting others* as outlined in Moore's ethics of utilitarianism, management actively engages in all three highly unethical forms of behaviour.

In conclusion, the core concepts of utilitarian ethics of Jeremy Bentham (1748–1832), John Stuart Mill (1806–1873), Henry Sidgwick (1838–1900), and G. E. Moore (1873–1958), as well as contemporary ethicist Peter Singer have been outlined in this chapter. They have been brought into a relationship with management to reveal the truth about management ethics. In the Hegelian concept of dialectics that is commonly associated with thesis → anti-thesis → synthesis, the thesis part has been represented by the core concepts of utilitarian ethics. The anti-thesis was presented by management in its real, non-textbook version (Harding 2003). Bringing both – thesis and anti-thesis or positives and negatives – into a relationship made it possible to highlight a number of syntheses on the issue of management ethics. Having applied this method to the most relevant forms of utilitarian ethics and management, the overall conclusion (synthesis) is that management negates virtually every single version of utilitarian ethics.

4
A Kantian Critique on Management Ethics

Perhaps *Immanuel Kant* (1724–1804) is modernity's single most important philosopher on ethics and morality (*Moralität*).[106] His *deontological ethics* defines rights by reference to the good that is commonly achieved through good actions. Kant separated two *imperatives* that both apply to every rational being, the *hypothetical* and the *categorical imperative*.[107] Hypothetical imperatives operate as *if-then* constructions, for example, *if* management seeks to be ethical, *then* it needs to do the following. This is a classical *hypothetical imperative*. Kantian ethics, however, is formulated exclusively in *categorical imperatives* where ethical statements or moral laws have to be formulated in *imperatives that are commands or orders*.[108] Kantian ethics does not exist in *if-then* formulas and there cannot be a condition attached to ethical formulas. They are simply a must. In contrast to wishes and desires, *categorical imperatives* bind us to act ethically. Kantian ethics does not offer management a choice other than to be either ethical or unethical notwithstanding any managerial desires or wishes. There is no middle ground and one's behaviour, and even more importantly one's intentions, cannot be both – ethical and unethical – at the same time.

Both the hypothetical and the categorical imperatives imply that ethics can only be created by rational human beings. For Kant, ethics is not an issue of religious scripture or God. Instead, ethics is to be established through logical arguments.[109] Kantian ethics needs to be free of any inclinations or feelings. It is guided purely by rational ethical laws that are recognised by rational human beings. For Kant, ethics is the purest expression of achievement of the human intellect. However, for management things are different. The purest expression of an achievement of the managerial intellect is a well-run company that produces shareholder values. The *human intellect* is only useful to management if it works towards *organisational goals*, the managerial codeword for profits. In contrast, Kant's maxim is often seen as to *act only according to that maxim whereby you can at the same time will that it should become universal law*. Kant's universal openness is in stark contradiction of many managerial practices that include, for example, non-disclosure clauses and are done behind closed doors. They are often termed *gentlemen's agreements* or, in more severe forms, monopolies or cartels. These are specifically set up not to be universal but to serve a narrowly defined situation. Because they exclude the free market they achieve the ultimate goal of management – profit-maximisation.[110]

Sometimes these cartels are created to hide corporate immorality from the law, sometimes they are simply unlawful. The aim of management, despite all corporate PR announcements, is to have a *business strategy* [that] *moves an enterprise away from perfect competition and in the direction of monopoly* which is the location of real profits. Anti-monopoly or anti-trust regulations all too often provide nothing more than a fig leaf for managerial actions. Sometimes a so-called high-profile case of anti-trust violation is publicised to make the public believe that the free market really exists. Simultaneously, however, most markets are dominated by a few players. These range from oil corporations, car companies, mass media, and container shipping companies to shopping centres, breakfast cereal producers, and condom manufacturers to name but a few. Management is often at pains to avoid being noticed by the few remaining anti-trust laws. In the least however they are interested in giving their oligopolistic market setups the appearance of being universal.[111]

Kant talks about humans and humanity, whereas management *derecognises humans* only to mention them as *others* (Magretta 2002). In other words, humans, people, individuals, workers, and all those *who make things* (Aristotle) appear only as *others* inside the managerial orbit. For Kant humanity is central while for management it is a mere *periphericum*. Humans, i.e. human material, human capital, or human resources, are lumped together with material that is to be allocated in a profit-generating activity. *The Struggle for Recognition* between Hegel's *Master and Slaves* – today's management and employees – has long been lost in favour of management that eliminates Kant's ethics of humanity.[112]

The pure essence of management is not to be found in treating humans as *ends* but in treating them as a *means* as outlined in the managerial goal of *creating performance through others*. Management represents the complete opposite of Kant's *Kingdom of Ends* which demands that humans be treated as ends, not as means. Management is the *Kingdom of Means*. Undeniably, there are exceptions but the very reason for management as an institutional setup inside companies and corporations is not to treat people as *ends* but as *means*. In the managerial world, humans are seen as a cost to management that has to be incurred in order to realise profits, *The Real Bottom Line*. But *costs also have to be kept down*. In both respects, management fails to live up to Kant's *means-ends imperative*. In Kantian terms, management's very existence is based on an unethical model. Management also treats people outside the company as *others* as these people are only of use to management if they can be turned into customers. It is the customer that *generates profits as a result* of managerial efforts. At work and as buying customers, humans have no value *in-themselves* (Kant) for management. They only become valuable when they can be converted from a human *end* into a *means* for profits and shareholder-values. The managerial and the consumptive regimes have no interest in humans beyond their roles as *human resources* – those *who make things* (Aristotle) – and paying customers.[113] Kant demands that we value the human *subject...as an end in himself....*[114] For management however, the value of humans rests only in their *function* inside a process. Therefore, on Kant's means-ends imperative management fails to carry any ethical value.

One way of *treating everyone as a means* is the use of *others* (e.g. employees) as an arbitrary *means*, a tool, or an instrument. On this Kant noted: *man and, in general, every rational being exists has an end in himself and* [is] *not merely a means to be arbitrarily used* by someone else's *will*. Hence Kantian ethics denies management the right to use others, indeed every rational being, as a means. The *right to manage* and the so-called *managerial prerogative* is, in Kantian ethics, an expression of the *managerial will* that turns *rational beings* into means while denying them to be ends. For management every *rational being* [that] *exists as an end in himself* is useless. It only becomes *useful* to management if it can be converted into an instrumental means that produces and consumes.

Kantian ethics rejects not only the arbitrary use of *rational beings* (Orwellian Oldspeak) or *human resources* (Newspeak) but also the idea of processing human *beings* into human *material* or human *resources*, thereby converting their ethical *end-in-themselves* into an unethical *means-for-management*. The concept of managerial prerogative has been invented precisely because management uses people arbitrarily. In Kantian terms this is something a *moral man will not do*.

Kant sees the *good will* as essential for ethics: *it is good only because of its will...it is good of itself*. When management acts out of *good will*, it acts ethically. However, in most cases management acts out of purposive rational and instrumental choices, and out of self-constructed and market- or monopoly-driven necessities. It is the absence of Kant's *good will* that makes management possible. The *good will* is deformed into a *managerial will* for profit maximisation. In short, management negates the Kantian *good will* by acting out of an invented, purposive rational *(Zweckrationalität)*, and, above all, *managerial will*.

The absence of the Kantian *good will* almost denotes a similar absence of Kant's *cultivated reason deliberately devoting itself to the enjoyment of life and happiness*. Management *cultivates reason* and rationality that may be deliberate but it does not *devote itself to the enjoyment of life and happiness*. Instead, managerial life is devoted to a life of market-driven confinements, shareholder demands, market shares, and the like. Buchanan and Badham (2008:41) found that *our organisations are not always the happy, harmonious, collaborative communities that management texts imply*. This environment alienates employees just as much as managers. Even the enjoyment that may be found in beating a competitor, in the latest market share figures, and in stock market numbers is both short lived and false.

Kant says *it is unavoidable for human nature to wish and seek happiness*. Management diverts such *human wishes* into organisational goals and converts the *human* quest to *seek happiness* into *organisational performance* to achieve managerial goals. This supports *The Real Bottom Line*, not an adherence to Kantian ethics. In order to convert human nature into *Organisation Men* (Whyte 1961), management has to repress Kant's *human nature that wishes and seeks happiness* with all the pathological consequences that follow. These pathologies are also an outcome of the denial of Kant's idea of self-determination.

Kant's concept of *self-determination* is an end in-itself.[115] It demands that human beings must be able to determine their own being and their own self. For management this is not possible. When management's sole existence is based on determining the lives of others, self-determination might easily mean the end of management. Therefore, management represents the very opposite of *self-determination*.[116] The managerial regime demands that people who fall under it are determined by management rather than by their own self.[117] Kant's concept of *self-determination* is circumvented by management by being turned into a managerial *means*. For management, self-determination has no value in itself. It rather constitutes a danger that has to be avoided. It can only serve as a tool to achieve managerial goals. In short, management represents the total opposite of Kant's ethical concept of *self-determination* as *an end in-itself*.

Motivation is at the core of self-determination inasmuch as Kant advocates *you to decide for yourself rather than to have somebody else or something else make a decision for you or on your behalf.* This is the essence of Kantian ethics but the exact opposite is true for management. It is management's very essence to make decisions for *others.* In line with the philosophy of *Essentialism,* this is not accidental but essential for management.

In fact, the so-called *Scientific Management* (Taylor 1911; cf. Klikauer 2007:143–159) determines that management represents the total opposite of Kant's ethics. It began by shifting workers' craft knowledge and skills into the arena of management who consequently started to make decisions while those *who make things* (Aristotle) carried them out. Inside corporations the very existence of management depends on making decisions for others by way of the so-called *managerial prerogative* or the *right to manage.* Both lie at the heart of management and sharply contradict Kant's dictum to decide for oneself.

One problem for management is manifested in its inability to make decisions outside their corporations. To a large extent managerial decisions are influenced by markets, monopolies, other corporations to which management reacts, share prices, the global economy, government regulation, new entries, competitors' behaviours, etc. The fact that management has only a limited ability to make decisions again violates Kant's ethics. Therefore, the very essence of management constitutes a negation of the Kantian ethics of *self-determination.* It turns management into a reactor to external influences, reduces its legitimacy, and narrows the need for its existence.

But this is not the only problem Kant's concept creates for management. Ultimately, management is defined as *achieving performance through others* and needs to rely on *others* to function. In many cases these others must make decisions on management's behalf that are out of management's control. As a consequence of management's negation of Kant's ethics of self-determination, it also has to negate the ethics on self-decision-making and therefore violates two core ethical principles of Kant. But by making decisions on management's behalf, those '*others*' – especially other managers and subordinates – always have some autonomy over decision-making that cannot be totally controlled by management or top-management.[118]

Just as self-determination, Kant also sees *truthfulness* as an end: *It is a duty to tell the truth...for a lie always harms another: if not some other particular man, still it harms mankind generally...to be truthful (honest) in all declarations, therefore, is a sacred and absolute commanding decree of reason, limited by no expediency.*[119] Kant's ethics of truthfulness creates a number of problems for management. For one, *information management* is a key component of management ever since Taylor's *(Un-)Scientific Management* (Klikauer 2007:149–154) removed craft knowledge from the hands of the workers and placed it into those of management. Kant's ethics of *telling the truth* cannot be honoured by management because *information-giving* and *information-withholding* are two key elements of managerial power (Klikauer 2008).

Secondly, management is not about truth at all. It is about managing and saleability. For example, McDonalds does not sell food with the intention of being *truthful* but because it generates profits. The only truth that is useful to management is managerial truth which services management's goals and comes at no cost to management. Prime examples of managerial truthfulness have been depicted by the tobacco industry, the fast-food industry, and even the pharmaceutical industry (cf. Table 1.1).

A standard definition of management denotes that it provides the *construction, maintenance, and improvement of an administrative system which co-ordinates, plans, allocates, and transforms human and material resources into profit-making operations.* The word *truth* fails to appear as it is not an essential component of management. Truth and truthfulness only become relevant inside a cost-benefit analysis when the true state of markets, share prices, products, employees, etc. is at stake. In short, while truth in Kantian ethics has an intrinsic value that represents a good *in-itself*, for management it only has a meaning when it is useful or when truth contributes to *The Real Bottom Line.*

At the level of individual managers, speaking the truth seems to be something that managers tend to avoid hence management and Managerialism both have developed their very own language.[120] Inside the world of management language, special *Weasel* words greatly assist management in hiding the truth. At the daily operative level, management and individual managers tend to do the opposite of what Kantian ethics demands. Inside the *Moral Maze* (Jackall 1988) of management truth telling is not encouraged but discouraged as most managers, and even management as such, cannot afford to tell the truth. It has to negate Kant's ethics on truth.

Often the outcomes and negative results of managerial non-truth telling are located outside the corporation or offloaded to other managers and subordinates. Instead of following Kant's dictum of truth-telling, management seems to contradict it by assuming that as long as it is not self-damaging and detrimental to the corporation, the truth does not need to be told. It appears that management is very economical with the truth because it could be used by a competitor. *One also needs to outperform competitors in order to ensure winning the battle and the war* and for that truth can be rather a hindrance than an advantage. In sum, management sees truth, almost like anything else, in zero-sum terms: telling the truth makes you win while I lose and not telling the truth might assist me in winning over you.

The asbestos and tobacco industries, as well as several others, have shown the withholding of the truth for years, if not decades. This has resulted in handsome profits for the industries and their managers while the effects of their unethical behaviour have been offloaded to smokers, the public, and health insurances. These effects range from lung cancer to mesothelioma, obesity, diseases, and industrial deaths. But in the managerial zero-sum game of '*truth vs. shareholder-value*' it is the latter that wins. Even in the infamous Pinto case the truth has been withheld so that Ford's profits would not be diminished even though *civilian casualties* and death were incurred.[121] In conclusion, the very essence of management disallows management to tell the truth unless it is profitable to do so. This is not what Kant had in mind. For Kant it is an ethical imperative to tell the truth but this is something management can ill afford. As a consequence management's use of truth as a tool directed towards goals that support management instead of seeing it as a virtue in-itself contradicts Kant's ethics.

A textbook-case, categorical imperatives, and means-ends

Perhaps the most central ethical theme of Kant's ethical philosophy in regard to management is his categorical imperative that implies to *act so that you treat humanity...always as an end and never as a means only*. This relates to Kant's *Kingdom of Ends* and goes to the very heart of Kantian ethics around which all other dictums centre (Korsgaard 1996). If one seeks to comprehend Kantian ethics in relation to management, one needs to understand his two ethical imperatives of universalism and means-ends. They also highlight the way in which *The Servants of Power* (Baritz 1960) in the form of textbook writers twist and turn Kant to make it look as if Kantian ethics was in support of management. The following nine critical reflections on a present day standard textbook (Boatright's 6th edition, 2009) will highlight how affirmative management writers seek to achieve this. It is a truly Kantian enterprise that follows Kant's *Trilogy of Critiques* (*Critique of Pure Reason* (1781), *Critique of Judgement* (1790), and *Critique of Practical*

Reason (1788); (cf. Sedgwick 2000) as it is written as *A Critique of Management Ethics*.

1. Humanity – the first problem

First of all, management does not *treat humanity* as being important *in-itself* as it has no relationship to humanity as such. Management seeks to pretend it exists in *splendid isolation* of humanity and only turns human beings into human *resources* and consumers. Concepts such as humanity, humankind, civilisation, and the human race have no meaning for management's *The Real Bottom Line*. They are absent from its thinking from business schools, as well as conferences, journals, and magazines. The moral term of *humanity* does not appear anywhere in managerial textbooks and is excluded from the everyday language used by managers (Klikauer 2007 and 2008).

Put simply, management and *The Servants of Power* have separated the world of management from the world of humanity. Each has become a separate entity that never meets the other. Outside the corporate world management only reaches as far as consumer and product markets. The world of humanity, in contrast, encompasses everyone. Management has cocooned itself from even knowing what the world of humanity entails and therefore cannot act in accordance with it. According to Kant's concept of universalism such a separation is not possible and therefore constitutes immorality when measured against his ethics of humanity.

2. Respect – the second problem

Kant's categorical imperative to *act so that you treat humanity, whether in your own person or in that of another, always as an end and never as means only*, does not mention the word '*respect*' at all. The word 'Respekt' does not even appear in Kant's German original. However, in Boatright's textbook on *Ethics and the Conduct of Business* (2009) it suddenly appears. The textbook pretends that respect is the core issue in Kant's ethics.[122] Kant's moral imperative is carefully re-interpreted by stating *these words are unusually interpreted to mean we should respect other people (and ourselves!) as human beings* (Boatright 2009:66).

The term *usually interpreted* translates into trust us experts and textbook writers and secondly tries to imply a majority opinion on Kant. The infamous '*we*' creates an inclusive idea of something we all do. The sudden inclusion of '*respect*' has several functions. Firstly, it diverts our attention away from Kant's means-ends ethics that sees the *Kingdom of Ends* as the final destination of ethics. Secondly, it makes Kant appear as if his ethics was about respect rather than the unethical use of humans as a *means* in the form of human resources/material. Thirdly, it denigrates Kantian ethics to the mere side issue of *respect* and thereby neglects the fundamentality of Kant's ideas on ethics. Finally, it invents and creates the highly agreeable notion of *don't we all respect other people*. In the textbook this is reinforced through the addition '*and ourselves!*' to create a personal feeling. This sort of rhetorical trickery is applied to distort Kant's ethics. The textbook departs further and further from Kant's means-ends dictum through phrases like '*the kind of respect*', '*ethics requires that we respect*', and finally, '*to respect persons, therefore, is to respect them as rational beings*' (2009:67).

It is hard not to conclude that the sudden introduction of a totally unrelated issue – *respect* – serves to misrepresent what Kantian ethics is about. It eclipses his ethics by diverting our attention away from Kant's real intention towards the simplistic issue of *respect*. Meanwhile in Kant's version of ethics, morality is about treating people as an *end in-itself* because this is what constitutes ethics and is therefore strongly linked to *universal humanity* rather than to *respect*. Universal humanity, however, is highly challenging to management. The invented issue of *respect* converts Kant's *critical ethics* into a more user-friendly version *for* management. Kant's ethics however has to be seen in the light of his *The Kingdom of Ends*. This is what Kantian ethics is all about.

3.   The Kingdom of Ends – the third problem

Rather than Kant's *Kingdom of Ends*, management represents a version of a *Kingdom of Means*. It cannot treat humanity as an end in-itself. Customers and employees can only be means.[123] Only as means do they have value for management. Management needs to negate Kant's *Kingdom of Ends* because their ideology is predominantly based on *means* and on achieving organisational outcomes through others. Kantian ethics would destroy the very essence of management. Management has to prevent this from occurring.

4.   Kant's word 'Only' – the fourth problem

In the common textbook reinterpretation of Kant the word '*only*' is turned into the prime target of *The Servants of Power* who service management by deforming ethics so that it fits those in power. The textbook equation of *management + ethics = management ethics* cannot be a truthful understanding of Kant's ethics as it does not allow the only possible conclusion under Kantian ethics which is *management = Kingdom of Ends*. To enable the distortion of his ethics, management writers need to focus on the word '*only*' to legitimise their ideology.[124]

The word *'only'* is used to state that treating people just a bit as a means is permissible to management as long as it respects them! Therefore the totality of management ethics is possible just because Kant has used one word – *'only'* – and management has over-interpreted and partly misused it. However, this is a somewhat strange way to understand Kant. But for management the task is not to understand Kant but to scavenge his philosophy so that his ethics can be made to fit into the prevailing managerial paradigm. The entourage of *The Servants of Power* is ready to accomplish this. Most commonly, this is attained by the use of the *taxi-driver* case (Boatright 2009:66). Here, standard textbooks argue that if you get into a taxi, you use the driver as a means to go from *A to B*. This is portrayed as normal hence an *'everyone does this'* is added. The twisters of Kant tell us next that we are not interested in the drive as an end *in-itself* but in the *means* of being driven. We respect the driver and in that way accomplish Kant's *end*. We are told this fulfils Kant's ethics.

A somewhat plausible but wrong case because of a number of issues: firstly the case cloaks the asymmetric power relationship that operates in the labour market. Having a taxi-ride does not equate to the asymmetrical power relations of employment. After all, most people exposed to managerial regimes are wage employees and not self-employed taxi-drivers, drivers on commission, or drivers who rent a taxi and radio inside the taxi. Secondly, one of Kant's core concepts is *self-determination*. One might argue that the economic determinants existing independent of human beings make one person a taxi-driver and the other an employee under management. Both scenarios deny real *self-determination*. A taxi-driver might – out of lack of other options – be confined to driving a taxi. Hence, money and market-driven structures of the real existence turn taxi-drivers into *means* rather than *ends*. This renders the assumption of economic self-determination a neo-liberal illusion (Offe and Wiesenthal 1980). Hence to be a taxi-driver or an employee is more often than not determined by economic necessity, not self-determination. As a consequence, the textbook analogy of *taxi-driving equals employment under management* is as false as the assumption that both represent Kant's self-determination.

5. False universalism – the fifth problem

By using the taxi-driver example, managerial textbook writers wrongly equalise the user of a taxi service with management. But the user of a taxi does not become the driver's manager which is the underlying false assumption presented in the case to support management. Using a taxi constitutes an individual act while management represents a structure of power relations that reaches far beyond that. This case therefore is a form of false universalism.

Since more people are employed working inside managerial regimes than driving taxis one wonders why an exceptional case – taxi-driving – is used to make a generalisation on management. Managers take on the specific form of organisational behaviour represented in the *Organisation Man*. And they convert human beings into human resources inside parameters set by management. None of these characteristics is exhibited by the ordinary taxi-driver nor are they depicted by the user of a taxi. Human behaviour (taxi-ride) and organisational behaviour (management) cannot be equalised.

6.   Hypothetical imperative – the sixth problem

Another problem of the taxi-driver case rests on the mistaken conversion of Kant's *categorical imperative* into a *hypothetical imperative*. Kant distinguishes between both. For him ethics exists in the realm of the *categorical imperative*. Therefore, others have to be treated as *ends in-themselves*. There cannot be any conditions attached to categorical imperatives. They are '*musts*' and not '*if-and-then*' constructions. There is no other option than to act morally. However, Boatright (2009:66) writes ...*we should respect other people*... Based on Kant's categorical imperative however we *must*, not *should*, respect other people. Kant's categorical imperative leaves no option other than to follow ethics. In sharp contrast to Kantian ethics, management and its affirmative writers have to turn Kant's categorical imperative into a hypothetical one in order to make it sound plausible that Kantian ethics supports management.

7.   TINA – the seventh problem

The invented taxi-driver example negates that there are other – non-market driven – forms of getting from A to B. It presents the case as TINA: there is no alternative. But there is. In Kant's *Kingdom of Ends* a person that seeks to go from A to B can do so as an *end in-itself*. In contrast to management who converts humans into customers and suppliers of a service, a person can move from A to B without becoming a *means* in the form of a customer. In the same way a taxi-driver can take someone from A to B without having to turn him- or herself into a means that supplies a service for profits or income. There are non-capitalist and non-managerial ways of getting from A to B even though that is outside of the imagination of *The Servants of Power* (Baritz 1960).

The point, however, is to show TINA, not alternatives to management. The alternatives are deeply enshrined in Kant's *Kingdom of Ends* but remain unmentioned in standard textbook cases whose task it is to use parts of Kant to manipulate his ethics so that it appears as if it supported management.[125]

8. The means-ends reversal – the eighth problem

The eighth problem management ethics faces is constituted in Kant's dictum to *act so that you treat humanity...always as an end and never as a means only*. For management it is the other way around: *act so that you treat humanity...always as a 'means' and never as an 'end' only*. This turns Kant into an unsustainable upside-down position. As stated earlier, humanity only has value for management if it can be used to convert people into *productive employees* and *shopping customers*. This great achievement of Henry Ford also makes our consumerism and material wealth possible.

Once management has achieved the conversion of *an end* (humanity) into *a means* (employees and customers), the Kantian reversal is fulfilled. The term *'only'* again assumes a central role. When people are profitable, not impairing profits, and adding to shareholder values, they can be also be treated as ends. But these remain the exceptions in a system that is based on human material/resources, markets, profits, cost-cutting, and *The Real Bottom Line*.

9. Kant's motives and intentions – the ninth problem

Unlike *utilitarianism* and *consequentialism* that only look at the outcome of an action when determining whether or not it is ethical, Kant's ethics examines an actor's motives and intentions. Inside Kant's means-ends dictum it is the intention that counts when examining the ethics of an act. If one constructs an alternative to the means-driven taxi-driver textbook example that is based on market-forces and instead looks at alternatives, then these alternatives may also convert the human relationship of the taxi-driver example from a means- into an ends-driven relationship and proceed from the *Kingdom of Means* to a Kantian *Kingdom of Ends*. In other words, instead of getting from A to B under the dictates of market-forces it could be accomplished under the dictates of ethics and humanity. It could make getting from A to B a human experience rather than a service performed for money. The very same applies to the employment relationship inside the current managerial paradigm that is presented as TINA.

In the invented taxi-driver example as well as in the somewhat different reality of employment relations it is not the moral intention and motive that determines whether an act is ethical or not as demanded by Kantian ethics. In neither case are the intentions based on Kant's ethical *end in-itself*. They are rather based on managerial *means*. In the more plausible employment relations case, the intention and motive of management is to treat employees as a means, not as an end in-themselves. After all, in the words of Magretta (2002), the task of management is to *achieve performance through others*. Once the motives and intentions of management for employment, for the use of humans, and for the conversion of human *beings* into human *material/resources* becomes obvious, the only conclusion Kantian ethics allows is that these acts are immoral. Consequently, the invented taxi-driver case and the managerial reality of employment both negate Kant's categorical *means-ends* imperative and also represent the total annihilation of Kantian ethics.

Under management's supervision ethics in general can only be a means to an end. It exists on the marginalised outskirts of management and is being reduced to the formula E+M=ME (ethics + management = management ethics). Even the Kantian version of management ethics is nothing more than a minor sub-discipline of management studies.[126] When needed, it can supply ethical appearance to management – which is always done under the maxim of making money. Ethics can be a contributor to *The Real Bottom Line* but only when deprived of the essence of Kantian ethics. It has to be reformulated as Kantian management ethics and converted into a pure *means*, never an *end*.[127] The *(mis)-use* of Kant by management represents reason deprived of Kant's *critical* element and knowledge. This is no more than Kantian ethics in the service of management, engineered by *The Servants of Power*. The conversion of Kantian ethics into a managerial support machine even negates Kant's prime motive for ethics: *the good will* of human beings.

Management's often attempted synthetic, but ethically unsustainable, separation of managerial technicalities from ethics does not pay tribute to what Kant called *good will*. It points to management's attempt to extract itself from *good will*. In Kant's ethics *human dignity, happiness*, and *good will* are seen in line with *the highest good in the world*. However, good will or the intention and motive of *the will to do good* is not the prime motive for management.

In sharp contrast to Kant's intentions and motivations to do good, management's intentions and motivations differ strongly from what Kant calls ethical. One of the prime intentions for management is to *create value for shareholders*. Their *highest good in the world* (Kant) is shareholder value. This is not supported by Kantian ethics. Substantial for management is not the intention to *do good* but the intention to do something for profit. Profits, however, cannot be seen as synonyms for *doing good* as an intention in Kantian ethics that has value in-itself and is self-determining. Having the intention to do something to achieve shareholder value reduces any action to a *means* that has no value *in-itself* and is not *self-determining* but *non-self* or externally determined.

Kantian ethics also sees human dignity as a prime goal of ethics which therefore becomes a categorical imperative. Again, management's essence does not rest in the achievement of human dignity but on the *Real Bottom Line* that is the prime *modus operandi* even if it means *to incur civilian casualties*.[128] This is the extreme opposite of Kant's idea of *human dignity*. For Kant, the ethical concept of *human dignity* applies especially to rulers and leaders. Obviously management is seen to be the ruler and leader given the vastness of managerial leadership literature, seminars, conferences, university degrees, etc. on leadership. On rulers and leaders, Kantian ethics denotes that it is the *moral duty* of rulers to *act as if you were a member of an ideal society in which you are both ruler and ruled at the same time*.[129] Kantian universalism demands anyone – and especially rulers and leaders – imagine themselves as being part of an *ideal society*. This is manifested in his concept of *The Kingdom of Ends*. But management, as the representative of *The Kingdom of Means*, does not see the *ideal society* as an end in-itself but as an entity to which their products can be sold. Society therefore is commonly reduced to *'the market'*. What is sought by management is the capacity to consume, not the *ideal society* as a moral entity.

Inside corporations, management has never established an *ideal society* either. Rather than representing the moral entity of Kant's *ideal society*, corporate reality reflects a *Moral Maze* inside which the non-democratic and authoritarian dictates of a few – the so-called top-management – are seeking to enshrine extreme inequalities and hierarchies. This represents the total negation of Kant's *ideal society*.

The second part of Kant's concept – *act as if you were both: ruler and ruled* – establishes an even greater problem for management. Management almost never puts itself into the position of those *who are ruled*. On the whole, management remains steadfast inside its own orbit where it is the sole rule-maker and rule-interpreter and has excused itself from rule-obeying.[130] Management has deliberately separated itself from those over whom it rules. The spectrum of separation ranges from minuscule issues such as different floor levels in office buildings, different parking spaces, and different refectories to more substantial issues such as different remuneration schemes, working time arrangements, contractual obligations, and general privileges.

But it gets even worse. Those *who make things* (Aristotle) are not even mentioned in standard managerial textbooks.[131] Management does not even recognise those who are *ruled*. Thereby it is incapable to follow Kantian ethics. By solely focusing on one side – the ruler – and excluding the other – the ruled – management has deliberately excluded itself from the Kantian concept of human dignity.

In Kant's writing there is, however, one sentence that signifies management like no other. Kant says:

> *as long as human nature remains as it is, human conduct*
> *would thus be changed into a mere mechanism in which, as in*
> *a puppet show, everything would gesticulate well but there*
> *would be no life in the figures.*

Management is very much interested in the 200-year-old fact that *human nature remains as it is*. Ever since the invention of capitalism and the social construction of management, the essential dichotomy between master and servant (Hegel), boss and worker (Marx), or manager and employee (Offe and Wiesenthal) has not changed. According to George Orwell (1949:210) *from the point of view of the low, no historic change has ever meant much more than a change in the name of their masters.* This is what management has achieved. It has changed the names – labourer → worker → employee → human resource → associate → team-member → human capital and so on – but never the principle. The fundamentals of Hegel's *Master-Slave* dialectics inside labour-management relations have never been altered.[132]

Management has, however, achieved that human conduct at work resembles a *mere mechanism in which* the Organisation Men, *as in a puppet show*, fulfil their managerial tasks. Like puppets, they are also remote-controlled through the most sophisticated HRM-techniques. *Key Performance Indicators*, Balanced Scorecards, and performance related pay make sure that human *beings* – now *advanced (!)* to human *material/resources* – act as if they were in a puppet show. Their puppet-like mechanical acting is further reinforced through work psychology (Arnold 2005). Once behind the corporate gates, human behaviour becomes organisational behaviour that is deprived of humanity. A digitalised barcode swipe-card grants access but also swipes off humanity and fills former human beings with the organisational conformity of *Organisation Men*. They are not beings *in-themselves* (Kant) but mere puppets who perform. In the words of Schwartz (1990:27): *the result is that social interaction takes place not between persons, but between performances*. In sum, the managerial world has become a world of performers rather than one with real people interacting at a human level. On the managerial stage of this *puppet show* the organisational performers carry out their *scripted behaviours*. They *gesticulate* and simulate management-guided images rather than living reality (Klikauer 2007:163). This represents the extreme opposite of the Kantian concept of self-determination.

Human life at work is reduced to what Kant described as *there would be no life in the figures*. French philosopher Baudrillard has described such humans as *Simulacra* (1994). They are not *self-determined* (Kant) but simulate what management demands from them without truly living it. It is an existence emptied of life like a static movement of *dead figures* (Kant), confined to a never ending wheel of competition, market shares, and *The Real Bottom Line*. The managerial world represents almost everything Kant envisioned as the extreme form of anti-ethics. In the world of management *human conduct* is reduced to the *mere mechanism* of management-driven performance management techniques. Real people are converted into wooden instruments with management holding the strings and pulling them in a marionette-like *puppet show* in which *gesticulated* movements are performed. Such a stage-managed theatre allows management to pull humans like *objects of an unseen power*, almost unnoticed to the casual observer. Such choreographed performance makes unconscious observers believe that the scripted behaviour is real. In reality however, the managerial script-writing is the only thing that remains real. Script-writing, rehearsing, and choreographing operate behind the scenes and allow management the ultimate excuse that immoral acts are not committed by management but by others.

This managerial puppet show reduces acting subjects to mere string-dummies that move almost in an automated way deprived of self-determination and morality. In 1788, Kant almost perfectly described what later happened under Taylor's task oriented division of labour (1911). He truthfully predicted work on Ford's assembly line (1930s) as well as every setting that applies Taylor's and Ford's methods today, ranging from McDonald's to call centres and to universities' *Student Processing Centres*. According to Kant, this reduces humans to non-ethical puppets and mechanical automats. It also appears to move them through an *alien hand*, thereby predating Hegel's and Marx' concepts of alienation. According to German philosopher Adorno (1903–1969) humans are condemned to live inside an alien world from which they are made to develop alien ideas about morality.[133]

For Kant however, the exact opposite makes us moral actors. For Kant, there is an ethical responsibility to create *self-knowledge*. Ever since Taylor's division of labour into brain (management) and hand (those *who make things*, Aristotle) these two have been separated (Klikauer 2007:153). Non-managerial staff is largely deprived of Kant's *ethical responsibility of self-knowledge*. Management instead seeks the creation of limited and functionally related managerial knowledge. Such a form of knowledge has no value *in-itself* and does not represent an end in-itself. It only represents a *means* to support managerial goals. *Self*-knowledge is useless to management unless it can be turned into *management*-knowledge.

Under the ideological auspices of Managerialism, the so-called *knowledge company* or *knowledge society* is not a company or society that allows Kantian *self-knowledge*. It rather fosters knowledge in support of Managerialism. Consequently, most of today's schooling is not directed towards the Kantian *ethics of self-knowledge* but towards knowledge that can be used in a managerial process.[134] Hence, schooling, colleges, and universities have become institutions that take out the '*self*' in Kant's *self*-knowledge and replace it with *textbook*-knowledge that is not self-determined (Kant) but scripted by Managerialism. This sort of highly functional knowledge and its degrees are accredited to so-called industry associations such as charter accountants, HRM associations, etc. that sanction managerial knowledge. Beforehand, school knowledge is produced by for-profit educational and textbook corporations. As a result, before human *beings* become human *material/resources* through employment, years of primary socialisation in schools and colleges have already produced conditioned pre-*Organisation Men* who only need minor adjustments during secondary socialisation (corporate induction programmes) to become fully functional *Organisation Men* or Kant's *mechanical puppet*.[135]

In sum, outside of corporations Managerialism has established an educational system that negates Kantian *self-knowledge* and instead produces managerial use-knowledge to be traded in exchange for employment. Inside of corporations self-knowledge does not exist either as management only needs managerial knowledge. Rather than nurturing

Kantian self-knowledge, management needs to avoid it by focusing on managerial knowledge. Managerialism always lives with the fear that the development of Kantian *self-knowledge* by individuals might encourage them to depart from management and its ideology of Managerialism. The *self* cannot be tolerated by an unethical system that needs *Organisation Men*.

Management has to contradict Kant's ethical concept of *self-knowledge* because it does not deliver anything to *The Real Bottom Line* unless knowledge is converted into managerial knowledge. The managerially engineered world that exists inside and outside of corporations testifies to the success of Managerialism. Managerial training courses at corporate, school, and university level have established highly supportive mechanisms for the conditioning of people. These training regimes have successfully eliminated Kantian *self-knowledge* and replaced it exclusively with knowledge in the service of management, taught by *The Servants of Power*. Such management trained human resources represent *non-self-knowledge*. They are deprived of almost all *self-determining* potentials and morality and are ready to be *used up* in the managerial process.

The Kantian concepts of self-knowledge and the *Kingdom of Ends* support ethical subjects and assist them in preventing what Kant called *self-deception*. Deception, however, is one of the core principles of management. Outside the corporation, management's marketing principles operate almost exclusively on deception, if not mass-deception.[136] But once management starts to believe in its very own ideology, self-deception is fulfilled. Management depicts a substantial degree of self-deception inside and outside of corporations. Instead of *avoiding self-deception so that you act ethically* (Kant), management and marketing foster both deception and self-deception.

If management wants to be successful, it needs marketing techniques such as emotional selling for mass-deception and has to annihilate Kantian ethics that teaches to avoid self-deception. The more managers take on the deceptive ways of marketing and Managerialism, the more successful they become. And the more these ideologies become part of a manager's self, the more self-deception is established. Subscribing to the deceptive and ideological ways of management leads to success but it does not lead to Kantian ethics. Instead, it departs further and further from it.

For Kant not only is the avoidance of self-deception important for an ethical actor but also a *moral cognition of one's self which seeks to penetrate into the depths of one's heart*. Management has to prevent this from happening for two reasons. Firstly, it does not foster *moral cognition* because it is not conducive to *The Real Bottom Line*. Any moral cognition by managers might even lead to several problems for management: moral cognition can foster self-doubt, pondering, self-assessment, and critical self-reflection. This can mean inaction as a form of moral cognition. Secondly, in some cases, moral cognition can also lead managers to bypass these problems by consciously and cognitively linking management to ethics, thereby claiming that some forms of managerial action are unethical and can not be solved through the application of management techniques.

Management needs the exact opposite of *moral cognition*. It needs to foster cognition of facts and figures.[137] These are relevant to management while moral cognition is not. Not surprisingly, Harvard Business School's *Decision Tree for Ethical Decisions* focuses on the questions *'Does it maximise shareholder values?'* and *'Is the proposed action legal?'* but not on *moral cognition of one's self*.[138] The concept of being *one's self in moral cognition* needs to be obliterated. Therefore, management has invented a raft of instruments inside of the so-called decision-making science. They focus primarily on facts and figures which are simply designed to take the ethically acting human out of the equation.[139] According to Magretta (2002), *quantification helps, sometimes enormously, to depoliticise the difficult decision*. What she really means is that the *de-politicisation* is a *de-personalisation* and *de-humanisation* so that the moral self is taken out when making so-called difficult decisions which are usually not directed towards management itself but towards those *who make things* (Aristotle). For management it is enormously important to take out the human factor (de-personalise) and Kant's *moral cognitive self*. In that way ethics does not *penetrate into the depths of one's heart* (Kant).

The managerial avoidance of self-determination and *moral cognition of one-self* also avoids what Kant called *to have the courage to make use of your own understanding*. Management not only seeks to circumvent being a self-reflective and a moral cognitive agent, it also cannot foster courage and self-understanding. Kant's ethics emphasises the four essential parts of *self-reflection, moral cognition, courage, and self-understanding*. Independently as well as together, they contradict management's *Organisation Men*. Management cannot tolerate people who have their *own understanding*.[140] Instead, it has to cultivate managerial understanding.

Kantian ethics always includes two ways of understanding that relate to the current state of affairs. One is *what is*, the other is a speculative and somewhat utopian way of thinking of *what ought to be*.[141] The latter is directed to Kant's ethical goal of *The Kingdom of Ends*. *What is* always includes a possibility directed towards *what ought to be*. In philosophy, one is not thinkable without the other. Both depend on each other and often one represents the negation of the other. For Kant both ways of thinking are relevant. For management however, things are different. *The only things that evolve by themselves in an organisation, Peter Drucker once observed wryly, are disorder, friction, and malpractice.* Management needs to prevent this from occurring by cementing *what is* at the expense of Kant's *what ought to be* and thereby negating Kantian ethics. In management the present order, efficiency, and managerial practice smother Kant's ethics.[142]

While management focuses on *what is* (*numbers that tell the real story about a corporation, facts and figures*, Magretta), ethics focuses on *what ought to be:* an ethical world directed towards Kant's *Kingdom of Ends*. Both constitute fundamentally opposing positions inside which management negates ethics and ethics negates management. This represents the final conclusion of this chapter. It has examined the core concepts of Kant's ethics such as means-ends, universalism, categorical imperative, The Kingdom of Ends, self-determination, self-knowledge, and moral cognition. It has brought Kant's ethics (thesis) into a relationship with management (anti-thesis) to reflect on Hegel's *truth of a thing* (synthesis). As a consequence, the only final conclusion permissible is the synthesis that management and Kantian ethics contradict each other.

5
Hegel's *Sittlichkeit* and Management Ethics

German philosopher Hegel's ethics (1770–1832) is almost unthinkable without his predecessor Kant and it is not helpful to understand him in isolation from Kant. For some, Georg Wilhelm Friedrich Hegel's importance ranks alongside that of Aristotle and Kant. Born in Stuttgart on 27th August 1770, the *French Bastille Day* became a personal holiday for Hegel who was a private tutor in Frankfurt and a lecturer at Jena University by January 1801. He was not paid a salary. The first salaried position came in the year 1807 when he was made editor of the newspaper *Bamberger Zeitung*. After that he became rector of a High School (1808–1816). In 1816, he was offered his first full-time academic post in Heidelberg. Hegel died of cholera on 13th November 1831.[143]

During his lifetime, Hegel published only four books, *The Phenomenology of Spirit*, also called the *Phenomenology of Mind* (1807), *The Science of Logic* (1811), the *Encyclopedia of the Philosophical Science* (1816), and *The Philosophy of Right* (1820).[144] For Hegel philosophy, and with it ethics, constitutes what he saw as being the kernel of his own philosophy: *philosophy is the only science that is free, because it alone exists for itself*. In other words, Hegelian philosophy and Hegelian ethics are not in the service of anyone or anything but the quest for philosophical truth. For Hegel there can never be an ethics that serves a particular goal. Hence ethics can never exist in the service of management and can also never be written by *The Servants of Power* (Baritz 1960). All of this would result in *'unfreedom'* as these writers are not free to engage in ethics because they serve managers and power rather than ethics and moral philosophy itself. For Hegel, ethics can never service power or be subservient to the demands of management. It has to be free from being written to service, to please, and to support management. Ethics can only ever service itself, it can only ever please itself, and only ever support itself. This is Hegel's definition of philosophy, ethics, ethical life, and *Sittlichkeit*.

Autonomy, freedom, and *Sittlichkeit* are at the core of Hegelian ethics. *Sittlichkeit* is a socially constructed morality that demands an independently acting individual (*Mündigkeit*) who exists autonomous of any forms of alienation.[145] Hegel constantly stressed freedom and autonomy. Importantly, however, Hegel teaches us that nothing falls beyond the reach of philosophy, not even management. If one seeks to establish an ethical life as *Sittlichkeit*, this needs to be done socially. Management is excluded from such an ethical project because *managers...cannot formulate ethical rules on their own, but neither can they come together as a community without tensions and differences* (Kelemen and Peltonen 2001:151).

Managers can never formulate ethics *on their own*. Instead they create a managerial world inside which they seek to be *on their own*. They actively negate the social elements that exist at work and also isolate themselves from society through the creation of an artificial institution, the company. In a world defined by competition managers see other companies as enemies. And their so-called *business community* is not the pretended romantic community of companies. The world of management is rather defined by Hobbesian competitors and strategic enemies that operate on the battlefield of market-shares, mergers, acquisitions, and take-overs.[146] Inside companies, the essence of management requires the exact opposite of autonomy. It demands what has been termed *organisational behaviour* – the behaviour of individuals inside the managerial organisation – in order to create *Organisation Men* (Whyte 1961). The sole *telos* of such behaviour is directed towards the organisation and its organisational goals. Management needs to create and maintain non-autonomous individuals. These *Organisation Men* have to be guided by OBM (*organisational behaviour modification*) which adjusts individuals to organisations by taking their autonomy away from them.[147] Management has to negate the first core principle of Hegel's *Sittlichkeit* as it depends on negative autonomy in the form of non-autonomous individuals that have been turned into *Organisation Men*.

Hegel's philosophy is based on the notion of the negative, the act of finding a new concept through the comparison of two opposites, in short, active dialectical thinking. Hegel's development of dialectics into a full system of philosophy has its origins in Greek antiquity. The dialectical method was used for the first time in human history by Socrates and Plato. It is probably as old as philosophy itself. The original as well as Hegel's version of dialectics is nothing but a method or a system of thinking that is based on discourse. As a method of discussion it brings positives and negatives into a relationship to ascertain truth. For management there is no such thing as an elaborate truth-finding discussion in a systematic way and there is no discourse that resembles the Greek's or Hegel's version of dialectics which are both based on the inclusion of the *other*. In contrast, management operates exclusively without *others*. It operates *through* others (Magretta 2002), not *with* them. Hence communication inside the managerial work regime more often than not reflects a command and control structure rather than a philosophical dialogue directed towards truth and ethics (Klikauer 2007 and 2008). The managerial form of communication is almost never conducted under the principles of *communicative ethics* (Klikauer 2008:215ff.).

In sharp contrast to the ideas of Socrates, Plato, and Hegel, management communication is not directed towards finding an ethical truth. Instead it seeks to find what is workable for management. It is *The Real Bottom Line* that counts, not discourses on moral philosophy. Socrates', Plato's, and Hegel's dialectical method of finding truth demands an exchange of pros and cons in which the better argument wins. This version of communication occurs in an autonomously constructed discourse independent of power and hierarchies. Management represents the exact opposite. It is based on hierarchy and power which both provide not only the foundation of management but also structure managerial communication. Autonomous thinking or autonomous people can never exist inside the managerial regime. As a consequence Socrates', Plato's, and Hegel's philosophical methods of autonomous dialogue for truth finding are hardly used by management.

Instead of Hegel's dialectics, management operates with several cut-down versions of communication. For example, one of the most prominent versions to examine pros and cons inside the managerial regime is termed: SWOT. In SWOT, the strengths, weaknesses, opportunities, and threats of a company are discussed. Such a narrowed down version of dialogue however is not reflective of Socrates, Plato, or Hegel. For one, it is narrowly tailored so that a specific goal is assessed, and it also does not allow anything beyond SWOT. It is not a philosophical engagement but a restrictive way of discussion that is not tailored towards truth but towards the company and shareholder-values. And that is exactly what management needs.

The common use of SWOT confines and directs management to think, communicate, and operate inside a box that is largely created and maintained by management. This sets tight parameters that coerce managers to think inside their self-created limits. Managers need to *think inside the box* because *the problem with phrases like 'thinking outside the box' is that they quickly become slogans, applied universally and somewhat mindlessly.* In management, *everyone is focused on the problem they have to solve* (Magretta 2002). In sum, management is not about a philosophical dialogue directed towards truth finding as outlined by Socrates, Plato, and Hegel who demanded thinking outside the box. That is why they developed the method of dialectical thinking. Management does not need this. It focuses on the problems at hand. It thinks, operates, and discusses issues inside a box that is often labelled SWOT and directs the managerial dialogue away from autonomy. In short, it restricts, distorts, and alienates dialogue based on the needs of its own essence (shareholder-value).

The existence of non-autonomous individuals inside managerially controlled work processes is closely associated with Hegel's concept of *alienation*.[148] Alienation occurs when human subjects are *estranged* (Weber and Durkheim) from its objects and the world around them. In the managerial process Hegelian alienation is established in two ways: firstly, humans are not in governance of the products they create. Those *who make things* (Aristotle) do not own the things they make. Their products are not objects *of* them but objects *of* someone else. Hence, individuals in the managerial process are alienated from *their* objects. Secondly, human subjects in the managerial process are alienated from their objective existence inside a process that is governed by *the Other* (Hegel). *The Other* is a central category for Hegel. According to Hegel's *Phenomenology of Spirit* (1807) in consciousness one thing exists for another. Consciousness regularly contains the determinateness of a movement of knowledge. At the same time, this *'other'* relates to consciousness. It is not merely *for* it. It also exists outside of this relationship. It exists *in-itself* as *the moment of truth* and is a condition of the Geist, one of Hegel's favourite terms. Hegel's term *'Geist'* has been translated into the English *'spirit'* but spirit does not characterise the German meaning of *'Geist'* properly. For example, Geist carries no connotation to spirituality but to Geisteswissenschaft (human science). Secondly, in Hegelian thinking the *'Other'* is needed to establish knowledge. But this *'Other'* also represents the *'Geist'* that comes from outside. Only by relating the *'Other'* to what is examined, the truth of a thing (Hegel) can be established.[149]

This challenges Kant's ethics of self-determination that exists *in-itself*. Hegel argues that one cannot know oneself in isolation. We need the

Other to know that *'I'* is *'I'* and *we* are *we*. Individuality without society is not possible. At work, Hegel's *Other* is represented in employees, general staff, management and in so-called corporate governance.[150] For most people inside companies, their working existence is not a human product of *the self* but a product of a distant and alien hierarchy. This constitutes a second level of Hegelian alienation. In sum, management fulfils Hegel's concept of alienation in three ways: there is alienation from the products employees create; there is alienation from the self through the negation of self-determination as organised by a distant hierarchy and control institution; and there is also alienation through management's conceptualisation of employees as mere others because *management operates through others* (Magretta 2002).Together, they establish another problem Hegel dealt with, the idea of freedom.

The idea of freedom represented a dilemma of an unsolvable contradiction for Hegel. He asked: *how can we achieve true freedom?* Hegel thought that we are free when *we can simply do what we want, when there are no external barriers preventing us from obtaining what we, as individuals, aspire to do.* Management negates Hegel's idea of freedom. In addition, critical philosopher Marcuse (1966) has argued *that economic freedom would mean freedom from the economy – from being controlled by economic forces.* Management, however, supports the exact opposite by emphasising that market forces are the single most important determinant for managerial action. In short, management can never adhere to a *freedom from economic forces* unless it seeks to cease to be management. It can never grant others, and above all itself, such freedom. Its essence lies in economic unfreedom. The major role of management is to create and maintain *external barriers* (that) *prevent us from what we aspire to do.* These are established through performance management, key performance indicators, company policies, procedures, and managerial rules. In short, management negates Hegel's ethics of true freedom.

Another way to circumvent true freedom in the managerial world is established by means of eclipsing the human aspiration and manipulating humans for management goals. This is achieved through so-called invented *hierarchies of needs* and the relocation of true human goals and aspirations into organisational goals, managerial aspirations, and the all important money and power code that converts every human aspiration into monetary value and power.[151] In sum, Hegel's ethical concept of true freedom cannot be realised inside companies that are managerially guided.

For Hegel true ethical life means to *overcome the separation between the individual and society* as society constructs a social version of ethics (*Sittlichkeit*). It also means that individuals are able to realise ethics free from external barriers. The core difference between Kant and Hegel can be seen in morality (Kant) and *Sittlichkeit* (Hegel). *The first denotes the morality of the heart or of the conscious. The latter denotes conventional morality, or the objective customs that are recognised as moral. The first is the individual conscience, the second the social conscience. Hegel would say that there cannot be Moralität without Sittlichkeit* (Sterrett 1892:178).

Management negates Hegel's ideas by constructing fences to prevent the construction of ethics as a social act. Instead a managerial ethics is constructed through managerial acts in the form of policy statements that are created in absence of any social involvement of organisational members. Management works towards hyper-individualism and an atomisation of organisational members through the use of key performance indicators, performance related pay, organisational psychology, individual employment contracts, individual bonuses, HRM, etc. Such an overemphasis on individuality destroys the social community that is needed for Hegel's ethics of *Sittlichkeit*. Management deliberately attacks social relations in general and at work in favour of individualism. Largely through HRM it has set in motion an apparatus that is exclusively geared towards the opposite of Hegel's ethical life as *Sittlichkeit* which is based on a social community. In sum, management represents the very negation of Hegel's ethical concept of *Sittlichkeit* by deliberately erecting barriers that prevent any overcoming of individualism and organisational community.

The realisation of Hegel's freedom that demands the overcoming of HRM-engineered individualism would also end the separation of the *self* and the *object*. This separation constitutes alienation in Hegel's ethics but is fundamental to management. Management can never allow the separation between *object* and *self* to end. It cannot permit those subjects *who make things* (Aristotle) to establish ownership of the outcome of their work (objects). Secondly, it cannot allow human subjects to take over managerial rule-making. Corporate governance cannot be converted into the Kantian and Hegelian ethics of self-determination. Management can never entail a democratisation of management.[152] In short, to realise Hegel's ethical concept to end the separation between objects and self means to realise ethical life. It would also mean the end of management. Management has to prevent this from occurring.

Management's almost classical double-morality announces and uses the individual but simultaneously disallows the creation of an autonomous personality (Brunsson 2002). The creation of *the self* is one of the core concepts of Hegel's *Sittlichkeit*. For Hegel, the ethical concept of *the self* and personality depends on the establishment of self-consciousness. In his *Introduction to the Reading of Hegel* (1947), Hegelian philosopher Alexandre Kojève (1902–1968) noted that *man is self-conscious* and intimately related human existence to our ability to understand ourselves as selves, have a consciousness and eventually develop self-consciousness. Hungarian philosopher Lukács (1922) added *man must become conscious of himself as a social being*. This consciousness relates to *social* being, not a *managerial* being. The managerial being, or rather human resource/material, is strongly fostered by management and organisational behaviour. It is designed to create *Organisation Men*, not the social being of Hegel, Kojève, and Lukács. The socially constituted being also represents an awareness of *the conscious self*. A personality creating *self* needs to develop self-consciousness and be aware of its personality as a *self*.

For Hegel, self-awareness, consciousness, and *the self* always describe consciousness. They can never be realised within the managerial system as management has no use for an autonomously thinking individual (*Mündigkeit*) that has developed a strong identity of *the self*. This would contradict management's need for *Organisation Men*. The same applies to Hegel's ethical concept of consciousness and to being conscious of the fact that consciousness exists. In corporate reality however, those *who make things* (Aristotle) should never develop a consciousness of what it means to be inside a managerial regime. And finally, they should never be aware of what consciousness means because being conscious about one's consciousness might lead to being conscious *of* oneself which subsequently might lead to being conscious *for* oneself. And those *who make things* (Aristotle) should not be conscious *for* themselves but work diligently for management. As such *the self* should never be conscious of consciousness. All three – self-consciousness, self-awareness, and being conscious about consciousness – have to be negated by management as they can lead to a high degree of autonomy that is independent of management.[153]

An autonomy that enables all three forms of self-consciousness to flourish would issue strong demands onto management's organisational independency. According to Hegelian ethics, turning humans into *slaves denies them personality*. The modern corporation under management needs to continue that line of operation. Inside the corporation human beings can never be allowed to develop a true personality. Ever since Taylor's (un-)*Scientific Management* (1911; Klikauer 2007:143–159) management allows, and even fosters, the establishment of *Organisation Men* – at first through the engineering principles of (un-)*Scientific Management*, then through behaviourist reinforcement, and finally through sophisticated HRM techniques linked to advanced forms of managerial communication, performance management, and workplace psychology (Arnold 2005; Klikauer 2008).

The history of management shows that instead of encouraging the development of human *personalities* at work, management has sought to create the very opposite.[154] During the 19th century, management took to the whip and later those *who make things* (Aristotle) were made to internalise the whip through psychological HRM techniques. In sum, management needs to negate *human* personalities and convert them into *organisational* personalities in order to make use of them. Thereby it negates Hegel's ethical concept of *personality*.

Organisational Men have to be compliant, docile, domesticated, and subdued. Individuals have to show organisational fit in a FIFO format – *fit in or f*** off!* Organisations can neither allow autonomy that could create the three Hegelian forms of self-consciousness nor can they assist the establishment of a true personality. In the past, management has done anything to prevent it. At all times, management has disallowed the creation of a *self* by forming an organisationally operative individual in highly standardised ways by using *barcodes*, access-codes, and employee numbers. It has prevented self-consciousness by overloading people with a one-dimensional management ideology and a managerial consciousness. This is supported by a raft of managerial measures ranging from induction programmes to organisational culture. On the ideology of capitalism, Lukács (1922) noted humans once *imprisoned in the modes of thought created by capitalism, experienced the gravest difficulties in comprehending the structure of thought in capital.* It is the task of Managerialism to prevent any critical comprehension of capitalism. The ideology of Managerialism is to *imprison* humans *in the modes of thoughts created by capitalism* so that they *experience the gravest difficulties in comprehending* ethics and morality. In short, the ideology of Managerialism actively works against the mode of ethical thinking. All of this is geared towards the prevention of self-consciousness, personality, and freedom.

For Hegel, the idea of freedom not only depends on the establishment of a personality but also on the concept of *private property: personal freedom is manifested in my possession of things.* The *Janus-face* of managerial double morality is manifested in two ways. Firstly, it denies those who create property the ownership of those things and products as they belong to the company. Secondly, those *who make things* (Aristotle) are overloaded with commodities through commercialised consumer wares and – *often useless* – things. Relentless marketing makes sure that people buy things they do not need with money they do not have to impress people they do not like. Marketing's almost exclusive goal is to sell things that people do not need. People buy the things that they need because of their use-value. But capitalism cannot be sustained through the sale of life's essentials. It has to market and sell things that are not really needed. For that it has invented brand-names, emotional selling, advertising, marketing, and *sign-values* (Baudrillard 1993).

Freedom, the common will and *Sittlichkeit*

The overloading of people with things creates *Affluenza* – where affluence becomes the sickness of Affluenza (Hamilton and Dennis 2005). It also shifts human beings from the consciousness of *being* towards the commercially driven consciousness of possessing and *having*. On the shift from *being* to *having*,[155] German philosopher Marcuse (1966) noted *the people recognise themselves in their commodities; they find their soul in their automobile, hi-fi set, split-level homes, kitchen equipment.*

Management depends on humans who were turned into Fordist mass consumers outside the corporation and who cherish minuscule property ownership as the high achievement of a petty-bourgeois life. According to Magretta (2002), when Ford instituted the five-dollar-day for workers, thus doubling the industry standard wage, the *Wall Street Journal* condemned him for injecting *'spiritual principles into a field where they don't belong'*. In reality however, the five-dollar-day wage turned workers into consumers who could afford cars. Magretta (2002) truly explained why the *Wall Street Journal* got it so wrong. It failed to see the *Brave New World* of mass consumerism that Ford had created by turning humans into customers.

The Fordist mass consumers assist management a great deal because human subjects can compensate *organisational unfreedom* and the negation of personality with the faked freedom of consumer choice inside the standardisation of consumption. Rather than self-determining their life choices, modern consumers are left with a pre-structured consumer choice over insignificant variants among commercial goods. In sum, management, the modern Fordist corporation, and mass consumption have established a near total negation of personality and turned the entirety of human existence, humanity, and ethics into consumption. The negation of Hegel's ethical concept of personality is paralleled by the asphyxiation of humans through an endless oscillation between the managerial and the shopping regime.[156]

With the negation of personality through standardised managerial procedures and mass consumption universal laws of ethics are further damaged. Depersonalised and dehumanised in the productive and reproductive spheres, individuals are rendered ethically impotent in two ways. For Hegel, ethics fulfils its destiny firstly in an area where *humans ought to act* and secondly in an area where *humans ought to be*. With the negation of human personality through managerial and marketing structures, depersonalised and dehumanised people are deprived of the ability to develop ethical behaviour that subscribes to Hegel's concepts of *ought to be* and *ought to act*.

Hegel's '*be*' has been destroyed by Managerialism and consumerism linked to corporate mass media while his '*act*' has been negated by the confinements and command-and-control structures of management at work and the preconceived mass-marketing of consumer goods. Hence we have lost our ability to act and be moral through such a double-detachment and double-alienation. Hegel's ethical concept of '*act*' has been negated through an existence inside a pre-fabricated world of mass-consumption and managerial rule which has converted the human options of *acting* into *being acted on*. The human space has turned from what we '*ought to be*' into an existence that is arrested inside managerially structured work- and shopping regimes. Both places – work and shopping – are not places where humans *ought to be*. In both places, *ethical life (Sittlichkeit)* is all but negated.

Hegel saw good moral behaviour as *the absolute end of the will*. But management turns personal *will* into consumer choice. In modern society the Hegelian *will* has been corrupted at two levels. Firstly, since social scientists mutated to *The Servants of Power*, modern managerial techniques in the form of organisational behaviour, workplace psychology, and management communication have been merged into the one-dimensional goal of converting the *human will* into an *organisational will*.[157] Secondly, since the conversion of the poverty-stricken proletarian, as described by Marx, Engels, and more recently Thompson (1963), into a Fordist mass consumer, the advertising and marketing industry became essential. It was established to ensure the conversion of the *human* will into a *consumer* will and into a conforming and diligent employee will (Beder 2000). In sum, management and its ideological outgrowth of Managerialism have converted Hegel's ethical *will* into an organisational and consumer will. The ethical will has been exterminated.

In his *Philosophy of Right* (1821) Hegel emphasised that *the will is the man, and the ethical man is realised in his social institutions* (Sterrett 1982:180). Hegel's will that represents ethics inside moral institutions can never be realised in modern management. After the event of modern mass-communication it can no longer be applied in such linearity.[158] Secondly, if Hegel's *will* has been compromised and distorted through modern mass-media, then so has his concept of the *ethical man*. Thirdly and finally, if Hegel's *will* and his *ethical man* have been compromised, his *man* can no longer *realise* himself *in his social institutions*. In sum:

- the managerial conversion of the human *will* into an organisational *will*,
- the conversion of a human institution into a managerial institution,
- the conversion of human *beings* into human *material/resources*, and
- the conversion of philosophical ethics into the pretence of management ethics

all negate Hegel's concept of *Sittlichkeit*. Humans cannot realise themselves *inside social institutions* that are constructed for managerial purposes rather than for the purpose of an ethical life (*Sittlichkeit*). They have been turned into *Organisation Men*. When humans no longer carry *ethical knowledge* (Hegel) but management's *knowledge*, Hegel's ethics of *Sittlichkeit* has been annihilated.

Similar to Kant, Hegel also sees the *right to knowledge* as essential to ethics. For management however the *right to knowledge* converts into the employee's duty to exclusively gain managerially constructed knowledge. The right to manage includes management's right to determine knowledge. Managerially constructed knowledge supports consumption and management. It represents the negation of Hegel's ethical concept of the *human right to knowledge* which is next to useless for management. Only managerially useful knowledge is knowledge that management needs. Knowledge *in-itself* (Kant) just as the human *right to knowledge* (Hegel) is useless for management because neither one contributes to *The Real Bottom Line*.

The redirection of Hegel's human *will* towards managerial goals – at work and in consumption – further negates what Hegel called the *moral will to universal welfare*. For Hegel, will always has two moral components attached to it, universality and common welfare. Management has converted the first into universal consumerism – Coca Cola, Disney, Pepsi,

Toyota, McDonalds, etc. Hegel's *will to common welfare* is useless to management unless it can be converted into *The Real Bottom Line*. Management and welfare are two sets of ideas that are highly contradictory to each other. For management only the will to universal consumption is of use. Hegel's moral will to universal welfare even constitutes a danger to management. After all, management's position on universal welfare has been perfectly expressed by Noble Prize Winner Milton Friedman (1970): *it is the social responsibility of business to increase its profits*, not to create universal welfare.

For Hegel *the moral sphere is one in which universal human nature, and universal welfare are dominant considerations.* For management, *universal human nature* is only a consideration if it can be turned into a *universal consumptive nature*. Only when humans can be turned into workers who in turn become *consumers* are they of value to management. Furthermore, *universal welfare* represents the exact opposite of what management seeks at work and in the consumptive domain. *Universal welfare* and universal human nature are not concepts to which management has ever contributed anything beyond an occasional statement. At best management is indifferent to it and in the worst case it represents the negation of both ethical concepts.

Hegelian ethics means the realisation of true freedom and autonomy in what he called *Sittlichkeit*. In *Sittlichkeit* '*the good becomes alive*'. The ethical life refers to *Sitte* as a general conduct of humans directed towards morality. A moral and social custom *(Sitte)* is what determines an ethical life. According to Hegel, *Sittlichkeit* means a life dedicated to a *purely natural will* in which *the soul of customs permeates through and establishes an actual existence. Sittlichkeit* as socially constructed existence is not just *negative freedom* which means freedom *from* interference, for example, of management. Hegel's *Sittlichkeit* also means *positive freedom*, the freedom *to* do something. This is what makes us who we essentially are.

Management needs to negate *positive* and *negative* freedom. Constructing a working environment free *from* managerial interference so that those *who make things* (Aristotle) can have freedom *to* do things would simply destroy management's very own existence. For management the idea of positive freedom means *to* favour commercial freedom in the market sphere. And it means freedom *from*, for example, state interference. Both forms of managerial freedom, however, are not ethical but commercial and political freedoms. While management seeks these two forms of freedom, it simultaneously denies Hegel's ethical freedoms at work. Management cannot remove control mechanisms and HRM methods used to manipulate those *who make things* (Aristotle) to affirm to managerial rules.[159] Freedom in Hegel's understanding is not an ethical virtue of management.

For Hegel, talk about virtues borders on empty rhetoric because it is about something abstract and indeterminate. Argumentative and expository talk of this sort is addressed to the individual as a caprice and subjective inclination. Hegel rejects the idea of management virtues as a form of *empty rhetoric* that seeks to construct and rely upon an individual that does not exist. Milgram (1974) and Bauman (1989) have conclusively shown that hierarchical organisations based on power are dominant when it comes to an *individual versus organisation* dichotomy. Individuals in organisations are converted into *Organisation Men* and deprived of being able to represent Hegel's *ethical man* or living an ethical life in society (*Sittlichkeit*). They cannot live a life inside an organic community but exist inside alienating companies under the non-democratic and non-self-determined regime of management. Being forced into such a *false life* (Adorno 1944), true ethical virtues in Hegel's understanding are not possible.

For Hegel, *virtues are defined as ethical personalities (sittliche Persön-lichkeit), or the life of the individual permeated and transformed by the ethical substance* (Sterrett 1892:185). The development of an *ethical personality* has never been part of almost any management programme. It is not the *ethical* person that management seeks but the *functional* person (Magretta 2002). Managerial induction programmes, for example, have the single goal of *modification of work behaviour* rather than modifying work and the managerial regime (Arnold 2005:276; Klikauer 2007: 194–202). The working life of individuals who were converted into *Organisation Men* is all but *permeated by ethical substance*. Instead, the *Organisation Man* is permeated by Managerialism that replaces *human* virtues with *organisational* virtues. It also eradicates Hegel's ethical substance that is fundamental to ethical *Sittlichkeit*. Such managerially constructed individuals are an image of the managerial ideology of individualism. They are not real. Management has assigned a lot of importance to its own figment of imagination of managerial virtues. Once established, these virtues can be manipulated into *subjective inclinations*. Hegelian ethics rejects the idea of management virtues as these virtues can never lead to *Sittlichkeit*. Even at a time when virtues were supposed to create an ethical life, this was not so. According to Hegel, *in the states of the antiquity, ethical life had not grown into this free system of an objective moral order.*

The Greek states of antiquity had developed virtues but they remained brutal slave states where slaves were conveniently excluded from developing virtues. They were also excluded from society as a whole. As such they were barred from living a *virtuous life* among equals which would have carried connotations of Hegel's *Sittlichkeit*. In modern management, modern *'slaves'* – now partially freed and labelled human material/ resources – are assigned managerial virtues by management. Quite similar to Greek antiquity, modern employees will never be able to live an ethical life inside the managerial regime. Now, as in the past, the asymmetrical power relationship at work prevents not only unfreedom but also an immoral order. Neither Greek nor managerial virtues will lead to *Sittlichkeit*. Even more than the slaves of Greek antiquity, today's employees are not even expected to live an ethical life of virtues. Instead, they are exposed to *the formative process of self-enfranchisement*. They are made to show *discipline of service and obedience* under a regime in which *fear remains formal*. The *Management of Fear* (Monk (1997:57) is enshrined in HRM's disciplinary powers. Often this includes the infamous *three strike rule*, on the spot dismissal, wage reductions for lateness, etc. This *objective negative element* of employment *is precisely alien* and an *external reality before* which workers *tremble*. Disciplinary powers are not only deemed relevant for the *Management of Fear*, they are also relied upon for the creation of the *Organisation Men* who represent the exact opposite of Hegel's concept of *having and being a mind of his own*. To *have a mind of his own* supports the ethics of self-determination, autonomy and *Mündigkeit*, however this is not what management can permit. Instead, *having a 'mind of its own' (der eigene Sinn) is simply* [seen as] *stubbornness (Eigensinn)* by management. Having a *'mind of its own' is a type of freedom* which challenges *the attitude of bondage*. This is not permissible to management.

Today, Hegel's *attitude of bondage* has been converted into the conformity of *Organisation Men* who are made to carry the custom of an ethics that has been prescribed by management and represents the reverse of Hegel's ethics of *having and being a mind of his own*. As a replacement for the own mind, management engineers a *subservient consciousness* (Hegel). This is created in two ways. For one, the managerial regime has created an extensive apparatus that ranges from business schools, to induction programmes, and from performance management to key performance indicators. This apparatus ensures that the subservient consciousness is being established. Secondly, Hegel's subservient consciousness is created through work itself. Hegelian philosophy tells us *through work and labour, however, this consciousness of the bondsman comes to itself*. Hegel's bondsmen are today's employees in the form of human resources. They are men in bond – bound to management. A bond is *a thing used to tie or fasten things together and physical restraints used to hold someone prisoner.* In other words, a bondsman is a manager who uses a thing (company and hierarchical power structures) to tie and fast labour together using work settings to hold them in their assigned place. Labour that is not conducted as a self-determining (Kant) and freedom establishing entity is everything but deliberating. Instead, it creates the managerially appreciated *consciousness of the bondsman* (Hegel). In modern HRM language, Hegel's *consciousness of the bondsman* is called corporate culture, being a team-player, contributing to the bottom line, and showing organisational initiatives.

According to Hegel *the bondsman is not finding his truth in the will of his master and in service.* This is supported in four ways. As long as human beings remain bondsmen – human resources/materials in modern terms – ethical life cannot be established. *Finding his truth* is not possible inside the managerial work regime where the bondsman is degraded to being mere material in the form of a human resource. Finding truth is a faculty of human *beings*, not of human *resources*. As long as an employee's will is directed by a master or manager, both – antiquity's *slave and master* and modernity's *employee and employer* – will never be able to *find truth*, ethical life, and *Sittlichkeit*. Only when the bondsman is freed from being a bondsman and when human resources become human beings again, their will is freed and can become an ethical *will* that services human ethics, not managerial functionalities. A *will in service* is not the self-determining will (Kant) that engages in ethical life as *Sittlichkeit*. In sum, present day management fulfils what Hegelian philosophy has laid out: *the bondsman is not finding his truth in the will of his master and in service.* By doing so, management contradicts everything Hegelian ethics envisions for an ethical life.

For Hegel, *the essence of consciousness is to be free* while for management it is to be in service for management. Morality (Kant) and an ethical life as *Sittlichkeit* (Hegel) demand that human beings can exercise their own free will and follow their own free consciousness. Most ethical philosophies, from utilitarianism and virtue ethics to Kant and Hegel, see a free consciousness as one of the primary pre-conditions for ethics. According to Hegel, this even constitutes the *essence of a thing*. The philosophy of *essentialism* separates the essence from the accidental. In other words, Hegelian ethics sees free consciousness as the essence of ethical philosophy, ethical behaviour, and *Sittlichkeit*.

Management, however, negates this in various ways. For management, a *free consciousness* is something uncalled for and unwarranted. Rather than the ethical free consciousness, management needs a managerial consciousness. Any consciousness that is developed by human beings beyond managerial consciousness is accidental and not essential to management. Management needs to convert free consciousness of the human being into managerial consciousness of the human resource/ material. In sharp contrast to this, the defining condition for ethics is a free consciousness that is undamaged and not colonised by managerial ideologies (Baillargeon 2007).

Quite similar to the states of the antiquity, in management too, *individuals are simply identified with the actual order so that ethical life appears as their general mode of conduct, i.e. as custom.* Management constructs humans as organisational members, corporate citizens, and *individuals.* They are *simply identified with the* managerial *order* so that ethical existence can be made to appear as a custom of a corporate culture. Hegel would have said that they are made part of *a general mode of conduct* – today's *corporate culture* – which is often not much more than *the way things are done around here.* The great advantage of this is that managerial ethics *has attained its right, and its right* is *validated* by management itself. In other words, management has created a self validating structure to the exclusion of *Sittlichkeit.*

This self-validating managerial order also prevents Hegel's concept of an ethical destination found in freedom. For Hegel, *the right of individuals to be subjectively destined to freedom is fulfilled when they belong to an actual ethical order* which constitutes Hegel's socially constructed *Sittlichkeit.* For management, however, the creation of a managerial order is predominant, not the creation of *Sittlichkeit.* Furthermore, management does not seek to create *subjects destined to freedom* but *objects of power* (Bauman 1989). Only through them organisational performance can be achieved. The negation of *subjects destined to freedom* negates Hegel's concept of an *ethical life.* Management sees most of its world, including ethics, as relative to *The Real Bottom Line.* For Hegel, *there are certain absolute principles* in ethics. The only *absolute principles* for management are profit-maximisation and shareholder values which all non-managerial staff should accept as the only *certain absolute practical principle.* Any consciousness of *Sittlichkeit* is to be avoided which carries two advantages for management. Hegel noted that *consciousness is, on the one hand, consciousness of the object, and on the other, consciousness of itself.* Hence, any consciousness of the object of management by non-managerial staff also entails self-consciousness. Self-conscious subordinates however might become aware of the fact that managerial behaviour prevents the Hegelian ethical order expressed in *Sittlichkeit.* As a consequence, management needs to eliminate all hints that could establish a *consciousness* in order to secure management's power structure. This is achieved in two ways: firstly, by denying and negating *positive freedom* (freedom to) and secondly, by denying *negative freedom* (freedom from). Management has to negate both. It cannot issue positive freedom because individuals cannot be allowed to behave and act ethically. They have to behave and act managerially. Secondly, management needs to uphold its policies, regulations, procedures, and rules and therefore has to continue to operate negative freedom. In short, humans in organisations cannot be free *from* management and cannot be allowed to have positive freedom *to* be self-determining. If management were to grant positive and negative freedom, Hegel's *master-slave dialectics* – today's employee-employer relationship – might be annihilated.

For Adorno (1903–1969), one of the principal Hegelian philosophers, Hegel's philosophy and ethical writings constitute *the irreconcilability of the contradictions in bourgeois society*. In his work *Hegel: Three Studies* (1993:2) Adorno saw fundamental differences between the ethics of bourgeois society and its daily functioning. Similar to Adorno's statement on society, there are also tremendous differences between management ethics and the daily activities of management. Management has come to be seen as being one of the core elements of modern society. In the words of one key management writer, Magretta (2002): *we all need management*. Hegelian ethics however has shown *the irreconcilability of the contradictions* between management and ethics.

Inside the managerial regime that is defined by a relationship between *master and slave* (Hegel), *bondsman and master* (Kojève), and modern human resources/materials and management, ethical *Sittlichkeit* can never be established. The contradictory forces between management and ethics point in fundamentally opposite directions. As long as this structure is the all-defining essence of management, management ethics in the understanding of Hegel's *Sittlichkeit* is impossible. Ethical truth and *Sittlichkeit* are not something *in-itself* but something that is in the Hegelian process of *becoming* (Adorno 1993:142). The conversion of Adorno's and Hegel's *becoming* into *being in-itself* (Kant) can never be realised unless Hegel's master-slave dialectics is overcome. The impact of this dialectics on ethics is discussed in the next chapter.

6
Hegel's Slave-Morality and Management Ethics

One of Hegel's core contributions to ethics, and to management ethics in particular, is his master-slave dialectics.[160] The master-slave relationship of antiquity has changed several times. It moved from a relationship between lord and peasant during feudalism to one between worker and capitalist during liberal capitalism. Eventually it became known as today's relationship between human resources/material and management. The names might have changed but the structure has remained the same. According to George Orwell (1949:210), *from the point of view of the low, no historic change has ever meant much more than a change in the name of their masters.* Therefore, the ethics of Hegel's master-slave dialects continues to some extent inside today's relationship between employee and management.

Hegel's concept of *master and slave* – just as today's relationship between management and employee – negates the concept of *positive* and *negative* freedom.[161] It eliminates the freedom *from* something or someone and negates the positive form of freedom as it negates the freedom *to* do something or to be someone. The master→slave and the manager→employee relationship still operate inside an asymmetrical power relationship.[162] Even though today people are no longer owned by others, the employee-manager relationship still confines both to act in somewhat alienated ways.

The more vulnerable element in the equation, the employee, can neither be granted freedom *from* management nor the freedom *to* establish Hegelian autonomy and self-determination. On the management side things are not much better. Management cannot relieve itself *from* the market and its own ideology of Managerialism either. It has next to no freedom *to* act independently *from*, or even against, the market and its ideology. Management also does not have the freedom *to* establish its own organisational autonomy independent from markets. At least two determinants prevent this: firstly, the economic structure based on markets and secondly, the ideology of Managerialism. In sum, both – management and non-managerial staff – are trapped inside Hegel's *Master-Slave* ethics whose fundamentals still define modern management-employee ethics in relation to freedom.[163] A modern Hegelian statement on management and freedom would read like this:[164]

> ...*management is something purely mechanical...Only what is an object of freedom may be called 'idea'. Therefore, we must transcend management! Every management must treat free men as cogs in a machine. And this is precisely what should not happen; hence management must perish.*

In short, Hegel rejects the idea that ethical life (*Sittlichkeit*) can be established inside management. Hegel's concept of ethics is very much in line with Kant's dictum on treating people as ends – the *Kingdom of Ends* – and not as means, or *cogs in a machine* (Hegel). Therefore, management exists in contradiction to *Sittlichkeit*. As a logical consequence of Hegel's philosophy, *management must perish* in order to establish an ethical order based on Hegel's concept of humanity, humankind's self-realisation, autonomy, and freedom.

Hegel's ethical understanding of management has been continued by the philosopher Kojève (1902–1968). Kojève (1947),[165] one of the foremost Hegelian philosophers, stated that *if the human being is begotten in and by the fight that ends in the relationship between Master and Slave,* [then] *man is nothing but his becoming.* Inside the 21st century understanding of Hegel's master-slave ethics the employee-manager relationship still reflects humans that are *begotten in a fight between employee and management.* As a result of this unsolvable dilemma, humans can be nothing more than becoming. In other words, inside the managerial regime humans cannot be humans. They can only *become* humans (Kojève 1947) once management *has perished* (Hegel).

As a consequence, Hegel's dialectics relentlessly confines both employee and employer in a position of *becoming.* They are not humans *in-themselves* (Kant). As long as the employee-employer relationship exists, neither one can escape from the structural determinants of this set up. Life cannot be life *in-itself* (Kant) inside the managerial regime. For that reason life can only ever *become* ethical life (*Sittlichkeit*). As a consequence, being confined to an existence inside the employee-manager relationship, neither one can live a Hegelian ethical life of true *Sittlichkeit*. Therefore, and according to Kojève

(1947), human beings inside the current managerial world can be *nothing but becoming* because *employee and employer* cannot enter into a form of ethical life that is based on Hegelian *Sittlichkeit*. The only solution presented by Hegelian ethics is that *master and slave must finally end in the 'dialectical overcoming' of both* (Kojève 1947). Unless the Hegelian *employee-and-employer* relationship can be *overcome dialectically*, Hegelian *Sittlichkeit* cannot be established. In other words, if management seeks to establish Hegel's ethical life based on *Sittlichkeit*, it has to *overcome* itself. Modern management however is actively working into the opposite direction.[166]

On Hegel's ethical understanding of both, Kojève (1947) noted *the slave is...the immediate and natural being while the master's behaviour is mediated. And consequently, his behaviour is also mediated...with regard to things and with regard to other men; moreover, these other men, for him are only slaves*. In short, Hegel's employee-employer dialectics defines the employee as *immediate and natural*. It sees employers and management as mediated because their existence is based on employees. This demands mediation and negates an immediate and natural life. It also determines management's relationship to *things and other men*. According to Magretta (2002), management *transforms human and material resources into profit-making operations*. For management *these other men... are only slaves*. This has been perfectly expressed in the idea of Human Resource Management where humans are pure human material, resources, assets, instruments, tools, and *means* (Kant). They have been degraded to *objects of power* (Bauman 1989) in the hands of management. Inside management's paradigm, management can never see its subordinates as anything but *objects of power* (Bauman 1989) that are *transformed (together with material resources) into profit-making operations* (Magretta 2002). For that reason, only when management overcomes itself and ends all asymmetrical employer-employee relations, can it *convert* itself from *becoming* to *being* and move from being *mediated* to being *immediate and natural*.

As a consequence of the current incomplete state of human affairs, Kojève (1947) noted that *since the slave works only for the master, only to satisfy the master's desire and not his own, it is the master's desire that acts in and through the slave*. In the modern managerial world employees work for management. They no longer directly *satisfy the master's desire* but their desire has been reformulated into a managerial desire which has been code-worded into *organisational objects, shareholder-values* often initialled as KPIs, ROIs – key performance indicators, return of investment – and *The Real Bottom Line*. However what remains the same is that employees do not work towards their own desire.

Inside the managerial regime, employees' desire can only be alienated as they are forced and enticed to negate their own desire which is replaced by the master's desire. *It is the Master's desire that acts in and through the slave* (Kojève 1947). The same has been expressed in less philosophical terms by management writer Magretta (2002) when stating that *management operates through people.* Management acts through employees inside Hegel's dialectics.

On the Hegelian Master-Slave dialectics Kojève (1947) concludes *it is, therefore, an unequal and one-sided recognition that has been born from this relation of master and slave.* Contemporary German philosopher Axel Honneth (1995) has also recognised this unequal relationship in his *The Struggle for Recognition – The Moral Grammar of Social Conflict.* Today, the *struggle for recognition* is still reflected inside the management relationship to *others.* The prevailing asymmetrical power structure of management cements the one-sided and unequal relationship between humans and results in the fact that those *who make things* (Aristotle) remain un-recognised by management (*achieving performance through others*) and only recognised by the *self* as a *self.* This recognition is established through work. Those who rule over those *who make things* (Aristotle) do not experience such self-recognition through their work. As a consequence, a gigantic apparatus of recognition has to be established in order to create the mere appearance of recognition for management (Marglin 1974). Simultaneously, management does not recognise those *who make things* (Aristotle). They only receive an unspoken non-acknowledgment as *others* (Magretta 2002).

This inflicts serious damage to the construction of *Sittlichkeit* (Hegel). Not to recognise employees as human beings and instead seeing them as human material/resources and numbers on a balanced scorecard represents an extreme form of anti-*Sittlichkeit*, the height of immorality and unethical behaviour. Because of the use of human beings in industry, American moral philosopher Stoops (1913:463) concluded that *industry can never be moral.* Without recognising the other as full human being, a common agreement on *what ethics is* and what it *ought to be* (Kant) can never be established. This negates any hope for management ethics. Kant and Hegel place strong emphasis on the mature, *mündige*, critical, self-reflecting, and, above all, self-conscious human being. The ethical human being is not a human resource. However, both management and its ideology of Managerialism deny the ethical existence of humans and therefore represent the extreme opposite of Hegelian *Sittlichkeit.* Without recognising the other as a human being, ethics is not possible.

According to Hegelian philosopher Kojève (1947) *the master is not the only one to consider himself master. The slave, also, considers him as such. Hence, he is recognised in his human reality and dignity. But this recognition is one-sided, for he does not recognise in turn the slave's human reality and dignity. Hence, he is recognised by someone who he does not recognise.* Kojève has described what is found in almost all modern textbooks on management. While management recognises itself as such, non-managerial staff is forced to recognise management based on the prevailing power asymmetry that is operative at work.[167] As highlighted by Hegel and Kojève, the recognition however is one-sided. It reflects the asymmetry of power inside the managerial regime. Those *who make things* (Aristotle) are forced to recognise management that in turn does not recognise them. This exterminates management's ethical behaviour.

According to Hegel's philosophy, humans have a desire to master objects, creatures, each other, and their own beings. In modern management, this is expressed in the mastery, leading, and managing of others (non-managers). Management has *a desire to negate the other person he sees before him* (Hegel). A quick look into any management textbook testifies to this as those *who make things* (Aristotle) are usually reduced to Magretta's *others* (2002) and are totally absent from management's recognition. There is a near complete non-recognition of workers inside managerial textbooks. This is an extreme form of MADD: *moral attention deficit disorder.*

Those who are not even named – workers – remain un-recognised and confined to an existence as *resources*. As if management wanted to add immorality to its own unethical behaviour, it sees itself as *allocating material and human resources*. The equation of humans with material represents the final degeneracy by management. Through this act, management has more or less extinguished itself as a moral actor. Without recognising other humans as ends in-themselves, Hegel's ethical life (*Sittlichkeit*) can never be achieved. To do this, first of all one needs to recognise the other as such.[168] Without a comprehensive acknowledgment of Hegel's slaves→employees, Hegelian ethics cannot be established. The recognition of employees by management is the utmost essential precondition for the development of any management ethics that lives up to Hegel's *Sittlichkeit*. Through management's non-recognition it denies other human beings their existence, their interests, their humanity, and their being in-itself (Kant). Simultaneously it negates their input into the development of ethics. Management negates the very foundation that is needed to achieve Hegel's ethics.

In the Hegelian Master-Slave morality *a slave is for a master an animal or a thing* hence, *mastery is the supreme given value for him, beyond which he cannot go.* In modernity, employees are truly treated as things in the version of *resources* as prescribed in HRM. Inside the modern managerial world, humans have become objects, materials, numbers, and resources that have to be allocated, controlled, performance measured, and used. In Kantian ethics, they are reduced to pure *means* for organisational objectives. They are the *means* (Kant) *through* which management acts (Magretta 2002).

In support of this, Magretta (2002) has emphasised management *co-ordinates, plans, allocates, and transforms 'human and material resources' into profit-making operations.* Somewhat trapped inside the self-reinforcing ideology of Managerialism, management cannot escape from its own essence that is expressed in *allocating human and material resources into profit-making* (Magretta 2002). For management humans are equated with material. It is the managerial logic of *human-material* equals *object-material* or *'material = human'* that defines managerial thinking, actions, and, above all, managerial ethics.

Hegel's ethics also tells us that *mastery is the supreme given value for* a master. In other words, mastery over others is an essential part of being a master. The very same applies to management and rafts of writings on leadership carried out by *The Servants of Power* (Baritz 1960). Management can only be management when it exercises management – *mastery* (Hegel) – over those *who make things* (Aristotle). If the master stops in his function of mastery, he ceases to be a master. Managing others gives value to management. Hence, management has to exercise its managerial prerogative and insist on the right to manage. In other words, while employees find their essence in working, management is only left with mastery without which it has no essence and therefore no legitimate reason to exist. Unlike those *who make things* (Aristotle), management needs an elaborate apparatus to make us believe that mastery is relevant. Otherwise its very own essence could be exterminated. This explains the explosion of management literature and the simultaneous decline of workers' literature. One needs an apparatus to make us believe that mastery is relevant while the *other* is working and gaining legitimacy through their work. By existing inside a self-reinforcing managerial ideology and practice, management has trapped itself inside a framework beyond which it cannot proceed without ending its own essence. The conversion of current core managerial principles to the ethical principles of Hegel's ethical life (*Sittlichkeit*) would bring the end of management in its current form. Therefore, the material existence of management disallows any move beyond the non-ethical employee-employer rigidities and also eliminates all potentials for *Sittlichkeit* as described in Hegel's concept of an ethical life.

Slaves, Hegel writes, also have *a positive ideal to attain; the idea of autonomy*. Such autonomy however cannot be granted by management because their very essence rests on the premise of not granting autonomy to those *who make things* (Aristotle). Management needs to convert humans into human resources, thereby making them *Organisation Men* (Whyte 1961) for whom autonomy does not exist. Management needs organisation conformity, non-autonomy, and dependency. As such, a term that could be called *organisational autonomy* does not exist in standard managerial literature, in management textbooks, or in managerial practice. It does not even exist in the history of management. *The Servants of Power* (Baritz 1960) have made sure of that.

Management has to negate autonomy. Almost by definition, this renders employees dependent, non-autonomous, and *unfree*. One of the core values of ethics, from the introduction of virtue ethics onward, has been freedom. It is one of the central principles of almost all versions of ethics. On Hegel's concept of freedom, Kojève (1947) noted *the slave knows what it is to be free. He also knows that he is not free, and that he wants to become free.*[169] In other words, employees know what it is to be free of the confinements of managerial work regimes. They equally know what it means not to be free – to be confined to a desk, a machine, a computer, etc. Hence, employees cannot be seen inside the factual stage of just *being* employees. The present condition prevents them from being *themselves* (Kant). Instead, they have to be seen inside the incomplete stage of pure *becoming*. They are always in a state of '*what is*' but also in '*what ought to be*' (Kant). It is for that reason that employees continuously contain an element of *dynamics* and of *un-being* because they seek to reach autonomy and *being themselves* rather than *becoming*. Employees always carry their own negation of what they are inside as long as they are constructed inside the managerial paradigm. They can never be anything but a dynamic power seeking to end their *becoming*. To reach their becoming, however, the essence of management would have to be altered.

Management, on the other hand, is constantly forced into a position where they need to invent ever new and ever more sophisticated apparatuses to fight this internal dynamics. It needs to ensure that employees remain unaware of the fact that they carry the negation of the employee-management structure inside them. To achieve this, management has invented, and continues to invent, performance management, corporate identities, organisational cultures, rewards, organisational behaviour, workplace psychology, promotions, mission statements, and a raft of additional measures. The prevention of self-awareness and self-consciousness is the main task of HRM, organisational behaviour, and organisational psychology.

Superficially, management and HRM make sure that non-managerial staff does what management expects them to and work diligently towards the so-called organisational goals as expressed in *The Real Bottom Line*. Underneath this, management has a second task to accomplish. It is also obliged to ensure that Hegel's prediction that *through work consciousness comes into itself* is not realised by employees. To prevent this consciousness, a raft of measures is set in place, geared towards socialisation in the form of internalisation of managerial values and codes of conduct. They are engineered at work and even before working life starts to ensure that people do not develop a consciousness of work in the Hegelian sense (critical reflection and *Mündigkeit*).

In this process *primary* socialisation (family, school, and corporate mass media) is as important as *secondary* socialisation (induction programmes at work and HRM techniques). Primary and secondary socialisation work hand in hand with corporate mass media's ideological support through depicting pro-business attitudes, a pro-management work ethic, and the 'work = money = success' equation (Klikauer 2007:183–204). Schooling, mass media, HRM, management, and Managerialism make sure that Hegel's critical *consciousness* of *Mündigkeit* does not *come into itself*. Instead a positive attitude towards the managerial regime is fostered from early childhood onwards. After all, Magretta (2002) noted *we draft great attitudes. If you don't have a good attitude we don't want you, no matter how skilled you are. We can change skill levels through training. We can't change attitude*. The creation of such a pro-management attitude starts in early childhood with regular feeding times for newborns to *a job well done* for toddlers, to Brownie Points at Kindergarten, and is fostered in good marks at school, successful degrees at university, etc. (Bowles and Gintis 1976, 1981, 2001).

Instead of enabling Hegelian autonomy, consciousness, and *Sittlichkeit*, management – with the assistance of the one-dimensional society (Marcuse 1966) – is actively working towards the prevention of employee autonomy, consciousness, and an ethical order expressed as *Sittlichkeit*. To do this it has created a raft of managerial instruments and the complementary ideology of Managerialism that has successfully infiltrated, colonised, and occupied human society. According to Hegel people *who do not work produce nothing stable outside themselves*. The fact that management does not represent those *who make things* (Aristotle) but those who manage turns them into people who *produce nothing stable outside themselves*. Instead, management creates insecurity, legitimacy problems, anxiety, apprehension, angst, and misgivings. According to Hegelian philosophy, it is exactly that problem that has historically driven management into using methods of subordination. By making others subordinate, they seek to negate the negatives of their fragile existence thereby trying to appear positive.

In order to create subordinates to enhance, stabilise, and maintain their own existence, management has often resorted to immoral methods. These ranged from 18th and 19th centuries' whips and beatings of employees to modern psychological methods.[170] Managerial control and subordination have been essential and a historical feature ever since the invention of management. Throughout its existence, management has gone through at least five stages of employee subordination (Klikauer 2007:166). It started with direct control though the immediate boss and then moved into technical control through the assembly line. This was superseded by bureaucratic control that came with the rise of the service industry. Methods of surveillance and neighbourhood watch systems enhanced this in teamwork settings until management was finally able to rely more and more on the socialisation powers administered to humans in society and at work. Primary and secondary socialisation is no more than the latest stage in management's endless quest to ensure that employees accept the imperatives of the managerial order. If they do, they implicitly lend legitimacy to management that *produces nothing stable except itself*.

As a final consequence of Hegelian dialectical philosophy, *there is no slave without a master*. Equally, *there is no master without a slave* and no management without employees or vice versa. In short, if management and employees ever want to enter into Hegel's *Sittlichkeit*, both need to overcome their inherent contradictions in terms of their differing interests that are part of their essence and not accidental or a by-product of management. These contradictions can only be solved and Hegel's ethical life (*Sittlichkeit*) be established through an overcoming of management and its alienating forms of employment. In order to achieve this, autonomy, critical self-consciousness, and *Mündigkeit* have to be established. As long as the more powerful player in this relationship (Marglin 1974; Offe and Wiesenthal 1980; Klikauer 2007) is actively working towards the negation of these Hegelian goals, the ethical potential of Hegel's *Sittlichkeit* remains unrealised.

Well aware of the shortcomings of corporations, Hegel wrote in 1821 in his *Philosophy of Right: the corporation, of course, must come under the higher supervision of the state, for it would otherwise become ossified and set in its ways.* The latter is exactly what 20th century deregulation as part of neo-liberalism has achieved. It has – for most parts – removed Hegel's *higher supervision of the state* by creating de-regulation, pro-management re-regulation, and the deceptiveness of so-called industry self-regulation.[171] This has been fostered through the corporate mass media induced and widely accepted call for an *End of Red Tape*. Hence, 21st century's corporations are increasingly *set in their ways*, just as Hegel predicted during the early 19th century. Today's corporations are even able to create their own ethics – the so-called corporate governance, corporate citizenship, and *Corporate Social Responsibility* – to ensure the corporations continue to follow their set ways.

Hegel argues correctly that *the corporation is not an enclosed guild.* Society cannot allow the corporation to create its own *ethical status.* The idea that *managers need to think inside the box* (Magretta 2002) and that corporate management ethics takes place disconnected from society is false. Business and management ethics cannot exist independent of society. Even the term *'management ethics'* is false as it pretends that there is a version of ethics specifically designed for management. This can never be a Hegelian understanding of ethics and *Sittlichkeit.* The *'business of business is business'* is as false as *'the social responsibility of business is to make profits'.*

By pretending that corporations and management ethics exist in a closed off space, *The Servants of Power* (Baritz 1960) seek to create a CCTV version of ethics that operates as a closed circle (CC) inside corporations. The hope is that this represents a managerial circle in which management *gains strength and honour* (Hegel). But Hegel's *Sittlichkeit* disallows management ethics to appear to the outside world as a CC affair. In Hegel's concept ethical actors are societal actors. This closes the option for management to insulate itself from society and also disallows it to *gain strength and honour* inside a circular motion. Hegel noted that corporations are not able to create their own ethics nor are they isolated from society. Rather the opposite is the case.

Through the invention of corporate, business, and management ethics as well as corporate social responsibility, the modern corporation admits itself to the *circle* of human society. By feeding off these self-invented circles management can never *gain strength and honour* in an ethical understanding of these terms. In short, the relationship between corporations and society is defined by a sort of *double negative ethics.* On the one hand – through deregulation – corporations have been able to continue their set ways pretending to have a version of ethics that is disconnected from society. On the other hand, they feed off society's ethics by entering into the domain of social ethics. There is no philosophy of corporate ethics. The essence of ethics has never been found in corporations but always in society and the human condition. Hence, the double-morality of corporations appears in a circular motion that seeks to present itself as independent of society through the invention of management ethics. Simultaneously, however, it cannot exist independent of society. It is from society that corporations and management ethics extract ideas about ethics. The conversion of those sections of human ethics that are deemed usable into management ethics is the task of *The Servants of Power*.

Corporations, managerially-driven employee relations and corporate management depict Hegel's master-slave ethics. These are advanced versions of what Hegel expressed as the ethics of corporations in an awareness that the essence of corporations does not rest on ethics. Hegel has noted that corporations, and with it management, are incapable of developing human ethics. However, he found another agent that he saw able to allow human ethics to flourish. Not surprisingly, he saw this in the rising modern state that replaced the old feudal order of estates. For Hegel *the state is the actuality of the ethical idea*. It *is the actuality of freedom* [and] *the essence of the modern state* is to be a *universal* actor.

Hegel did not see corporations as the location of ethics, freedom, autonomy, self-actualisation, self-reflection, self-determination, and universalism. This could only be found in the modern state which was to be based on direct democracy and governed directly through the will of the people, thereby representing a gigantic step in the direction of Hegel's *Sittlichkeit*. The core experience for this idea was the French Revolution. It radically altered centuries of feudalist rule by replacing it with the people's rules. For ethical philosophy, this meant that for the first time in human history people themselves were able to decide what ethics should be and how an ethical state should conduct itself. For Hegel, the French Revolution opened the door towards *Sittlichkeit*, the ethical life of people. For Hegel *Sittlichkeit* was only possible as an affair of a democratically elected state rather than the un-democratically installed managerial regime found in corporations.

But Hegel's high hopes towards *Sittlichkeit* under a democratic state were negated by the way many states were functioning during the 19th century. Instead of adopting democracy, they turned authoritarian. Anti-democratic institutions were found at state level as well as at work. Even the late introduction of democracy did not fulfil Hegel's dream of an ethically acting state. Today management's ideology of Managerialism has neatly separated the domain of state, society, and democracy from the domain of management.

German philosopher Marcuse (1966) wrote *free elections of masters do not abolish the master or the slaves*. In other words, if the Hegelian master-slave dialectic is to be overcome, it cannot be done through democratic elections of the master through the slave, the ruler through the citizen, or the election of management through their employees. As long as relations in society and inside the managerial regime are based on hierarchies, authoritarianism, and top-down structures, not even democratic elections will alter the entrenched positioning of people. It remains the essence of management to create servants who are subservient to the managerial will. Whether or not management is democratically elected by subordinates can never alter the fact that the institution of management remains hierarchical, authoritarian, and controlling. It also includes power as a core concept, the right to manage, and management as the sole agent that rules with disciplinary action.

Instead of ethical life in the form of *Sittlichkeit*, so far only a name change has occurred from slave to peasant, to worker, and to human resource/material. In the other domain the names changed from slave owner to feudal lord and finally to modern management. Neither of these name changes has altered the essence of Hegel's master-slave ethics. For Hegel, Orwell, and for management itself democracy does not mean much as long as the basic structures remain untouched.[172] The immorality of the slave-owner is manifested by the fact that he owns slaves, whether he is elected or not. The immorality of the medieval lord is manifested by the fact that he keeps peasants in bondage, whether he is elected or not. And finally, the immorality of management is manifested by the fact that management rules over its subordinates.

Democratic elections of management have become relatively scarce after the successful prevention of attempts to introduce industrial democracy during the 1970s. Such elections would only have meant for management a slight impairment on their right to manage. It would never have challenged management's position of power (master). The same applies to parliamentarian democracy. Voting for party A or party B exists independent of the domain of management. But democracy still fulfils an important role. It diverts attention away from the economic foundation of society which is governed undemocratically. Not surprisingly, the term *'democracy'* is absent from the place where most people spend most of their daytime – the workplace. It is also absent from any textbook on management. The term *'democratic management'* is non-existent. Democracy only exists during a few minutes inside a polling box every three to five years. Management has insulated itself from democracy. Simultaneously, however, every manager can claim to be a democrat.

Having overcome the microscopic challenge of democracy to the managerial rule during the 1970s, from the 1980s onwards, management faced a radically different state of affairs. In describing a situation that carries connotations to the British philosopher *Thomas Hobbes* (1588–1679), Hegel wrote when *two men encounter each other, each viewing the other as an obstacle in life, a battle ensures compromise.* During the battles in the developed world of the 19th, and partly 20th century, workers and trade unions revolted against management. Today, however, these battles are largely over and a 20th century compromise with *big labour versus big management* and management's 21st century ideological offensive of Managerialism have ensured and secured management's rule. This has not ended by enhanced alienation.

Nevertheless, management realises that employees continue to evaluate them. As a result there is still an odour of alienation. It is enshrined in the managerial process. Management requires others because it *is achieving performance through others* (Magretta 2002). These *others* are human beings and they face a dilemma. Because management has a desire to conquer others, it converts the human will to self-determination and freedom into *Organisation Men*, thereby threatening the consciousness of these humans. This managerial threat to consciousness is substantiated in a raft of pathologies that range from the *Moral Mazes* (Jackall 1988) to Schwartz's *Narcissistic Process and Corporate Decay* (1990) and Schrijvers' *The Way of the Rat* (2004).

The managerial power structures disallow Hegelian *Sittlichkeit*. But they also deny something else. One of the foremost Hegelian philosophers, Theodor Adorno (1903–1969) called this *there is no way of living a false life correctly.* Managerial and organisational life is a false life because it converts human beings into human resources/material and negates self-determination and the will to freedom. Freedom is the single most agreed upon *telos* of ethics. Almost all versions of ethical philosophy agree on that. But management needs to negate it and convert freedom and the life of human beings into the life of the *Organisation Men*. According to Adorno, such a life cannot be a correct life and it is also impossible to be an ethical life of *Sittlichkeit*.[173] There is simply no possibility of knowing and doing the right thing inside this false life (Adorno) nor is there *real living*. For Adorno, the power structure of management does not open up any space to develop Hegelian *Sittlichkeit*. Managerial life constitutes a *false life* inside which humans are denied to have a real life. The modern management regime *provides for nothing good in-itself*. Hence, organisation life *is nothing more than mere survival*. For Magretta (2002) it is life *in the survival zone* that constitutes management, administration, bureaucratisation, and the commodification of human life. But it is not real life and not ethical (*Sittlichkeit*) either.

For Adorno, the underlying cause of false life is not so much socio-economics but resides in managerial rationality itself. This rationality removes humanity from human beings and converts them from *being an end in-themselves* (Kant) to being a *means*, an apparatus or an instrument inside the managerial process. This reverses Kant's means-ends dictum. Humans are a managerial *means* used to achieve organisational goals and *The Real Bottom Line*, both managerial code-words for profit. This framework is set up by management and legitimised through the ideology of Managerialism. Inside management, the term *evil refers to the widespread and systematic tendency* by managers to be *forced to choose* (Bauman 1989). The same applies to non-managerial staff who is often *forced by* management *to choose*. Hence *choice* became the overall ideology and *The Servants of Power* (Baritz 1960) have invented the *prisoner dilemma, decision-making science*, and *rational choice theory* as an ideological and semi-scientific support mechanism.

Inside the managerial orbit the prisoner dilemma gained prime importance. It is a reflection of *Sophie's Choice* (Styron 1979; Bauman 1989). Humans inside the managerial framework experience *their own unfreedom by adjusting to and accepting* managerially constructed *norms* and *pursuing* managerially *given ends* (Adorno). This turns rationality against humans. To achieve this, management has successfully transformed Kant's critical reason into *instrumental reasoning* that is based on *the calculations of the most efficient means to given ends*.[174] Inside the forces of selection under the dictates of instrumental rationality, subordinates are exposed to daily choices. In some cases, top-management expresses their choice to lower- and middle-management as resemblance of *Sophie's Choice: cut 10% of the staff in your department or you will be removed as an incompetent manager.*

Consequently, almost all management decisions can be seen as '*if-then*' constructions in which rationality becomes a weapon of the powerful against the powerless. For management, Kant's hypothetical imperative (if you want 'x', then you ought to do 'y') depends upon empirical and numerical motivations to pursue a given end: cut 10% = bonus; cut 20% = double-bonus, for example.[175] It is the clear cut cost-benefit rationality that is applied mercilessly by the powerful against the powerless. In the words of Magretta (2002) *management has developed its own specialised vocabulary, much of it quantitative* because of two factors: a) *management requires the discipline of quantifications* and

b) *numbers are essential to organisational performance*. In short, management has assigned itself to the world of zero-sum, i.e. *if I win then you lose*. The world of empirical and numerical motivation assists the pursuing of management's self-created goals (*The Real Bottom Line*). Inside this, a de-moralised, de-personalised, de-humanised, and immoral framework is at work that is supported by a *specialised vocabulary* (Magretta 2002) and by a non-ethical way of thinking and acting.

Management positions itself inside instrumental rationality that reinforces its *institutionalised pattern of unfreedom* (Adorno). It uses knowledge not for ethical ends but for the immorality of *unfreedom*. This is the very opposite of the historical promise of the Enlightenment period that saw all knowledge as *critical knowledge* (Ward 2006). Knowledge always represented a critique directed towards the historically older order of feudalism. But management has decapitated Enlightenment's critique from rationality and converted Kant's *Critique of Pure Reason* (1781) into pure instrumental reason. Through that, it has created ethically disabled human beings with no control over their own *Sittlichkeit*. Management has immobilised Kantian critique and his ethical categorical imperatives. It has also become habituated to seeing and treating those *who make things* (Aristotle) merely as tools to be manipulated through *behaviour modification* (Arnold 2005). It exploits them for their own ends. As a consequence, management has also become habituated to seeing and treating other subjects likewise.

By ethical conduct Kant meant *not treating others ever only as means but as ends*. Management writer and *Harvard Business Review* editor Magretta (2002) denotes the exact opposite of Kant: *management transforms human and material resources into profit-making operations*. Three philosophers of ethics, Kant, Hegel, and Adorno, have warned in different words that treating people as *means* and not as *ends* is unethical. Management, however, does exactly that. It transforms human and material resources (means) into profit-making operations (ends). This reverses ethics and thereby eradicates it. The essence of ethical philosophy determines human beings as ends in themselves. The essence of managerial operations sees human beings as pure means, now called human resources/material.

The conversion of human *beings* into human *resources* is not only unethical but also negates Hegel's concept that denotes that *human agents are driven by a powerful common interest in rational freedom*. Management seeks to negate this by converting Hegel's *human agents* into *Organisation Men* thus denying them the development of a *powerful common interest*. For management, the only interest those *who make things* (Aristotle) should have is to work towards organisational interests such as share-holder values. Management converts Hegel's ethics into their own thinking that *human resources/materials are driven by the managerial interest.* This conversion ends ethics.

If management would foster, encourage, and allow the development of human interest in rational freedom, it would cease to be management. The only interest that succeeds is management's interest in *The Real Bottom Line* and shareholder-value as well as its interest in self-preservation. If an ethical principle contradicts or threatens management's interests, management would always select self-preservation. When it has to wage one against the other, it is management itself that wins. In some cases, management positions itself in the location of *'self-preservation vs. ethics'.* In other cases, it chooses the location of *'self-preservation vs. shareholder-value'.* In all scenarios, however, self-preservation wins. Implicitly, management follows the French religious ethicist *Blaise Pascal* (1623–1662) who outlined the moral dilemma of waging one against the other. In his cases, it was to *'believe in God'* vs. *'not to believe in God'.* In *The Wager* he concludes that the ethical choice for any person living in medieval Europe has to be to carry on believing in God. God secures your existence and preserves you in the face of evil. In this spirit, management would always take the same option: *do what you have always done.* For Pascal it was the *belief in God,* for management it is the *belief in-itself.* They are the safe options when self-preservation comes into play. This is one of the foremost guiding principles of management.

To have a purpose and to serve a purpose

The managerial interest in self-preservation also negates Hegel's concept of ethics that relates to a *universal purpose* of *benevolence.* Firstly, management has never had an ethical universal purpose. According to Magretta (2002) *it is the purpose of business to generate profits* [but] *the real purpose of any business is to create value for its customers and to generate profits as a result.*[176] Neither of these constitutes a universal purpose in the understanding of ethics. Instead, there are two managerial purposes – to generate profits and to create values – but they do not constitute what the moral philosopher had in mind when he formulated the concept of a *universal purpose* for mankind. Secondly, *benevolence* has never been a management virtue. In sharp contrast to virtue ethics, managerial *'virtues'* are not to be found in kindness, generosity, and open-handedness. Instead, management sees *others* as either a cost (those *who make things,* Aristotle) or as a customer whom to sell their products or services to.

According to Magretta (2002), management sets up a *business model on how an enterprise works* which includes *paying out all the costs that go into a product (the labour, the raw materials) before they can sell it and recover their costs.* She continues *the anxiety of competition* demands that management *must keep costs down.* Instead of kindness, generosity, open-handedness, and benevolence, the non-ethical *virtues* of cost-cutting, anxiety, and competition build the core of management. These, however, could never satisfy the standards of *virtue ethics* and Hegelian *Sittlichkeit.* In sum, management does not engage in the Hegelian concepts of *universal purpose* and *benevolence.* Instead, its essence is directed towards the complete opposite of it.

Beyond *universal purpose* and *benevolence,* Hegelian ethics also demands that *human beings should not 'serve' purposes, they should 'have' purposes.* In management, however, human beings (now converted into resources) are allocated to *serve* the purpose of managerial profits. Hegel's distinction between *'serving'* and *'having'* a purpose raises further problems for management. For one, when serving someone else's purpose, people tend not to be engaged in their own *self.* They service Hegel's *'Other'.* This serves an *external* rather than an *internal* purpose and diminishes the human capacity for ethical behaviour, self-reflection, and, above all, Kant's self-determination and Hegel's self-actualisation.

Serving an external rather than an internal purpose also leads to *alienation* (Hegel) as it represents a form of estrangement from the self. In order to conceal this, management relies on numerous sophisticated techniques of work-psychology, organisational behaviour, and communication. It also relies on an advanced apparatus of HRM practices conducted by *The Servants of Power* who, in fact, also behave unethically as they too serve an external source (those with power = management) rather than an internal one (themselves).

Despite all efforts, management has not been able to totally annihilate the alienating fact of *serving others* rather than one-self. Organisational existence under the managerial regime remains essentially *directed by others* rather than *self-directed* and therefore unethical. The same applies to life outside of corporations. The meaning of life can never be found in serving a purpose, only in having one. People who have no purpose in life have almost lost their life. The purpose however is not to be found in consumerism. Otherwise one would not see the pathologies of consumerism as an outcome of serving the purpose of the marketing industry. And one would not see the pathological outcomes of serving an alienating work process that serves management instead of the self. As a final consequence, neither serving the purpose of management nor the purpose of consumerism creates Hegel's purpose in life which is the most important condition for living an ethical life (*Sittlichkeit*).

In fact, the immorality of *serving a purpose* rather than *having a purpose* is strongly supported by Magretta (2002). She states management is done through leadership and not through *self-organisation* which sounds *seductive* but is *wishful thinking*. As a concept of management self-organisation is *fundamentally flawed*. In short, management and self-organisation are contradictory terms. Management totally negates Kant's *Moralität* and Hegel's *Sittlichkeit*. For management, self-organisation would lead to *self-determination* (Kant) which would result in the destruction of management. Yet to keep up the appearance of self-organisation, management has installed so-called self-managed work teams while the non-textbook reality of management demands leadership that confines self-organisation into the world of mysticism or as Magretta put it: '*self-organisation is a flawed concept*'.

For serious management writers who deal with the reality of management rather than textbook inventions, self-organisation is nothing more than a seductive buzzword. As a concept it is fundamentally flawed. Ethics sees this fundamentally different. For Kant's ethics, the concept of self-determination is fundamental while Hegel considers the concept of self-actualisation to be crucial. Kantian ethics can never be achieved without self-determination nor can Hegelian ethics ever be achieved without self-actualisation. What is fundamentally flawed for management – self-organisation – is fundamentally important for Kantian and Hegelian ethics. For ethical philosophy it is self-determination, self-organisation, and self-actualisation that give life a purpose.

One of the final problems with Hegel's ethics of *having* a purpose rather than *serving* someone else's purpose arises through the meaning of *having a purpose*. Hegel tells us that those *who make things* (Aristotle) also develop a purpose which they subsequently *have*. This purpose is not the same as the purpose of management. There are inherent contradictions in the managerial process. Three fundamentally different purposes are outlined in the following. These divide the purpose of management from the purpose of those *who make things* (Aristotle).

According to Offe and Wiesenthal (1980), the purpose of wages constitutes a *cost factor* for management while for those *who make things* (Aristotle) it represents their livelihood. The purpose of management is to increase working time. For those *who make things* (Aristotle) the purpose is to lower it. The shorter the working time, the more life they have. Finally, for management to allow good working conditions serves a purpose: productive employees. For those *who make things* (Aristotle) it means to have good work. Despite the ideology of Managerialism, management has not been able to overcome the Hegelian difference between having and serving a purpose. They remain in contradiction with each other. Hegel's ethics of *having* rather than *serving* a purpose challenges management at two levels. Firstly, management cannot allow self-organised, self-determined, and self-actualised employees who *have* a purpose. They need employees who have none of that and instead are supposed to *serve* a purpose. If employees were allowed to *have* a purpose, they might also realise the true potential of self-organisation. And this in turn might extinguish the need for management. Secondly, self-organisation would constitute a movement towards Hegelian ethical life expressed as *Sittlichkeit*. In the interest of self-preservation management has to prevent this.

Hegel's concept of *having a purpose* also demands that *the final purpose* of human existence is *a distinctively moral one: the realisation of freedom*.[177] For Hegel, human self-organisation, self-determination, and self-actualisation are elements that direct humanity towards the *final purpose of the realisation of freedom*. The essence of management as well as its history has prevented Hegel's ethics from becoming reality. The *realisation of freedom* denotes two things for those *who make things* (Aristotle). Firstly, it means freedom *from* management. In its current format management is not an ethical institution inside a Hegelian understanding of ethical institutions. Secondly, it denotes freedom *to* realise oneself inside moral institutions as part of an ethical society. This is what Hegelian philosophy calls *Sittlichkeit*, a moral life inside moral institutions. Management's need for self-preservation however must negate Hegel's philosophical ethics of *Sittlichkeit* that denotes a social existence in a society of ethical institutions.

Management ethics as camera obscura

During Hegel's lifetime philosophy began to influence social theory and Karl Marx became Hegel's immediate philosophical successor. He engaged himself mostly in economics, politics, and philosophy. His critical analysis of capitalism outlined in his work '*Das Kapital*' followed Kant's three critiques (1781, 1788, 1790).[178] Marx's essential masterpiece, '*A Critique of the Political Economy*', is a further development of Kant's critiques. Rather than being a critique of philosophy, it is a critique of the political economy. Marx never wrote specifically on ethics. Despite this, he thought that *the production of ideas, of conceptions, of consciousness, is at first directly interwoven with the material activity and the material intercourse of man, the language of real life. Material activity and intercourse of man* denote the place where production takes place, today's corporation. For Marx, this is the place of *real life*. Today's society has almost no other place where the production of goods and services takes place. The corporation is also the place where the production of ideas, including the production of ethical ideas, takes place.

Marx also noted that in all *ideologies men and their circumstances appear upside-down as in a camera obscura.*[179] For management this denotes, for example, an organisational chart that depicts the position of people inside a corporation with the CEO at the top, employees at the bottom and management in-between. This shows the world in an ideological way. If organisational charts want to be a true reflection of human ethics, they have to be turned upside-down. In other words, they should show the society of human beings without top and bottom. But this is not the case because management, hierarchies, top-down structures, and organisational charts testify to the single most relevant dictum of Marx' ethics: *the ruling ideas of each age have ever been the ideas of its ruling class.*

Marx claims that each age – slavery, feudalism, and capitalism – had ruling ideas that paralleled each societal formation. For example, the virtues of man in Greek antiquity reflected those in power (men) rather than the powerless (women and slaves). During feudalism Christian morality confined peasants to the soil. This was made to appear as moral and God's work. In capitalism, management ethics is again created by those in power or those serving the powerful in the form of *The Servants of Power*. They represent nothing but the ideas of those who rule.

The ruling ideas have always been created by those who rule over others. In modern managerial capitalism, many of the ideas on production, consumption, morality, and about society in general are created by management. Societies have moved from the morality of slave-owners via the morality of feudal lords to the morality of management which governs today's society. At each age, morality has been created to stabilise those in power. It also ensured that the others – slaves, peasants, and workers – stayed in the place assigned for them by those who rule. According to Marx, *the history of all past societies has consisted in the development of class antagonism.* Moral codes of conduct and ethical concepts have always existed inside this antagonism.

They have been created by one group who ruled over another. Their morality and ethics are nothing more than instruments that those who rule invented to further their advantage and sustain their position. This might explain why management represents nothing but a contradiction of Hegelian ethics. It contradicts Hegel's key concept of self-actualisation as a realisation of *Sittlichkeit* in the form of ethical institutions directed towards ethical life. The ethics of *Sittlichkeit* demands that humanity be treated as a Kantian end in-itself, not as a means to achieve something. It is not to be found in the conversion of humans into human resources/ materials when those human resources/ materials are made to *serve* a purpose rather than *having* one. In conclusion, as long as the division between master and slave is preserved and Hegel's master-slave ethics is operative, there cannot be an ethical life of *Sittlichkeit* and management cannot be ethical.

7
Kohlberg's Moral Manager I: From Impulsiveness to Punishment

The morality of Laurence Kohlberg (1927–1987) is somewhat different from all previously discussed philosophers on ethics. Kohlberg's work applies to almost every single form of ethics ever developed by philosophers. It also applies to all forms of human conduct and to all institutions (Kohlberg 1958, 1973, 1981, 1984; Kohlberg and Kramer 1969). Kohlberg's moral philosophy ranges from stage zero, the pre-adult stage where impulsiveness governs human behaviour, to stage seven at which morality relates to a holistic and *cosmic* view that includes plants and animals. This chapter includes an introduction to Kohlberg's ethics and his first two stages. The complexity and extent of bringing the moral stages three to seven into a relationship with the essence of management demands another chapter and will be discussed in Chapter 8. But before this is done, a short introduction will sketch out the main elements of Kohlberg's contribution to ethics.

As an addition to the classics of ethical philosophy (Greek virtue ethics, Kant's morality, Hegel's *Sittlichkeit*, utilitarianism, etc.) the recent con-cept of American ethicist, philosopher, and psychologist Kohlberg is brought into a relationship with modern management to examine *the truth of a thing* (Hegel). The truth of Kohlberg's ethics is somewhat different from classical philosophical elaborations on ethics. While many philosophers on ethics have dealt with different levels of morality, his theory of gradually increasing levels of morality delivers the foremost comprehensive concept of ascending morality. His stages are universal, sequential, and irreversible. He also shows that one cannot skip a stage and that each consecutive stage is superior to the previous one. Because of a strict focus on the *ascending scale of morality*, it has to be discussed rather differently from all proceeding philosophers when related to management.

The beginnings of Kohlberg's contemporary ethics have their origins in World War II and the Nazi-Holocaust. The Holocaust was partly carried out by using modern techniques, rational planning, organising, selecting, controlling, and administering the death of millions. Management's ideology of Managerialism likes to eclipse the fact that the death of millions of people has something to do with modern management techniques; it prefers to show it as being committed by evildoers and monsters. Bauman (1989) has proven otherwise. The killing of such a large number of people could only happen because textbook management techniques were applied. In other words, the utmost immorality in human history has only been possible by merging immorality with management. Kohlberg's ethics explains how this was done and is therefore highly relevant today.[180] Being determined by the inhumanity of *Auschwitz*, his ethics is not only to be seen historically in the context of the singularity of Nazi atrocities but also carries connotations to Adorno's '*Mediation on Metaphysis: After Auschwitz*' in his masterpiece '*Negative Dialectics*' (1973). Kohlberg worked out an ascending scale of moral development as a result of studies he conducted in the immediate aftermath of World War II.[181]

Through a field trip to Germany in the early post war years Kohlberg tried to answer what perhaps has been the foremost pressing question about Germany: *How could such a developed nation be so evil?* His fieldwork, subsequent research in the USA, and finally the answer to his

Table 7.1　Kohlberg's Seven Stages of Morality: General Moral Orientations

Stage	Orientation
0	Impulsive and amoral
1	Obedience and avoidance of punishment
2	Personal benefits and rewards and getting a good deal for oneself
3	Conforming to social expectations and gaining approval
4	Protecting law and order; maintaining existing systems of official arrangements; and supporting existing structures unquestioned as a given
5	Promoting justice and welfare within a wider community, as defined in open and reasonable debate
6	Defending everyone's right to justice; supporting and promoting universal welfare; and the universal application of all ethical actions
7	Respecting the cosmos as an integral whole; an openness that extends well beyond humanity

question was developed inside the tradition of a philosophical understanding of humanity. It also related to ethics, morality, and developmental psychology.[182] To answer the above question, Kohlberg developed
seven stages of moral development. These stages provide a Kantian
universalistic foundation and an analytical framework inside which
any morality – including management's moral conduct – can be discussed, evaluated, and examined.[183] To outline Kohlberg's work, the
seven stages of moral development will be shown in two tables. The
first table provides a general overview of the stages while the second
one highlights Kohlberg's moral motives.

Table 7.1 shows an overview of Kohlberg's seven stages of moral
development. In fact, Kohlberg listed eight stages. However he regarded
the first stage (0) as somewhat irrelevant to moral development. Stage
zero indicates an early infant stage. He argued that newborns cannot
develop moral understanding because of insufficient self-determination
and self-reflection based on limited interactions with the outside world.
In other words, Kohlberg, like Hegel, thought that in order to develop
an understanding of oneself, of ethics, and of morality, one depends
on Hegel's 'Other' – a mature person. Ethics and morality are socially
constructed with *the Other* as a point of critical reflection. Moral behaviour is not inherent in human nature (Darwin 1871; Kropotkin 1902).
Kohlberg defined this non-ethical stage as zero (0) because moral
development is hardly possible at this level. Since management is not
run by babies or newborn infants and one of the core objects of management – those *who make things* (Aristotle) – are not newborns either,
Kohlberg's stage zero is not relevant to management ethics. Nevertheless
it is an early and vital stage of human moral orientations as the Table 7.2
indicates.

In Table 7.2, moral motives for each stage are outlined. The philosophy of ethics delineates two basic versions of moral orientations, one
that looks at the outcome (consequentialism), the other that considers
the intention and motives of an action (Kant's Deontology). The first
version does not examine *moral motives* at all. Instead it only observes
the outcome or consequence of an action. If the outcome of an action
– disregarding its motives, intentions, and purpose – produces an
ethical good, then such an action is deemed morally good. This is
the philosophical idea of *consequentialism*. When management, for
example, favours a design of a commercial good that is cheaper
to produce and therefore increases profit margins but is also safer for
consumers to use then such an action is seen as morally good. Even
though management's original intention was to produce a cheaper

Table 7.2 Kohlberg's Seven Stages of Morality: Management's Moral Orientations

Stage	Moral Motives of Management
0	None (unconscious stage of babies and newborns), pre-ethics
1	People act irrational to the threat of punishment through management Guiding principles are fear of those in managerial authority
2	Management gets selfish pleasure and gains are for managers Calculating managerial risks and payoffs of management actions
3	Avoiding disapproval by other managers and top-management Wanting to be praised, liked and admired, rather than shamed
4	Performing managerial and formal duties and responsibilities Meeting company standards as set by management Working for the best interest of the company
5	Following principles that serve the best interest of the great majority Striving for reasonable, just and purposeful managerial action
6	Applying well-thought principles to management and the company Share information in an open debate beyond corporate boundaries Act non-defensive with other managers and employees
7	Respecting, preserving, and supporting all intrinsic values of the cosmos with its wider environmental harmonies (animals and plants)

good and only as a by-product it is also a safer good, it is still seen as morally good in terms of *consequentialism* that only looks at the outcome – not the intention – of an action.

Kantian morality is the extreme opposite of *consequentialism*. Kant focuses our attention on moral motives. Only when one has good intentions can an act be good. Therefore, in Kantian ethics, management cannot claim to have acted morally in the above case as its intentions were not directed towards morality – a safer good. While consequentialism favours outcomes, Kant focuses on intentions and motives.

Kohlberg's ethics of moral development follows Kantian ethics rather than consequentialism. Kohlberg, like almost all other moral philosophers, was interested in the orientations, intentions, and motives that drive moral and immoral behaviour as shown in the table above. Like Kant, Hegel, and many others, Kohlberg based ethics on people's intentions. For both, the outcome of an act has to be morally good. But Kant, Hegel, and Kohlberg do not stop there. The intentions with which an act is conducted are of foremost importance and relevance when considering whether or not this act is ethical. Another example for an ethical concept that looks at the importance of orientations, motives, and intentions is Kant's most famous moral imperative.[184]

While the Kantian categorical imperative focuses on *'yes-and-no'*, being ethical or not, and on acting morally or not, Kohlberg's morality sees seven levels at which this can occur. He linked ethics to different stages. Recently, Hinman (2008:300), for example, has also sought to connect *some traditional moral theories* to Kohlberg's stages. For instance, he linked stage five to *social contract theory* and *utilitarianism* while stage six reflects on Kant's *universalism* and Rawls' justice. Somewhat more detailed than Hinman (2008:300), the following table provides an overview of Kohlberg's seven (+zero) stages and the corresponding ethical theories that provide background theories for each one of his categorisations:

Table 7.3 Kohlberg's Morality and Its Philosophical and Ethical Background

Orientation	Philosophies and Philosophers
0 Impulsive and amoral	Common themes in primate ethics (Singer 1994)
1 Obedience and avoidance of punishment	Milgram (1974), Bauman (1989), Foucault (1995)
2 Personal benefits and rewards; getting a good deal for oneself	Ethical egoism, some virtue ethics, moral relativism
3 Conforming to social expectations and gaining approval	Some virtue ethics, Hegel's *Other*
4 Protecting law and order; maintaining existing systems of official arrangements; supporting existing structures unquestioned as a given	Pascal's Wager, Thomas Aquinas, Locke, Nietzsche, Kant's duty, Rawls' justice, Consequentialism, Hegel's theory on the state, Hobbes
5 Promoting justice and welfare within a wider community as defined in open and reasonable debate	Utilitarianism, Hegelian *Sittlichkeit*, social contract theory, Habermas (1990 and 1997), Rawls' Justice, Nozick (1974)
6 Defending everyone's right to justice; supporting and promoting universal welfare; and the universal application of all ethical actions	Kant's universalism, Hegel's *Mündigkeit*, Adorno and Horkheimer, Marcuse, global ethics,[185] the ethics of human rights, Existentialism, Zizek, Habermas (1990 and 1997)
7 Respecting the cosmos as an integral whole; An openness that extends well beyond humanity	Animal ethics (cf. Singer's *Animal Liberation*, 1990), Environmental Ethics (cf. Taylor's *Ethics of Nature*, 1981)

Overall Kohlberg's eight stages of morality range from *pre-conventional morality* at stages zero and one – that has been highlighted in Milgram's *ethics of obedience* (1974) and in Bauman's sociological theory of morality – to the highest level of stage seven. Stage two represents the '*Me, Myself, and I*' approach that carries connotations of *moral egoism*, egocentricity, and selfishness. Stage three is the *good boy/nice girl* stage of conformity while stage four represents rules, duties, law and order. Stage three and four form Kohlberg's *conventional morality*. Stages five, six, and seven build his *post-conventional morality*. Stage five represents the ethics of *utilitarianism* and elements of Habermas' *Theory of Communicative Action* (1997). Both Kohlberg and Habermas demand an open debate among discourse participants. Stage six also corresponds to Habermas because his *communicative ethics* (1990) and *theory* (1997) demand an engagement beyond simple communication, a social action theory (Klikauer 2008:215–245). This is also the morality of, for example, Mother Teresa, Gandhi, Martin Luther King, and Nelson Mandela. It carries connotations of Hegelian *Sittlichkeit* as it is a form of deliberately, purposefully, and socially constructed ethics. The final and highest stage carries connotations to environmental ethics and animal ethics as represented in Singer's ethics of *Animal Liberation* (1990) and *All Animals are Equal* (2007) as well as Taylor's *The Ethics of Respect of Nature* (1981).

The concept of universal moral development starts with the very beginning of human life, the age of babies and newborns who generally have no concept of morality and ethics. This stage has been depicted as the pre-ethical stage of awareness. Management relates to this by feeling that it is not in need for ethical consideration showing extreme forms of MADD (*moral attention deficit disorder*). Rather than applying ethics and morality, management is determined by functionality. This is especially the case when management claims to operate outside the ethical realm based on an engineering ideology – Taylor's *Scientific Management* (1911) – seeking to pretend that it only deals with factual, technical, mechanical, neutral, objective, value-free, and scientifically proven facts. Management often operates a strange version of value reversal. On the one hand it seeks to relieve itself from being influenced by values (and morals!) through the appearance of being value-neutral, technical, engineering-like, and scientific as prescribed in Taylor's *Scientific Management* (1911), on the other hand, when it comes to *The Real Bottom Line*, the maximisation of profits, cost-cutting, and shareholder-*values*, suddenly all the talk of *value* and its self-announced *value-neutrality* is conveniently forgotten (Brunsson 2002; Klikauer 2007:151). In short, not ethical values but monetary values are the ones that count. As a reflection on stage zero, management sometimes likes to present itself as value-free and morally neutral based on its invented engineering ideology while at other times it likes to pretend the complete opposite. Instead of stage zero, however, managerial behaviour relates more strongly to Kohlberg's stage one.

At stage one, management's moral motives are no longer eclipsed by the pretence to be scientific, technical, engineering-like, and value-neutral but to be found in methods of punishment, sanctioning regimes, and disciplinary actions. What is demanded from non-managerial staff is obedience to the managerial will. At stage two, management essentially follows the moral motives of *ethical egoism* as it is primarily interested in getting a good deal for itself. This is the classical realm of trade-offs, cost-benefit analyses, and zero-sum games in which one wins (management) while the other loses (employees, society, environment, etc.). At the next stage, management moves on towards a version of morality that depends on *Others* (Hegel) who are needed as suppliers of approval. Management's moral motives are geared towards acting in a way to find approval from others. It also seeks the admiration of others and avoids being shamed by them for its actions. Management's moral motives at stage three rest solely on the approval or disapproval by others.

At stage four, management moves back into its secure realm of managing. It is less and less dependent on the '*Other*'. Its moral motives are based on performing what is perceived as being the formal duty and responsibility of management (Weber 1924 and 1947; Marcuse 1964). In many cases, these standards are set by corporate behaviour inside which individual management formulate their duties and responsibilities (Mander 2001). However, the prevailing maxim is: *you scratch my back, I'll scratch yours*. This is essentially a version of managerial motives based on *whatever is working in the best interest of management*. At level five a real shift in management's moral motives takes place. For the first time, the motives of self-preservation, getting a good deal for oneself, and the best for the corporation are superseded and replaced by a genuine concern for what lies beyond the boundaries of management and corporations. At this stage, management's moral motives are no longer based on management and the company itself but on developing ethical principles in order to serve the best interest of the great majority rather than the narrow minority of management. With this management enters into the ethics of *utilitarianism* as stage five is a reflection of *The Greatest Happiness* principle. This is also the stage were managerial actions carry connotations of Rawls' ethics of justice.

At stage six the utilitarian *Greatest Happiness* principle and concepts of justice are also exposed to an entirely new form to create ethical behaviour. In Kantian and Hegelian understanding, ethics moves from categorical imperatives (Kant) into a socially constructed form of ethics (Hegel). In other words, management's moral motives move from the ethics of moral principles into the socially constructed ethics of Hegel's *Sittlichkeit*. At this level, management and non-managerial staff are seen as equals in the construction of moral foundations. The concept of sharing information in an open debate beyond corporate boundaries includes the wider society as well as forms of *ideal speech* as outlined by Habermas (1997; cf. Klikauer 2008). Such forms of moral communication have to be conducted in a non-defensive way in a non-hierarchical and domination-free environment between management, employees, and the wider society. This can lead directly to the final stage of Kohlberg's ethical model where management respects, preserves, and supports all intrinsic values of the cosmos within a wider environmental harmony (animals and plants). Having briefly outlined an overview on how management relates to Kohlberg's seven stages of moral development, the following section will discuss stages zero and one in greater detail:

0. Stage zero: Impulsiveness. Stage zero represents a level of morality based on the maxim of *whatever I want at any time is seen as right*. This is regardless of the consequences and without any form of social concern. It represents the complete opposite of utilitarianism and consequentialism that both see the outcome of an action as the sole indicator for ethics. Naturally, newborns are not capable of such reflections. There is a genuine unawareness of *cause-and-effect* relationships at this age. Only later in life do humans develop an understanding of this relationship. By that time, the moral conscious has also developed. Many observers have determined that time to be about 16 years of age when humans start making comprehensive connections between an act and its moral consequences. Moral developments of *cause-and-effect* relationships are not fully understandable to most humans before they reach their late teenage years. Since management is usually conducted by mature people capable of comprehending moral values, managers *should* be able to make connections between an act and its moral consequences. They *should* also be able to reflect critically on this relationship.

Yet management has been, and still is, using children in the managerial process. This has historical roots but is also current practice in many sweatshops which also use child-labour. As a matter of convenience, these are artificially kept distant from management and corporations through subcontracting, outsourcing, and franchising. These work settings carry animal-like patterns of enforced behaviour. Historically, this practice reached a high when management converted itself into Taylor's (un)-*Scientific Management* (1911; cf. Klikauer 2007). The so-called scientific method demanded a workforce that resembled child-like, impulsive, *reflexive* rather than *reflective*, scripted, and stimulus-response like behaviour.[186] The engineer and inventor of scientific management, Taylor, actively promoted that the treatment meted out to workers should go below that of a human being. He advocated that workers should have the understanding – or rather non-understanding – of '*ox*' and '*gorilla*' (cf. Klikauer 2007:150) which testifies to the unscientific character of Taylor's work. But Taylor's early ideas were only a reflection on what the second most important management inventor, Henry Ford, later complained about: *Why is it that whenever I ask for a pair of hands, a brain comes attached?*[187] It was also *Henry Ford who took command and control to a pathological extreme.*

In other words, Taylor's *horizontal and vertical division of labour* (Klikauer 2007:153) was taken up by Henry Ford who, just as Taylor, wanted hands, not brains. Both essentially demanded an *ox-* and *gorilla*-like workforce that operates below the level of humanity and morality. *The Servants of Power* (Baritz 1960) have labelled both management ideologies as technical, engineering, and even scientific. They negate all human moral development and ethics and are closer to ideology than to science. While the two most prominent management writers – Taylor and Ford – advocate a stage of pre-morality, almost all philosophers on ethics see the ability to think, reflect, and be self-aware as the most essential dividing line between the animal kingdom and human society. Humans without *brains* (Ford) who depict the animalistic behaviour of *ox and gorilla* (Taylor) are the extreme opposite of ethics.

However, even today Taylor's monotone work regimes that treat humans like animals (ox and gorilla) and the exploitation of children are still part of the current managerial system. They have been largely outsourced to non-advanced countries where they are hidden behind a web of sub-contractors. In advanced, and even more so in developing countries, work is still arranged by management in a way that *the factory worker is degraded to the lowest level of dullness. In many parts of the world, the mass of the population is condemned to the stupefying, unhealthy, and insecure labour of factories, manufactories, mines, and so on* (Marcuse 1941). In a sense, the use of child-labour has been '*relocated away*' from the developed world. This is nothing more that an attempt by Managerialism to push highly unethical forms of work out of the media spotlight. Management acknowledges that this is necessary as child exploitation in advanced countries is no longer welcomed today as it was in the past where child-labour was part of every form of early capitalism ever developed (Engels 1892; Thompson 1963). During those early years, Taylor's *widely adopted systems were totally dehumanising, reducing skilled work to tedium, and a recent report in the American Machinist suggested the ideal workers for them would be the mentally retarded. The author advocated a mental age of 12* (Roper 1983:73). Under today's Managerialism dehumanising work and child-labour exploitation come under the maxim of *out of sight is out of mind*.[188] This seems to occur not so much out of ethical concerns but out of a structural change in capitalism (manufacturing → service industry → knowledge industry). Today, marketing, research, development, finance, etc. are kept in the developed world while production is outsourced to developing countries. Even some of the most advanced network-structured corporations continue to '*indirectly*' employ child-labour. The nebulous web of sub-contractors, joint-ventures, and franchising-networks in developing countries is run by management located in the developed world. They manufacture so-called '*brand-labelled*' clothing that is sold on every High Street in every advanced country.[189]

In the advanced world of managerial capitalism, industry, and a differentiated workforce, management had to develop new forms of work. As a spin-off these new work forms also happen to appear more mature and moral even though child-labour is not exclusively an issue of the developing world.[190] Nevertheless, even mature and morally conscious behaviour of adults can be targeted through *scripted behaviours*. This occurs when those *who make things* (Aristotle) carry out managerially set work tasks with little or no conscious awareness. One of the core tasks is to replace conscious, reflective, and even moral behaviour with *scripted behaviour*. Essentially, people who are forced to conduct scripted behaviours follow a managerially pre-organised *script* – almost like a movie script – without much critical reflection. *Scripted behaviour* is reflective of Kant's *human nature...that can be changed into a mere mechanism in which, as in a puppet show, everything would gesticulate well but there would be no life in the figures.* A classical case of scripted behaviour is found in the motor car industry where the assembling of motor cars occurs inside a 55-second cycle time and in roughly seven meters of space along the still moving assembly line. It is also found in what has been called SOS: *standard operation sheet*. Like scripted behaviour,

SOS determines every move a car worker has to make. It is at the core of a highly routinised, scripted, essentially dehumanising, and un-ethical work regime that does not treat those *who make things* (Aristotle) as humans but as human robots or *hands-without-brains* (Ford).

In today's car industry work regimes with highly standardised and routinised activities are conducted in extremely confined, managerially arranged, and over-familiar settings. They provide clear schemata for tidily regimented work patterns, just as prescribed by Taylor, and are carried out in an absent-minded or mindless fashion. The reason for this is often deeply embedded in the managerial scripts which are covered up by the managerially constructed ideology of efficiency. At least this is what individuals are made to believe when confronted with such rigid work patterns. They are explained as being the most *efficient* and absolutely rational work patterns and are applied to hide the inhumanity of the industry as well as the immorality of such man-agerial work regimes. Management applies instrumental reasoning to give self-invented managerial engineering processes legitimacy. Those on the operative side – those who are managed rather than those who manage – are made to feel that they do not need to monitor the morality of an action that is carried out as *scripted behaviour*. In short, inside the dilemma of managerial efficiency vs. moral behaviour, it has always been management that determines the process. Through these processes however management exterminates humanity and ethics.

In sum, almost all of the world's mass-manufacturing still follows Taylor's and Ford's model. This is the way to make the cars we drive, the TVs we buy, and every computer and keyboard we use. It is highly monotonous, ritualised, standardised and, above all, a highly immoral form of work that is enforced upon those *who make things* (Aristotle). Immorality is enforced by those who claim to be required to manage (Marcuse 1966; Marglin 1974). As a consequence, Taylor's dehumanising and immoral horizontal and vertical division of labour enshrined in SOS is still alive and operative today. It still resembles *scripted behaviour* that has been condemned so strongly by Kant. Hence, management in general does follow the morality of stage zero when work regimes for mass manu-facturing are concerned. The fact that most of our present work regimes in countries of advanced capitalism hardly contain such methods any-more does in no way negate the fact that they are prevalent in those countries that deliver mass manufactured goods to the so-called devel-oped world. In countries that have made the transition to the advanced world, more advanced work regimes are dominant. Kohlberg linked these to *obedience and punishment* in his first stage of morality.

1. Stage one: Obedience and Punishment. Obedience to authority and punishment including the fear of punishment still play powerful roles in human lives.[191] Behavioural scientists such as Skinner have noted the effects of punishment and the fear of it. They found that people can be manipulated by the fear of punishment and their behaviours can be re-designed (Lemov 2006). Punishment – along with positive and negative reinforcement – became a core element of Skinner's theory on conditioning. Smith (1982:58) noted that in the mechanical Skinner model people were regarded as reactive victims of environmental causal forces with no freedom of choice or capacity for self-direction.[192] Skinner's conditioning theory has been eagerly picked up by The Servants of Power. It entered the domain of management in the form of organisational psychology.[193] These models are also applied to management and marketing. Not surprisingly, today's managerial workplaces represent Jackall's (1988) Moral Maze as designed by behaviourism. According to Lemov (2006), the maze has been the core experimental construct used to test and condition animals and humans.

In Chomsky's critique (1971:33) on Skinner's manipulation of human behaviour he noted, *except when physically restraining, a person is the least free or dignified when he is under threat of punishment.* For ethics, behaviourism is full of moral problems. Radically opposing the idea of life under punishment is, for example, the ethics of *existentialism.* The following premises rest at the core of existentialism: there is *no inherent human nature;* the concept of *radical freedom* is linked to *self-determination; being human* means *being free;* the invention of so-called *'I must...'* necessities are delusions; and *radical freedom means accepting responsibly. Existentialism* rejects behaviourism as immoral. However management and organisational psychology rely heavily on it. Managerial performance measures like key performance indicators, performance related pay, etc. are based on the managerial assumption that *human nature* exists and that it can be manipulated. This is often uncritically accepted as a given like *Maslow's* endlessly rehearsed *Hierarchy of Needs* (Arnold 2005:313ff.; Klikauer 2007:279). But *existentialism* rejects the concept of *human nature* and with it the idea that there is a natural hierarchy of needs. According to *existentialism,* rather than depicting human nature, management invented a hierarchy of needs which is *pre*-scriptive rather than *de*-scriptive. This is the reason why so many textbooks contain Maslow's hierarchy. It pleases political masters, management, and the market for managerial textbooks instead of producing truth. Similarly, existentialist ethics also contains the concept of *radical freedom.* This is negated by management who rather creates conditions of *unfreedom* under the ideological cover of self-invented necessities such as the usual justification of market-determined business needs and economic necessities (Beder 2006). Such managerially constructed determinism deforms human life and negates human freedom. Finally, if existentialist ethics denotes that *being a human* means *being free,* then management negates this by creating humans who suffer *unfreedom.* To management, humans are no more than *human resources/materials* who represent a cost-factor and *costs have always to be kept low* (Magretta 2002).[194]

Freedom is one of the core elements of almost all versions of ethics ranging from Aristotle to utilitarianism, Kant, Hegel, Rawls, Bauman, and Adorno. The fear of punishment constitutes an extreme impairment of human freedom and dignity. In other words, it is not only punishment itself but the fear of it that eradicates the ethics of freedom and dignity. The fear of punishment is only superseded by physical restraints as being the strongest form of denial of freedom. Management hardly ever *physically restrains* their subordinates. But the threat or fear of punishment has not ceased. In Skinner's model of obedience, *punishment avoidance* operates a highly dictatorial system that favours people in authority. For example, adults who were raised in an authoritarian home under strict, harsh, inconsistent, and emotionally repressive parental regimes are left with a weak ego and low self-esteem. They are the ideal human material to be converted from human *beings* into human *resources.* They have been made totally dependent on pleasing (positive reinforcement) and obeying their parents. This structure is carried over into schooling, the army, colleges, even universities, and later into management.[195] It is the total negation of Kant's ethics of self-determination and Hegel's ethics of *Mündigkeit.*

Inside behaviourism there are always those who control others and those who are controlled whether in laboratory or managerial situations (Lemov 2006). Skinnerian conditioning is a controlling top-down activity that suits management's need for control. Simultaneously, it diminishes ethical equality, self-actualisation, *Mündigkeit,* justice, and freedom. Those exposed to behavioural methods of mental manipulation are denied any access to shaping the methods that create obedience and punishment. Crucially, those manipulated are not even aware of the fact that they are being manipulated. Unawareness, rather than Kantian self-awareness, self-reflection, self-determination, and Hegelian self-actualisation is essential for behaviour modification (Kreitner 2009: 416ff.; Arnold 2005). It constitutes the very foundation of organisational psychology, HRM, and workplace behaviour modification. In this model, managerial rules are created in a non-democratic, authoritarian, and dictatorial top-down way. They are formed without any input or awareness of those to whom the rules are applied. It is a deceptive *behind-your-back* method that negates almost all versions of ethics known today. The managerial maze and Skinner's maze-laboratories represent a strict division between two entities, those for whom punishing models are designed and those who design and administer them. In management as in Skinner's animal testing the rules of punishment and punishment avoidance must be precisely obeyed. This however destroys ethics and moral behaviour.

Management does not administer Skinner's electrical shocks and the days of the whip are long gone, at least in the so-called developed world. However, on the basis of Skinner, *the Servants of Power* have invented somewhat more sophisticated sanctioning regimes for management that are administered to human *beings* now converted into human *resources*. In managerially constructed work regimes, disobedience to the managerially outlined punishing regime will lead to penalties such as fines, demeaning work tasks, demotion, and the loss of income and employment. For those *who make things* (Aristotle) this is to be avoided. But management not only creates regimes that punish, it also creates the organisational setup that diminishes the likelihood of punishment.[196] To achieve this, corporations have been, and still are, in dire need for supportive, uncritical, and affirmative academic faculties such as organisational psychology. With their assistance, management creates corporate cultures, induction programmes, reward structures, behavioural adjustment methods, and organisational behaviour to achieve the goal of the *Organisation Men* (Whyte 1961). Once human *beings* have successfully been converted into management-supportive human *resources* who internalise the organisational rules of sanction regimes, punishment becomes less important.[197]

Management demands strict rule-following by those on the receiving end. The driving force behind this is self-preservation. It becomes an all-important mode of existence. Through alienating control and sanctioning regimes individuals are solely preoccupied with the demands of those in managerial power and how to avoid causing them anger.[198] Many observers have detected the rise of the *psychopath* in management.[199] The non-textbook reality based view of management also supports the concept that management is a *narcissistic process*.[200] Narcissistically operating managers also tend to manage through *Management by Fear* (Monk 1997:57) that is based on giving and receiving orders as the sole determinant of managerial conduct. Adorno (1944:22) has summed this up as *the ones who help because they know better, turn into the ones who humiliate others through bossy privilege*. Constructed in this way, managerial regimes are highly authoritarian, governed by domination, and directed to follow strict top-down hierarchies.[201] This is the epitome of *command and control* (Magretta 2002).

At this stage managerial authority – the power associated with a position within an organisation – is enshrined in what constitutes the hierarchical relationship.[202] Magretta (2002) noted the essence of management is that it *must keep the cost down* through *co-ordination and co-operation that come with hierarchy (that is, with ownership)*. It establishes *command-and-control structures*. Without hierarchy authoritarian management relationships are hardly possible. Each actor in this structure has a clearly defined position and even those at the bottom are still made to believe that they have subordinates: wives, husbands, children, pets, neighbours, pub acquaintances, and friends. The core patterns of such cemented hierarchies define authoritarian, asymmetrical, aggressive, violent, pathological, unequal, and domineering relationships inside work and society that have been accepted by the authoritarian structure of society and Managerialism. Both are built on the *Banality of Evil* (Arendt 1994) based on the maxim of *each level has authority over the immediate below and over all echelons below that*.[203]

Hierarchy and authoritarianism are structurally set against those at the bottom (employees) rather than against those who manage. For example, those in lower positions are left less of a chance to be promoted to the top. For them promotion is pure illusion hence the greater is the need for management to keep the illusion alive.[204] Such authoritarian hierarchies exist in almost all companies. Under authoritarian rule they are of particular significance. Each promotional level provides additional barriers *against* promotion which asphyxiates individuals inside rigid, sharply divided, and hardened borders that are set against organisational mobility.[205] Hierarchies, authoritarianism, and conformity are created for stability and sustainability of the managerial authority. As an addition to the illusion of promotion, managerial authority is also based on pay structures, managerial praise, as well as obedience and the avoidance of punishment.[206]

Apart from behaviourist psychological manipulation, the illusion of promotion, and the creation of psychopaths as managers, *obedience and punishment regimes* carry two more elements. One is what Bauman called *soliciting the co-operation of the victims* in his ultimate masterpiece *Modernity and the Holocaust* (1989), the second is to be found in the famous *Milgram Experiment* (1974) that highlights *The Ethics of Obedience*.[207] For British philosopher and ethicist *Zygmunt Bauman*, the Holocaust was not a failure but a product of modernity. It was not created by insane monsters but through the administration of rational managerial means, the *rationality of irrationality*.[208] Modern means based on rationality were applied to the mass extermination of Jewish, Sinti, Roma, communists, trade unionists, homosexuals, and countless other groups seen as a threat to Nazi-rule or defined as non-Aryans. It served the most irrational goals such as the goal of a pure Germanic race. Hence, *the Holocaust was not an antithesis of modern civilisation* (Bauman 1989:7) but the application of modern managerial means. The concentration camp *Buchenwald was* part *of our West as much as Detroit's River Rouge*, Ford's car plant (Bauman 1989:9).

In carrying out mass murder, *the Nazis could count on Jewish co-operation* (Bauman 1989:118) by installing the so-called *Judenrat*. Elderly Jewish people of small villages, towns, cities, hamlets, the Warsaw ghetto, and so on were assembled by the Nazis and given the choice between delivering a certain number of Jewish people to them for '*resettlement*' (extermination in gas chambers) or, if they failed to do so, the SS would take twice as many away for '*resettlement*' (the Nazi term for mass murder), including the *Judenrat* itself. Given the choice, the *Judenrat* diligently delivered time and time again until no one was left and the *Judenrat* itself was put into a cattle-train destined for Auschwitz. It was *Sophie's Choice* (Styron 1979) executed thousands of times turning *choice* into a weapon against those who were already constructed as *objects of power* (Bauman 1989) inside the German management of death. In that way, *the Jews were part of that social arrangement which was to destroy them* (Bauman 1989:122).

The relentless managerial logic of mass extermination was based on the motto *we do not decide who is to die; we only decide who is to live*. On that premise *many Judenrat leaders wished to be remembered as benevolent, protective gods* (Bauman 1989:140) because they were able to save a few while otherwise oiling the Nazi death-machine. And so *the death machinery of the calculation of loss avoidance, cost of survival, lesser evil, was set in operation. In such a situation the rationality of the victims has become the weapon of their murderers. But then the rationality of the ruled is always the weapon of the rulers. In short, the co-operation of the victims with the designs of their persecutors was made easier by the moral corruption of the victims* (Bauman 1989:142–144). Bauman (1989:149) concludes, *almost everything was done to achieve maximum results with minimum costs and efforts. Almost everything (within the realm of the possible) was done to deploy the skills and resources of everybody involved, including those who were to become the victims of the successful operation.* In Bauman's (1989:150) final words:

> **The Holocaust could be made into**
> **a textbook on scientific management**

In other words, according to Bauman's discussion of the Holocaust, the greatest mass murder in human history has only been possible through the application of modern management techniques. It made one of the most hideous crimes possible by using just three rather banal core elements against those to be killed. Firstly, the victims were turned into *objects of power;* secondly, the Nazis relied on *the co-operation of the victims;* and thirdly, they were made to be part of the logic of death when rationality and choice was used as a weapon against them. These three core underlying managerial principles can be found in any modern corporation. Firstly, human beings made part of the managerial process through their conversion into human *resources* represent *Menschenmaterial* (human material in Nazi-language). This confines them to an existence as *objects of managerial power.* Two core elements of all management derive from this: the *right-to-manage* and the *managerial prerogative.* They are reserved exclusively for management. Inside the managerial process human beings are assigned the unethical status of being *objects of power.*

Secondly, the managerial machine does not function without the *co-operation of the victims* who are totally excluded from managerial decision-making. Simultaneously, they are exposed to managerial power.[209] Management is faced with one of the most enduring contradictions. It needs co-operation but also hierarchy and control over those with whom it is co-operating. This is a contradiction not gone un-noticed by many. Just like choice has been used against those who co-operated in the case of the *Judenrat,* management uses the very same methods of rationality when co-operating. For example, it constructs cases where *costs must be kept down* (Magretta 2002). They give lower managers and non-managerial staff a choice inside a tidily controlled setup engineered by management. For example, management demands that 20% of operating costs have to be cut otherwise the whole department will be dissolved. To achieve this, management often sets up its own version of the *Judenrat* in the form of teams and committees comprised of victims who, just like the *Judenrat,* co-operate with management to achieve the cost-cutting. It represents nothing more than the standard mode of operation exercised day-in-and-day out in thousands of companies. It also represents the height of inhumanity.

In that way, those *who make things* (Aristotle) are made *part of that managerial arrangement which was to destroy them* (Bauman 1989:122). The relentless managerial logic of cost-cutting is based on the maxim: *we do not decide who is to be* dismissed; committee members *only decide who is needed in the department. Many* committee members *wished to be remembered as benevolent, protective gods.* They saved the department from being dissolved by sacrificing a few! And so, *the* cost-cutting *machinery of the calculation of loss avoidance, cost of survival, lesser evil, was set in operation.* In such a situation the rationality of *those who make things (Aristotle)* has become *the weapon of their* managers. *But then the rationality of the ruled is always the weapon of the* managerial *rulers.* In short, *the co-operation of employees was made easier by the moral corruption of the* employees. The simple example of departmental cost-cutting highlights the similarities between the management, Nazi deaths, and the management of any department in any company.

Thirdly and finally, employee participation is made to be part of the managerial logic of cost-cutting. In other cases, workers' involvement is used for different issues such as quality control, outsourcing, downsizing, relocation, etc. The issues at hand may change but the destructive and unethical logic of choice stays the same. Rationality and free choice are used as weapons by management. In sum, by applying these three core concepts of all modern management, the *Holocaust* can indeed be *made into a textbook of scientific management.* Beyond that, the immorality of management is exposed when management operates at Kohlberg's stage one that contains the *fear of punishment.* In the managerial case dismissal due to cost-cutting is the version of punishment. It is administered to those who fail to live up to the managerially engineered standards.

Next to punishment, stage one also contains *obedience.* With his work on *Obedience to Authority* (1974), Stanley Milgram became the foremost expert on obedience. Next to punishment regimes – *disciplinary action* in HRM-language – *obedience to authority* has always been one of the core elements of management. Through laboratory experiments Milgram found that the willingness to inflict pain on others increases with distance.[210] In short, it is easier for top-management to be cruel to those on the bottom of the scale. The example of the Union Carbide plant in Bhopal, India illustrates this point. With a relatively longer geographical distance between the USA and Bhopal, the suffering and deaths of Indian people became a distant issue. The same applies to the case of Ford's Pinto cars. Ford's top-managers never met the victims of exploding gas tanks. The victims of Ford's cost-cutting exercise died in a position where management could distance themselves from their victims. The same goes for Nestle's baby food, the tobacco, asbestos, fast-food industries, etc. There is an *inverse ratio* between executioner and victim. The greater the distance between managerial decisions and those affected by it, the greater the cruelty of management.

In short, it is hard to dismiss your personal assistant but easy to close a plant in some distant country. To ensure that, management, and even more so top-management, has structurally isolated – and more importantly insulated – themselves against those *who make things* (Aristotle) through a raft of measures ranging from separated car parks to refreshment areas, from different floor levels (height = power) to business class air travel (front = power). In sum, most top-managers never see, touch, or even hear those who are affected by their cost-cutting measures, especially when they occur in an overseas production facility. Hence a hierarchical separation between cause (management) and effect (dismissal of workers) has to be engineered as the essence of management without which it cannot do. It not only requires physical but also moral distance. Since MADD (*moral attention deficit disorder*) increases with distance, management is at pains to engineer such a distance. Hierarchy and chains-of-command assist management to distance itself from moral responsibilities.

Milgram noted *indeed, mediating the action, splitting the action between stages delineated and set apart by the hierarchy of authority, and cutting the action across through functional specialisation is one of the most salient and proudly advertised achievements of our rational* management. The meaning of Milgram's discovery is that, *immanently and irretrievably, the process of rationalisation facilitates behaviour that is inhuman and cruel in its consequences, if not in its intentions. The more rational the organisation of action, the easier it is to cause suffering – and remain at peace with itself* (Bauman 1989:155). In other words, management operates through *mediated action* by setting up a strictly hierarchical and pyramid structured organisation. It has layers of layers between CEO, CFO, top-management, divisional-management, regional-management, plant-management, departmental-management, middle-management, line-management, section-leaders, shift-supervisors, team-leaders, and so on.[211] With this management fulfils what Milgram (1974) sees as an unethically structured institution.

Hierarchies of authorities have to be maintained in the managerial world. Management has done this ever since its invention. It sees self-organisation as flawed (Magretta 2002). And despite decades of managerial talk of *'flattening the hierarchy'*, de-layering, and restructuring, there is no corporation without hierarchy. The process of rationality is equally important to management. This is manifested in Magretta's (2002) quote *numbers are important* and in the rational act of *allocating resources (material and human)*. This sort of rationalisation converts managerial decisions from active into passive ones. It is no longer *the CEO* or *manager X who has decided* but *accounting demands..., the market needs...*, etc. The deception through language use knows no end in management (Klikauer 2007 and 2008). Immorality is hidden behind the veil of managerial language that rationalises, naturalises, and eventually neutralises managerial decisions in order to appear moral where immorality is exercised. It appears that the more moral managerial language becomes, the more immoral are the acts that follow.

Finally, according to Milgram, *the more rational the managerial organisation of action, the easier it is to cause suffering*. Suffering is never administered as such but inside a managerially constructed process of rationalisation. Even the words with which suffering is administered are rationalised. People are no longer *fired* and *kicked out* but *retrenched*, *set free*, and *let go of*. This seeks to neutralise ethical standards in the face of immoral behaviour. The rationality of obedience to authority seeks to neutralise the suffering of those *who make things* (Aristotle) and creates a protective shield of self-deception for management. While acts of immorality are committed, rational managers *remain at peace with themselves* because they are not to blame.[212] It is the job that is responsible, the career, the demands of top-management, the market, trade unions, economic circumstances, the weather, and so on. Management has only done its job in a rational way and according to neutral cost-benefit rationalities.

According to Milgram, *one of the most remarkable features* of the managerial *system of authority is, however, the shrinking probability that the moral oddity of one action will ever be discovered* (Bauman 1989:159). The greater the distance between top-management and those who suffer from its immoral action, the less likely it is that top-management is discovered to be immoral. In general, the blame for immoral action can be put onto those lower down the line. This sort of *ethical cleansing* shields top-management from any blame to have acted unethically. In the Bhopal case, the fault rested solely with the plant manager or some individual employee – never with top-management or the CEO who retired wealthy but quietly into some New England estate inside the protective shield of US law. In the Ford Pinto case, it was down to bad engineering or even bad driving. And in the cigarette industry it is down to bad personal habits, not to the billions spent on advertising and the five decades of mass-deception that engineered the public myth that smoking is harmless. It had nothing to do with falsifying research, deceptiveness, lobbying, PR-campaigns, paying off others, marginal-ising, and outright lying. In no way is top-management to be held responsible.[213] No Union Carbide, no Ford, and no cigarette industry CEO has ever faced up to their ethical and criminal responsibilities and received a jail sentence.

While relieving itself from ethics and loyalty, management still demands loyalty from employees. According to Milgram, *loyalty means performance of one's duty as defined by the code of discipline* (Bauman 1989:161). Management demands loyalty and relies on the duty to be carried out by others (*management is achieving results through others*, Magretta 2002). And it is management that solely defines the *code of discipline*. Hence, Milgram concludes that *it is psychologically easy to ignore responsibility when one is only an intermediate link in a chain of evil action but is far from the final consequences of the action* (quoted from: Bauman 1989:161). In other words, the responsibility for unethical and sometimes even criminal action is dissolved inside the managerial hierarchy. Everyone is just a part of a chain of managerial actions so that nobody is responsible. The managerial setup seeks to dissolve all ethics. Those who claim managerial responsibility only have the respons-ibility to find someone to blame. Once they have offloaded their res-ponsibility, management is able to insulate themselves from all moral obligations.

Milgram's findings also indicate that it is best for management to be as far removed from the place of immoral action as possible. The further management is removed, the less likely that any responsibility will fall onto it. Hence, the layers of management that represent a *clear command-and-control* structure (Magretta 2002) also act as a shielding undercoat for top-management against unwarranted ethical intrusions. It allows management to allocate work tasks towards those lower down the ranks while simultaneously deflecting morality from top-management. Just like work tasks, responsibilities for immoral action can also be allocated to middle-management, departmental-management, line-management, supervisors, workgroups, and eventually to indi-vidual employees until nobody is responsible. In short, rather than being an institution of morality, management is an institution inside which morality is made to disappear. The more layers of protective coating are applied, the more diversified a company is, the more locations it has, and the greater the distance between them and the head-office, the more likely it is that ethics inside it *vanishes into thin air.*

Milgram's final conclusion is that *the readiness to act against one's own better judgement, and against the voice of one's conscious, is not just the function of authoritative command, but the result of exposure to a single-minded, unequivocal and monopolistic source of authority.* Hence, *pluralism is the best preventative medicine against morally normal people engaging in morally abnormal actions* (quoted from: Bauman 1989:165). In sum, Milgram highlights the fact that lines of authorities and monolithic organisational structures do not support ethical conduct. They tend to prevent it. Unethical behaviour is born out of an exposure to a *single-minded, unequivocal, and monopolistic source of authority.* Management is such a *single-minded* institution as its structures are not based on *checks and balances.*[214] There are next to no dissenting voices inside management. Neither managerial power nor the ideology of Managerialism leaves any room for them. Management represents TINA: *there is no alternative.* Hence, it is not a place for self-determination, *Mündigkeit* (Hegel), critical self-reflection, and autonomy (Kant). Rather the extreme opposite is the case – a one-dimensional institution (Marcuse 1966) with an *unequivocal and monopolistic source of authority*: management itself.

Finally, if *pluralism is the best preventative medicine against morally normal people engaging in morally abnormal actions,* then management represents the near total opposite. What Milgram (1974) and Bauman (1989) view as the best way to prevent unethical behaviours is negated in management. Management is not based on the ethics of *pluralism.* It has deliberately excluded anyone from acting in a pluralist way inside the monolithic modern corporation. This is called corporate culture – a common set of beliefs to which everyone subscribes. Management rather represents singularity and one-dimensionality, the managerial code words for which are *organisational culture, mentoring, stewardship,* and *strong leadership.* Management has rendered itself incapable of ethical actions because its very own setup acts against ethical behaviour. This setup actively and structurally enables managers to engage in unethical behaviour. In sum, operating at Kohlberg's stage one does not contradict many of today's managerial practices. Managerial authority often demands obedience while managers still use punishment – e.g. *disciplinary action* and *three-strike-rules* – to enforce organisational conformity and rule compliance when the managerial system of benefits and rewards fails. How the system of benefits and rewards operates is the starting issue of the next chapter.

8
Kohlberg's Moral Manager II: From Rewards to Universalism

Having outlined the basics of Kohlberg's ethical concept of morality, his non-ethical stage zero, and the first real stage of management's moral motives of punishment and obedience in *Part I: From Impulsiveness to Punishment*, this chapter discusses the moral stages from *rewards to universalism*. It highlights those stages of morality that are highly relevant to management. Part I has shown that many of today's managerial practices do not contradict stage *one*. Managerial authority often demands obedience and managers still use punishment. Often this is called *disciplinary action* in HRM language or the most commonly exercised form of the so-called *three strike rule*. It is designed to enforce organisational conformity and rule compliance. These methods to create obedience and avoid punishment sometimes fail to ensure the designed outcome, the creation of *Organisation Men*. It is at this point when the managerial system of *benefits and rewards* starts to manifest itself as the essence of management's moral motives. This is highlighted below.

2. Stage Two: Benefits and Rewards. At moral stage two, management acts essentially in its own interest, carrying connotations to selfishness, egocentrism, and *ethical egoism*.[215] For moral egoists, the key problem of life is not how to be good, how to be happy, and *what shall I do* but rather: *what should be our personal aim in life?* Their answer is rather easy: It is the individual ambition to be materially wealthy. But moral egoism goes even one step further. It argues that the quest for personal wealth should be achieved in disregard of other people. The Hegelian *Other* is all but excluded from individual preferences. The maxim is: whatever other people may think and feel is largely irrelevant. Even though there may be reason to accept their advice, this would in no way challenge the quest for material things. It is also no impairment to perform certain actions only as long as I can do what I want to. In sum, moral egoism carries strong connotations to *moral selfishness*.

The ethical concept of moral selfishness has been part of virtue ethics ever since its development in Greek philosophy. The philosophical ethics of selfishness is enshrined in the *virtue of selfishness* that has simple self-interest at its core. As part of the philosophy of *moral egoism*, moral selfishness is conducted independently from *others*. Again, the Hegelian idea that ethics is only possible in relation to *others* is negated. The *Other* provides no guiding signpost for moral selfishness whose moral core is constructed by and around the individual. It is perceived to be independent of Hegel's *Others* and of society. Most obviously, *moral selfishness seeks to promote the satisfaction of my own interest.*[216]

This makes ethical egoism highly attractive to management ethics as it relates to Kohlberg's concept of ethics based on *rewards and benefits*. Since moral egoists are primarily driven by their own benefits, getting rewarded for an action serves their moral intention of getting a good deal for themselves. The only remaining problem is that of Hegel's distinction between *having a purpose* and *serving a purpose*. Rather than having a purpose in life, they serve the purpose of getting personal benefits. Not the action itself is at the centre but the goal (benefit) it serves. According to this philosophy, moral egoists are supposed to do whatever they like as long as it serves the purpose of receiving a benefit. Whatever furthers their aim in life – material wealth – is good. If this can be achieved through rewards and benefits, then this goal supersedes the concept of *doing whatever one likes*. The credo is to *do whatever achieves a personal benefit*. Hence, Hegel's concept of *having a purpose* (human fulfilment) is negated by the concept of *serving a purpose* where an action is carried out because of the expectation of a reward that serves the goal of getting rich.[217]

Management is the sole authority over punishments and rewards. While punishment represents the first stage of Kohlberg's morality, rewards are represented at stage two. In the clear cut managerial world *being in charge* always means there is someone who is *not in charge* – those *who make things* (Aristotle). In fact being or not being in charge divides management from non-management most clearly. The authority over the allocation of rewards defines the managerial process. Management is just as much defined by distributive as by retributive powers which also represent the dividing line between reward-giver and reward-receiver. This poses a problem for management.

Management can give rewards (Kohlberg's stage two) but it can also hand out punishment (Kohlberg's stage one). Those *who make things* (Aristotle) are on the receiving end of both. For management things are different because it is the sole decision-maker. In some cases, however, the hand-out of rewards to subordinates diminishes management's rewards. According to Magretta (2002), management is a *zero-sum game*. The asymmetrical structure of the managerial regime is represented in relatively large rewards for management and smaller rewards for non-managerial staff. In short, it appears as if the hierarchical structure of organisations puts management in a favourable position when it comes to rewards. Moral egoism services management more than it services non-management. It favours those who are in the position to issue or withdraw rewards. Consequently, moral egoism also gives management the argumentative upper hand.

With moral egoism, management is able to argue that it follows the very core of human life, the self-serving interest of humans. Hence, they can safely abstain from the ethical task of having to care for others. More than care, a good working life, and *organisational happiness*, subordinates want financial rewards. Secondly, subordinates' self-interest makes them seek rewards in place of everything else. Moral egoism determines both these interests. But they are not the only issues management can divest itself of. Moral egoism also demands that management only takes advice – moral or otherwise – when it wants to and when it favours its interest. This suits management since their primary task is to follow their own interest. Moral egoism supports management's need to satisfy its own existence and always places this above the satisfaction and in disregard of others.[218] Furthermore, management cannot be distressed by the distress of others as this would violate the ethical demands of moral egoism. Therefore, the philosophical idea of moral egoism creates a positive and highly valuable morality for management. It is the philosophical underpinning of one of the lowest moral stages developed by Kohlberg.

Management's use of moral egoism is contradicted by Hegel's concept of the *Other*. Management has to deal with the *Other* because it *creates performance through others* (Magretta 2002). It has to acknowledge that making deals with others may be necessary in certain situations. However such deals are purely governed by management's self-interest.[219] This is enshrined in the *virtue of selfishness*.[220] Selfishness takes place when it serves management's benefits that are prevalent in the age of *me-first* management and the culture of *'me, myself, and I'*. If at all necessary, dealing with others is reduced to *win-lose* or *zero-sum* strategies based on cost-benefit calculations. For example, any information that is provided to others is viewed as a loss to management inside the win-lose paradigm.[221] In other words, the ethics of management is not to be found in openness and access to information. The secrecy surrounding every single allocation of remuneration is presented as confidential and the higher the ranking, the more secretive it becomes. In sum, the use of information is a bargaining tool because *you have to make tradeoffs in order to achieve results* (Magretta 2002). Information is not seen inside the ethics of sharing but as an instrument that can be used for managerial advantages (Klikauer 2007 and 2008).

Consequently, management ignores others and refuses to communicate whenever communication with them is deemed non-beneficial, unnecessary, and unproductive to *The Real Bottom Line*. Anyone at lower levels is treated and made to feel as if they were cogs in a machine unless they are useful for the benefit of management. This negates Kant's *Kingdom of Ends*. For management, communication and information represent a *Kingdom of Means*. Once human beings have been turned into cogs in a machine, the Kantian concept of self-determination is all but unwanted by management, as is the Hegelian ethics of self-actualisation. It also negates the single most important unifying idea between various forms of ethics (virtue ethics, utilitarianism, Kant, Hegel, and Rawls' ethics of justice): the ethics of freedom. It is negated by constructing employees as cogs in a machine who are kept at bay by rewards and benefits. But management goes even further by framing *lower cogs* as *objects of managerial power* (Bauman 1989) who may be rewarded or punished. This forces them into scaffoldings inside which they are reduced to the aspiration to become a bigger cog in expectation of bigger rewards and bigger benefits. They are made to become *Organisation Men* and eventually *Organisation Supermen* in the true sense of Nietzsche's philosophy. HRM calls this career, performance management, talent, and leadership.

This is also the stage of pure *Machiavellianism* where the key to success is the desire to manipulate others for one's own benefit. It is the selfish anti-ethics of '*me, myself, and I*' and represents Hobbes' ethics of *all against all*. Strategy is used as deception of the enemy (Klikauer 2007:129–142) and managerial forms of deviousness and deception may be applied whenever required to get ahead. Machiavellian management personalities can be found working successfully in many managerial occupations, particularly in those that deal with people such as HRM. They excel in bargaining and even more so in bargaining a better deal for themselves.[222] Many elements of moral behaviour linked to stage two can be found in today's management. If, however the immorality of benefits and rewards fails to asphyxiate non-managerial staff inside the managerial paradigm of *serving* a purpose rather than *having* a purpose, other methods are used to make those *who make things* (Aristotle) conform to managerial expectations.

3. Stage Three: Conforming to Expectations. At stage three, management seeks to position others in a way which forces them to be supportive to management in order to prevent them from taking on any position that is critical or contradictory to management. This assures management that its self-interest is not hurt. Non-managerial staff is deemed to be loyal and seen as living up to managerial expectations. This stage represents the opposite of Hegel's ethical concept of *Mündigkeit* as management negates the independently thinking and acting human being who strives towards self-realisation (Hegel). It also negates Kant's concept of autonomy because an autonomous person can hardly be made to conform. Instead, the conduct of management at this stage is based on obedience, compliance, submission, duty, and conformity all of which carry strong connotations to Christianity.[223]

The medieval religious philosopher Blaise Pascal (1623–1662) advocates in *The Wager* that believing in God is the safer option and compliance to the church is the moral duty of humans.[224] Similarly, management advocates the believing in management is the safer option and compliance to management is a moral duty of humans. Compliance is no longer achieved through punishment, benefits, and rewards but through the approval, affirmation, and endorsement of management.[225] The structure moves from a *monetary* incentive (rewards and benefits) towards a *non-monetary* incentive (conformity to managerial expectations). This is a classical textbook case of HRM who can prove to other managers (finance, marketing, operations, etc.) that HRM is worthwhile. It can save money by moving those *who make things* (Aristotle) from monetary incentives (high cost) to non-monetary ones (low cost) which is important because management *must keep the cost down* (Magretta 2002).

At stage three, management also no longer needs to show aggression towards others to achieve its goals. According to Adorno and Horkheimer (1944:12) a managerial ruler no longer attacks other people's lives, body, and property. Management does not need to operate by using phrases like *you must think as I say or die* (stage 2). Instead, the managerial maxim of this stage is *you are free not to think as I do*. Non-compliance, however, is sanctioned through exclusion: *from this day on you are a stranger amongst us*. Compliance on the other hand is supported inside the managerial regime. It is constructed around the managerial use of the language of *trust*, loyalty, and a one-dimensional so-called *shared interest*, all of which are closely linked to managerial reward structures. To convey this image, management strongly relies on the ideology of *we are all in one boat.*[226] It pretends to be inclusive. The corporate message is that compliance works best for the company, for management, and for oneself. It pretends a *win-win* situation where in reality there is only one clear winner.

At this stage management creates the appearance of being more inclusive compared to the strict *Machiavellianism* of '*me, myself, and I*' and Hobbes' *all against all*. Management can afford this because it moves towards support through compliance and conformity. When needed, it constructs social inclusion but also uses social exclusion for those people deemed non-compliant to the managerial demands. Punishment and rewards diminish as conformity increases. Management relies on the formula: *non-conformity = punished by exclusion* while *conformity = rewarded by inclusion*. Non-managerial staff is forced to value management for its own sake. Self-preservation is no longer linked to the fear of punishment but to compliance, conformity, and living up to management's expectations. This represents the opposite of Hegelian *Mündigkeit* and self-actualisation and Kantian autonomy and self-determination as an end in-itself which are both annulled through enforced, engineered, and supervised conformity.

The *Management by Fear* (MBF) of earlier stages has been superseded by the *Management by Compliance* (MBF→MBC). Both operate under the cover of the managerial language of MBO (management by objectives). Engineering MBF and MBC leads straight to MBO which directly leads to profits (MBF→MBC→MBO→profits). MBF, MBC, and MBO are part of the managerial ideology of Managerialism. Inside this framework non-managerial staff is seen as being in need to adapt themselves to management while self-sacrificing Hegel's ethics of *Mündigkeit*. Management on the other hand seeks to make others believe in a *shared common interest*, expressed in the ideology of *organisational culture* and the catchphrase *we are all in the same boat* (Klikauer 2007:198). It identifies all interests as managerial interests.[227] A *sectarian* management interest is converted into a *universal* interest but such a faked universal interest is ideological and not ethically grounded. It negates Kant's universalism as it is not by self-determination that people are part of the managerial interest that masquerades as a universal interest. Instead, they are made part of it through the managerial apparatus that remains unethical as it denies the fundamentals of Kantian and Hegelian ethics.

Management demands a certain level of *self-alienation* in order to turn subordinates into conforming *Organisation Men* (Whyte 1961). This negates Hegel's ethics that sees the end of alienation as a moral end. Instead of eliminating alienation, management enhances it by advancing itself to the all-encompassing ideology of Managerialism. Magretta's (2002) claim that *we all learn to think like managers* is a true representation of this ideology which has colonised the non-managerial *lifeworld* (Habermas 1997) turning everything in its way into a management issue. While the Kantian *Kingdom of Ends* represents a de-alienated world, management's *Kingdom of Means* stands for an alienated world camouflaged by Managerialism in which the only virtue left for human beings is egoistic self-management. Virtually all ethical imperatives of *virtue ethics* are negated when non-managerial staff is subconsciously made to identify itself with externally constructed goals such as the managerial *Real Bottom Line*. Hegel's idea of *having a purpose* moves to *serving a purpose* and virtue ethics such as Aristotle's morality of *friendship* and Plato's *life of philosophical contemplations* are negated. This negation serves management in achieving what it had set out to achieve. The managerial *socialisation* of *others* denies almost all ethical philosophy.[228]

It has been shown that individuals who have been socialised towards managerial regimes *carry institutional roles as conforming workers to transient settings that simulate the authority setting for more permanent organisations* (Katz and Kahn 1966:304). When people move from *primary* socialisation – family, school, homes, etc. – into employment (*secondary* socialisation), they carry the values set up before employment into the managerial regime. Whatever has been conditioned, trained, and learnt for years and whatever individuals have been adapted to during the pre-employment period is *carried* into work. It is a form of *pre-work-adaptation-to-work*. The sole idea behind it is that people adapt themselves to work regimes based on previous experiences that are largely constructed through authoritarian structures.[229] Previously experienced conformity to the authority of family and school will continue to work against the individual by preventing autonomy, self-determination, and self-actualisation. The authoritarian structure confines human beings even when they move between work and consumption.[230] Once people reach the managerial realm, they have already undergone years of conditioning to system compliance and conformity. At company level, system conformity is further fostered through the non-democratic and authoritarian ideology of corporate management, Managerialism, and mass consumption that is generously supported through corporate mass media.[231] After years of primary socialisation to authority, people recognise the symbols that demand conformity to the managerial settings. In short, the *school principal's office* becomes the *manager's office*.[232] The conditioned adult respects and complies with the demands set forth by the manager's office. This negates virtually all ethical philosophy that underpins freedom (Kant, Hegel, Rawls, Adorno, etc.) and happiness (utilitarianism).

Inside the managerial regime, conformity to authority is established through clearly defined managerial rules and rigid work related requirements linked to reward systems. They carry forward the rules and regulations internalised at earlier stages. These are not the ethical universal rules of Kantian philosophy but rules that contradict Kant's ethical *universalism* and Rawls' *ethics of justice*. These managerial rules define a particular purpose that was created without the input of those who are affected by these rules. Conformity to these managerial rules is policed through a system of hierarchical structures that mirror the structures previously adopted at home and at school. Authoritarian parents and authoritarian teachers are replaced with authoritarian managers without any interruption. Primary socialisation through home and school and secondary socialisation through work regimes have only one function and one goal: conformity to authority. This always entails the *exclusion-inclusion* regime. *You are free not to think as I do* but *from this day on you are a stranger amongst us* (Adorno and Horkheimer 1944:12). Expulsion or the threat of it to non-conformers has been part of the authoritarian system ever since. Conformity has been internalised and handed down through generations of authority-conforming workers, employees, and today's human resources/materials. When conditioned individuals move from home and school into the managerial regime, human *beings* are denied being *ends in themselves*. They are *objects of power* (Bauman) in the hands of the authoritarian family, the authoritarian school, the authoritarian soccer team, the authoritarian university, and finally the authoritarian management regime. Such *alienated* human *resources* (Hegel) carry a tremendous amount of conformity-enhancing attitudes.

As long as individuals behave inside the conforming boundaries set by family, school, and management and accept these boundaries as legitimate, the structure of authoritarian conformity lives on.[233] This guarantees not only the silent acceptance of authority and authoritarianism, it also ensures that almost all social institutions are perceived as being normal as long as they signify authoritarian structures. As a result, institutions that disturb or challenge authority such as democracy, democratic management, anti-authoritarian models and alternative forms of education, non-conventional lifestyles, or even free love are not seen as part of life but as a disturbance and as alien. If they do not depict authority, they are perceived as unruly, disorderly, unworkable, controversial, and even utopian and pathological. The portrayal of democracy through corporate mass media underscores this. Corporate mass media provide external support for a seemingly endless self-reinforcing structure of conformity to authority established from authoritarian kindergarten onwards. There are virtually no areas of human existence where challenges to authority are allowed. Nothing can infiltrate the authority enhancing settings of home, school, and work. Hence, in adult life democracy has been isolated as much as possible and, just as the nonsensical term *democratic management* portrays, democracy has been reduced to yet another authority-conforming ritual that is dutifully conducted at frequent intervals.

Overall, conformity to managerial regimes and to mass consumption occurs in the total absence of democracy. It has also insulated consumption and management from consumer or employee choices and inputs. We work diligently as told by management and we shop diligently as told by the multi-billion-dollar industry of modern marketing. The denial of real life choices and democracy in the consumptive and managerial domains occurs through two fantasies: in mass consumption, real choices and input are eclipsed by an endless array of miniscule consumer choices; inside the managerial regime the idea of democracy is made to appear as utterly preposterous. Both fantasies are easy to establish. A lifetime of artificially created authoritarian experiences has taught individuals that what is needed in management as well as in society as such is not democracy but conformity to authority. Therefore, many social and managerial activities are directed to an existence that conforms to authority and simultaneously negates the ethics of freedom and happiness. But conformity to authority is not an all-encompassing system. For those who fail to adapt to it, there are rules, laws, and the managerial order itself that confine them to authority. This is outlined in Kohlberg's stage four.

4. Stage Four: Maintaining Rules, Laws, and Order. At stage four, management expects that their subordinates are fulfilling their roles by performing managerially set duties.[234] Management invents and enforces these corporate roles and official duties. Simultaneously it excludes those for whom the rules are made from the process of rule creation which violates Rawls' ethics of justice. The managerially created corporate standards uphold HR policies, formal regulations, rules, laws, and procedures.[235] Their creation follows Hegelian master-slave ethics rather than Kantian universalism. Management is the sole creator of these rules and establishes the managerial order, deceptively called *organisational culture* (Alvesson 2002) to mystify its true origins and authoritarian character. Management sees those who have to live inside the rules solely as *rule-abiders*. Inside the managerial hierarchy, the *rule-creator* is reserved to management while the *rule-interpreter* is allocated to a sub-branch of management: HRM. This division positions HRM as a buffer between Hegel's *master* (management) and those *who make things* (employees). The whole setup reflects Hegel's *master-slave ethics* rather than his concept of *Mündigkeit*. It is the unashamed denial of *Mündigkeit*, self-consciousness, self-determination, and autonomy.

Kant's *means-ends* concept of ethics determines that rules can either serve ends or be used as means. If they serve as a *means* to the managerial *end* of turning human beings into *objects of power* (Bauman 1989), such rules are unethical. These rules are also used as a *means* for maintaining rule-governed *scripted* behaviour and the upkeep of the managerial order (Klikauer 2008:163). Compliance to managerial rules always channels compliance to management itself. Management's rule-governing generalisations tell people what to do and how to behave in a managerial and corporate regime. They use technical and bureaucratic language that enforces rule compliance. Inevitably however, rules must be linked to those who are supposed to follow them. Only when rules are made *follow-able*, are people turned into *rule-followers* and made submissive to them. They become *rule-supporters* rather than *rule-breakers*.[236] In addition, rules are perceived as being *descriptive* so that the common man understands them as descriptions of certain issues. In reality however, they are *prescriptive* as they direct people's action towards how management wants *them to behave* and direct behaviour away from Kant's self-determination.

Rule-governed behaviour must be *adjustable* so that those who do not conform can be exposed to managerial rule-adjustment initiatives. In the past this was administered through retribution, sanctions, corporal punishment, and the whip. Modern management however uses sophisticated HRM techniques. Non-conformity is constructed as system destabilising. This is deemed pathological while the blind submission to managerial rules is rewarded. Therefore the pathological behaviour is individualised and framed as being in the need of re-adjustment or correction. The correctional facilities HRM uses are, for example, EAP, the so-called *employee assistance programmes* where maladjusted behaviour to the managerial code is constructed as a psychological defect and in dire need of corrections. Firstly, EAPs individualise the contradiction between *human* and *organisational* behaviour. Secondly, they offload the problem to the employee. Thirdly, they deflect the problem of adjustment away from management. Finally, they also construct the employee as the being *the problem* (Marcuse 1966:110–117). In general, rule-deviance is evaluated *negatively* inside the managerial framework of performance management while conformity and compliance are evaluated positively. The adjustment of employees to managerial rules is the prime task of HRM's performance management.

Managerial rules are kept impersonal and as such decrease the visibility of the asymmetrically constructed power relations between management and its subordinates. De-personalised rule-based patterns of behaviour – cementing the management-employee relationship – can be portrayed as free of power and conflict because managerial behaviour expectations are based on neutral-sounding, technically formulated, and logically constructed rules. By taking on a neutral and natural appearance they reflect the asymmetrically constructed rules of the authoritarian society.[237] Through that, they assume acceptability. People in companies are made to adapt to the natural force of the managerial rule that reflects the natural forces of authoritarian rules that conditioned the individual from kindergarten onwards. The role of the individual is seen as being a compliant contributor to the good of the business and to make special efforts to act consistently with managerially defined *official* rules, duties, HR-policies, and standards. People are made to subscribe to properly formulated rules and procedures which are designed to appear more serious to them than to those who make the rules. In that way, people are captured in the ideology of rule-obedience which is mirrored through the ideology of being a *law-abiding citizen*.[238] The height of managerial rule in Kohlberg's stage four has been expressed by Adorno and Horkheimer (1944:12): *immovably, they insist on the very ideology that enslaves them.* In sum, the morality of obeying formal rules, laws, and being a law-abiding corporate personality strongly appeals to management as it supports hierarchy and authority.

Linked to rule-abiding is also the idea of *duty*. For Kant, *duty involves the pure and unconditioned self-determination of the will.* In stark contrast, management's idea of duty is to be compliant with management which represents the total negation of Kant's concept. But even management itself is not totally free to determine its own will. The demands of the market, the challenges of competitors, and employees that management rule over set tight parameters for management. On the employee side things are different. Management must disallow them *the self-determination of the will.* If employees saw self-determination as their *duty*, the managerial prerogative would be seriously challenged. Therefore, any suggestion directed towards Kant's ethics of self-determination has to be annulled by management. Kant's ethics denotes that *in the case of moral rules, the will of a rational being is not only subject to the rule but is subject to it in such a way that it makes the rule which it obeys*. In other words, the duty of rule-abiding comes from two sources. Firstly, a rule must be a moral rule. Most managerial rules support management and do not necessarily equate to moral rules. Management's intention is not morality but manageability. Secondly, Kant wants those *who obey rules* to be those to *make the rules which they obey*. In democratic societies the process of rule-making – even though mediated through parliamentarianism, lobbyists, corporate mass media, etc – is done by the people who obey the rules. Managerial rules however have no democratic legitimacy. Instead they are invented by HR-managers and signed off by top-management in total exclusion of those who are supposed to obey them. Therefore, managerial rules contradict two fundamental principles of Kantian ethics: There is no *self-determination* or involvement by those who have to obey the rules and they do not represent moral rules in Kant's sense. Nor does the managerial order represent Hegel's *Sittlichkeit* (ethical life). Much like Kant, Hegel saw the involvement of individuals in the establishment of an ethical life as essential. Managerial rules and orders in contrast do not represent ethical life and morality. They represent the very opposite of Kantian and Hegelian ethics. It appears as if management fails on the ethics of rule-making. In sum, almost all previous stages of morality – stage one (punishment), two (moral egoism), and three (conformity) are more suitable to management.

5. Stage Five: Promoting Justice, Welfare, and Openess in Debates. At stage five, management depicts even more serious failures. The problematic areas for management are to be found in several aspects of ethics: utilitarianism, Hegelian *Sittlichkeit*, Kant's moral rules, and Rawl's ethics of justice all of which have been discussed previously.[239] Just like Hegel, Kohlberg also saw the *wider society* as absolutely relevant for the development of ethics. Management however represents a clear contradiction to a socially based ethics that includes the wider society. Its focus and location is the company. Throughout its historical existence, management has been largely unable to show much interest in the wide-ranging betterment of social affairs, as well as human, civil, political, economic, retributive and distributive justice (Rawls and Nozick), and human welfare.[240] Despite ideas about stakeholder values in the textbook version of management (Kreitner 2009:121), in the real world of management the prime objective is the reality of *shareholder values*.[241] To achieve this management confines itself largely to two spheres of operations, internal and external affairs. At company level legal boundaries also represent ethical boundaries. Management-to-management relationships are represented largely through competition, buying, and selling all of which represent *contractualism*. Management confines itself to internal affairs and external competition. Neither one is engaged in the philosophical *telos* of ethics. Apart from turning human beings into customers, management's interest rests preliminarily *inside* the company with its prime motives being profits and shareholder value maximisation.

In sharp contrast, Kohlberg's ethics of stage five is positioned largely *outside* companies. Ethical behaviour is located at the interface between management and outsiders as it is this interplay that establishes morality. It is impossible for management to insulate itself from the moral demands of Kohlberg by simply issuing *corporate social responsibility* (CSR) statements; it would have to actively engage in creating a better society. This however ranges well outside of management's essence. At the internal company level, ethics has been reduced by management to having in place an *ethics policy* and an *ethical code of conduct*. Both are part of what has become known as OC or *organisational culture* (Alvesson 2002). OC and CSR are incapable of producing ethical outcomes and are more likely to function as alibi measures that eclipse ethics. To management the ethics of justice and social welfare is no more than an obstacle on the way to the profit maximisation and a hindrance to cost-cutting. Hence Kohlberg's moral imperatives can almost never contribute to *The Real Bottom Line*. The ethics of social justice and welfare for the wider community represents nothing but a cost to management that is to be avoided. Shareholders (*the real owners of the business*, Magretta 2002) determine such behaviour. However, in some unlikely cases, when the ethics of justice and social welfare creates only microscopic costs to management or even adds value to the business, it is highly welcome.[242]

For management the ethics of justice and societal welfare is often reduced to being a kindly afforded surplus or an auxiliary issue to the managerial process that can create a better corporate reputation. For managers who see *numbers as essential to organisational performance* (Magretta 2002), it is a rather nebulous concept to invest in. It can however be added to the company if management wishes to do so because it can communicate a positive corporate image.[243] In Kohlberg's ethics at level five open and reasonable communication and debates become part of the ethical make-up. The determinants *open and reasonable* have been outlined in Habermas' concepts of *Consciousness and Communicative Action* (1990) and *The Theory of Communicative Action: Reason and the Rationalisation of Society* (1997).[244]

Essentially Kohlberg's *open and reasonable debate* and Habermas' *communicative ethics* are directed towards an ethical *communicative relationship* that is based on the acceptance of *truthfulness, comprehensibility*, debates directed towards the *truth*, and *rightness* (appropriate in light of existing social norms and values). Together these elements create what Habermas has termed *ideal speech*. Kohlberg's open and reasonable debate and Habermas' *communicative ethics* represent forms of communication that are free of domination, hierarchy, and authoritarianism. Their concepts are based on the power of the best argument rather than the power of management. The four basic conditions that establish an ideal speech situation can be divided into *external* and *internal* conditions. *Internal* conditions guide communication once the frame of ideal speech is established. In the outer area social conditions that are considered ethical in society that have to be met. Kohlberg's and Habermas' conditions for *communicative ethics* display a clear picture that can be summed up as follows:

> *The concept of communicative action refers to the interaction of at least two subjects capable of speech and action who establish interpersonal relations (whether by verbal or by extra-verbal means). The actors seek to reach an understanding about the action situation and their plans of action in order to coordinate their actions by way of agreement. The central concept of interpretation refers in the first instance to negotiating definitions of the situation which admit of consensus* (Habermas 1997:86).

For Habermas, the complete framework of *communicative ethics* – *truthfulness, comprehensibility, truth*, and *rightness* – must be established in full and without any damage (Klikauer 2008: 231–245). Communication will be seen as disturbed even when one of these conditions is missing.

Furthermore, when communication among people is not directed towards reaching understanding, a vital condition is not satisfied. Communication becomes an instrument of *system integration* that structures communicative exchanges under conditions of deception and distortion. This leads to an objectively false consciousness that gives rise to *structural* violence.[245] These violations of important structural elements of *communicative ethics* create systematic restrictions on communication.

Once *communicative ethics* has been violated, distortions become established. They prejudge communicative objectives and distort the social and subjective assertions between communicating people. In these cases the domain in which ideal speech was supposed to take place has degenerated into manipulation.[246] Management is in a position to do exactly that. The power of management enables those in charge of an organisation to manipulate others in a way so that they act against their own interest. Managerial claims are turned into pure illusions of truthfulness. The forces of instrumental action only ever satisfy systematic restrictions. In such cases, *communicative ethics* cannot be established and maintained.[247] Only an unhindered environment free of domination allows the flourishing of *communicative ethics* that is directed towards ethical goals.

Once applied to management, Kohlberg's and Habermas' *communicative ethics* faces two challenges. Management operates on a fundamentally different logic. While Kohlberg's morality is directed towards the debate about ethics of justice and societal welfare, management's discussions are geared towards *The Real Bottom Line*. One of the most serious challenges *communicative ethics* poses on management however positions human communication for justice and societal welfare away from the imperatives of managerial forms of communication (Klikauer 2007 and 2008). This would highly endanger management's position and is therefore rejected by management.

In conclusion, Kohlberg's stage five is directed towards open and reasonable debates about the ethics of justice and social welfare. However, the essence of management negates all three versions of Kohlberg's ethics: ethical justice, moral welfare, and communicative ethics. This is because management restricts itself to company-internal affairs and *shareholder* (reality) rather than *stakeholder* (textbooks) values. Consequently, management is unable to move away from forms of communication based on power, hierarchy, and authoritarianism towards Kohlberg's *open and reasonable debate* and Habermas' ethics of communication. The essence of management determines that it has to negate Kohlberg's ethics of justice and welfare in society. The universal application of these ethical principles is outlined in Kohlberg's level six.

6. Stage Six: Universally Applied Justice and Welfare. Kohlberg's stage six encompasses the application of well thought-out ethical principles applied universally as intended by Kant. To reach such ethical principles, the previous stage demands an open, truthful, and domination-free debate. Stage five has already shown that management is incapable of engaging in *communicative ethics*. It cannot debate such principles openly as its interest (*The Real Bottom Line*) prevents management from domination-free discussions. Neither can it adhere to the non-defensive principle demanded by stage six. It would represent a failure of management to move away from self-serving managerial goals and towards Kantian universalism. Well thought-out ethical principles on universal justice and welfare do not represent the essence of management. Management can never apply justice and welfare to the wider society (stage 5) nor can it apply these principles universally (stage 6). Instead of respectful, non-distorted, and open discussions management's aim is *to make other modes of thoughts impossible*. This has been called TINA: there is no alternative. Management promotes the singularity of a corporate identity and one-dimensional Managerialism, commonly known as *corporate culture*.

Historically, societal and universal justice and welfare have never been part of management nor is management likely to include these principles in the future. Management's reliance on instrumentalism confines them to self created cost-benefit calculations that seek to exclude ethics. Management exists under the self-constructed excuse of *The Real Bottom Line* and relentless competition constructed as *a fight of all against all* (Hobbes). Therefore it cannot establish a relationship of trust with other organisational actors, least of all with its competitors inside the mythical *business community*. And it can never apply justice and welfare universally as this would result in the complete destruction of the asymmetrically distributed power that stabilises the managerial regime. Management's aim is the opposite: *to make other modes of thoughts impossible*. This however negates the demands of Kohlberg's ethics of level six which are directed towards enabling rather than disabling. It would be extremely counterproductive for management to act in fulfilment of Kohlberg's ethical imperatives. The essence of management as conducted ever since it has put itself into existence (Marglin 1974) demands the near total negation of everything Kohlberg has laid out for moral life. Kant's universal concept of morality and Hegel's concept of *Sittlichkeit* have shown this comprehensively.

The essence of management is first of all to process human *beings* into human resources and construct them as *objects of power* (Bauman 1989). These objects of power are further weakened by Taylor's *Division of Labour* (1911) that has resulted in horizontal and vertical divisions (Klikauer 2007). In the moral orbit of management those who make things are the managerial *means* to achieve managerial goals (*The Real*

Bottom Line).[248] Management turns everything at its disposal into means. It needs the *means* of money, the *means* of labour, the *means* of output, the *means* of allocation, and so on. In fact, management represents an apparatus that is designed and hierarchically structured with the authority to turn everything and everyone into a *means*. Management is nothing but the *Kingdom of Means* in total negation of Kant's *Kingdom of Ends*.

Historically, Kant's universalism has been directly opposed by management in the 18th century version of mercantilism. On this, Kant noted that it is essential not to confuse the point of *ethical duties* with duties as such. Because a *merchant who acts neither from duty nor from direct inclination but only for a selfish purpose* does not act inside what Kant sees as moral duty. For Kant, *an action performed from duty does not have its moral worth in the purpose which is to be achieved through it but in the maxim by which it is determined*. Kant uses the example of a shopkeeper who sees his duty in being honest in dealing with customers because it is good for business. For Kant, such a shopkeeper does not act morally because his *inclination* and moral motives for acting dutifully are not based on ethical principles but on the need of the business. Morally acting managers need to act out of moral motives and ethical consideration. Management's prime inclination for acting honestly however is because honesty is good for business. And if it delivers a little by-product in terms of ethics, so be it. Kantian ethics determines that it is the universal motive that makes a duty ethical. Conducting a managerial duty for *good business* can never establish Kant's morality as it lacks the all important universal-moral inclination.

Kant has also formulated a number of universal laws for ethics. One of the most important ones stipulates to *act only according to that maxim by which you can and at the same time will that it should become a universal law*. This would create a world in which all Hegelian contradictions were solved because Kant's *Kingdom of Ends* would be established. Management can never follow this maxim because it represents what Korsgaard (1996:78) called a *practical contradiction*, a contradiction that would be self-defeating if universalised. Management represents internal contradictions that cannot be solved without ending management itself. Secondly, management does not *act in accordance with universal law* (Kant). It represents a sectarian self-interest, not a universal interest.

If management were to assume the status of Kant's universal ethics, several changes would occur. Firstly, the family of a male manager (still the dominant case) composed of wife, mother, and children, would convert into a *wife-resource* and *children-resources* who would be employed to achieve family goals (profits).[249] For this, they were to receive wages. This scenario shows that the basic maxim under which management operates cannot be universalised. Managerial universality is already defeated at family level. Therefore, managerial maxims do not represent Kantian universalism. According to Korsgaard (1996:87) *the contradiction emerged when an action or instinct is used in a way that is inconsistent with its natural purpose.* It is not the natural purpose of a family – not even the family of a manager – to be turned into a managerial entity. Such contradictions indicate that a managerially restructured family can never assume the status of Kant's universal laws of ethics. Hence, *one sees immediately a contradiction in a system of nature whose law would be to destroy life,* says Kant. The example of the managerial family depicts the non-applicability of the managerial system to Kant's universal ethics. Management's maxim contradicts Kant's maxim of ethics. Management represents all but the complete opposite of Kant's universalism and with it the negation of Kohlberg's ethics at stage six.

7. **Stage Seven: Universal Humanity as a Holistic Perspective.** At stage seven, ethical rights are extended to issues that are totally useless to management. Here, human rights are applied to a wider holistic context instead of being restricted to humans alone. Ethical awareness reaches beyond humanity. It embraces other forms of life such as animals and ecological systems regardless of their social utility.[250] Animal ethics sets principles for the ethical treatment of animals. The application of these principles would totally annihilate management's need to create value from animals by exploiting, misusing, abusing, and eventually destroying them. In the deceptive managerial language this is called *utilising nature.* It already starts with the managerial use of plants in mono-*culture* plantation. The managerial process uses pesticides, herbicides, and genetically modified organisms for profits. The elimination of the term *culture* in agri-*culture* leaves it as agri-*business.* It occurs through the conversion of nature and animals into manageable and productive units.[251] This violates what has been termed *Environmental Ethics,* Biocentric Ethics, ecological philosophy, land ethics, ecofeminism, the ethics of preserving nature, ecological human rights, rights of nature, ecological intergenerational justice, primate ethics, and animal ethics.[252]

The so-called *utilisation of nature* (Orwellian Newspeak) ranges from oil spills to the torturous treatment of animals in chicken farms and cosmetic testing laboratories. In an attempt to falsify reality, many corporations have sought to distance themselves from animal mis-treatment and environmental destruction through elaborate, nebulous, but always sophisticated webs of managerial make-ups that *make* something *up* that is not real. These setups include freelancing, sub-contracting, outsourcing, supply-chain-management, the (mis)-use of universities, and so on and through them corporations seek to avoid the unavoidable by creating a distance. However, as Milgram (1974) has comprehensively shown, though this creates *Obedience to Authority,* it can never exempt management from moral responsibility. Often cor-porations claim to be *only* a financer, *just* a supplier, *simply* a buyer, or a *mere* seller. Bauman (1989) and Arendt (1994) have scrupulously shown that these excuses cannot be sustained. These managerial mea-sures, frequently rehearsed by corporate PR experts, may be able to eclipse unethical practices but they can never isolate management from ethics or eliminate their ethical responsibilities.[253]

Since management's sole responsibility is directed *inward* (share-holder-value) and not *outward* (animals and nature), it can never develop an awareness of the integrity of the environment and other systems as ethics demands. It cannot even link itself to human society and nature outside of the confines of the company. Any ethical awareness of the environment is negated because management is only responsible to shareholders, not to animals, the environment, or nature. Since man-agement is financially disassociated from all things natural, they only ever feature as a cost, never as objects of well-being. Kant's ethical concept of *well-being* is not seen as being universal. Instead, it is res-tricted to shareholders. The environment can never be important to management who are focused on shareholder values. To exchange profit maximisation with environmental care and animal welfare would constitute the eradication of management. Management's conduct through the history of Managerialism testifies to the fact that manage-ment's essence represents the total opposite to Kohlberg's stage seven.

It has constructed an asymmetrical relationship between environment and management. This relationship can never be free of domination because the essence of management is domination. CEOs dominate top-management, top-management dominates middle-management, middle-management dominates line-management, and line-management dominates those *who make things* (Aristotle). But management not only dominates those below, it also dominates whatever is outside the company in the form of animal and plant life. It can never adhere to the philosophical principle of truth as truth does not directly contribute to *The Real Bottom Line.* Hence, corporate records on environmental destructions are hidden behind glossy magazines. To cover-up the truth, corporate PR managers create isolated environmental initiatives that appeal to the public and serve as alibis, thus masquerading the truth.[254] Kohlberg's highest level of ethics represents nothing more than the total opposite of management's actions. The highest stage of Kohlberg's scale entails a managerial utopia that can never be realised as long as the essence of management remains what it currently is.

In *The Ethical Respect for Nature* (1981 and 2004) philosopher Paul W. Taylor shows that human ethics stems from a *human-centred* standpoint and that ethics needs instead a *life-centred* standpoint.[255] Taylor's ethics includes two moral principles: firstly, *every organism, species population, and community of life has a good of its own which moral agents can intentionally further or damage by their actions*; secondly, *essential to the morality of respect for nature is the idea of inherent worth*. Given management's lack of human-centred ethics it is hard to imagine how a life-centred ethics could be realised.[256] *Life-centred ethics* includes nature. For management, however, nature – just like any other resource – is just another material or facility to be allocated and utilised towards the goal of shareholder value, profits, and *The Real Bottom Line*. Instead of moving from *human-centred ethics* towards a *life-centred ethics*, management is locked into a management-centred ethics. It also negates Taylor's two *life-centred principles* as management is more likely to intentionally damage than further nature. In addition, human nature has no *inherent worth* for management. Its worth derives from its usability and is thereby all too often destroyed. What has *inherent worth* to management is not nature but shareholder value. The same applies to animals as Singer (1990) has outlined.

In *'All Animals are Equal...'* (1990) Australian ethicists and philosopher Peter Singer argues that *the basic principle of equality does not require identical treatment; it requires equal consideration. Equal consideration for different beings may lead to different treatment and different rights.*[257] The ethical concept of *equal consideration* is not, however, part of the essence of management who always considers itself first. Instead, management operates in the spirit of George Orwell's *Animal Farm: some pigs are more equal than others*. For example, the – always as *necessary* announced – dismissals and retrenchments are almost never done under equal considerations. It is not management but foremost those *who make things* (Aristotle) who are down-sized, right-sized, and *sui-sized*. Similarly, when it comes to bonuses, it is management who considers itself first and as the exclusive recipient of bonuses. Inside the *Moral Maze* (Jackall 1988) of management plant life and animals rank even lower. Animals tend to be regarded as coming third, if considered at all. The essence of management determines that it must conduct *unequal* considerations that contravene Singer's ethics. Singer (1990) also argues that

> *precisely what our concern or consideration requires us to do may vary according to the characteristics of those affected by what we do: concern for the well-being of children growing up...would require that we teach them to read; concern for pigs in a place where there is adequate food and room to run freely. But the basic element – the taking into account of the interest of the being, whatever those interest may be – must, according to the principle of equality, be extended to all being, black or white, masculine or feminine, human or nonhuman.*

Singer's ethics demands that management sees animals not as material and resource to enhance *The Real Bottom Line* but consider their interests. Given the present structure of management, any consideration of animals' interest would reduce the surplus value management has to extract from animals. *Milton Friedman has argued: the shareholder must always come first* and *it is the social responsibility of business to increase its profits.* This is the essence of management and their ethical imperative.

Singer (1990) also highlights Bentham's utilitarian concept of *suffering/enjoyment* denoting: *when a being is able to experience suffering or enjoyment it is our ethical duty to take this into consideration.*[258] Singer continues to argue that racists give greater weight to their race, sexists give greater weight to their gender, and *speciesists* give greater weight to their species.[259] *The pattern is identical in each case.* If Singer's ethics is applied to management they give greater weight to their managers because it *allows the interests of their own managers to override the greater interests of members of others.* In short, management favours their managers. The essence of management determines that it sees *a stone*, a *mouse*, and all non-managerial humans as resources. Management *allocates and transforms human and material resources into profit-making operations* (Magretta 2002). It does so in near total disregard of the enjoyment or suffering of these resources. Singer's ethics determines that *if a being suffers there can be no moral justification for refusing to take that suffering into consideration.* Because management violates this, it acts immoral. When taking Kohlberg's holistic ethics into account by linking it to animal and environmental ethics, management fails on both accounts. Because it can never transcend beyond its self-created confinements of *The Real Bottom Line*, it has to treat everything as a resource. This negates nearly everything Kohlberg's morality at level seven determines.

As an overall conclusion on Kohlberg's morality, management appears to reflect the morality of Kohlberg's stages one to four (from obedience to law and order). It fails to reach stages five to seven (from justice/welfare to animal/environmental ethics). The essence of management determines that it is company focused. It engages with the outside world predominantly in the form of competition. As soon as ethical issues such as wider communities, universalism, communicative ethics, and nature/animal ethics come into play, management has shown to be rather amoral. Instead of depicting Kohlberg's upper levels (5–7), management is confined to the lower ones (1–4). In sharp contrast to that, almost all ethical philosophy takes place at levels 5 to 7 as this is the truthful area of ethics. Management is incapable of accessing this vital area.

9
Positive Management Ethics

Positive management ethics commenced at the same time and in the same location where philosophy and ethics started, in Greek antiquity. The *Sophist* philosophers were a group of thinkers who divided *facts* from *values* and perceived the world as split into *physics* (facts) and *nomos* (thinking). Management follows this division by separating managerial facts and figures from value-creation. The latter is exclusively established for shareholder values while management simultaneously claims that it is itself value-free, unbiased, and neutral. For the Sophists, human values, along with ethics, were of prime importance. For management values relate to markets, dividends, ROI (return of investment), bonuses, and the like. Ethics for management is a somewhat peripheral issue that has no value for *The Real Bottom Line* but can be effectively managed. Epictetus advised in 100 AD: *remember that you ought to behave in life as you would at a banquet.* His observation is the best to portray management's *'the winner takes it all'* morality. Therefore, Epictetus and the Sophist's understanding of values are still meaningful for management today.

For management, ethics is a question of values that only interferes with their world of facts. What counts is value-creation for shareholders and the hard facts of business. Furthermore, management's *physics* is not found in the *nomos* (thinking). Their essence rests on the creation of the physicality of money and profits.[260] But Sophist values still support management because their philosophy offers an artificial separation between *facts* and *thinking*. The real support of ethics for management can be found in much more contemporary philosophy that starts with the ethics of intuitionism and subjectivism. Similarly, the ethics of moral egoism provides good assistance to management ethics just as moral relativism and nihilism. Apart from Hume, Hobbes and Nietzsche remain two of the most relevant philosophers on ethics for management. Being historically located before Nietzsche, British philosopher Dave Hume's ethics of intuitionism and subjectivism is laid out in the following paragraphs.

The managerial ethics of intuitionism and subjectivism

David Hume (1711–1776) has been associated with the ethical theory of *intuitionism*. He argued that *reason is subordinate to feelings*. As such, it only serves the purpose of desire and feelings. Intuitionists argue that there is *no principle that can be used to justify our actions*. What defines moral behaviour is not rationality but intuitive actions that are not intrinsically wrong. Intuitionism further claims that ethics cannot be reduced to a single set of ethical principles. In fact, there is simply no such thing as a single ethical principle. Once management takes up the multitude of ethical viewpoints, it acts ethically. Management only needs to act in accordance with desires and feelings. Therefore, as Hume outlined, it should never follow any single principle of ethics. Instead management should pursue its intuitions as only then are managerial actions ethical. This strongly relates to the *doctrine of double effect* according to which there is a distinction between what an *actor's intent* is and what *actors can foresee*. This suggests that when management acts it cannot always foresee the outcomes but can always claim it had good intentions. This is perfectly legitimate under Hume's ethics.

For ethical intuitionists, morality is a fact of life that exists outside of rational arguments and is therefore closely associated with our feelings. Hence, there is no need for management to justify its actions rationally. Morality operates above rational justification. Management does not need to adhere to the idea that reason holds the answer to every moral question. In such an understanding of morality, management is excused from the demands to rationally justify its actions morally. It frees itself from the ethical constraints that non-intuitionist morality enforces on them and turns a negative – the demand for justification – into a positive. This is the freedom to do as you like and still be able to claim that the outcomes are ethically based on intuitionist morality.

Quite similar to an intuitionist understanding of ethics is the idea of *ethical subjectivism*. It argues that it is simply impossible to find the *right* answer when challenged on moral grounds. Moral answers are only to be found by individual subjects. It is impossible to reach a correct conclusion through objective reasoning. Many, if not all, questions of morality do not even have *right* answers that can be found through philosophical contemplation. The idea that every moral question has a right answer is nonsensical to subjectivism. Inside the framework of ethical subjectivism, management can negate the demand to have an answer to ethical questions. And it does not need to justify its actions because all moral problems are purely subjective and not based on objective truths.

Management is well advised to use *objective language* [that] *removes all emotion and nuance from the action that people initiate*. This is perfectly legitimate because management deals with hard objective facts and not subjective feelings on morality. Magretta (2002) also recommends to management the use of objective language. After all, it negates all demands directed towards management to engage in moral reasoning. When management uses objective language it seeks to practice the art of rhetoric. It is *the art of being persuasive in speech and writing; its goal is success, not truth*.[261] Therefore, managerial communication is good when it is successful. Management's essence is not truth but success. Marketing strategies, advertising concepts, PR slogans, TV-commercials, etc. do not need to be truthful as long as the product sells and a good company image is preserved. To many, being successful in the market is proof of being right. Similarly, managerial decisions do not need to be truthful but successful. Hence, management's *communicative ethics* relates directly to Plato's '*beautiful lies*'. The art of rhetoric is perfect for management because it legitimises the use of Plato's *beautiful lies* to achieve success, thereby releasing management from unreasonable and unwarranted demands to be truthful. It supports success which is, after all, one of the core essentials for management. Success is not only what makes management but also shows management what its purpose is: the aspiration to be successful, triumphant, and wealthy.

The managerial ethics of moral egoism

The key question for moral egoism is '*what should I aim at in life?*' and its answer is '*aspiring to be rich*'. But moral egoism goes even a step further. It argues that whatever other people may think and feel, there is only one good reason to accept the advice of others – when it advances me. Moral egoism also denotes that seeking things and performing certain actions are only deemed necessary insofar *as I want to*. This is enshrined in the *virtue of selfishness* that has a healthy self-interest at its core that is independent from others. It is the '*me-first*' and '*me, myself, and I*' of moral philosophy. Most obviously, it seeks to promote the satisfaction of *my own interest* which takes primacy over the satisfaction of the interests of others. The underlying idea is that people only do what they want to which becomes the only moral reason for doing something. As a consequence, a moral egoist is *not distressed by the distress of others.*

With moral egoism, management is able to argue that it follows the very core of human life, the self-serving interest of humans. Hence, it would be morally wrong for management to care for others. Moral egoism demands from management that it only takes advice – moral or otherwise – when it wants to and when it favours its interest. Management's most important task is to follow its own interest. Nothing else can be morally justified on the basis of moral egoism. Management needs to satisfy its own existence and has to always place this above the satisfaction of others. Moral egoism is a philosophical idea that creates a positive morality for management.

Moral egoism also extends to the sanctioning of negative and unwarranted behaviour by management. This is commonly associated with *disciplinary action*. The idea of managerial punishment regimes – from three strike rules, warnings, demotion, reprimanding, pay-cuts, dismissals, etc. – is extremely useful to management. It is *a means for suppressing or eliminating certain behaviours* (Arnold 2005:287). After all it is the task of management to eliminate unwarranted behaviour and to turn disorderly behaviour into organisational behaviour. To achieve this retribution is needed. But beyond such immediate functions, punishment also serves another, even more useful, purpose for management.

Organisational wrongdoing – not following managerial orders and duties – is a clear violation and *negation* of the managerial *right to manage*. Punishment and sanctioning re-establish management's original right to manage. For an ethically egoistic management, punishment and disciplinary actions are not evils. They restore the original managerial right through righting a wrongful act committed by an employee. Punishment seeks to correct non-organisational behaviour and reaffirms management's right to manage. Maintaining the managerial order and securing management's existence is one of the prime motives behind sanctioning, punishment, and disciplinary action when viewed from the standpoint of ethical egoism. It operates with a zero-sum approach to management morality.

Zero-sum is a construction of the *prisoner dilemma*. It is one of the most useful methods for management's ethical egoism.[262] It allows the exclusion of nearly all unwarranted socially constructed realities that are positioned external to corporations. It is based on a somewhat artificial and unreal laboratory setting inside which human subjects are requested to make individual choices.[263] This setting is based on the underlying assumption that all people act at all times in their own best interests. A raft of artificial *prisoner dilemma* settings and laboratory experiments have continuously proven that management is right, ethical, and that philosophical egoism is what drives humans. In sum, the ethics of the prisoner dilemma is highly supportive of management ethics. In other words, those who have invented and used *Sophie's Choice* have been right.

Ethical egoism also denotes that the essence of ethics rests on personal gains that can be achieved even *at the expense of others*. For management, this means that it is ethically right when it favours its own good over others. Therefore, it may be necessary that the achievement of *organisational goals* comes *at the expense of others*. These *others* are usually people in the form of employees and human resources/materials. Chomsky's *Profits over People* (1999) reflects nothing more than ethical egoism that states that it is ethically correct when management acts at the expense of employees and customers. Under ethical egoism, management can plan to achieve its goals at the expense of employees and still act ethically. Therefore, *ethical egoism* is one of the most suitable versions of ethics management can subscribe to. It is just as important to management as ethical relativism.

The managerial ethics of relativism and moral solitude

Today *moral relativism* exists in the margins of standard philosophy and ethics (Moser and Carson 2001; Levy 2002). It holds that truth-values of moral claims do vary from individual to individual, from group to group, from country to country, from culture to culture, from company to company, and from management to management. This has also been termed *cultural relativism*. Like many other philosophical concepts, the philosophy of moral relativism was coined in ancient Greece supporting the view that morality is culturally specific. Moral relativism represents the view that whatever was morally right in the culture of the *Greeks* might be morally wrong in the culture of the *Callatians*. It implies that there are no objective and, more importantly, no universal rules for ethics. Therefore, there can never be a universal moral rule that applies to all managements in all countries.[264]

Furthermore, moral relativism assumes that management inhabits a unique universe inside which it is governed by *moral solitude*. In other words, management ethics is different from society's ethics and represents a solitary actor in its own right that exists independent from other societal institutions. Management's unique setup and factual existence creates management's *moral solitude*. There are no *outward obligations*. The concept of moral solitude demands from management to take care of its own affairs, not of other people's affairs. For relativists the moral solitude of corporate ethics exists independent of others. Therefore, management is under no obligation to concern itself with external affairs and externally constructed moral demands. Equally, external agents (e.g. states, academics, NGOs, trade unions, consumer groups, etc.) are simply ill-advised when judging whether or not a managerial act is deemed ethical or unethical. Such a judgement cannot be forced onto management from the outside because the position of moral solitude demands that judgements can only be made from the inside of management. In other words, if management follows the idea of *moral solitude* for its corporate affairs, it frees itself from several responsibilities that are enforced by external agencies. These include *corporate social responsibilities*, being society's moral actor, and *sustainability*. In short, the philosophical idea of *moral solitude* demands that corporate ethics ends at the boundaries of the corporation. It also ends all moral obligations beyond that point.

The second form of moral relativism is *subjectivism*. It relates not only to *intuitionism*, as outlined above, but also to *non-cognitivism*. It is the key idea that ethics is not a matter of knowledge. In this version of moral relativism, the notion that one can define ethics and moral behaviour through cognition and thinking is not possible. Ethics is believed to be part of the human existence that does not need any kind of cognitive operation. This idea has been closely associated with the philosopher David Hume (1711–1776).[265] He advocated that one cannot derive '*ought*' from '*what is*' because statements of facts (*what is*) cannot themselves have prescriptive value. They cannot tell us what to do. In short, one cannot literally see what one ought to do *from what is*. If this position holds true, management does not need to develop any ethical code as every human being knows intuitively what is ethical and what is not. Even the development of so-called ethical '*facts*' (what is) can never tell management what it *ought* to do. In short, management should stay away from making ethical determinants.

Hume also argued that there are two separate spheres. One consists of *matters of fact*, the other of *relations of ideas* in which reason can operate. Management is set to exist in the sphere of *matters of facts* as its prime essence is the area of facts and figures. After all, management sees its *strength in numbers* (Magretta 2002). Hume's *sphere of ideas* where ethics is located is not the sphere of managerial thinking. Hence, there is a strict separation between management's operative sphere – marketing, operations management, HRM, and finance – from the sphere of ethical ideas. Management does not even need to negate ethics in a nihilistic fashion because ethics is simply located in a sphere not connected to their own.

The managerial ethics of nihilism

Moral Nihilism has been closely associated with one name, Friedrich Nietzsche (1844–1900). Nietzsche represents the view that there are no moral facts at all.[266] *The most extreme form of nihilism*, according to Nietzsche, *would be the view that every belief*, and everything we *'consider-to-be–true', is necessarily false because there simply is no true world*. Nihilism – the dark philosophy of nothingness – establishes two separate groups.[267] The *error theorists* believe that moral claims are false and an error; the *noncognitivists* claim morality is not an issue that can be either true or false. The first group believes that *objective ethics* is impossible.[268] Morality and ethics can only be established through common ethical customs which in the managerial world are part of the *organisational culture* (Alvesson 2002). To establish this culture, employees and management need to create a set of basic patterns that are shared among people. Ultimately, these shared patterns of an organisational culture are related to emotions, feelings, and morality which vary from company to company. Therefore, there is no universal organisational culture and there cannot be a universally set form of management ethics. Instead, morality depends on the organisational culture of a specific corporation. In general, there cannot be anything that constitutes management ethics. We might only be able to understand management and management science when we use numbers.

For Magretta (2002) management means that *numbers matter*. When management relies on scientific language we can understand management but we can never understand ethics in the language of management. Such an objective scientific language is of no use when describing ethics that is based on emotions and culture. In sum, it does not make sense for management to engage in a field that is disconnected and inaccessible through scientific managerial language. Hence, management is better off leaving ethics to the ethicists and management to managers.

Nihilism believes that there is nothing in the world that could constitute morality. It is purely a human invention, not a fact but a kind of storytelling or a narrative told by people with certain interests. Here management finds its true home as it claims to act on hard facts, not on human stories. If morality is nothing more that just another human narrative, management should not be concerned with it at all. In addition, management's world is determined by decisions about what is true and false. According to the *non-congnitivists* – those who think that ethics can never be understood through cognitive processes – management should not be dealing with ethics at all. Ethics is all about making decisions based on what is true and what is false.

In Nietzsche's understanding of nihilism ethics is the morality of the flock, the drove, and the herd, Nietzsche's famous *herd morality*.[269] Accordingly, morality is nothing more than an invention orchestrated by Christianity to corral people into a herd. Once the herd mentality is established among people, it turns humans into herd-followers and as such they blindly follow the will of the Christian church.[270] For Nietzsche, the herd constitutes a great mass of ordinary people that can be guided more by fear than by hope. Most members of the herd are afraid to stand out. Not surprisingly, there is the MBF aspect = *management by fear* but no MBH = *management by hope*. Management tends to operate much more with fear than hope when corralling their flock into following their will. MBF ranges from the fear of demotion, the fear of job loss, and the fear of relocation, to the fear of downsizing, restructuring, outsourcing, and so on.

But management can itself assume the characteristics of a herd as even for them it is hard to avoid falling into the trap of Nietzsche's herd mentality. Any management meeting, the boarding of business class at any airport, any lunch in any CBD testifies to management's herd mentality. Managers dress the same, read the same newspapers, attend business schools, have read the same textbooks, know the same buzzwords, talk the same language, make the same deals, discuss the same issues, dine in the same places, and buy the same business shirts in the same shops. Managers do what other managers do and thereby display the morality of the managerial herd.

In Nietzsche's work the *Genealogy of Morality* he associated the birth of morality with slave society. This society created a *slave morality*. The moral values of the slaves were derived from their masters.[271] What they represent is no more than the negatives of their masters' ethics. The foundation of slave morality rests on the feeling of resentment towards their masters. The morality of slaves is designed to attack them. Morality is nothing other than an invention of the weak to justify their weakness and to force the strong into a position of guilt. Because weak slaves resent their masters, they have invented morality through their resentment. As a matter of fact, morality is not quite morality but a tool of propaganda. Hence, if management (the strong) were to follow morality, it would only give in to the demands of employees (the weak). In other words, morality is an invention of *those who 'make' things* (Aristotle) to force those *who 'do' things* (management) into doing what the weak want. This is not morality but a weapon in the hands of the weak.

In *The Republic* Plato argued that *justice is nothing other than the advantage of the stronger*. Hence, whatever management (the stronger) thinks justice to be is justice for the weaker part. Those *who make things* (Aristotle) are exposed to management's justice. According to Plato, it is a fact of life that the strong are needed to rule the powerless. In order to do so, managerial rulers should even develop laws that further their interests rather than the interests of someone else. Consequently, whatever the ruler demands is right and just. For Plato, morality is enshrined in the dictum that *the greater the amount of control they* [management] *exercise over people, the greater their own gain. Hence tyranny...is the best form of* management. Not surprisingly, managerial rule has hardly ever been democratic. Throughout its history management has represented exactly what was described by Plato. In the 21st century management may, for the most part, no longer rule by domination and totalitarianism but as MBF – *management by fear*. Consequently, the idea of *democratic management* is a tautology and totally absent from management literature.

In a somewhat Aristotelian sense, managers would be *highly esteemed at the courts of tyrants; they make themselves pleasant companions in the tyrants' favourite pursuit, and that is the sort of man they want*. Historically and structurally, there seems to be a problem with *democracy and management* because these are two sets of ideas that are never allowed to meet. Rather to the contrary, it appears as if *authority, authoritarianism, tyranny and management* are better matches. Management displays characteristics that carry connotations to authoritarianism enshrined in the authority of strong top-down hierarchies. These are used to control subordinates in a rather autocratic, domineering, and even tyrannical fashion. Not surprisingly, the history of managerial capitalism is splattered with support for countries ruled by tyrannies despite public appearance of the opposite. Management can exist and function well in tyrannies and dictatorships. Modern world history testifies to that. As an example, there was significant support for the Nazis in Germany from an anti-democratic managerial class while Nazi-Germany remained a thoroughly capitalist society with handsome profits for virtually all

German companies. Similarly, the *use* of Jewish and POW labour in German factories was managed to perfection (Bauman 1989).[272]

Hence, democracy and justice should not be part of management. Management's essence demands that it is neither democratic nor engaged in the issues of justice. Instead, it is *the unjust person who happens to gain more out of life, precisely because of their injustice.*[273] Unjust persons will cheat on taxes when there is little chance of being caught. They have no scruples about taking bribes and will gain hugely. Bribe-taking is not uncommon in management, ranging from small gifts to billions as the annual statistics of *Transparency International* shows year by year. In line with bribes and other injustices, the Greek philosopher Thrasymachus, for example, thought that *the greater the injustice, the greater the payoff, the more power and strength it brings.* In some forms of management, this could well be a leading business maxim. It could also be a hidden and somewhat *unofficial* corporate mission statement. Some of today's managerial practices could hardly be described any better. After all, the very essence of bribes and injustice is that it brings greater payoffs. Payoffs, organisational goals, shareholder value, and the bottom line are nothing more than the managerial code-words for profits and profit-maximisation. Management's core task of making profits has been achieved by cutting costs. For example, saving on safety equipment and bribing state officials to overlook it is good for cost-cutting and *cutting cost is always important to management* (Magretta 2002). It may cost lives, create injuries, accidents, industrial disasters, diseases, and even epidemics and pandemics (mad-cow-disease, swine- and bird-flu as a result of mass-manufactured meat-production) but it creates great payoffs for management. This is especially the case when these *costs* (i.e. human suffering) can be *'externalised'*, the codeword for offloading suffering onto others – usually the general public, health-funds, society, and the taxpayer. The world is not free of industrial accidents and not all of them can be disposed of in management's favourite way: blame the victim.

Thrasymachus' dictum *the greater the wage injustices, the greater the payoffs* holds truth for management in a very special sense. According to Magretta (2002), wages are a zero-sum game for management. In short, the higher the wages, the lower the profits for management and vice versa. Hence the rising gap between workers' average wage and CEO remuneration and the creation of special processing zones, sweat-shops, child and bond-slave labour. The more management can exclude institutions of justice, the more power and strength it gains. Hence, the relative justice of the state has been attacked and wound back inside the ideological framework of deregulation. Similarly, trade unions have been excluded from the sphere of management (Kreitner's *Threat of Unionisation*, 2009:42). Excluding both – state and unions – brings *more power and strength* to management. It is commonly known as *Macho Management*.

Finally, Thrasymachus provides the ethical underpinning for cartels, monopolies, oligopolies, and management's relentless quest for market dominance. It all follows the managerial maxim: a *life of injustice is more rewarding than a life of justice* (Thrasymachus).[274] The ethics of the managerial money and power code is further enshrined in Thrasymachus' statement: *my claim is that morality is nothing other than the advantage of the stronger party*. Hence, those with money and power (management) have the advantage of also being moral. Management sets morality and defines what is ethical. If it wishes, it can even avoid recognition of the weaker party and their ethics. Being in the stronger position also allows management to define those in the weaker position, primarily those in non-managerial positions. In sum, management takes full *advantage of being the stronger party* which also positions management in a location where it has the sole defining power over others (the weak).

Plato's Callicles advocated that *one should be given free rein to one's appetite and desires* and *it is only natural that the strong control the weak* culminating in *successful injustice is better – more natural and rewarding – than justice as defined by the conventional rules of society*.[275] Unlike many real ethical philosophers, it turns out that Plato's imaginary Callicles may be one of the foremost philosophical figures of management ethics. He described in near perfect terms what management ethics should be once management has gone beyond its true essence of *The Real Bottom Line* and the maximisation of shareholder values. Centuries after Plato's Callicles, his ethical ideas have been extended further by Thomas Hobbes.

The managerial ethics of Thomas Hobbes

Managerial contracts are related to the morality of *social contract theory* and *contractualism*. One of the main proponents of this was the rather pessimistic Thomas Hobbes (1588–1679). He coined the phrase that life is *solitary, poor, nasty, brutish, and short*. Inside management's hierarchical setup a *poor, nasty, and brutish* existence becomes ever more evident the lower in the hierarchy someone is positioned. Those at the top of the managerial hierarchy enjoy privileges while the lives of those at the bottom are exposed to less fortunate settings. Hobbes' description however is more likely to be seen in, for example, an Indonesian sweat-shop than inside the CEO's Manhattan office that runs such a sweat-shop through outsourcing, sub-contracting, and franchising. The managerial reflection of Hobbes' idea creates what is called *structural violence*. Inside the asymmetrical structure it is directed against those at the bottom of the managerial pyramid. But structural violence is required to create order. It is a price we have to pay, according to Hobbesian moral philosophy. Humans in their natural stages are confined to live in a chaotic state of affairs that is brutish and short and can only be overcome through social contracts with each other. This is highly positive for management who genuinely believes that without management there would only be chaos inside organisations and society.

Hence, management creates order through contracts in the form of employment contracts, supplier contracts, delivery contracts, banking contracts, and so on. Contracts establish and enforce managerial order. Without a legal contractual framework that underpins management, chaos would reign. For Hobbes, ethics is created through a contractual agreement. And it *requires a ruler to enforce it*. In the world of management, the ruler that enforces rules can only be management. Virtually every employment contract underpins management's right to manage. Through this contract, management establishes itself as the ruler to guarantee order and *to enforce it*.

The ethics of *contractualism* is what creates society, human relations, and management. It sets out obligations humans make towards one another. Once management has made a contract and employees have been made to accept it – often in a *take-it-or-leave-it* fashion – employees are obliged to abide by it. The foundation of the employment contract is the *free will* of two parties in the ideology of management and the result of asymmetrical power relations of the labour market in reality (Offe and Wiesenthal 1980). For management, the former is the very origin of ethics. In Managerialism, ethics is created through a *voluntary* contract into which we enter. It establishes and enforces obligation onto us but is the lesser evil because without it chaos would reign, as we are made to believe, and turmoil would be the greatest evil of all.

To avoid chaos and enforce order, management *must have some coercive power to compel men equally to the performance of the covenants* and contracts (Hobbes). Management should do so *by the terror of some punishment, greater than the benefit they expect by the breach of their covenant*. Management has *the terror of some punishment* in the form of coercive powers usually called *disciplinary action* in modern HRM-language. Apart from that there is a raft of instruments that can range from real terror to the fear of job loss. It can also include managerial bullying, harassment, demotion, demeaning work tasks, etc. They are used to compel humans into managerial performance. All too often, management has planted terror into people through these and other measures.

Hobbes' noted that the *punishment* must be *greater than the benefit* of the breach. In managerial language this is called cost-benefit analysis or zero-sum game. It can be observed in almost any negotiation between management and employees and their trade unions. In fact, almost the entire ideology of management is geared to convince people that the benefit lies in doing what management wants while those who recant will be punished. It is the clearest expression of Epictetus' writings on *A Stoic View of Life* written in 110AD. He says *if I do not punish my slave-boy, he will turn out bad*. One only needs to exchange Epictetus' *slave-boy* with the *subordinate* and add a modest amount of modern HRM terminology to make it work. A little bit of *disciplinary action* here and there and modern managerial ethics is completed. In managerial terms Epictetus' dictum would read today: *if management has no company policy on disciplinary action in place, my subordinates will not act in accordance with organisational behaviour.* Employees are made to believe that such HR-policies are needed because the natural state of people is chaos. Only management makes them *managerial-able* by establishing order.

Hobbes' original starting point was the assumption that in the natural state of affairs humans were not members of a group or tribe but raw human nature would exist in its uncontrolled state, like *a war of every man against every man*. This is highly applicable to management because without contracts, mergers, acquisitions, trusts, cartels, monopolies, etc. companies would descend into a war of all against all. It needs the form of contracts and legal frameworks, otherwise the much admired competition would turn into Hobbes' *war of every man against every man*. It would turn Magretta's (2002) *battlefield with human casualties* into a perpetual war. State regulation prevents this. Modern competition is nothing more than a mild version of regulated warfare. Management's ideological quest for *deregulation*, the *elimination of red tape, winding back the state,* and *the end of the bureaucratic burden,* are essentially measures to make competition more warlike.

Managerial contracts help to regulate this war by establishing order, human relationships, and Hobbes' ethics. Hobbes also outlined what happens when management fails to establish a contractual order and his war of *all against all* becomes a way of life: in *this war of every man against every man...nothing can be unjust. The notion of right and wrong, justice and injustice have no place.* In short, on the battlefield for market shares and company-internal power, management actions are beyond moral issues such as justice and injustice, right and wrong. They have no place there. After all, management's goal is performance directed towards shareholder values and profit maximisation. In that pursuit ethical issues such as justice and injustice are of no value.[276]

But there is also a second reason for being offensive rather than defensive. Some managers are *taking pleasure in contemplating their own power in the acts of conquests* (Hobbes). We must be aware of the fact that *some human beings are not moderate persons (like ourselves!).* They are *dominators who take pleasure in imposing their wills on others and they enjoy their power as an end in-itself.* Hence, Hobbes' ethics tells management that it needs to be prepared for an attack and be offensive in a *'shoot before they shoot you!'* version of ethics. According to Hobbes, ethics gives the managerial ruler a right to command and to be obeyed. Without rulers life would be *poor, nasty, brutish, and short.*

In order to win the business war *on the battlefield* (Magretta 2002), management must *compete* with other companies. When a market share war or a take-over battle is won, management can enjoy the *glory* that comes with winning. Hobbes tells management that there are no common standards for what is good and evil. What is considered good by one company, another perceives as evil. Therefore, there are constant disputes in which only winning counts.[277] The contest is not between winning in ethics but in market shares, profits, and take-overs. Hobbes makes it clear that in order to win a war no actual fighting needs to occur. There are many methods in the managerial arsenal that lead to winning. Any one of them can to be used to secure a corporation's existence and to win over others.

One of the prime responsibilities of management is to safeguard companies just as Hobbes outlined: *when going to sleep, he locks his door; even when in his house he locks his chests.* In modern management, he may not need to *lock his chests* but there are safes, access codes, barcodes, passwords, securities, insurances, protective measures, internet-firewalls, and CCTV. Management needs to be on guard against industrial espionage, the protection of brand names, and patents. It is a world of protection and mistrust rather than openness and trust. Hobbes states *there can be no security to any man.* Indeed, management's all-defining treadmill of perpetual competition ensures that no manager can be safe inside the managerial world.

Hobbes correctly predicted what has become the essence of management: *competition*. For Hobbes this is established when *two men compete for one thing*. Competition is perhaps the foremost defining act in which management engages. It sets the parameters for all managerial actions and is the most fundamental cornerstone of management.[278] Its world is constructed of competing interests, competing with other companies, competing for market shares, and competing with other managers. Hence, for management as for Hobbes competition is the all-defining issue of life. Not surprisingly, losing the competitive game is feared by management.

For Hobbes the strongest notion is the *fear of death*. It is a fear that compels us to fight. While modern managers hardly fear death, they fear the death of their company, a fall in market shares, and the decline in shareholder values just as much as they personally fear dismissal and demotion. When failing to secure the company's survival, they themselves are at risk. Just as Hobbes predicted, management becomes very active when faced with being taken over, liquidated, closed-down, downsized, merged, or annihilated by a competitor. Hobbes also denotes that *the passions that incline men to peace, are fear of death*. In the world of management, the fear of death comes with the fear of mergers, acquisitions, take-overs, buy-outs and the like. They not only create fear and the willingness to fight a *battle with civilian casualties* (Magretta 2002) but also create a passion for peace. This is often established through methods that end companies' competition with one another. One such form is the cartel. It creates a temporary or permanent monopoly or oligopoly. When management is unable to win the war against another company or a company is not strong enough to destroy others, then Hobbes' *fear of death* creates a *passion for peace*. The truce ends the competition. Magretta (2002) writes,

> *a monopoly is excellent for us, because we can exploit it to make and keep people dependent on us. In our economy, business people, professionals and technicians profess gladly to embrace free market competition. Let's face it: it's all a sham. Given half a chance, any business would become a monopolist like a shot so that it could set the rules in its own interest.*

The monopoly is the ultimate source of Hobbes' peace because it eliminates competition altogether just as peace eliminates war and destruction.

Not surprisingly, management feels that it has every right when there *are no external impediments to my doing what I want to do*. For

Hobbes, this is the *Right of Nature*. For management, it is the *Right to Manage*. Hobbes declares that there is a *liberty each man has to use his own power as he will himself*. Management uses its power for its own advantage. Inside Hobbes' framework, the use of managerial power means to *seek and use all that helps and advantages war. On the battlefield* (Magretta 2002) management needs to win the business war and it can do so by using *all means* needed to defend itself. To do so is not only ethical but the moral duty of management.

According to Hobbes, management *has a right to acquire whatever it can* and to secure itself. To do so, Hobbes says *the bonds of words are too weak to bridle men's ambition, avarice, anger, and other passions, without fear of some coercive power*. He advocates not to trust words but to have enough coercive power in place to ensure that others do what management wants it to do. Coercive power is not unethical. It serves the acquisition and security of whatever management wants. Management should never trust words when dealing with men's ambition, avarice, and anger. Instead it should rely on fear and coercive powers.

To use coercive power against others is not wrong because *human beings are not equal by nature*. Hence there is no need for management to treat them as equal. Hierarchical structures are the natural structure of life for management. As a consequence, some have power while others do not and those with power need to use it to advance their course. When management is accused of using coercive power wrongfully, it has *the right not to incriminate itself and the right to self-defence*. This is important as it relieves management from externally created demands such as *corporate social responsibility* which have been forced onto it. It is management's legitimate right *not to incriminate itself* by blaming others, blaming the victim, the market, the economy, trade unions, the weather, and so on.

In order to create a defensive shield, management needs to create unity within its own ranks. According to Hobbes, *in unity resides the singleness of power*. Management depends on this power and therefore needs to have a one-dimensional structure, one corporate culture, one hierarchy, one leader, and one mission. Once this is achieved and management has *constituted* [itself] *as sovereign, it cannot be deposed*. Today, there is hardly ever any challenge to managerial power. The ideology of Managerialism is deeply entrenched in society. Cases where management has been deposed are virtually impossible. Management has literally managed to install a general acceptance of itself into the wider community and into those working for it.

Similarly, it has adopted the enlightened self-interests of egoism and determinism that are widely accepted inside management and society. On this basis, management *always needs to act in its own self-interest*. Portrayed as the guiding principle of the managerial world as well as of society, thousands of corporate PR experts, affirmative journalists, privately owned newspapers, TV stations, and *The Servants of Power* (Baritz 1960; cf. Lynd 1939) are standing by to broadcast management's propaganda.[279] The ideology has reached God-given status in modern society. This applies even to Mother Theresa. Through helping the poor she received media recognition, awards, and the acknowledgment of the Church and the Pope. Some have even argued she only acted selfishly towards what she desired for her own good, thus depicting self-interest as the ultimate end – something hardly any manager would deny.

Management achieves the realisation of self-interest through the rational application of managerial tools directed towards shareholder-values. It is only logical to management to promote its own interest and use reasonable tools to achieve this. Management has developed *quantifying methods, finance, decision science, and negotiation because they provide a systematic and rational way*. With these tools management has achieved the unachievable. It has managed to appear objective, using rational tools directed towards two specific goals: the realisation of its self-interest and the maximisation of shareholder-values. In sum, the ethics of rational egoism forms a major part of management. Its ideological expression of Managerialism has managed to portray it as rational and anchor it in the mind of the public. For Hobbes, acting against one's self-interest is like acting against human nature and would constitute acting against the nature of management. However, there is nothing *natural* in management. It is a socially constructed human invention.

Many are also made to believe that self-interest is an expression of modernity and an enlightened and ethically based management. For Hobbes as for management, ethics starts with the self, the person, and with the immediate needs of management. Management's essence does not lie in a distant idea of Hegel's *Other*. Just like any other issue in the orbit of management, ethics is one aspect that has to be managed. This carries strong connotations to Nietzsche's idea of *slave morality*. According to Hobbes and Nietzsche, management has to see morality as a strategic device to defend and protect itself.

The managerial ethics of Friedrich Nietzsche

For Nietzsche the idea of morality came with Christianity which he called *mankind's greatest misfortune*. It grew out of Christian pity. Nietzsche considered this to be rather unhealthy for conducting life in modern societies. Instead, he thought it important that humans free themselves from the mental and ethical shackles of Christianity. In order to do so, people would need to develop a *Will to Power*. The question *'what is good?'* finds its answer in *all that heightens the feeling of power, the will to power,* and *power itself in man.* On the question *'what is bad?'* his response is everything *that proceeds from weakness.* For management, this means it should never proceed from a position of weakness and it is perfectly legitimate to *heighten the feeling of* managerial *power, the will to* have managerial *power,* and *power itself in* management. In Nietzsche's understanding management would find itself in the allocation of power rather than of resources.

The fight between good and bad is an essential part of life for Nietzsche. Hence, the fight between weak and bad as well as strong and good in management is a part of corporate life. Management must be strong and it must win. It must strive for power. Nietzsche advocates that one needs to live life *not out of weakness but out of strength.* Therefore, it is management's task to gain a position of strength. Management should never operate from a position of weakness and it should always fight any attempts to become weak. In addition, it always needs to show the weak (employees) that management (the strong) is in charge. This is supported by a raft of management books, journal articles, conferences, textbooks, etc. that all emphasise the importance of leadership (Kreitner 2009:331–457). For Nietzsche's managerial ethics nothing exemplifies the strong more than leadership. Strong leadership and strong management create a *man for whom nothing is forbidden.* Thus, managerial life means the *exercise of strength and will to power.* The best corporate outcome is achieved when management gets what it wants. Consequently, *the life of self-denial is less good than the life of self-assertion.* This could be the overall motto of almost everything that management represents.

The ethics of Nietzsche provides a number of positive elements for management. It favours the *Will to Power* almost unconditionally. Today, management is the prime exposé of power in our society. Almost all managers need to have the *Will to Power* in order to become managers.[280] In modern managerial language this is called *'leadership qualities'.* Management in general is not a place where *'the weak'* meet. It is the location of the strong. According to Nietzsche *it is only natural that a living thing seeks above all to discharge its strength.* Management does this on a daily basis.[281] Hence, it is only too natural – *Human, All-Too Human* (Nietzsche) – when management seeks to discharge its strength. After all it was given to them for a purpose and managers are humans, just as Nietzsche outlined. If management fails to act in this way, it fails to act naturally. If it fails to discharge their strength, Nietzsche's answer to such managers would be: *you alone are to blame for yourself!* To avoid this, management has taken charge. It provides leadership to control *the herd* (Nietzsche).

Leadership is the essence of management. Thousands of management books, textbooks, seminars, classes, MBA school curricula and so on teach the virtue of being strong and being a leader. Powerful management leaders have always been held up as examples, ranging from Getty to Gates and from Enron's to Lehman Brothers' CEOs. The *Will to Power* is probably one of the most important virtues modern managers need to have, despite all the talk of being a moderator, a facilitator, and a team player. Strong leaders are free to operate as they wish without ethical constraints imposed from the outside.[282] In adopting Nietzsche's ethics, management can create positive foundations for its actions as well as for its existence.

Managerial leadership and self-assertion is in line with the Sophist's concept that *following moral precepts is foolish*. For Nietzsche, morality is not just foolish but a sickness that has been ingrained in us by Christianity and the weak. Our ideas of *good and evil* originate from weakness. In short, the religious and Christian origins of pity, sympathy, and kindness have led to what is today called morality. If management follows this, it commits a foolish act and even prevents management from making money. Management needs to be free of any Christian baggage, religious pity, and moral sympathy as it arrests management inside an ethics that has been created by the weak to trick the strong into following the will of the weak. Management however operates from the non-religious and non-Christian position of the strong. It needs to negate all ethics. Instead, what creates management is the *will to power* that represents the *essence of the world*. For Nietzsche, managers are *the members of a higher ruling order* according to the formula: *good = noble = strong = powerful = beautiful = happy*. For management the formula reads: *successful = self-righteous = managerial power = attractive = wealthy = happy shareholders*. In Nietzsche's understanding, management ethics has to reverse the Christian understanding of *Good and Evil* that sees the weak and wretched as good and the powerful and rich as evil, cruel, and lustful. Now it is the other way around. Management is good and powerful and the weak (employees, other companies, states, unions, etc.) are evil and cruel. Management ethics seen from the viewpoint of Nietzsche's *Beyond Good and Evil* declares itself as the superior actor who represents the good. In reality, there is no doubt that many managers see themselves as a force of good.

Nietzsche also denotes *the people who are acted upon, those who are below them are bad or contemptible.* This is perhaps one of the clearest expressions of management. Many managers see themselves as belonging to *a higher ruling order* who rule over *people who are acted upon.* Finally, it has not been unheard of that management treats those who *are below* them with *contempt,* for example in cases of downsizing, restructuring, and outsourcing.[283]

To manage downsizing, restructuring, and outsourcing, Nietzsche's *herd mentality* becomes highly valuable for management. Once constructed as a *herd,* those *who make things* (Aristotle) can be made to *follow their instinct of fear* [because] *fear is the mother of all morals* (Nietzsche).[284] MBF or *management by fear* engineers the fear of downsizing, relocation, closure, cuts in bonuses and wages, demotions, dismissals, etc. It has always been a powerful tool in management's arsenal that has been used throughout management's history. It started with corporal punishment during the 18th and 19th century and currently uses more sophisticated psychological HRM techniques.[285] These tools are needed to manage the herd that is seen as unable to act on its own. If it does act, it acts aimlessly, unstructured, without direction, and often chaotic. Management provides order, stability, and direction for the herd of employees.

The herd's task is to react to management while management acts.[286] In responding to management, the herd protects itself though it comes to resent their masters and all they stand for because they seek revenge. Management sees those who resent management such as trade unions, whistleblowers, troublemakers, agitators, recalcitrant people, NGOs, and even states as rebellious elements inside the herd. The reason for their protest, resistance, recalcitrant behaviour, fights, strikes, boycotts, etc. in the eye of management is not because they seek the greater good and work for general betterment but because they seek revenge. Therefore, according to Nietzsche's understanding, ethics is nothing more than a tool of revenge.

For Nietzsche morality is just another invention of the weak to torment the strong. The strong vs. weak argument is nothing new in ethics. *Two and a half thousand years ago the Greek sophist Thrasymachus argued that ethics is something imposed on the weaker by the stronger* (Singer 1994:17). Nietzsche however sees it exactly the other way around.[287] For him morality and ethics stink. Ethics in the world of management would come down to something used by those *who make things*

(Aristotle) to attack management, not because they seek to equalise themselves with management but out of resentment towards the strong. All they want is to become strong. Therefore, ethics is nothing more than pure hypocrisy depicted by the weak. Because they resent strong management, their self-invented morality represents small-mindedness.

According to Nietzsche, to be strong *one does not need reason because reason is the cause of our falsification of the evidence of the sense*. Reason clouds management's actions and therefore it is prudent not to rely on it.[287] Management is better advised to operate with ideological devices, self-beliefs, and belief-systems such as emotional selling, charismatic leadership, and simple convictions such as *cost-cutting is always good*, or *you are not as efficient as you think you are*. In order to cement managerial power, management needs power and ideologies instead of reason. Reason only serves management to a certain extent but can never be enough to secure its existence. Instead, it can *falsify the evidence* (Nietzsche). For management and Managerialism *power and ideologies* are by far more important than reason, logic, and rationality.

An ideology such as Managerialism serves management because *we have no categories at all that permit us to distinguish between a 'world in itself' and a 'world of appearance'* (Nietzsche). We simply cannot know the difference between what management factually is and how it appears to others. Hence, management needs to create an impression of what it actually is. This is called *impression management*. A number of instruments have been invented to achieve the *world of appearance*. These include myths, mission statements, corporate PR, company videos, leaflets, policies, image consultants, branding, etc. Because *management in-itself* cannot be separated from *management of appearance*, the border between impression and reality is constantly moved by management. The crucial difference between both, however, is that ideologies such as Managerialism and *impression management* are more powerful than facts and figures. In Nietzsche's terms, management needs to project the *Will to Power* (1880) rather than the *Will to Facts*.

The Managerial Will to Power can even overcome the rather deterministic technological and *mechanical necessities* of the managerial process.[289] They are *not facts: it is we who first interpreted them into events* (Nietzsche). Hence, *necessity is not a fact but an interpretation*, writes Nietzsche. The meaning for management is twofold. Firstly, management is open to interpret *technological necessities* at will and free from technological constraints. Managers understand that the so-called *facts of technological necessities* are in reality nothing more than their own interpretations. Once management achieves the freedom to select between *not-interpreting* and *interpreting*, the way to presenting technology as a necessity and/or an interpretation is opened up.

Once management has selected the interpretive option, the second path opens.[290] This gives management the ability to interpret *technological necessities* inside the ideological framework of Managerialism. This option is purely ideological because it uses *technological necessities* to support managerial power. In a third step, management is in the dominant position of information, interpretation, and communicative control (Klikauer 2007 and 2008). For one, it has the exclusive option to sell *technological necessities* to non-managerial staff as a *fact of life*. In addition, it can also interpret these *necessities* in ways so that they become acceptable to those *who make things* (Aristotle).

In an ideal scenario those *who make things* (Aristotle) are made to support technological necessities. Management only has to interpret them properly and present them inside a managerial framework that allows only one understanding which follows TINA: there is no alternative. Done properly, it can achieve the seemingly unachievable: those *who make things* (Aristotle) support management even when it means cost-cutting, wage-cuts, or dismissal for them.[291] On the basis of its sole control over communication, management is positioned in a *win-win* situation. In sum, Nietzsche's philosophy hands over the options to management that can be used at will to sustain its existence. *The Will to Power* is deeply ingrained in management. It is more important than truth.

Truth, for Nietzsche, *is therefore not something…that might be found or discovered*. It is rather *something that must be created and that gives a name to a process*. It also gives a name *to a will to overcome that has in itself no end. Truth* is *a 'processus in infinitum', an active determining – not a becoming – conscious of something that is in itself and determined*. For management, the philosophical concept that *there is no truth* is most welcoming. Management's essence has never been linked to truth, only to saleability, profit-maximisation, and shareholder values. In management, Managerialism, and management studies, the idea of truth concerns academics rather than management. However, truth can be relevant to management if it assists in annihilating a competitive enemy or can be used inside the strategic management paradigm. Truth can also be called upon when it supports management and Managerialism. In those cases, the *Servants of Power* (Baritz 1960; cf. Lynd 1939) are important because they can adjust truth to management and use it ideologically to legitimise and support management.

On the whole, management is free to use truth as *something that must be created and that gives a name to a process*. When management creates a managerial process it also creates its own truth.[292] Therefore truth is *not something there, that might be found or discovered – but something that must be created*. Management has the means and the power to create its own truth. In line with all ideologies – including Managerialism – there is some truth in whatever management does. The core of any ideology is that at all times it relates to truth. There is also always some truth inside management, waiting to be wheeled out when it is in management's interest. In general, Nietzsche's idea of *creating truth* correctly highlights the essence of management.

In conclusion, there are several ideas inside ethical philosophy that are highly valuable to management. Quite often, they denote the exact opposite of most forms of ethics. Intuitionism, for example, believes there is no rational explanation for ethics as it is intuitive. Similarly, subjectivism denotes that ethics is related to the individual subject and not an objective world. Both assist management in deflecting ethical demands directed towards them. A non-defensive and more positive view for management comes from moral egoism because it supports management's idea that whatever is of personal advantage is moral. This can be shown to be relative because relativism believes that ethics differs from company to company and from management to management. Again, ethical nihilism denotes that there is no objective truth in ethics and that the idea of *good vs. bad* is false. This is more in line with Nietzsche than with Hobbes who saw the perpetual fight of all against all as the only base for ethics. In such a struggle the strong should use everything at their disposal to win over the weak. Nietzsche advocated this and stated that ethics is no more than a tool of the weak directed against the strong. In sum, most versions of ethics presented in this chapter assist management in deflecting ethical demands. This is of great importance to management who is not primarily concerned about ethics but about *making things work*.

10
Conclusion: The Practical Ethics of *Sittlichkeit* and Communicative Ethics

The concluding chapter has three tasks: it sums up the core arguments presented so far, delivers a conclusion, and provides a solution to the problem of management ethics. It starts with a summary of the key elements of previous chapters and extracts the essence of what management and ethics are and how, if at all, they fit together. To do this, Hegel's concept of the *'Other'* is required in order to identify *what is* and *what is not*. Hegel's *'Other'* will also show *what management* and *ethics* are not. *'What is'* is never just something in-itself (Kant) but always represents positives (*what it is*) and negatives (*what it is not*). In other words, we know day because we also know night. The negation of things makes them what they are. In the case of management ethics one needs to rely on the non-textbook version of real management which shows what management is and what it is not. For example, it is not predominantly an ethical enterprise. Ethics, as far as it appears in management at all, is a side-issue that may or may not service management. In Hegel's terms, the essence of management does not contain ethics as a core element. In the philosophy of *essentialism* ethics for management is something *accidental* – something non-defining – rather than a constitutive element.

Chapters 2 to 6 indicate common thoughts on ethics including Greek virtue ethics, utilitarianism, Kantian universalism and categorical imperatives, as well as Hegelian *Sittlichkeit*. Yet, they all largely contradict the non-textbook version of management. In Hegel's terminology, management is nothing but the negation of ethics. Almost all standard concepts of ethics contradict management. Management and ethics have different goals, concepts, motives, duties, origins, demands, objectives, categorical imperatives, foundations, underlying assumptions, outlooks, justifications, and purposes. The chapters on Kohlberg – *Kohlberg's Moral Manager*

I: From Impulsiveness to Punishment and *Kohlberg's Moral Manager II: From Rewards to Universalism* – provide an insight into the most inclusive version of ethics ever formulated, an overall concept of an ascending moral scale in which any issue of human and managerial conduct can be located. It shows that non-textbook management operates foremost on the lower levels of Kohlberg's scale of morality and is largely confined to obedience of non-managerial staff and punishment regimes, called *disciplinary action* in HRM-language.

At Kohlberg's second level, management's *telos* reflects rewards and personal benefits, in managerial terms performance management and performance related pay. This is the realm of *ethical egoism*. Management also relates to Kohlberg's stage of law and order. Its law and order approach seeks to maintain the existing structure of corporate affairs. This stage also describes the stage inside which today's managerial practices can be located. In Kantian terms, this stage represents *what is* rather than *what ought to be* while all subsequent stages represent *what ought to be* and constitute severe challenges for management. In Kohlberg's stages five, six and seven, the pathways of management and ethics diverge further and further.

Management, however, is not a totally unethical enterprise. Apart from most mainstream forms of ethics such as Greek virtue ethics, utilitarianism, Kant's categorical imperatives, and Hegelian *Sittlichkeit*, there are a few ethical theories that relate positively to management (McCarthy 1994). *Positive Management Ethics* has been outlined in Chapter 9 and includes intuitionism, subjectivism, moral egoism, ethical relativism, nihilism, and finally the ethics of Hobbes and Nietzsche. These philosophical and ethical writings provide many positive ideas for management. However, from the historical origins of Greek moral philosophy onwards management experiences strong challenges from almost anything moral philosophy has to offer. For example, unless management seeks to contradict itself, it cannot apply most parts of Greek virtue ethics because its relations are not based on the Aristotelian virtue of friendship but on hierarchy, managerial power, top-down structures, authority, and, above all, competition. Taking into account most recent moral philosophy, management can also never subscribe to Rawls' ethics (1972) whose goals are universal justice, justice as fairness, and equality. Management lives from treating people unjustly and unequally by using hierarchies, power, competition, and so forth.

Finally, management can never operate under Kantian formalism of categorical imperatives and under Hegelian *Sittlichkeit*. Instead of representing Kant's *Kingdom of Ends* management represents the *Kingdom of Means*. This is a fundamentally immoral concept in Kantian ethics. Unlike management ethics, Hegelian ethics is connected to an ethical community and society. Management represents the opposite. Hegel's moral concept of self-actualisation demands the inclusion of the *'Other'* in the formulation of ethics. For Hegel, *Sittlichkeit* carries connotations of *customary morality* constructed through critical self-reflection as *social custom, usage, and Sitte*. Therefore, *Sittlichkeit* refers *to a way of living and not to a theory*.[293] Freedom and *Sittlichkeit* are established through *the relation of many individuals* in a social and moral order (*Sittlichkeit*). Hegel sees *Sittlichkeit* as a product of solidarity because *without solidarity, society dissolves into a heap of atoms* that represent the *abstract private person whose personality has no ethical life* (Wood 1990:201f.). For Hegel, all *human individuals are products of their social order*. *Sittlichkeit* also demands that societal codes of ethics be articulated by self-determined human beings, otherwise ethics does not exist. In *Hegel's Ethical Thought* (1990:256ff.) Wood concludes

> *Hegel's ethical thought does not dissolve ethics in sociology or reduce it to politics, but social relationships and institutions do play an important role in the way Hegel's theory grounds ethical standards on the self-actualisation of freedom. A free society is one in which individuals are with themselves in their ethical institutions. Hegel attacks the subjectivistic, atomistic, and moralistic foundations of modern liberalism, and he provides an alternative rationale for quite similar social institutions based on a combination of communitarian principles and the radical German idealist conception of absolute freedom.*

In applying Hegel's concept of *Sittlichkeit* to management, one has to depart from Kant's *categorical imperatives* that denote ethical determinants as a must and move on to Kant's non-ethical *hypothetical imperatives*. These are *'if-then'* constructions. For Kant, these are not suitable to express ethics. In the present form, however, management is not able to engage in ethics on the level of a Kantian *categorical imperative* as shown in Chapter 4. To an overwhelming extent management ethics can only be expressed in Kant's *hypothetical imperatives*, a form of expression that negates ethics. Management can only establish *Sittlichkeit* when socially based forms of ethics include *'space'* for human self-actualisation. Management's actualisation of *Sittlichkeit* requires *ethical institutions in which individuals are with themselves* (Hegel). However, such ethical institutions do not exist *inside* current managerial practices. It is possible to establish them somewhat apart from management but still located *'inside'* companies and corporations.[294] Such an ethical institution might constitute an *Ethics Council*.[295]

An *ethics council* represents Kant's, Hegel's, Kohlberg's, and Habermas' tradition of ethics. For one, it is a representation of Kant's autonomy because it needs to be set up as an autonomous body to management. It cannot be part of management due to management's proven record of ethical failures and communicative structures that are not conducive to ethics (Klikauer 2007:205–219 and 2008:160–178). At present, the essence of management largely contradicts the essence of ethics. An *ethics council* is a manifestation of Kant's *self-determination*. Because of its independence of management it can determine its own structure, setup, and *modus operandi* within an ethics of self-determination. Secondly, *ethics councils* also represent Hegel's *self-actualisation, Mündigkeit,* and *Sittlichkeit.* They are designed to set their own rules of engagement and are critically-independent (*Mündigkeit*) as they represent commonly agreed social wills of their members. Therefore, they are capable of constructing socially based ethics. This is what Hegel calls *Sittlichkeit.* Finally, in the process of developing a socially constructed version of ethics, members of such *ethics councils* need to communicate. Habermas (1990 and 1997) developed a set of rules that govern ethical discourses. The *ethics council* is not only an *ethical institution in which humans can realise themselves* (Hegel), it is also an institutional assurance for ethical behaviours of management. It assists in improving a somewhat damaged historical track-record of management ethics. The *ethics council* acts as a *clearing house,* advisory body, and moral overseer of management with the legal right to veto unethical management decisions.

Once such a socially based *ethics council* is established by management, it replaces *managerial individualism* with *Hegelian solidarity* and *managerial atomism* with a *communitarian ethos.* It also supplants all managerial forms of communication with forms of human *self-articulation* (Hegel) and *communicative ethics* (Habermas). In contrast to standard *managerial communication,* Hegel advocates a socially based form of ethics that is enshrined in the actualisation of ethics. To establish the Hegelian vision of a socially and community based *ethics council* inside a company, people need to communicate at a social level that includes communicative elements that are part of Hegel's concept of *Sittlichkeit.* In the 20th century, Hegel's 19th century ideas have been taken up by German philosopher Adorno (1903–1969). In Adorno's work *Hegel: Three Studies* (1993) he presented an up-to-date version of

Hegel (cf. Kojève 1947). Adorno's student – Jürgen Habermas – developed the concept of socially based ethics further. This resulted in: *'Discourse Ethics, Law and Sittlichkeit'*; *'Communicative Ethics and Sittlichkeit'* (1986: 245ff.); and two seminal theories: *'Moral Consciousness and Communicative Action'* (1990) and *'The Theory of Communicative Action: Reason and the Rationalisation of Society'* (1997).[296] Habermas' study on *Moral Consciousness and Communicative Action* (1990) outlines the need for communication during the process of creating ethics. In his subsequent masterpiece, Habermas (1997) established the parameters for a version of communication inside which Hegelian *self-actualisation* can take place. This communicative self-actualisation is based on Hegel's concept of articulation. It establishes a socially based form of ethics that Hegel calls: *Sittlichkeit*, an ethical life.

The following section outlines practical steps for a company based *ethics council* in order to achieve an ethical life of *Sittlichkeit*. These practical steps are designed to set up *human-to-human* communication that frees up managerial determination, negates alienation, and prevents the colonisation of communication. In a final step, it converts individualism, competition, and atomism into *communicative ethics*. As a side-effect it also eliminates the current deficiencies in management ethics by converting it into Hegelian *Sittlichkeit*.

Essential to *Sittlichkeit* is an open and reasonable debate that establishes Habermas' vision of *communicative ethics*. It creates a *communicative relationship* that is directed towards domination-free communication enshrined in *ideal speech*. Its foundation is manifested through an acceptance of a) *truthfulness* among all participants of an *ethics council*. In addition to *truthfulness* three more elements are needed for *communicative ethics* represented in *ideal speech*. These are b) *comprehensibility*; c) debates directed towards the *truth*; and d) *rightness* that represents appropriate contributions to the *ethics council* in light of existing social norms and values (Klikauer 2008:141–178). These elements create *ideal speech* as communication that is free of domination. Communication inside the *ethics council* is based on the power of the best argument rather than the power of management. These four basic conditions can be divided into *external* conditions that have to be met from the outside of a speech situation as well as *internal* conditions that guide communication once the frame of ideal speech is established. In the outer area, institutional and social – not linguistic – conditions for ideal speech have to be met. In the inner area, validity claims are based on the four elements of *comprehensibility, truth, rightness*, and *truthfulness*. They guide all ethical dialogues.

Habermas' conditions for ideal speech, *communicative ethics*, and communicative action display a clear picture of communication inside an *ethics council*. This can be summed up as follows:

> *the concept of communicative action refers to the interaction of at least two subjects capable of speech and action who establish interpersonal relations (whether by verbal or by extra-verbal means). The actors seek to reach an understanding about the action situation and their plans of action in order to coordinate their actions by way of agreement. The central concept of interpretation refers in the first instance to negotiating definitions of the situation which admit of consensus* (Habermas 1997:86).

The complete framework of *communicative ethics* and ideal speech must be established in full and without any damage. This is not a shopping list from which one can *pick and choose*. Communication will be seen as disturbed when even one of the conditions is missing. It renders the *ethics council* dysfunctional and unethical.

Furthermore, communication among members of such an *ethics council* must be directed towards reaching common understanding. This is a vital condition. If this is not satisfied, communication becomes an instrument of *system integration*. Therefore, the *ethics council* operates exclusively on *social integration* (Klikauer 2007:74). Traditionally, managerial system integration has structured communicative exchanges under conditions of deception, distortion, and manipulation (Klikauer 2008:34–140). These alienating forms of communication have to be prevented from colonising the *ethics council* as they would lead to an objectively false consciousness that gives rise to *structural* violence.[297] The prevention of *structural violence* is an important element that has to be met. It has to be excluded if *communicative ethics* is to prevail. Once the stages of structural violence and communicative deformations have colonised an *ethics council*, distortions become established and damage all conditions of speech acts. This has the power of communicative malpractices where misrepresentation and prejudgment occur. They distort all social and ethical assertions of the members of an *ethics council*.

In such cases, *communicative ethics* inside an *ethics council* has degenerated into a communicative forum open to manipulative elements.[298] It enables those in charge of an organisation to manipulate other organisational members against their own interest. In these cases, ethical validity claims are turned into pure illusions. This occurs when ethical claims are made under the forces of instrumental action whose *telos* is not truth. Here, ideal speech and *communicative ethics* can no longer be established and maintained. According to Heath (2003:4) *the key idea in Habermas' theory of communicative action is that speech acts cannot be planned or executed with entirely strategic intent.* In other words, communicative action cannot be instrumentally guided towards managerially induced strategic goals. They need to fulfil conditions that free ethical communication from all system interferences. Only an unhindered environment free of domination allows the flourishing of *communicative ethics.* Once this has been achieved, it can direct communication towards positive ethical changes and moral outcomes.

Ten rules for ethics councils

The following section will discuss in detail ten key elements of universal and practical communication inside the proposed *ethics council.* It outlines general conditions of ethics councils while also drafting workable parameters for them. The section also delineates practical steps that establish and maintain *communicative ethics* inside an *ethics council,* starting with rules that can govern participation. It issues general ideas about communicative rationality and deals with communicatively established rules. It closes with discussions on attitudes, time, and places as a framework for the council and also outlines a draft for a workable *ethics council.* These elements will provide a real and hands-on solution to establish communication. It charts layouts; rules governing moderators and speakers; the problem of different skills and levels of knowledge that people bring with them; contract zones and vetoes; rules of speech participation; methods of ideal speech; the problem of principles vs. case orientation; the danger of group thinking; forms of agreements; and finally conflict resolutions. But before detailing this, a few general principles on the issue of participation should be clarified.

1. Participation: Participants of *ethics councils* should not be prevented from taking part in any discourse relevant to the subject at hand. Their statements should not be hindered.[299] However, there are limits to the size of an ethics council. If too many participants are included, discussions can become unworkable because individuals are unable to fully participate. An ethics council should never become an undifferentiated crowd of people. This might have a destructive influence on discourses and the ethics of *Sittlichkeit.* Those who seek to participate in an ethical discourse should have valid reasons to do so and be able to justify these. They should provide a sincere, genuine, and authentic interest in participating on an *ethics council*. However, participation can never be an end in-itself. Furthermore, nobody should assume a position based on privileges or power structures. The ethics council must exclude the money and power code just as much as hierarchy, managerial authority, force, coercion, and the like.

2. Communicative Rationality: While *ethics councils* can be established at work, they need to exclude any form of *communicative colonisation* through managerial system imperatives that hinder *communicative ethics*. *Communicative ethics* should be applied inside *ethics councils* when making statements during discourses.[300] These statements should subscribe to the demands laid out in Habermas' *Theory of Communicative Action* (1997). Participants in ethical discourses should try to come to an understanding about appropriate speech acts that serve discussions directed towards communicative understanding. Communication should also be based on ethical relevancy. This means that communication can only be established when dialogues are based on an ethical self-awareness (Kant) and self-actualisation (Hegel). Both need to be linked to Kohlberg's (1981 and 1984) morality of stages five to seven.

3. Communicative Rules: Commonly achieved understanding can only be reached in an open and fair exchange of ideas that are reflective of *Sittlichkeit*. Rules and procedures for such a discussion should subscribe to the pragmatics of argumentation (Klikauer 2008:173ff.). All communicatively established rules need to have the moral substance of Hegel's concept of *Sittlichkeit*. Similarly, all participants can raise problematic statements as long as they can support them and these statements are linked to the discourse at hand. Overall, rules supporting communication should be comprehensible and understood by all members of an *ethics council*. It is relevant for participants that they constitute such a council through their own participation. Once discourse participants have communicatively reached an understanding and established rules, these should be applied consistently. At the same time, participants need to be able to change rules if a demand to do so has been issued. This is the same demand that guides all forms of communication. Changes to rules can only occur when '*all*' participants have reached an understanding for such a change.

Any participant can – at any time – introduce new claims into the discourse, much in the same way as they can introduce expressions about their own views, attitudes, desires, wishes, and needs. They should be able to express their own opinions and interpret them for others. It is an imperative to consider what Hegel termed the '*Other*'. On valid grounds, these views and attitudes can be opposed or supported. By issuing their views and attitudes, participants can enter into an ethical discourse. Their views need to stand up to previously issued arguments by other participants. If they do not, participants must be asked to explain their arguments further. Participants must reflect on the sincerity and inviolability of contributors. All issued statements during the course of a discourse should be viewed with respect and treated in a non-judgmental way.

4. Time, Places, and Layouts: Limitations of time, space, place, and resources should be eliminated as much as possible in order to establish a fruitful discourse. Today's world of work is closer than ever linked to time sequences, time management, and general time constraints. However, *communicative ethics* can occur *at* work as well as *off* work, therefore, *ethics councils* can be established at work or outside of it. Off-work *ethics councils* are just as likely as at-work councils as they can be constructed free of system imperatives that have potentials for colonisation that hinder *communicative ethics*.

At a much more tangible level, the demands issued above can be converted into more workable elements by creating some basic principles for *communicative ethics*. The drafting of such principles that support discourse can be divided into several sub-sections. These principles provide an overview of the rules that govern *ethics councils*. The rules are never a *once-and-for-all* set recipe to be followed in order to establish *communicative ethics*. They are a general guide for participants.

The ideal layout for *ethics councils* suggests an assembling of elected representatives and competent participants in an ethical forum in order to enhance the quality of discourse. Ethical quality also translates into the exclusion of all power plays, hidden or otherwise. A sub-council of a standard *ethics council* can be designed to work on specific moral problems. There is also an option to set up different *ethics councils* to work on the same or similar problems in order to compare outcomes once each *ethics council* has reached common understanding. The same applies to *ethics councils* that have been split into smaller groups to work on different moral problems. Each of these organisational forms of *ethics councils* should be subject to communicatively reached understanding and agreement. This is the guiding principle for all ethics councils and sub-units. A group of participants in such councils and sub-forums may decide to consult with outside experts when necessary. This may only happen after an agreement on such experts inside the *ethics council* has been reached.

5. Moderators and Speakers: A capable, competent and responsible speaker or moderator can be chosen as an independent voice. This serves the establishment of a somewhat more *neutral* or *impartial* person. However, such a person should never assume a decisive position of power over other participants. The key is to find someone who supports *communicative ethics* directed towards common understanding and agreement. The moderator or speaker should never be a leader or move into a leadership position. *Communicative ethics* demands horizontal, not vertical levels of discussion and equality instead of hierarchy. Therefore, it is vital to prevent the colonising elements of *management leadership* from infiltrating ethical forms of discourse inside *ethics councils*. The introduction of any kind of hierarchy is to be avoided as it is highly destructive to any ethical discourse and annihilates *communicative ethics*. The spokesperson should be prevented from moving into a position of being an expert, leader, boss, ruler, or judge. In sharp contrast to this, the much acclaimed *business leader* is to be barred from taking a foothold. Instead, a spokesperson or moderator should oversee communicatively established rules, foster open discourse, and refrain from using personal preferences to advance sectarian goals. In some instances, this person can even assume the role of a *devil's advocate*. It can stimulate Hegelian dialectics inside the *council* by representing an *anti-thesis* to a council's *thesis*. Through contrasting pros and cons an ethical *synthesis* can be reached that is supported by *all* members of the *council*.

6. Different Skills and Levels of Knowledge: Whenever one participant is treated differently from another, the reason for this must be explained. Any unequal treatment must be established communicatively and agreement on it must be sought. Reasons for different treatment of participants can include un-equal experiences and backgrounds. Participants must avoid that unequally treated persons become leaders in order to avert asymmetric power relations inside the *council*. Instead, the fundamental principle of equal participation must be enforced. Despite disparities and differences in levels of knowledge and skills among participants any utilisation of special and sectarian interests has to be limited. In exceptional cases, it can occur inside communicatively established rules but a person inside an *ethics council* should never be excluded because of their different skills or knowledge.

7. Contract Zones and Vetoes: One option is the introduction of a *contract zone.* It is available only when it is supported by all participants. Contract zones can be established when an agreement cannot be made communicatively. They enable an *ethics council* to go forward in the case of non-agreeable situations. Any discourse can lead to non-conclusive outcomes and disagreements. In such cases *contract zones* provide a preliminary outcome that can, at a later stage, be re-examined by a subsequent *ethics council* or by a sub-council. Such subsequent ethics councils, sub-councils, and *contract zones* can be vital for the communicative process. They are relevant only if participants have reached an agreement about the introduction and use of contract zones. This is the case when conclusive outcomes occur due to the overcoming of a veto. A *right to veto* can function as a *trump* in any discourse forum. The strongest advantage of a *right to veto* can be found in the power to protect minority voices. Such vetoes are able to block majority decisions through the right of minorities. The *right to veto* forces ethical discourse to focus on finding common agreement that is communicatively established and denies the majority to over-rule the minority.

On the negative side a *right to veto* can block an ethics council and can hinder its workability by effectively preventing positive outcomes. In some cases it can lend enormous and even unreasonable power to some. It can even prevent insignificant viewpoints issued by a participant or a relatively small group of participants. A *right to veto* provision can also lead to an ethical discourse because everyone is aware of the strong power that carries with it the real possibility of disabling or delaying common agreement inside an *ethics council.* As such, the *right to veto* should be used carefully because it can point to the opposite direction of communicatively established agreements. Finally, it only serves its designed purpose when a communicatively established understanding has failed to establish *communicative ethics.* More than anything, a *right to veto* provision is an indicator for an *ethics council* that it has already left behind simple communication and is moving closer towards positively engaging ethical action.[301]

8. Speech Rules, Ideal Speech and Group Thinking: Inside *ethics councils* the process of reaching agreement means that participants should not contradict themselves. Each participant should only engage in communication about those issues that carry connotations to the moral interest of the council. All statements made during council meetings should reflect *seriousness.* They should formulate ideas that morally support the argument that is put forward. All participants who aim to apply a predicate 'X' to an object '1' must also be prepared to apply 'X' to every other object that contains similar elements as expressed in '1'. It applies to all relevant occasions. Finally, different participants should not articulate the same expression with different meaning. Any link between expression and meaning must be coherently presented.

A participant of an *ethics council* who attacks the statement of another participant, an already established norm, or a code of conduct that is not subject to the discourse must explain the reason for doing so. Only when such an attack is supported through a communicatively established agreement can it become part of a discourse. Otherwise, the attack has to be withdrawn. Participants can issue new arguments and statements when they are requested to produce further arguments on the subject matter.

Finally, there are issues related to the participants and their interests. Participants have to apply certain options and criteria to discuss issues objectively. These basic rules are related to the i) participants of such forums, to their ii) interests, iii) opinions, and finally iv) to the application of objective criteria during discourses. The four basic rules assist the structuring of discourses inside an *ethics council*. The first rule is that problems should be separated from persons. The second rule denotes that it is vital to focus on interests rather than on positions. The third rule is about options for mutual gains, the final rule about objectivity. It demands that one should insist on using objective criteria when making valuable ethical claims and statements.

These four basic principles for *ethics councils* show the importance of assisting the establishment of conditions supportive of *communicative ethics*. They suggest that communication can be established when participants focus on issues rather than on themselves or other people. *Communicative ethics* is designed to follow a set of communicative rationalities that are enhanced when discourses focus on the issues at hand. While the overall interest of *communicative ethics* is directed towards achieving communicatively established understanding, *communicative ethics* is not achieved by *winning* or *losing* an argument. Discourse is never about *having* an opinion. Instead, it lives from arguments that are exchanged in solidarity and humanity. They should never be exchanged from a view that turns the argument into something that is *owned* by someone. Just as Hegel's ethics of *Sittlichkeit* is not a thing in-itself but an actual way of life, it is the way of an ethical life when people can achieve self-actualisation. Arguments are therefore not seen as a position or an object that can be lost. *Communicative ethics* is about finding common understanding through interest mediation.

Options for mutual gains are able to enhance discourse. Within *communicative ethics* there are several mutual gains – such as the prevention of unethical behaviour and bridging the communicative divide between employees and management (Klikauer 2008) – to be made along the way to establish common understanding. These should be utilised to the fullest extent. Finally, there should also be a focus on using objective criteria. The idea is not the denial of subjectivity but a reduction and elimination of bias, prejudice, unfairness, favouritism, and irrational preferences. All of this, however, might still not be enough to prevent one of the greatest dangers to an *ethics council*, commonly known as *group thinking*.

Group thinking is a version of group dynamics commonly regarded with negative connotations.[302] It can develop inside relatively isolated groups that are established as closed forums (Janis 1982). Such groups operate as social groups in which highly pathological social behaviour determines wrong outcomes of discussions. *Group thinking* is a social, psychological, and pathological – not a linguistic – phenomenon.[303] Councils need to introduce a version of *communicative ethics* that is capable of guarding against the dangerous and harmful effects of group thinking. Janis (1982) has established several useful rules that support *ethics councils* governed by *communicative ethics*. They assist in reducing or avoiding the dangers of *group thinking*. Each participant should critically assess an ethics council's course of action as demanded by Kant's and Hegel's ethical concept of *self-reflection* and *Mündigkeit*. In an open and fair *ethics council*, a climate of receptive and positive criticism should be encouraged. The same applies to the acceptance of criticism. The three best guards against *group thinking* are, firstly, mutually acceptable critique; secondly, Kant's dictum *in modernity everything has to be exposed to criticism;* and thirdly, Hegel's concept of dialectics. Under dialectical thinking, any discourse issue has to be presented as a *thesis* or *theme* and always needs to be exposed to a counter-theme, a negative, or a contra-point. This is what has come to be known as *anti-thesis*. Linked to Kant's *what is* and *what ought to be*, the concept of *thesis and anti-thesis* results in *philosophical synthesis*. Participants in discourses and discourse moderators need to assess all claims in the light of these ethical and philosophical determinants.

9. Forms of Agreements: Full, Working, Mini, and Quasi: *Full agreement* can be reached once discourse participants are in mutual understanding about an issue and have reached a commonly established platform for consensual agreement. However, there might be cases when full agreement is not possible. As a measure to build provisional or preliminary consensus, the introduction of *working agreements* may be considered. Such an agreement is seen as a somewhat under-theorised, under-justified, and sub-ethical agreement made in cases where a common understanding or a full agreement could not be reached. It is, however, supported by arguments that reflect communicative and ethical qualities and values.

The lower level of *mutual acceptance* can provide a foundation for a working agreement. Here, the strength of *communicative ethics* is somewhat weakened and the level of support has moved downward from mutual *understanding* to mere *acceptance*. Consequently, the likelihood of reaching agreement decreases but can move upward again once a working agreement is used that provides a bridge to a full agreement. A *mini*-consensus can also be reached when discourse participants come to an intermediate conclusion. It occurs through the exclusion of disagreements. This form of dialogue emphasises positives directed towards agreeable issues. It is not to say that conflicting issues are to be avoided. Rather the opposite is the case. Conflicting issues need to be part of any discourse as they are very important in moving forward. Similarly, a *quasi*-agreement can be reached when discourse participants are not able to reach mutual understanding but are aware of the reasons why. Such an agreement on the cause of disagreements can then be used as a foundation for further discussions to reach a full agreement. Quasi-agreements can be used to overcome previous disagreements. These different levels of agreement operate in an upward scale with 1) being the highest and 5) the lowest level of agreement: 1. *Communicative Ethics* → 2. Consensual Agreement → 3. Working Agreement → 4. Mini-Consensus → 5. Quasi-Consensus.

This also shows an upward scale of discursive tools that can be applied to move towards a level of mutual understanding that translates into ethical action.[304] Levels three to five are only interim levels of consensual agreements that demand further discourse. Levels one and two provide a borderline between communicatively established consensus that reaches an agreement on the direction of ethical action and ethics itself. Discourses at levels three to five carry strong connotations of ethics. Those at levels two and one switch from communication to communicatively established action. The upward scale however is not to be seen as a model with levels that have to be passed in order to reach level one. It needs to be understood as an indicator that discourses can occur at different levels. The ultimate goal of a communicative understanding that fulfils the demands of *communicative ethics* remains. The scale does not indicate that passing one level takes discourse participants automatically to the next stage. It also does not mean that participants cannot skip one or several levels. There may be situations where participants enter a discourse at level two and proceed to level one. In other cases, they might only reach one of the preliminary levels of discourse. Participants however need to communicate further to reach level one and overcome all existing internal conflicts. During all stages conflicts among participants can arise even though they should decrease as discourse moves upward towards level one. At level one, communicative action is not conflict oriented but conducted in a way to achieve communicative understanding and agreement.

10. Conflict Resolutions: Conflicts among participants can occur in any form of group discussion or discourse. Disagreements are standard occurrences and often have two possible sources. Firstly, one or several participants may indicate interpretive differences that appear unsolvable. Secondly, discourse participants have different preferences over the outcome of a discourse. This can be the case when different interests meet. In the corporate world differing interests are inherent in almost every communicative relationship between different organisational actors. In standard managerial practice this often leads to asymmetrical communication based on hierarchy, domination, and power which are forms of instrumental communication rather than *communicative ethics*. Management has produced strong structural determinants that hinder attempts by discourse participants to move towards the ethics of Habermas' *communicative ethics* and Hegel's *Sittlichkeit*. Therefore, it is by far easier to achieve communicative *action* and communicative *ethics* when management is strictly separated from *ethics councils*. This avoids many of management's colonisation attempts and also reduces communicative distortions that management intentionally or unintentionally carries with it. Only when an *ethics council* is established independent of the managerial domain, can it remain free from colonisation and communicative distortions.

Discourse-participants in such *ethics councils* often spend considerable time on discussions to interpret the reality of management and its ethical implications. This is necessary as different discourse participants interpret reality in different ways despite having similar interests. Interest similarities are high in management because management is supported by its own ideology of Managerialism. It *prescribes* non-ethical actions to management (Magretta 2002). The management domain's power provides strong tendencies for an ideological colonisation of an *ethics council*. This has to be prevented. Otherwise, any analysis, critical evaluation, or ethical consideration of *'what reality is'* and *'what ought to be'* (Kant) can be distorted.

Serious conflicts are more likely to arise when participants from both domains – the management domain on the one hand and the *ethics council* on the other – leave their respective domains and meet in the exchange domain where management meets members of the ethics council. Here, conflict resolution is much harder to achieve and underlying differences in interest play a larger role. Participants are by far more able to reach understanding and common agreement if they remain within their respective domain – *ethics council* or management. Domain internal disagreements can be easily overcome through domain-specific consensus formation. This is often based on power in the management domain and on *communicative ethics* in the domain of the *ethics council*.

In the domain of the *ethics council*, there is a substantial need to discuss *how* ethics should be applied and what kind of means should be used to establish *communicative ethics* directed towards ethical goals. Once such goals are agreed upon, discourse participants can discuss how *communicative ethics* translates into ethical action. At this stage clarification of *means* can be reached through *pragmatic discourse* that focuses on rather *mechanical* issues. Such discussions should never occur without ethical reflections.[305] A reflection on ethical issues should be conducted in accordance with Kohlberg's model of morality that discusses ethical goals. Such discourses on ethical goals are always in demand, especially when disagreements over these goals are discussed. The ethical goals need to be linked to the discourse participants' values. In contrast to the functionality of management's domain, members of an *ethics council* must always seek to combine and mediate between several ethical viewpoints (virtue ethics, utilitarianism, Kant, Hegel, Rawls, Kohlberg, etc.). This demands that any discussion includes elements of *pragmatic discourse*. It also needs to be linked to a discussion reflective of *ethical discourse*. Practical, ethical, and realistic solutions can never be separated from agreements on meanings, interpretations, and the means of achieving ethical goals. Disconnecting *pragmatic* from *ethical* discourses will not lead to conflict resolution inside *ethics councils*. Such a disconnection can never move a discourse towards ethical action.

Much in the same way in which *pragmatic* and *ethical* discourses need to be linked to one another, consideration of practical issues inside the *moral discourse* can never be excluded from discourses inside *ethics councils*. Unlike management's instrumental communication, ethical discourse inside *ethics councils* demands a linkage between the three forms of discourse: ethical, pragmatic, and action oriented. They are of significant relevance in order to establish *communicative ethics* directed towards ethical action. Ethics can never be a simple *add-on* and ethical values can never simply be attached to instrumental discussions as is often the case in the managerial domain. Put simply, non-ethical discourse inside *ethics councils* is impossible. There can never be any pretension of being value-free or value-neutral. All discourses in *ethics councils* have to be ethical discourses. They can move between pragmatic, ethical, and action-oriented discourse but can never neglect ethics as the foundation of all forms of communication. This can create conflicts among the three aspects but conflict resolution inside *ethics councils* is fundamentally different from conflict resolution in the management domain. For example, inside an *ethics council* nobody has a privilege like the managerial prerogative, nobody has the right to disciplinary action, and nobody operates with power and authority. The ethics council represents the opposite of all this.

There are, however, exceptions. Even a perfect application of all rules and discourse aids will not necessarily prevent a communicative failure inside an *ethics council*. Firstly, there is the issue of *bounded rationality*. Secondly, *ethics councils* are set in sharp contrast to managerial, neoliberal, cost-benefit, efficiency, strategy, and economic rationalist views. They do not operate under the false equation of perfect access to information leading to perfect decisions. Nobody has perfect access to all available information. Therefore, an economic-rational view based on instrumental rationality is structurally impossible. Instead, participants inside *ethics councils* are aware that ethics, management, companies, corporations, workplaces, HRM, company policies, markets, competition, business plans, corporate behaviour, and even the *ethics council* itself are socially constructed entities. When participants of *communicative ethics* reach common understanding on the structural impossibilities of managerially structured communication, considerable doubts about the perfection of managerial solutions can be raised (Klikauer 2008). Such an understanding has severe consequences.

Today management and Managerialism tend to follow the ideology of economic 'ir'rationalism. This belief system denotes a worldview that seeks perfect models but excludes almost everything ethics demands from us. In the mind of the so-called *rationalists*, there are perfect models but imperfect realities. In sharp contrast to the ideological trappings of

Managerialism, *ethics councils* are much freer in admitting ethical imperfections and morally incomplete solutions. Their setup and *modus operandi* are the result of a self-determining and socially constructed world that is not based on the confining demands of the ideological worldview that is represented in Managerialism. Consequently, *communicative ethics* as applied inside *ethics councils* can more openly deal with these imperfections.[306] *Ethics councils* are able to overcome managerially directed instrumental communication by gaining a realistic and critical view on information access. Information is also examined for possible ideological contents and deformities engineered by market-driven economic *'ir'rationalism* and Managerialism. *Ethics councils* can identify the shortcomings of managerial assumptions and pathological models. The awareness of the deficiencies of managerially structured communication by *ethics councils* enables them to critically analyse discourses. It also allows for a critical self-examination of their own abilities. Without Kantian *self-reflections* and a Hegelian *self-actualisation* all ethical discourses remain severely limited. Being aware of these limitations however does not weaken the ability of the *ethics councils*. Rather the opposite is the case. It strengthens the council's concerns about managerial fallacies as participants of *communicative ethics* enter into moral discourses. The awareness of these fallacies enables *ethics councils* – often more than management – to see the imperfections and immoralities of instrumental rationality manifested in managerial actions.

Managerial standards, management science, and traditional communicative science (e.g. sender→receiver-models) seek to deliver technical engineering outcomes that are fault-free (Klikauer 2008:17–32). The application of *communicative ethics* makes one aware that they can, and do, fail.[307] Similarly, the rationality of discourse inside *ethics councils* should not be taken as an absolute certainty. The aim of a council's ethical recommendations and communicative aids, for example, is to assist management and stakeholders in the application of ethical standards geared towards positive ethical change. In many discussions inside *ethics councils*, the use of *communicative ethics* can still create dilemmas and these are often unsolvable.[308] One such example is the conflict between time-consuming communications to reach consensus versus demands for urgent action to avoid moral failures of companies. As discourses are often linked to considerable time constraints, discourse participants will be exposed to some form of unjust restrictions. Some of these can be:

- some voices and arguments may have to be excluded from discourses;

- some discussions might be distorted even under conditions of *communicative ethics*;
- even discourses under conditions of *communicative ethics* might bring about unfair and unwarranted outcomes;
- discourses under conditions of *communicative ethics* might still include unjust and unfair processes;
- even good discursive procedures and discourse participants that subscribe to *communicative ethics* might consider their own discourse outcomes as bad but in such cases these discourse participants can decide themselves whether such outcomes are valid or not;
- as of yet, there is no procedure in place that automatically guarantees the correct results; and finally
- a communicative process that is able to produce better common understanding geared towards positive ethical life (*Sittlichkeit*) than the concept of *communicative ethics* is not in sight.

These are some of the most severe restrictions often experienced when engaging in *communicative ethics*. As much as it is regrettable, some participants have to be excluded from discourse arrangements that are geared towards ethics. For example, participants interested in means-ends or cost-benefit rationalities, prisoner dilemmas, strategy (the generalship of deceiving an enemy), instrumentalism, and instrumental communication may have to be excluded. Councils need to fight colonisation attempts from the managerial domain. Some forms of communication and discourse outcomes might still carry elements of distortions even though participants have already been excluded. In general, participants need to be aware of the danger of *system integration* that seeks to colonise *communicative ethics*.[309] If successful, these attempts can convert *communicative ethics* into instrumental communication. This, in many cases, marks the end of *communicative ethics*.

As communication under conditions of *communicative ethics* progresses, unfair, domineering, and unwarranted argumentations may still occur. During the course of such discussions, participants need to intervene whenever they detect elements contradictory to the demands of *communicative ethics*. They need to exclude them because there is no automatic guarantee for moral outcomes in *communicative ethics*. Even if conducted within all guidelines as outlined above, *communicative ethics* can never mechanically guarantee moral achievements. The basic idea behind *communicative ethics* is that it only sets parameters for moral discourses. It never determines the outcome and moral outcomes are not to be understood as assured. There is no inescapable and inevitable logic built into *communicative ethics*. It never establishes an instrumental necessity nor does it routinely and automatically lead to certain out-comes. However, in sharp contrast to managerial forms of commun-ication, it is able to direct participants towards reaching a shared, ethical, and, above all, communicatively established understanding. From there, participants can convert *communicative ethics* into moral action geared towards positive ethical change.

In sharp contrast to managerial institutions, *ethics councils* are able to establish conditions of *communicative ethics*. In symmetrical *com-municative ethics* settings that are free from domination by market forces and management intervention, all participants have an equal chance to employ constructive, regulative, and representative speech acts free from distorted communication. Moral goals have to be established communicatively using the concept of *communicative ethics*. All parti-cipants have an effective equality of chances to take part in the dialogue. Conditions for *communicative ethics* are not linguistic but social-ethical in character.

Their social-ethical disposition may demand that councils overcome *internal* constraints that are found in the unconscious reflection of man-agerial hierarchies and other forms of domination prevalent in industrial settings. *External* constraints are engineered by managerial purposive and instrumental rationality such as, for example, the managerial SWOT analysis that aims to identify actual and potential strengths, weaknesses, opportunities, and threats. But SWOT can infiltrate and colonise *com-municative ethics* confining communication to managerial techniques.[310] This has to be avoided as it constructs boundaries of communication by hindering *communicative ethics*. Such instruments pre-determine com-munication by shaping some ideas and excluding others. They often follow the concept of TINA: there is no alternative. But ethics in the managerial context is all about alternatives.

To avoid TINA, symmetric conditions have to be established so that the force of the better argument can flourish. Conditions that seek to enhance a co-operative search for a truthful representation of ethics have to prevail.[311] *Ethics councils* need to be able to raise problematic validity claims. Discussions under conditions of *communicative ethics* are not quick fixes or fast solutions. The goal remains to establish com-municative agreement for moral action. Seeking consensus and social action have to be seen as interrelated practices that move commun-ication towards moral action. Both also need to avoid communicative distortions and the colonisation of communication through patho-logies and manipulations. Communicatively established understandings have to be within morality and ethics both of which can never be disassociated from social conventions and history. Elevating moral standards in this way avoids pathologies, manipulations, distortions, and the colonisation of communication. Participants need to focus their attention towards *communicative ethics* directed towards a revitalisation of possibilities for moral action. *Communicative ethics* can also uncover expressions that have so far been buried alive. Traditions of morality, liberation, and emancipation that have historically included potentials of resistance against unethical behaviours need to be reactivated.

Participants need to withdraw from instrumental communication and turn their intentions towards moral forms of communication that are not neutral (Habermas 1986:223ff.). They move towards specific ends that are defined by the possibilities of ameliorating the human condition. Discourses among *ethics council* members seen as moral actors need to isolate themselves from managerial and hidden transcripts. This might have to occur *off-stage* and beyond direct and indirect managerial surveillance and has the potential to turn relations of *domination* into relations of morality. Management's domination, unfairness, injustices, hierarchies, power, and authoritarianism have always provided the anti-thesis to ethics. Their exclusion often leads to the synthesis of positive moral change. It also provides a structure of checks and balances to the managerial process. By assuming the role as a working group, *ethics councils* can create a diverging and, in some cases, even dissident forum beyond official managerial power structures. This can free up communicative space in which undistorted ethical communication is possible.

The strict separation of the domain of the *ethics council* from the managerial domain creates Kant's ethical demand for autonomy and self-determination. It links different levels of moral actions to communication including the expected outcomes of different practices and the use of different languages.[312] It positions the language of morality in opposition to the language of Managerialism. Hence, *language-in-use* relates differently to the management domain than it does to the moral domain. In the *ethics council* domain, speech is conducted inside the framework of *communicative ethics* and directed towards moral improvements. Under conditions of goal-achieving instrumental action management's language use is directed towards measurable success, means-ends rationalities, cost-benefits, shareholder values, and *The Real Bottom Line*. At the point of outcomes, *communicative ethics* manifests itself inherently with potentials for human emancipation from domination. Management's instrumental language use leads to fundamentally different outcomes. It creates pathologies and immorality. The immorality of corporate life is found in goal-achieving strategies that are established managerially, not through *communicative ethics*.

One of the clearest indicators of these pathologies is the fact that management is in constant need to readjust the Hegelian *'Other'* to the pathologies of corporate life. It has to convert human *beings* into human *resources;* it has to convert *human* behaviour into *organisational* behaviour; and it has to convert men and women into *Organisation Men* and *Women.* Any dissent from management's view has traditionally been labelled *organisational misbehaviour.* To eclipse these managerial pathologies, management has invented a raft of communicative distortions that are used in specific sections of managerial communication (Klikauer 2008). In sharp contrast to managerial communication, *communicative ethics* acts as some sort of *switching station.* It creates ethical and communicative energies and converts them into human solidarity and positive moral changes.[313]

To conclude, a detailed investigation into m*anagement ethics* has been able to uncover the fact that management's essence of instrumental rationality (profit-maxim, cost-benefit, cost-cutting, shareholder value, *The Real Bottom Line*, etc.) renders management unable to operate as a moral actor. It renders management also incapable of establishing moral conditions for *communicative ethics.* Management's relationship to ethics is at best contradictory and at worst manifested in blatant violations of ethics ranging from immoral behaviour to outright criminal activities. In order to make management more accountable to society's ethical demands, the introduction of an *ethics council* has been proposed. Such an independent and autonomous body can move beyond pre-structured managerial communication, raise managerial awareness on ethics, avoid MADD (*moral attention deficit disorder*), and align management with morality. An *ethics council* based on ethical communication truly opens up avenues for Hegel's *Sittlichkeit* and moral action. Communicative forums such as *ethics councils* have to be established in a domination free environment. This allows interactions through discourse organised by organisational members that are separated from management. Unlike management they need to be legitimised democratically. *Ethics councils* have to meet conditions of *communicative ethics.* They need to engage in reaching common understanding and agreement about moral action. This must be established among all participants of such a council. The concept of consensus is a basic demand for discussions on moral action. It is absolutely central to articulation (Hegel) directed towards the improvement of morality. Once a communicative and ethical consensus on morality has been achieved, such *moral actions* can be converted into *organisational actions*. They are directed towards positive moral change inside companies and well beyond the boundaries of companies and management.

Notes

1 Critical *Management Ethics* is about management, not business. It focuses on managerial, not on business issues. Management issues are predominantly internal to companies while business issues relate to a large extent to the outside market. In focusing predominantly on *internal* affairs (managing companies) and not *external* affairs (market exchanges, relations to supplies, and customers), management ethics, not business ethics, is at the centre (cf. Harrison 2005:10f.).

2 Ideology is an unconscious tendency underlying technical, scientific, political, and managerial thought to make facts amenable to ideas and ideas to facts in order to create a managerial image convincing enough to support the collective and individual identity of management (Beder 2006). Ideology masks the fact that managerial images are credible even though they differ under different socio-economical conditions. Therefore, the term ideology refers to *knowledge in the use of power*. The essence of ideology has been outlined in *Žižek's The Sublime Object of Ideology* (1989); cf. Bell (1960); Fox (1966); Marcuse (1966); Eagleton (1994).

3 On this German philosopher Marcuse (1966) emphasised the *absorption of ideology into reality does not however, signify the end of ideology*.

4 According to German philosopher Fichte (1762–1814), *philosophy has to display the basis or foundations of all experience*. It seeks to understand the philosophical and ethical foundations of values. For management values are often expressed in *shareholder values*. These are mere indications of financial values of corporations. While management claims to be scientific it also has to rely on philosophy. On the *philosophy vs. science dilemma* German philosopher Karl Jaspers (1883–1969) noted: *without philosophy, science does not understand itself*. Hence, without ethics and morality, management can never understand itself. *Science and philosophy* as well as *ethics and management* are inseparable. The concept of philosophy itself that originates in Aristotle's term *philia* carries connotations of *loved, dear* and *friendship*. It also relates to *philia* and Sophia meaning *friend* and *wisdom*. Neither of these terms – *loved, dear, friendship, friend, wisdom* – is associated with today's management. This reflects on the fact that modern management is neither *loved*, nor seen to be *dear*, does not include *friendship*, and that managers are not seen as *friends* carrying no *wisdom*. German philosopher Hans-Georg Gadamer (1900–2002) noted that the task of philosophy is to *mediate the employment of man's cognitive and constructive capacities with the totality of our experienced life*. Finally, there is Marx' dictum that *philosophers have only interpreted the world in various ways; the point, however, is to change it*. On this, German philosopher Adorno thinks that *philosophy must express the ineffable* (Finlayson 2002:11); while Hegel emphasised that *philosophy is not supposed to be an account of what happens*. Hegel saw critique as the task of philosophy. The task of philosophy is not, as

216

Kant thought, merely to assemble truth (cf. Hegel 1803/4, 1807, 1821, 1830).

5   A full list of ethical misconceptions is outlined in Sikula's *Applied Management Ethics* (1996:104).

6   For management, ethics and morality are not only an *add-on* but also supply legitimacy if needed when certain areas of managerial actions are carved out and managerially determined to be ethical or morally indifferent (Clegg and Rhodes 2006:5)

7   Perlmutter's *Manufacturing Visions of Society and History in Textbooks* (1997); Harding (2003); Jones et al. (2005:1); Schwartz (1990); it is also reflective of a *closing of the mind* and blissful ignorance.

8   Marcuse (1941) notes on Hegel's dialectics that it *is a process in a world where the mode of existence of man and thing is made up of contradictory relations* (cf. Singer 1994:115).

9   A good example for the marginalisation of philosophy is Collins' (2000) article on the first 1,500 articles published in *Journal of Business Ethics*. Among the six major research topics, philosophy is all but absent. The word 'philosophy' wasn't even worth an index entry.

10 A near perfect example is Melé's *Business Ethics – Seeking Human Excellence in Organizations* (2009). Melé's (2009) cases include Anderson Consulting, Enron, Worldcom, Siemens – *Several Bribes Hit The Company* (not that Siemens was the main culprit, NO 'poor' Siemens was 'hit' by briberies!), GAP – Combating Child Labour (well, thanks for GAP! – nobody really needs the ILO!) Mattel, Nike, and finally 'Bhopal – *Could the worst industrial disaster have been avoided?'* skilfully directing attention towards a debate that occurred 25 years ago while avoiding questions such as what happened to those responsible (nothing, Chairman and CEO of Union Carbide, Warren Anderson is not even mentioned by Melé) and what happened to the victims: also nothing – no compensation, no medical help (wikipedia.org/wiki/Bhopal_disaster).

11 Jones et al. (2005:3) noted in *business ethics, it seems clear that 20th century philosophy is almost completely excluded.*

12 Kant thinks in concepts because for him, *thought is knowledge by means of concepts* (1781).

13 A second, and even more dangerous, re-interpretation results from Kant's word '*only*'. For affirmative textbook writers Kant has ruled out treating people *only* as a means. In other words, treating people just a bit as a means is okay. These writers often insert claims on Kant's '*only*' as *hypothetical imperatives* in '*if-then*' construction (*...if management respects workers then...*) clearly violating Kant's *categorical imperative*. Following that, the totality of management ethics is made possible just because Kant put the word '*only*' in his categorical imperative. This is not what Kant had in mind. For him there is no secret little escape-door in the form of 'only' through which a whole discipline of management ethics can escape his categorical imperative. However, the task of *The Servants of Power* (Baritz 1960) is to twist Kant so that his ethics fits and supports the prevailing managerial paradigm.

14 Often, this comes as a CD-ROM attached to *your* (sic!) textbook that not only looks and feels like a *Cosmopolitan* magazine but is also similarly

structured and made up. The *easy users* (sic!) can switch from an airhead-like magazine to an airhead-like textbook without noticing which is which (cf. Gare's *The Triumph of the Airheads and the Retreat from Commonsense* (Ch. 8: Management for Airheads (2006)).

15 Managerialism is the ideology of management (cf. *The High Cost of Managerialism* (Rees and Rodley 1995). According to French philosopher Louis Althusser (1918–1990), *ideology (as a system of mass representations) is indispensable in any society if men are to be formed, transformed, and equipped to respond to the demands of their conditions of existence*. Hence, the ideology of Managerialism is indispensable to management because it forms (organisational psychology), transforms (humans→human resources), and equips people to respond to the demands of work regimes and consumerism.

16 A classical example of the M+E=ME method is presented in Kreitner's 11th edition of *Management* (2009) where 13 out of 546 pages – or 2.37% – deal with ethics. This represents roughly the space ethics is being allocated in real management. Throughout his textbook, Kreitner mentions ethics several times as a stand alone word without any meaning attached to it. Reading his book creates the impression that ethics is placed in there because it is fashionable to do so. But it is deprived of meaning. Tellingly, the foremost important 20th century French philosopher, Jean-Paul Sartre (1905–1980) noted in *Being and Nothingness* (1992): *the bourgeois who call themselves 'respectable citizens' do not become respectable as the result of contemplating moral values*. In short, management who calls itself respectable management does not become respectable as a result of contemplating moral values.

17 For Nietzsche (1844–1900) there are no facts. In *The Will to Power* (1883–1888) he emphasised *against positivism, which halts at phenomena – there are only facts – I would say: No, facts is precisely what there is not, only interpretations. We cannot establish any fact 'in itself': perhaps it is folly to want to do such a thing*. Facts and their interpretations are in a dialectical relationship. Once exposed to the power of dialectical thinking, *the dialectical method destroys the fiction of the immortality of the categories, it also destroys their reified character and clears the way to a knowledge of reality* (Lukács 1922). Dialectics destroys the immortality of managerial categories themselves and those of management ethics by exposing them to the negatives that are internal to both and it links management to society. On the society-scholarship link, German philosopher Gadamer (1990–2002) noted *the scholar – even the natural scientist – is perhaps not completely free of custom and society and from all possible factors in his environment*; see also the ultimate masterpiece on *Traditional and Critical Theory* in: Horkheimer (1937); cf. Habermas (1987); Searle (1996); Klikauer (2007:76–97).

18 On critique, German philosopher Karl Jaspers (1883–1969) noted, for the scientist, criticism is a vital necessity, He cannot be questioned enough in order to test his insights. Even since Kant's dictum *in modernity everything has to be exposed to critique* ethics, management, and with it management ethics have to be examined critically (cf. Horkheimer 1937 and 1947, Klikauer 2007:76–96).

19 On the issue of empirical knowledge and ethics, Kant noted in his *Foundation of the Metaphysics of Morals* (1785), that everything empirical is not only wholly unworthy to be an ingredient in the principle of morality but is even highly prejudicial to the purity of moral practice themselves. In his *Critique of Pure Reason* of 1781 (his masterwork), he noted *our empirical knowledge is made up of what we receive through impressions.* We are part of society and individuals with a developed consciousness. We can never be totally objective because we are human subjects with a subjective consciousness. Essentially we are, as Kant noted, restricted by *sensibilities* and *understanding.* The former gives us objects, the latter thought.

20 There appears to be an almost endless list of corporate failures testifying to the problematic of ethics vs. management (Corporate.Watch.Org); Baxter and Rarick (1987); Minkes and Minkes (2008); Leap (2007); Haigh (2006); Petrick and Quinn (1997:32); Punch (1996:85–212); *International Corruption Perception Index; Transparency International; WWW.Corporate. Watch;* http://www.google.com/Top/Society/Issues/Business/Allegedly_ Unethical_Firms/etc.; American International Group (following the 2008 bailout, AIG-managers engaged in a $444,000 retreat featured spa-treatments, banquets and golf outings) Bernie Madoff was the former NASDAQ stock-exchange chairman.

21 On *examining* (norm vs. norm), Hegel noted in *The Phenomenology of Spirit* (1807), *for an examination consists in applying an accepted standard and in determining whether something is right or wrong on the basis of the resulting agreement or disagreement of the thing examined.* Inside a *norm vs. norm* examination, ethical standards are applied to management to determine whether management is right or wrong; whether ethics agrees or disagrees with *what management is* (Magretta 2002).

22 The concept of *the essence* relates to the philosophical tradition of *Essentialism.* All objects have at least some essential properties (cf. *maximal* and *minimal* essentialism). These distinguish the *essential* from the *accidental.* This reaches to the core of things and their true being rather than their appearance. It is a form of *deep-structure* rather than *surface-structure*; (cf. Johnson 2008:140f.; Smith 1987:119). Aristotelian philosophy understands philosophy as *a deduction that reasons dialectically to a contradiction.* Despite his fame and prominence today, Aristotle died as a poor and forgotten man. The Socratic-method was the practice of dialectic that turned an opponent's words inward into contradiction. Plato extended the dialectical thinking by theorising anyone could discover a truth by studying arguments and contradictions. Plato believed all contradictions are removed through logic, the true would be revealed in the form of *perfectly absolute concepts.* Hegelian dialectics, according to Johnson (2008:129), *is both an epistemology and an ontology, namely, a mobile, dynamic knowledge-process that, in its function [and, more importantly, malfunctioning], simultaneously reveals the very configuration of being itself;* cf. Plato's *The Republic* (5th century BC).

23 Quite similar to the *deep-structure vs. surface structure* concept, French philosopher Bergson (1859–1941) noted *thanks to philosophy, all things acquire depth.* Hence, it is not surprising that most management students who acquire PhDs have neither reflected on the 'P' in PhD (P=philosophy), nor have they

read any philosophy, nor touched upon philosophy in their management-PhD. It is blind ignorance of any philosophy that defines almost all management-PhDs. Consequently these PhDs are low on depth but high on managerial buzzwords, code-words, functionality and instrumentalism.

24   Magretta (2002:7 and 196). In the following chapter all text that appears in italics is taken from her book when not otherwise referenced. The chapter is not designed as a negative view of management but as a realistic view as put forward by the former editor of the *Harvard Business Review* (HBR). After years of being the HBR-editor, Magretta's subsequent book truthfully divides the *Essential* from the *Accidental* (cf. Essentialism). There may be accidental articles in various journals and chapters in textbooks that contradict Magretta's overview of management but her book does not rely on the occasional or accidental article but on the essence of *What Management Is* (2002). Hence, this chapter seeks to represent her views as authentic as possible, even though some might argue that one cannot elaborate on the essence of management by relying on one single book. Firstly, the chapter relies predominantly on her work and on a few other sources as well. Secondly, the HBR is, after all, the most widely read journal in management. Thirdly, it strongly reflects mainstream views on management and with it the essence of management (cf. the philosophy of essentialism). Fourthly, Margretta's book is not just *a book* but combines years, if not decades, of experience in editing the HBR; and finally, there might be sources that contradict the HRB editor – even inside the HRB itself – but they, unlike Magretta (2002), do all too often constitute marginalised, accidental, isolated, etc. viewpoints that are not representative of mainstream management. Hence, the texts on management indicated in italics in the proceeding chapters are taken from her work as a truthful representation of the essence of management.

25   Magretta (2002); Kreitner (2009:5); Jones et al. (2005:167). Magretta (2002) emphasised that management operates through people and essentially consists of people (even though HRM is grossly undervalued by management). There is also a tendency to downplay the social or organisational context inside which individuals act. It negates the fact that humans are social beings and would not even know themselves without *The Other* (Hegel). Hegel was correct in stating that human need *The Other* to know that '*I am I*'. Humans live inside social context. Without social ethics humans would not exist. Despite this, there are still people claiming that ethics is a subject of the individual, the ego, and the self without recognising that *social* and *ethical behaviour* is not the same as *organisational behaviour* (cf. Ackroyd and Thompson's *Organisational Misbehaviour* (1999)). Schwartz (1990:135) sees management as *nothing but the management of the work process*. Petrick and Quinn (1997:3) see it as *reaching organisational goals by working with and through human and non-human resources* levelling people with things. This is the Nazi language that equates *Menschen* with *Menschenmaterial* – human resources (Poole 2006).

26   Cf. Singer's critique on ethics in his *The Oxford Reader on Ethics* (1994:58).

27   For Hare (1989) ethics is *the study of moral arguments* as a branch of logic and moral philosophy (formal arguments). In contrast, management is *not the study of moral arguments* but of means to increase shareholder values. It

is fundamentally different from ethics. It is almost as if two totally alien worlds collide when ethics meets management.

28 Quoted from Driver (2007:1). In Moore's *Pincipia Ehica* (1903) *ethics is the general enquiry into what is good.*

29 For Magretta (2002) *numbers are essential to organisational performance* and *numbers that truly matter are the ones that tell a story about how the organisation is doing*; it is the *management-by-numbers approach*. In the coal industry, for example, industrial accidents are calculated through 'deaths per million tons'. This reduces human lives and deaths to just another number on a managerial scorecard (Kaplan & Norton 1992, 1993, 2004).

30 Ethical philosopher Driver (2007:1) argues when we *do something that could harm or benefit someone else then arguably this is a moral matter.* Despite all the claims of being neutral, technical, ideology-free, scientific, engineering-like, etc. management can never escape moral questions. The key to management, according to Magretta (2002) is *quantification* [because it] *helps sometimes enormously do depoliticise difficult decisions.* It moves managerial decisions from a political or ethical sphere into a numbers sphere giving it the appearance of rationality, engineering, and mathematical soundness; cf. Klikauer (2007 and 2008). *Normative ethics* is concerned with standards for right conduct and moral evaluation. *Normative management* is concerned with *functional rules.* They are not for the right conduct but for those conducts that deliver outcomes. It is not concerned with moral evaluation but with management evaluation often expressed in financial controlling and the position of the business in the market place, etc. Normative management would not be interested in *right conduct* but in *profitable conduct.* After all *management makes organisations possible and good management makes them work well* (Magretta 2002:5). If management is right or wrong is not seen as an ethical question but a question of directing functions to the most profitable outcomes.

31 The idea of critically examining everything from two sides dates back to Greek philosophy advocating *elenchus* as a *cross-examination* or an *art of refutation* (cf. Barthes 1987).

32 Hegel, according to Marcuse (1941) noted that *to grasp the world in its veritable being we must grasp it with the categories of freedom, which are to be found only in the realm of thinking subjects. A transition is necessary from the relation of being to the relation of thought* (cf. Smith 1987:119–120).

33 In *Eight Theories of Ethics* (2004:12), Graham argues that *moral reasoning is no different from the sort of reasoning that goes on in a court of law* where one side (the accused[+]) meets the defence[(-)] to come to a conclusion or judgement (synthesis[#]); (cf. Smith 1987:118).

34 So-called honourable and respectable management journals, a closed-up troop of so-called peer groups that run journals like CCTV, gatekeepers, conference committees and the like make sure that marginal views are exactly that: marginal. By doing so careers of affirmative management writers are built, professorships are handed out. Simultaneously critique is isolated, diminished, and marginalised. Many observers have realised that such socially created imperfections in the *marketplace of ideas* cement management's position as an indestructible paradigm. This also creates insecurities shown in the need to marginalise contradicting viewpoints.

As Smith (1987:110) outlined, *all science, just like all societies, is the result of a cumulative process of negation whereby both thought and life are tested not against some externally imposed criteria of adequacy but against their own self-imposed standard of truth.*

35   For the concept of *becoming, Hegel recognised no finality in temporal institutions* (Sterrett 1892:195). As hard as it may sound for management gurus, affirmative management writers, and their entourage, management as a social institution is temporal and not infinite.

36   For Hegel, *being (phenomenal existence) and nothingness (phenomenal absence) are thesis and anti-thesis* representing dialectics which has been a tool of thinking ever since Greek philosophy. Marcuse (1941) noted that one must *break through the false fixity of our concepts and show the driving contradictions that lurk in all modes of existence and call for higher modes of thought.*

37   For example, a book entitled '*What is Management*' constitutes an impossibility. It fails to realise that management is a relationship that cannot just '*be*' but moves toward *becoming*. Management is always a relationship between '*being*' and '*becoming*' and between positive and negatives.

38   Management has even successfully distanced itself from its own employees by negating what used to be called *labour* or *industrial relations* that had been based on the sociology of relationships. Seeking to convert a structure based on social relationships towards Managerialism, they established *Human Resource Management* as the management of *Menschenmaterial*. For management the core rests on HRM's top-down and relationship-denying mode of operation. Management is not interested in *pursuing philosophical truth, ethics and Sittlichkeit*, as outlined by Hegel.

39   The Greek term *telos* meaning goal, aim, and purpose was originally used to describe a branch of philosophy dealing with final causes. During Enlightenment it was believed that things have an inherent and a given target and end.

40   According to Marcuse (1941), *definitions must express the movement in which a being maintains its identity through the negation of its condition. In short, a real definition cannot be given in one isolated proposition, but must elaborate the real history of the object, for its history alone explains its reality. In short, a thing cannot be understood through its qualities without referencing to other qualities that are actually excluded by the one it possesses* (Marcuse 1941); cf. Levinas (1961).

41   The problem of the rat race is: even if you win the rat race, you are still a rat!

42   Aristotle would see the endless pursuit of profits as: they *live on an endless treadmill of desire that never reaches a final goal, and they remain ever empty* (Arrington 1998:66).

43   *The contemporary virtue theorist Alasdair MacIntyre (1981) has argued that the figure of the manager, as a contemporary character, is incapable of virtues in a genuinely Aristotelian sense* (Jones et al. 2005:66).

44   Cf. Schwartz (1990); Punch (1996); Schrijvers (2004).

45   In the words of Adorno and Horkheimer (*Dialectic of Enlightenment* 1947), modern mass consumption is based on the ideology that *something is provided for all so that none may escape...consumers appear as statistics on*

research organisation charts, and are divided by income groups into red, green and blue areas; the technique that is used for any type of propaganda. See also: Walsh and Lynch (2008).

46 In *'The Laws'*, Plato argued *citizens shouldn't have anything to do with money* (Walsh and Lynch 2008).

47 Aristotle (often described as the quintessential Greek philosopher though he was Macedonian) believed that slaves and women are defective reasoners and could not possess full virtues. In ancient Greece it was permissible to own slaves and women should be sequestered (cf. Marcuse 1941). *The Greek philosophers never really raised the problem of slavery* (Midgley 1983:378).

48 Ethics' core question of *'what shall I do?'* leads to the wrong path because the 'I' indicates individuality whereas ethics is a social project (from Aristotle to Adorno) not a project of the individual (ethical egoism, etc.). Without Hegel's *'the Other'* ethics would not exist. Historically, not the individual but the community (tribes, collectives, etc.) created human history and human ethics. Marcuse (1941) noted that *the community comes first.* Ethics has always been an issue for human communities who initially developed codes of conduct on how to live together. History is not individual but universal consciousness. Perhaps, this is best represented in the consciousness of a primitive group with all individuality submerged in the community. Feelings, sensations, and concepts are not properties of individuals but are shared among all. The common – not the particular – defines consciousness and ethics.

49 On ideology, French philosopher Althusser (1918–1990) noted *ideology is as such an organic part of every social totality.* The ideology of Managerialism has been made an organic part of the social totality of management.

50 Management *allocates, and transforms human and material resources into profit-making operations* (Magretta 2002). *In The Organisation Men, William Whyte describes social ethics* as *organisational* and *bureaucratic ethics. It is a pervasive form of dull conformity* (Jones et al. 2005:148).

51 Magretta (2002) argues management *must create a nervous edge that keeps* [others at] *arm's-length...on their toes* [so to speak to keep] *the anxiety of competition* going.

52 It is Plato who analyses the virtue of *pure pleasure* (Levinas 1961).

53 Even though management has no use for friendships based on pleasure and virtues, this is not to say that individual managers do not have friends. They do. But what is at stake here is the essence of management and not the behaviour of individual managers.

54 A list of Aristotelian virtues is presented in: Arrington (1998:76).

55 Aristotle lived in a society based on the surplus value of slaves. Today's society lives on the surplus value of labour. Those who govern the process of surplus-extraction were called slave-owners. Today, these overseers are called management.

56 Perhaps not all too surprising is the fact that among all organisational behaviour, organisational change, organisational culture, organisational members, organisational practice, organisational action, organisational strategy, organisational knowledge, organisational learning, organisational commitment, organisational performance, organisational development, organisational

structure, and on and on and on, a term called *organisational happiness* is totally absent from management's vocabulary and thinking.

57   Management contradicts even utilitarian virtues. Mill (1861) noted *the multiplication of happiness is, according to the utilitarian ethics, the object of virtue.* Management's project is not *the multiplication of happiness* but *the multiplication of* shareholder-values.

58   For the foremost philosopher on justice, John Rawls (1921–2002), *justice is the first virtue of social institutions.* Management as a *social institution* would need to produce justice, including wage justice. However, management has never established what the medieval religious philosopher *Blaise Pascal's* (1623–1662) called *justice of the wager.* There is still no wage justice between men's and women's earnings. This testifies to the fact that management is, in Rawls' conception, not only unjust but also unethical.

59   Greek philosophy saw only men as relevant. But even in antiquity some suspected that there is no difference between men and women.

60   According to Magretta (2002) *numbers are essential to organisational performance...numbers...truly matter.*

61   This has been outlined in Schrijvers' *The Way of the Rat* (2004), Jackall's *Moral Mazes* (1988), and Punch's *Dirty Business* (1996). These three authors reflect on the reality of management and the role virtues play inside it.

62   The ideology of individualisation engineered through textbooks and corporate PR has been negated by managerial standardisations (standard employment contracts, standard operational policies, standard job descriptions, standard mission statements, standard CSR-statement, standard performance measures, etc.). Instead, Managerialism demands the ideology of individualism. This ideology needs to be established at work and also in the off-work sphere of consumption. The standardised *Organisation Men* (Whyte 1961) have been paralleled by the standardised consumer purchasing standardised mass-products for equally standardised body-parts (M, S, L, XL, and A-cup to E-cup). This has been linked to the ideological mass-deception of individual choice. Simultaneously, real life choices are reduced to consumer choices which confines humans to a narrow band of consumer-work oscillation for most of their existence. This sort of *society tears the individual away from family ties* as detected by Hegel (1821).

63   Managers have developed a kind of schism between the world of corporations and the world outside of them. *At home, they moan and groan. They say what they really feel: the boss is a pig, the department is arrogant, employees think only about themselves.* They are made to believe that they can be highly moral in their private lives and *leave their conscience at home* when entering the corporate world. On this Adorno and Horkheimer (1944) noted *the bourgeois whose existence is split into a business and a private life, whose private life is split into keeping up his public image and intimacy, whose intimacy is split into the partnership of marriage and the bitter comfort of being quite alone, at odds with himself and everybody else, is already virtually a Nazi replete both with enthusiasm and abuse; or a modern city-dweller who can now only imagine friendship as a 'social contact'.* In other words, there is a self-constructed fantasy of separating private from company life. This carries pathologies that cannot *bring one's emotions and dispositions into the*

harmony of an inner peace of mind. Rather, the opposite is the case. It dilutes virtue ethics and personal well-being, and obstructs *harmony and inner* – and outer! – *peace.*

64 Management is not about *preserving human life*, as Aquinas wrote, but the exploitation of human life. This is done even if it costs human lives (cf. Ford Pinto). The essence of management is to give preference to profit not to *preserving life* as demonstrated in: a) Bakan's *The Corporation: The Pathological Pursuit of Profit and Power* (2004); b) Chomsky's *Profit over People* (1999) among others (cf. www.babymilkaction.org/pages/boycott; and c) numerous websites: WWWs: wikipeida.org; geocities.com; breast-feeding.com; mcspotlight.org). These exemplify managerial misbehaviour and the fact that the virtues of management do not adhere to the principles acknowledged in the *Biblical commandments (thou shalt not kill, thou shalt not steal, and thou shalt not bear false witness).* Management have killed (from *Nestle's baby formula* to *Bhopal, Pinto*, etc.); they have stolen (from colonial exploitation to industrial spies), and they have borne false witness (senate inquiries, court cases, Enron, World.Com). None of the three commandments – *kill, steal, lie* – are in the essence of management. Instead the exact opposite has been executed by management ever since its invention (Taylor 1911; Marglin 1974; Klikauer 2007:97ff.).

65 The philosophy of trust dates back to Aristotle's idea of being *a trustworthy person. For that one must be a person who can be counted on.* One needs to be able *to take care of those things that others entrust to one and whose ways of caring are neither excessive nor deficient.* A distinction between *full* and *special* (in some cases only) trustworthiness has also been made. On *sincerity*, Jean-Paul Sartre (1992) noted *the essential structure of sincerity does not differ from that of bad faith since the sincere man constitutes himself as what he is 'in order not to be it'.* Therefore, management always needs to pretend to be *sincere* in order not to be seen as insincere. Given the managerial power and dominance over corporate communication (Klikauer 2007 and 2008), this has been achieved successfully. Management has been able to present itself as *sincere* – having corporate social responsibility (Subhabrata 2007) – and even as being an ethical actor (Beder 2000). On trustworthiness, Adorno (1944:38) noted *only that which they do not need to know counts as understandable; only what is in truth alienated, the words moulded by commerce, strikes them as trustworthy.* For Adorno, it is only when language has been recast in the absence of management that trust can be established. In the managerial use of language, words are deprived of their real meaning and put to use as deception. It is then, when people are asked to believe managerial *Weasel Words* (Watson 2003).

66 The core virtue of management is precisely not *calling one's self into question.* It appears as if management *is carried out in a morally indifferent and even selfish world, a world that is somehow placed beyond good and evil* (Jones et al. 2005:58). For Hegel (1821) selfishness has been enshrined in *the colonisation of new markets and the sphere of industrial activity* creating human *isolation* that *reduces him to the selfish aspect of his trade.* Hence, in Hegel's ethics of *Sittlichkeit*, the fundamental elementary structure of capitalism creates selfish human beings, preventing them from developing true human values.

67 Management is in a somewhat self-contradictory position. On the one hand, it does not acknowledge workers. On the other hand, conflict between management and workers still exists. Hence, conflict is pretended to be another issue that management has to manage, just like ethics. Therefore, *The Servants of Power* (Baritz 1960) have the tricky task of mentioning conflict without aiding the legitimacy of those who work under management.

68 For Adorno *Mündigkeit* also entails the ability of *not co-operating with a bad life* even though this might lead to *frustration, isolation, alienation, and despair* because co-operation with a bad life will not create a *good life of fulfilment and happiness*.

69 Even the often rehearsed textbook case of 3M does not show how an individual – despite management – contributes to the company's profits but it shows that *Mündigkeit* is not something management can use.

70 At the time when a banking CEO (Mr Moss) received $2,400/hr (even in his sleep!), workers are downsized (Orwell's Newspeak) or fired, while an unemployed person gets just $224/week (Horin 2009), any ethical claim by management is destroyed by its own actions.

71 Cf. utilitarian philosophers are also Francis Hutcheson (1694–1746) and Lytton Strachey (1880–1932).

72 This is in sharp contrast to Kant who demands that ethics be based on one's intentions. Management does have moral intentions. Its exclusive intention is however not *saving a fellow creature* but shareholder maximisation; cf. Williams' *A Critique of Utilitarianism* (2006).

73 Happiness and well-being carry connotations of hedonism (Epicurus 341–270 BC) that Mill developed into a hedonistic theory of value. This has been further modified into the *Swine Morality*.

74 In *Utilitarianism* (1861), Mill noted, *happiness intends pleasure and the absence of pain*. Management does not have the intention to create happiness. Its essence is not working towards *the absence of pain*. Accidentally, management might create happiness as a by-product of its action. If it creates pain (usually to others) management is sometimes at pains to justify it. It is often legitimised with '*it will be hard at first, but in the long run it will pay off*'.

75 The offloading of harm to others is an issue for corporate management in regard to customers (cf. Ford Pinto). The tobacco industry can relate to this.

76 Habermas' *Theory of Communicative Action* (vol. II; 1997:267–273).

77 Quoted from Driver (2007:59), cf. Layard's *Happiness – Lessons from a new Science* (2005).

78 Instead of treating individuals equally, management does the exact opposite. On top of that, it views the key organisation that seeks to achieve equality – trade unions – as the *Threat of Unionisation* (Kreitner 2009:42).

79 On consciousness, Marx (1844) noted: *consciousness can never be anything else than conscious existence, and the existence of man in their actual life-process*. According to Sidgwick, consciousness can be inherently good. But actual managerial processes and the *labour process* (Ackroyd and Thompson 1999) turn humans into objects of managerial power (Bauman 1989). The natural *inherently good consciousness* (Sidgwick) has been deformed by an

artificial process of management negating moral and ethical consciousness with the *Organisation Men* (Whyte 1961).

80 Cf. Mill's *Utilitarianism* (1861).

81 Not surprisingly, managerially governed workplaces are not places of happiness but rather represent what Layard (2005:48) called the *Hedonistic
Treadmill, where you have to keep running in order that your happiness stands
still.*

82 Happiness is also at the core of *Eudemonism* (Aquinas 1250 and Aristotle
35 BC). It states that *an action is good if it promotes or tends to promote the
fulfilment of goals constitutive of human nature and its happiness.*

83 Cf. Hegel's concept of satisfaction as intellectual and moral mastery
(Smith 1987:121).

84 On the unmentioned employees, Graves (1924) noted decades ago *the
organisation is a sort of hierarchy which chooses to ignore 'the little fellow'*
(1924:48); cf. Marsden and Townley (1996); Klikauer (2007:138).

85 Cf. Luxemburg (1870–1919) on *Democracy and Dictatorship* in: *The Russian
Revolution* (1919); Deetz's *Democracy in an Age of Corporate Colonization*
(1992); Canfora (2006); Klikauer (2008:95).

86 On this, Adorno and Horkheimer (1944) noted *the way in which a girl
accepts and keeps the obligatory date, the inflection on the telephone or in the
most intimate situation, the choice of words in conversations, and the whole
inner life as classified by the now somewhat devalued depth psychology, bear
witness to man's attempt to make himself a proficient apparatus. This is similar
to the model served up by the cultural industry.*

87 Cf. Arnold's *Satisfaction Measure* (2005:258) and *Modification of Work
Behaviour* (2005:276ff.).

88 Management hardly ever employs philosophers just as business schools
hardly ever employ them except in cases where a bit of *alibi-ethics* by *The
Servants of Power* (Baritz 1960) is in demand to give management the
appearance of being ethical. Having a mission statement on CSR is part of
The Myth System. Watson (2003:29) illustrates this in the following way:
*James and J. S. Mill wrote books that changed the course of history while
working for the East Indian Company, a multinational. Today they wouldn't.
Today they would be attending countless meetings, seminars and conferences to
update their knowledge of work-related subjects, all of them conducted in the
mind-maiming language of Managerialism.*

89 One of the godfathers of management, *Henry Ford, reportedly complained:
'Why is it that whenever I ask for a pair of hands a brain comes attached?'* Just
as the invention of the so-called and daily rehearsed *Scientific Management* talks about ox and gorilla in (dis)respect of workers, Ford also
thought that non-intellectual workers are the ones management needs.
Anti-intellectualism might even be in the essence of management.
Management is not an intellectual enterprise and so are those who support it. From business school professors to textbook writers with the very
occasional exception, of course (!), management has all but excluded intellectuals and replaced them with functionalists. Not surprisingly, standard
textbooks such as Kreitner (2009) not only look and feel like *Cosmopolitan,*
they are structured in a very similar way. Cosmopolitan and management
textbooks are easy to consume, have nice pictures, sell well, and, above

all, they are non-intellectual so that Drucker's *donkey* (Magretta 2002) can understand them.

90 In those few cases of commercial laws where corporate lobbying fails to achieve pro-management outcomes, management has the usual Hirschman-Options (1970) of *exit, loyalty, and voice*. It can ignore or bypass regulations (exit). If forced by courts management simply obeys them (loyalty), even at a cost to management, or it can fight them through the courts and lobby politicians for a more pro-management regulation (voice).

91 Schrijvers (2004:76) writes *a monopoly is excellent for us, because we can exploit it to make and keep people dependent on us. In our economy, business people, professionals and technicians profess gladly to embrace free market competition. Let's face it: it's all a sham. Given half a chance, any business would become a monopolist like a shot so that it could set the rules in its own interest.* The fourth version of power relates to back-up sources. *Most organisations have people who can make your life easier or harder. If you are able to acquire such a source of power yourself, consider yourself extremely fortunate, one down!* (cf. Schrijvers 2005).

92 *The important thing is to have a good memory so that you don't contradict the lies you have already told* (Macklin 2007:266).

93 One of the most insightful studies on this has been Nestle's corporate lying during the baby food scandal (cf. World Health Organisation).

94 Kreitner (2009:143–234); cf. Horkheimer (1937 and 1947); Horkheimer and Adorno (1947); Klikauer (2008:62–75).

95 For example, none of Whittington's four strategic options – *classical, evolutionary, systemic, and procedural* strategy (2001) – are related to ethics.

96 The motive of one of the foremost ethical philosophers, *Jeremy Bentham*, for writing his *Introduction to the Principles of Morals and Legislation* (1789) has been his resolute indignation about the fact that English governors preferred to exploit everyone and everything for their own benefit and advantage rather than serving the common good and not creating happiness but rather unhappiness. On unhappiness, Marcuse (1966) noted *'false' [needs] are those which are superimposed upon the individual by particular social interests in his repression: the needs with perpetuate toil, aggressiveness, misery, and injustice....the result then is euphoria in unhappiness.*

97 In his non-textbook study *The Morally Decent HR Manager*, Macklin (2007: 266) found *the important thing is to have a good memory so that you don't contradict the lies you have already told*. Sun *Microsystems'* CEO put an essential part of a reputation that way. *'Promises'*, he says, *'are still promises until somebody delivers the goods'*. Implicitly, he separated promises from delivery. The two are totally separated for management.

98 In *The High Cost of Managerialism*, Rees and Rodley (1995) have shown how things are off-loaded onto the public. This ranges from health costs of smoking, fast-food→obesity links, the months-long slow and painful choking and coughing death of asbestos victims without compensation, Ford Pinto's gas-tank explosions, Nestle's dying babies, the still unpaid victims of Bhopal, and so forth.

99 *We all need management* (Magretta 2002).

100 For Magretta (2002) *in a competitive world, doing a good job of creating value is only the necessary first step toward superior performance*; one also needs to

outperform its competitors. The other side will be defeated. This is what strategists call 'a zero-sum game'. Any victory for A is necessarily a defeat for B. Strategy in management is about winning.

101 Probably the only emotion management is truly capable of is *'love oneself'* as outlined in Schwartz's *Narcissistic Process and Corporate Decay* (1990).

102 By the time capitalism established itself and Mill wrote *Utilitarianism* (1861) management also started to manifest itself. Only 50 years later in 1911 management elevated itself to *Scientific Management* (Klikauer 2007:143–159).

103 Enlightenment has been seen as the negation of feudalism overcoming feudal limits of science and philosophical worldviews. Enlightenment's rationalism replaced the irrationalism of religion. When rationalism was elevated to an all-inclusive theme of Enlightenment, Kant developed his *three critiques* in response to that. Cutting off the critical element from Kant's *Critique of Pure Reason*, capitalism and management was left with *pure reason*. Management needs reason and *instrumental rationality* to operate. It does not need critique. However, without Kant's *Critique instrumental rationality* remains handicapped and insufficient. Nevertheless, management's *instrumental rationality* became one of the utmost distorted versions of the original Enlightenment project. One example is the allocation of labour based on instrumental rationality. Initially labour was told that technology and mechanisation will set them free from the bounds of feudalism but *mechanisation, the very means that should liberate man from toil, makes him a slave of his labour* (Marcuse 1941); cf. Kreitner (2009:13ff.).

104 Magretta (2002) quotes *Warren Buffett* who emphasised *somebody once said that in looking for people to hire, you look for three qualities: integrity, intelligence, and energy. And if they don't have the first, the other two will kill you.*

105 According to Schrijvers (2004), managers operating inside the *Moral Maze* (Jackall 1988) specifically set out to *hurt others* (cf. Schrijvers 2005).

106 In *Žižek's Ontology*, Johnson (2008:13) noted, *the prior sequence of various philosophies doesn't become 'Philosophy' per se until the advent of the Kantian 'Copernican' revolution.* Kant's *Copernican revolution* represents morality (Moralität) based on abstract formulas. His predecessor, Hegel, saw ethics as *Sittlichkeit*. This is based on social relations (Sterrett 1892:177). Hegel once called Kant's philosophy *Ursprungsphilosopie*, the original and first philosophy (Smith 1987:103).

107 Darwin follows Kant in his *The Origins of the Moral Sense*. Darwin said that *the difference between man and lower animals is a moral sense or conscious.* This *is by far the most important difference.*

108 Kantian ethics is based on *categorical imperatives*, not on hypothetical *'if-then'* constructions. However, nearly every textbook on management ethics contains sentences that use these constructions. They contravene Kant's ethics because they violate his categorical imperative. They are unethical in the Kantian meaning of ethics. Kant's categorical imperative renders claims that 'management should...', 'management needs to...', and 'management could...' obsolete. In Kant's *categorical imperatives* there is nothing to choose from. Either one follows Kantian ethics or one does not. Management represents the latter.

109 Kantian ethics is the negation of intuitionism and ethics based on feelings.

110 Marcuse (1941) thought that *the individual is determined not by his particular but by his universal qualities*; cf. Marcuse's *Kant* (1971:79ff.). Schrijvers (2004:76) writes: *a monopoly is excellent for us, because we can exploit it to make and keep people dependent on us. In our economy, business people, professionals and technicians profess gladly to embrace free market competition. Let's face it: it's all a sham. Given half a chance, any business, would become a monopolist like a shot so that it could set the rules in its own interest.* Magretta (2002) added: *business executives are society's leading champions of free markets and competition. Truth be told, the competition every manager longs for is a lot closer to Microsoft's end of the spectrum than it is to the dairy farmers. All the talk about the virtues of competition notwithstanding, the aim of business strategy is to move an enterprise away from perfect competition and in the direction of monopoly;* cf. Beder (2000).

111 The more problematic issue for management is Kant's formula which says: *act in such a way that you treat humanity, whether in your own person or in the person of another, always at the same time as an end and never simply as a means.* This is the most devastating *categorical imperative* for management. The essence of management is that it *operates through people creating performance through others* (Magretta 2002; Brunsson 2002). This raises a number of ethical dilemmas for management because management and Kantian ethics are *contradictions in concept* (Kant/Hegel). Cf. Sartre's *Condemned To Be Free* (1946); Nozick's *Anarchy, State and Utopia* (1974); Jones et al. (2005:45).

112 According to Jones et al. (2005:5) *the employment contract is treated as if it is not of concern for business ethics.* This is despite, or perhaps because, of the existing asymmetrical relationship between management and workers (Offe & Wiesenthal 1980). It was none other than one of the great inventors of management, Henry Ford, who claimed *'why is it that whenever I ask for a pair of hands a brain comes attached?'*; cf. Hegel (1807 and 1821); Kojève (1947); Honneth (1995); Sinnerbink (2007:101–122).

113 *Often, 80% of its profits come from 20% of its customers…it is universally true that some small numbers of 'x' (decisions, products, customers, distribution channels – you name it) will account for a disproportionately large percentage of results.*

114 On Kant's concept of the subject Johnson (2008:13f.) noted: *Kant, instead of Descartes, is the true founder of the notion of the subject…Kant's transcendental idealism focuses on the category of the 'subjective objective'* (cf. Negri 1970). Kant's successor Hegel negated Kant's concept of *the thing in-itself*. It falls apart once exposed to Hegelian dialectics.

115 German philosopher Fichte noted in his *Wissenschaftslehre* (1797–1800) that *a clear consciousness* is linked to *self-determination*. For management, this has to be avoided because most subordinates should never develop self-consciousness. They should not engage in self-determination either because this might lead to an awareness of the undemocratic, top-down, and hierarchical order enforced by management.

116 On self-determination Schrijvers's (2004) noted: *nothing instils greater fear in an organisation than people doing their own thing.*

117 If management grants some sort of partial self-determination inside, for example, semi-autonomous work teams, then it assures it always retains the controlling power over these teams. Thereby it negates Kant's ethics.

118 A classical case is the management of overseas subsidiaries by central management. Central management has three choices. It can send a local manager overseas, it can use an overseas manager, and it can use a so-called third-country national. Ultimately, any one of these three must make decisions on central management's behalf. In all three cases central management retains some control over decision-making. Some managers will exert more autonomy while others will use less when making decisions on behalf of central management but they all violate Kant's ethical concept of self-determination.

119 In his *The Fear of Freedom* (1960:215), the philosopher Erich Fromm noted *that truth is one of the strongest weapons of those who have no power*. This is exactly why the essence of management is not related to truth but to power.

120 According to Schrijvers (2004:14) *of course, we choose neutral terms, scientific terms, and we describe the law as follows: 'Managers give priority to the interest of the organisation in those situations where a conflict of interest occurs…we make use of scientific jargon to describe how we obstruct our boss and exclude our colleagues…objective language removes all emotion and nuance from the action that people initiate'* (Klikauer 2008:96–108; cf. Macklin 2007:266; Watson 2009).

121 Magretta (2002) writes it is important to have an overall sense of the direction when marching towards *management's real bottom line*. Management uses *strategy* inside a *battleground* even if this incurs *civilian casualties*.

122 Management is self-centred and ignorant of workers who Magretta (2002) merely calls *others*. It leads to the contradiction of: a) workers have been disrespected, reduced to mere *others*, and have been deliberately unrecognised (cf. Honneth's *The Struggle for Recognition*, 1995) while b) Boatright's standard textbook on *Ethics and the Conduct of Business* (2009) tells us that management '*respects*' them (cf. Sage 2007).

123 On Kant's *thing in-itself* Johnson (2008:17) noted: *the Ding an sich* [thing in itself] *evidently involves a paradox, an unsustainable contradiction*.

124 For that, affirmative textbook writers have to rule out treating people *only* as means. They cannot admit that management's essence, in accordance with Magretta (2002), is that *management operates through people*. They can also not admit that this totally contradicts Kant's idea of the *Kingdom of Ends* because it denigrates people to pure means, instruments, tools, apparatuses, and others and that their only purpose is to service management when it *operates through people*. In sum, the fact that the essence of management rests on the formula *management creates performance through others* does not allow for any other interpretation. If Kant contradicts the very essence of management, something else must be used to support management.

125 An example of this has been outlined in *Bowie's Version of Kant*, (Jones et al. 2005:43–48).

126 In Kreitner's 11th edition of *Management* (2009) 13 out of 546 pages are on ethics (2.37%). The rest is on the technicalities of management (97.63%).

127 In that way, ethics becomes a means to an end rather than being an *end in-itself*. It is also a form of managerially created knowledge. The worst expression of such ethical knowledge is when managers self-invent their own ethics in the absence of philosophical knowledge. In such cases, their self-invented quasi-knowledge on ethics is claimed to present ethics based on common sense. Kant labelled all versions of *common sense*-based knowledge *vulgar and unsophisticated*. For Kant common sense does not lead to ethics however critical reflection does (cf. Lukes 1985:100–138).

128 Management uses *strategy* inside a *battleground* even if this incurs *civilian casualties* (Magretta 2002). Schrijvers (2004:22) agrees with Magretta (2002). *People who know the battleground are better prepared than their opponents*. Inside the *Moral Maze* (Jackall 1988) of management there *is excitement about dirty tricks at corporate level* when *big companies with cruel and fraudulent CEOs* use *backstabbing and treachery to set the tone* in order to win on the battlefield (Schrijvers 2004).

129 Historically, Kant's universalism was directly opposed by management in the 18th century version of mercantilism. On this, Kant noted that it is essential not to confuse the point of *ethical duties* with duties as such. Because a *merchant who acts neither from duty nor from direct inclination but only for a selfish purpose* does not act inside what Kant sees as moral duty.

130 For example, the rule-obeying for *performance related pay* is designed for staff members while golden parachutes, CEO payouts, share options, special allowances (school fees, health insurance, free housing, etc.) and other bonuses are disconnected from actual achievements.

131 A good case in point is Kreitner's 11th edition of *Management* (2009) where workers appear as *workforce* on pages 61–66, a mere five pages out of 546 pages. It testifies to the claim that management and management textbooks *have a lot to say about those who manage, they are rather silent on those who are managed* (Klikauer 2007:129). Kreitner (2009) supports the claim that management has not much to say about those over whom they rule (cf. Honneth's *The Struggle for Recognition*, 1995).

132 Cf. Hegel (1807 and 1821); Kojève (1947); Adorno (1993); Sinnerbrink (2007:101ff.)

133 For two successors of Kant, German philosopher Hegel and later Marx, alienation is linked to employment and work. On this Marx (1844) noted: *alienation shows itself not only in the result; but also in the act of production, inside productive activity itself. Therefore, he does not confirm himself in his work, he denies himself, feels miserable instead of happy, deploys no free physical and intellectual energy, but mortifies his body and ruins his mind.* To prevent critical, reflective, and self-knowledgeable employees, management has invented a raft of measures starting with organisational behaviour to create the *Organisation Men* (Whyte 1961). Management needs to eclipse all feelings of misery and workplace pathologies (cf. Lukes 1985).

134 Bowles and Gintis' *Schooling in Capitalist America: Educational Reform and the Contradictions of Economic Life* (1976, 1981, 2001) delivers the reason for the fact that *almost all schooling is boring* (Albert 2006).

135 Cf. Whyte (1961); Beder (2000:193–272); Klikauer (2007:183ff.)

136 This is evident in just two examples. One is the wide, open, and empty country roads visible in nearly every car advertisement while the reality

for most drivers are jammed up city streets. The deception of the empty country road sells cars by deceiving drivers about the reality of car traffic. Secondly, almost every cereal box is at least one-third empty because a large box simply sells better and less content increases profits. It also means deceiving customers about the real content. Once you have internalised what 20-second advertisements tell you over and over again, self-deception starts. Similarly, when management's marketing experts start believing that those are good car advertisements and good cereal boxes and both are good for society, self-deception is established. On advertising, German philosophers Adorno and Horkheimer (1944) noted: *advertising today is a negative principle, a blocking device: everything that does not bear its stamp is economically suspect.* Inside corporations, management's use of deception ranges from faked promises of promotion to pay increases, workloads, etc. Corporate and managerial deception is truthfully depicted in Michael Moore's first documentary 'Roger and Me' (Moore, M. 1989. *Roger & Me* (documentary), Warner Brothers, December 20, 1989 (USA), 91 min. English).

137 *The numbers that truly matter are the ones that tell a story about how the organisation is doing* (Magretta 2002).

138 Bagley (2003:19) and Kinicki and Kreitner (2008:29).

139 In Kreitner's management textbook (2009:143–234) decision-making takes up 91 pages while ethics takes up a mere 13.

140 Several managerial ideologies are brought into gear to prevent this from occurring. These instruments prevent non-managerial staff from reaching their own understanding. They also advance a one-dimensional *managerial understanding* through the creation of a one-dimensional framework inside which the world of work is to be understood. It is not possible for management to follow the demands of Kantian ethics that are directed towards allowing non-managerial individuals' self-understanding. Management has to negate Kantian ethics in order to secure its own position. The managerial ideologies are established in management schools, induction programmes, corporate culture, leadership seminars, teamwork, corporate communication via newsletters, emails, brochures, as well as in more structured managerial initiatives such as promotions, remuneration, benefits, and bonuses.

141 Jean-Paul Sartre noted in his *Being and Nothingness* (1992) that *Kant's 'You ought, therefore you can' is implicitly understood.* Everything that *ought to be* always carries in it the seed of potentialities and of practical transformations.

142 The one-dimensional TINA approach of management remains stuck in *what is* while refraining from all utopian and speculative ideas about ethical possibilities. After all, management *includes all the activities associated with making something...and...all the activities associated with selling something.* For management any speculative thinking has to be confined to *selling something*, thus exterminating any form of ethics based on *what ought to be*. *Selling and making* are all about the self-invented so-called *hard facts* of business and *The Real Bottom Line*. What counts for management is not ethical speculation on *what ought to be* but thinking associated with making and selling. The essence of management, therefore, rests on *what*

is (making and selling) and not on *what ought to be*. Not surprisingly, neither management nor the discipline of management studies run by *The Servants of Power* (Baritz 1960) has been known for advances in ethical thinking (cf. Singer 1994; Shafer-Landau 2007; Shafer-Landau and Cueno 2007; Pogge and Horton 2008).

143 In his *The Problem of Hegel*, Watson (1894:548) calls Hegel '*the* philosopher *par excellence*' while Nietzsche talked about the enormous and still living influence of the Hegelian philosophy (Smith 1987:122). Kant's ethics is based on morality (Moralität) emphasising *abstract formulas*. Hegel (1803/4) saw ethics as *Sittlichkeit*, something that is based on social relations (Sterrett 1892:177); cf. Zizek's *Enlightenment – with Hegel*, in: Parker's *Slavoj Zizek – A Critical Introduction* (2004:36ff.); Kedourie (1995:93); cf. Sinnerbrink (2007).

144 This book has also been called *Phenomenology of Spirit*. But Hegel wrote on matters of the '*mind*' (Geist in German) and not on matters of *spirits* and *spirituality* (cf. Kedourie 1995:193–196; Speight 2008:27–50).There is also '*The Philosophy of History*' by G. W. F. Hegel (1830) which is not a real book published by Hegel but a series of lectures he gave during the winter term of 1830 and 1831. Its English language versions appeared in 1956 (recently republished in 2004). The same applies to his 1803/4 work on the *System of Ethical Life* (cf. Speight 2008:24 and 47–48; Sinderbrink 2007).

145 To achieve a sufficient level of *Mündigkeit*, philosopher Adorno saw that humans needed to be educated towards *Mündigkeit*. In his *Erziehung zur Mündigkeit* (1971), Adorno outlined how this could be achieved. What was needed is the Dealing with Germany's Nazi-Past, Philosophy and Teachers, TV and Education, Teaching as a Profession, Education after Auschwitz, Why Education, Education towards Non-Barbarian Principles, and Education towards *Mündigkeit*; (transl. into English); cf. Stoops (1913:459); Marcuse's Hegel (1971:95ff.); Taylor's *Ethics of Authenticity* (1991:8). Hegel rejected utilitarianism – on similar grounds to Kant – because it erodes the autonomy of reason.

146 Cf. Gadamer's *The Heritage of Hegel* (1983:38–68); Kelemen and Peltonen (2001:151).

147 Arnold (2005:625); Whyte's *The Organization Man* (1961); Ackroyd's and Thompson's *Organisational Misbehaviour* (1999).

148 The idea of a concept (Begriff) is essential for Hegel. As Adorno once outlined, *to think conceptually is to identify* and to identify issues is vital for philosophy (cf. Bernstein 2001; Speight 2008:62).

149 Cf. Levinas' *The Trace of the Other* in his *Totality and Infinity* (1961).

150 Cf. Wolff (2008). On the corporation, Hegel (1821) noted, *the corporation, of course, must come under the higher supervision of the state, for it would otherwise become ossified and set in its ways*. This is exactly what 20th century deregulation as part of neo-liberalism has achieved. It has – for most parts – removed the Hegelian *higher supervision of the state* by creating industry self-regulation that adheres to the widely accepted call for an *End of Red Tape* (Beder 2006). Hence, 21st century corporations have been increasingly able *to set* their *way*, just as Hegel predicted during the early 19th century.

151 According to Magretta (2002), *measurement is necessary* because *numbers truly matter* [for] *organisations*. Therefore, *good managers use numbers to create…purposeful action*.

152 On democracy, German philosopher Herbert Marcuse (1898–1970) noted, *a comfortable, smooth, reasonable, democratic unfreedom prevails in advanced industrial civilisations, a token of technical progress*.

153 As Schrijvers (2004) noted, *nothing instils greater fear in an organisation than people doing their own thing*.

154 On historical understanding, German philosopher Gadamer (1900–2002) noted, *the historical consciousness has the task of understanding all the witnesses of a past time out of the spirit of that time, of extricating them from the preoccupations of our own present life, and of knowing, without moral smugness, the past as a human phenomenon* (Baritz 1960; Thompson 1963; Foucault 1995; Arnold 2005).

155 Cf. Fromm's *Man is not a Thing* (1957) and *To have or to be?* (1995).

156 In the words of Magretta (2002) it *turns workers into consumers who could afford cars;* cf. Bauman (2009); Eagleton (2003:28) noted, *capitalism needs a human being who has never yet existed – one who is prudently restrained in the office and widely anarchic in the shopping mall*.

157 Marcuse (1966:87–126); Arnold (2005); Klikauer (2007 and 2008).

158 Cf. Enzensberger (1974); Habermas (1988); Zengotita (2005); Adorno (2006); Gore (2007); Klikauer (2007).

159 On the affirmation to social and managerial rules Marcuse (1966) noted, *under the conditions of rising standards of living, non-conformity with the system itself appears to be socially useless*.

160 Today, modern slavery largely exists in the form of economic bondage and sex-slaves to which any website (e.g. *International Labour Organisation*) will testify. On the whole, slavery has largely disappeared from advanced counties but carries on regardless in developing countries.

161 One of the immediate successors of Hegelian philosophy was Karl Marx (1818–1883). His main work is *Das Kapital – A Critique of the Political Economy*. It contains next to nothing on ethics, however, Marxian ethics still states that our concepts of ethics, justice, and injustice are *moulded to serve the interests of the ruling class* (Singer 1994:18; cf. Kedourie 1995:166–191). Marx, not unlike many other philosophers (Aristotle, Ahrasymachus, and even Nietzsche) saw that ethics is often created to aid one side's rule over the other. For Marx, management ethics would constitute nothing more than a structure of rules and principles created and enforced by a ruling group to rule over others. This is mirrored in all of today's corporations where one side – management – is the rule creator while the other side – those *who make things* (Aristotle) – are deemed to obey managerial rules and managerial ethics. Only in very few isolated cases has management ever invited those *who make things* (Aristotle) to participate in the creation of corporate ethics. And in next to no company has there ever been an ethical statement made by management that has been exposed to any form of democratic legitimacy. In sum, management truly fulfils what Marxian ethics had predicted during the mid-19th century (cf. Lukács' *History and Class Consciousness*, 1922).

162 Power is seen as a discursive phenomenon located in the context of material interest that represents different social formations. According to Dahl (1957), power has four properties attached to it: a) *base* as the base of power expressed in resources, opportunities, acts, objects, etc. that can be exploited in order to effect the behaviour of others; b) *means* or instruments such as threats or promises; c) *amount* of an actor's power expressed in probability statements such as '9 out of 10'; and d) *scope* that consists of responses that an actor receives during the application of power. Power can be seen as machinery in which everyone is caught, those who exercise it as much as those over whom it is exercised. Mumby (2001:588 and 595) emphasised *power resides not simply in relations of cause and effect* (as Dahl suggests), *but in structured relations of autonomy and dependence that are an endemic feature* of working life. Power's communicative aspect emphasises: *power is defined in terms of the ability of individuals or groups to control and shape dominant interpretation* at work (cf. Žižek 1989:31 & Habermas' *money and power code* 1997).

163 *Hegelian dialectics*, according to Johnson (2008:129), *is both an epistemology and an ontology, namely, a mobile, dynamic knowledge-process that, in its function [and, more importantly, malfunctioning], simultaneously reveals the very configuration of being itself.*

164 Taken from Hegel's *First Programme for a System of German Idealism* (co-authored with Schelling), paraphrased and adjusted to the world of management.

165 Cf. Watson (1894); Marcuse (1941); Taylor (1975); Gross (1976); Rockmore (1981 and 1992); Ritter (1982); Singer (1983); Cook (1984); Min (1986); Smith (1987); Honneth & Gaines (1988); Wood (1990); Luhmann (1991); Sterrett (1892); Adorno (1993), Žižek (1993); Kedourie (1995); Althusser (1997); Pinkard (2000); Baynes (2002); Belmonte (2002); Deranty (2005); Grumley (2005); James (2007); Speight (2008).

166 Cf. Magretta (2002), any textbook on management, on management ethics and any article in the popular management press and academic management journals testifies to that: *Administrative Science Quarterly, Academy of Management Executive, Academy of Management Journal, Academy of Management Review, Asian Pacific Journal of HRM, British Journal of Management, California Management Review, Harvard Business Review, Human Relations, Human Resource Management, Human Resource Planning, International Journal of HRM, Journal of Management, Journal of Management Studies, Journal of Organizational Change Management, Management Forum, Management Science, Personnel Review, Personnel Management, Personnel Psychology, Organisational Studies, Organisational Research Methods, Sloan Management Review, Strategic Management Journal,* etc.

167 Cf. Marcuse (1966); Marglin (1974); Offe and Wiesenthal (1980); Klikauer (2007).

168 On the recognition of the '*Other*' French philosopher Emmanuel Levinas (1906–1996) noted *we can recognise it in the desire for an other who is another [autrui], neither my enemy (as he is in Hobbes and in Hegel) nor my complement (as is still the case in Plato's Republic)...the desire for another is born in being that lacks nothing* (cf. Honneth 1995).

169 According to Jean-Paul Sartre's (1905–1980) *Being and Nothingness* (1992), we should refer here to Hegel's statement: '*Wesen ist was gewesen ist'.*

Essence is what has been. It indicates that everything that is (being) always includes something that has been.

170   Thompson (1963); Schwartz (1990); Foucault (1995); Bakan (2004); Schrijvers (2004); Arnold (2005); Macklin (2007).

171   Examples of industry self-regulation and the absence of state regulation can be found in: Boatright (2009:1, 25–26, 29, 55–56, 61, 82–83, 87, 105–106, 109, 133–134, 137, 160–162, 167, 197–198, 204, 242, 152, 259, 266, 305, 312, 336–341, 347, 370–373, 378, 408–410, 416, and 443–447).

172   In civil society, democracy has always replaced the bludgeon with a pen. Half a million years ago, men were hitting each other until one was left standing who was then declared the leader. Today, this is done by a pen. We vote for a leader but we still have one. We have made zero progress except for replacing the bludgeon with a pen.

173   Adorno (Finlayson 2002:8) noted there must be a critique on the *totally administered world* that represents a *concrete denunciation of the inhumanity* that such a world produces.

174   Management ethics tends not to focus on Kant's *categorical imperative* as the only permissible category of ethics. Instead, it focuses on Kant's hypothetical imperative which is Kant's category for non-ethics (cf. Fromm's *Fear of Freedom* 1960; Taylor's *Ethics of Authenticity* 1991:5; Korsgaard's *Kingdom of Ends* 1996).

175   'Mit entsprechendem Profit wird Kapital kühn. Zehn Prozent sicher, und man kann es überall anwenden; 20 Prozent, es wird lebhaft; 50 Prozent, positiv waghalsig; für 100 Prozent stampft es alle menschlichen Gesetze unter seinen Fuß; 300 Prozent, und es existiert kein Verbrechen, das es nicht riskiert, selbst auf Gefahr des Galgens. Wenn Tumult und Streit Profit bringen, wird es sie beide encouragieren. Beweis: Schmuggel und Sklavenhandel.' (P. J. Dunning, quoted in: Karl Marx, *Das Kapital* (1890), vol. I, p. 801, Dietz-Verlag Berlin, 1961). Translation: With adequate profit, capital is very bold. A certain 10% will ensure its employment anywhere; 20% certain will produce eagerness; 50%, positive audacity; 100% will make it ready to trample on all human laws; 300%, and there is not a crime at which it will scruple, nor a risk it will not run, even to the chance of its owner being hanged. If turbulence and strife will bring a profit, it will freely encourage both. Smuggling and the slave-trade have amply proved all that is stated here.

176   Magretta (2002) also states that management does what is *best suited to the organisational purpose.*

177   In Hegelian philosophy, society moves *in a progressive direction towards greater degrees of freedom for ever-larger numbers of people* (Smith 1987:117).

178   According to Smith (1987:99), Kant saw critique as an inquiry into the nature and limits of rationality. Hegel saw it as a form of an internal and intrinsic examination of the various sources of deception, illusions, and distortions (Lukes 1985; Ward 2006; cf. Baillargeon 2007).

179   See *Karl Marx, the philosopher*, in: McNeill and Feldman's *Continental Philosophy* (1998:215ff.); Marx/Engels' *Material Basis of Morality*, in: Singer's *Ethics* (1994:41–43; cf. 1980); Marx' *Das Kapital*, in: Russell's *Philosophical Classics* (2007:193ff.); cf. Kedourie (1995).

180   Samson and Daft (2009); Bauman (2009:31ff. and 1989); Hinman (2008: 299–300); Klikauer (2008); Driver (2007); Martin (2007); Shafer-Landau (2007); Wiggins (2006); Linstead et al. (2004); Singer (1994); Deetz (1992 and 2001); Rest (1999); Habermas (1990); Blum (1988); Reed (1987); Gilligan (1982); Goodpaster (1982); Kohlberg (1971, 1981, 1984).

181   Cf. Mumby (1988, 1997, 2000, 2001); Deetz (1992 and 2001); Rest et al. (1999:1–34); Habermas (1990); Blum (1988); Reed (1987); Goodpaster (1982); Kohlberg (1971, 1981, 1984) and Habermas (1990:116ff.).

182   Kohlberg also conducted research in Malaysian aboriginal villages, Turkey, and the Yucatán, Mexico to verify that his theory is not culturally based but universal.

183   For a good and critical adaptation to Managerialism see Linstead et al. (2004: 260–264).

184   A good example is Kant's categorical imperative to *act in such a way that you treat humanity, whether in your own person or in the person of another, always at the same time as an end and never simply as a means.* Immorality is the treatment of others as a *means.* Morality is the treatment of others as *an end in-itself.* This is what Kant meant by his *Kingdom of Ends* as the final and universal destination of every human being. In the case of moral management that designs a cheaper and safer commodity Kantian ethics differs fundamentally from *consequentialism.* In Kantian ethics the intentions and motives make management moral, not an accidental outcome. Management acts moral when it has the moral intention of creating a safer commercial commodity, not when it just happens as a by-product. For consequentialism only a good outcome is needed: if the product is safe, management has acted ethically. For Kant, good management is not morally good when it – accidentally or essentially – produces morally good results but when management is moral. This is perhaps the clearest case that exemplifies the power of Kantian ethics.

185   Mander (2001); O'Connell Davidson (2005); Pogge and Horton (2008); Monbiot's *Bring on the Apocalypse – Six Arguments for Global Ethics* (2008).

186   Cf. Klikauer (2007:143–159 and 163) on *managerial engineering ideologies* and *scripted behaviour.*

187   On the need for control Petrick and Quinn (1997:15) noted: *their managerial orientation is downward toward the reliable control of organisational operations;* cf. Townley (2005:306). According to Petrick and Quinn (1997:43), at the turn of the century, *Henry Ford (Ford vs. Dodge) wanted to share profits from his automobile company with his employees to improve their lives, but the Supreme Court sided with the position of Dodge that the fiduciary moral relationship with investors precluded the ethical sharing of profits with employees.*

188   Apart from the very occasional mentioning in mass-media, child-labour has, for the most part, disappeared from standard news headlines. Corporations in advanced countries have been able hide the use of child-labour through spatial elements (outsourcing to non-OECD countries) and corporate elements (subsidiaries, franchises, and loosely knitted network companies, etc.). In that way, child-labour has moved into the background for most people in advanced countries. The maxim *'if it's not on TV, it doesn't exist'* gives the appearance that the *problem* no longer exists.

189 Milgram found *the inverse ratio of readiness to cruelty and proximity to its victims. It is difficult to harm a person we touch. It is somewhat easier to afflict pain upon a person we only see at a distance. It is still easier in the case of a person we only hear. It is quite easy to be cruel towards a person we neither see nor hear* (Bauman 1989:155; cf. Connerton 1980).

190 Cf. http://www.unicef.org/protection/index_childlabour.html, http://www. hrw.org/children/labor.htm; Haspels and Jankanish (2000); Lieten (2004); O'Connell Davidson (2005).

191 Cf. Kafka's *'The Penal Colony'* (1919); Orwell's *Nineteen-Eighty-Four* (1949); Foucault (1995); Feldman (1998); Arnold (2005). On this, Adorno (1944: 74) emphasised that *Bettelheim's observation on the identification of the victims with the executioners of the Nazi camps contains a judgment on the higher seeding-grounds of culture, the English 'public school' [original in English], the German officer academy. The absurdity perpetuates itself: Domination reproduces itself all the way through the dominated.* The fear of punishment appears to be deeply enshrined in Christian value systems. In an article on *US Evangelists are Twisting the Bible*, Giles Fraser (2006:16) wrote *he that spareth this rod hateth his son: but he that loveth him chasteneth him betimes (Proverb 12:24)...Somehow, after eight of 10 licks, the poison is transformed into gushing love and contentment;* cf. Marcuse (1971); Beder (2000:193ff.); Baillargeon 2007:210ff; Passer and Smith (2007:627–631) .

192 Cf. Chomsky (1959, 1971); Beder (2000:93ff.); Baum (2005); Martin and Pear (2007).

193 Cf. Jacoby's *Conformist Psychology* (1977:46–72).

194 The ultimate way of *keeping labour cost low* (Magretta 2002) is the use of slave labour. In common mythology slave labour is a thing of the past and not the present even though it still exists (http://www.antislavery. org/ and http://anti-slavery.org); Bales and Trodd (2008); Craig et al. (2007); Nazer (2005); cf. Connerton (1980).

195 Cf. Marcuse (1941 and 1966); Adorno et al. (1964); Bauman (1989); Bowles and Gintis (1976, 1981, 2001).

196 On punishment and rewards, Magretta (2002) quoted *Peter Drucker* who had the last word. *One can never simply hire a hand, he wrote, the whole person always comes with it. And that is the problem.* In management, *workers had only to do exactly what they were told, and supervisors made sure they complied.* Management is about *having the authority to reward and punish – being in charge.* Skinner assumes that *punishable behaviour can be minimised by creating circumstances in which it is not likely to occur* (Chomsky 1971:33); cf. Apel (1980:180ff.).

197 This is in line with Foucault's predictions (cf. *Discipline and Punish*, 1995).

198 Cf. Reich (1946); Arendt (1951, 1958 and 1994); Bauman (1989).

199 A not uncommon view is that *my boss is a feudal psychopath, an incompetent nitwit who threatens everyone; he surrounds himself with boot-lickers* (Jackall 1988:97). Next to *psychopaths* (Punch 2008:107) there are also managerial *opportunists, fast trackers, and chameleons* (Petrick and Quinn 1997:62) while Petrick and Quinn (1997:103–104) noted that management is full of *arrogant people, greedy people, envious people, gluttonous people, jealous people, slothful people, hateful people, and resentful people.*

200 Cf. Schrijvers (2004); Schwartz (1990); Taylor (1991:14f.).

201 Concurrent with turning humans into *'objects of power'* goes the fostering of mechanisms that disallow these *'objects of power'* to ever realise what they are made into (Baillargeon 2007). Adorno (1944:22) has commented on this. He wrote, *part of the mechanism of domination is that one is forbidden to recognise the suffering which that domination produces, and there is a straight line connecting the evangelical lecture on the joy of life to the construction of slaughter-houses for human beings so far off in Poland, that everyone in one's own ethnic group can convince themselves they don't hear the screams of pain* (cf. tenBos 1997).

202 People are often degraded to *others* and eliminated from most management writings that testify to the total absence of the term *labour*. In contrast, Karl Marx called these *others 'producers'* because they – not management – *make things*. Standard management texts are blissfully ignorant to *labour*. This indicates Karl W. Deutsch's definition of power: *power is the ability not to learn* (Offe and Wiesenthal 1980). It also shows that management is in a powerful position. Management and its affirmative writers can afford to be ignorant because they have power.

203 The banality of evil has been expressed by Arendt (1994) and *Management by Fear* is discussed in Klikauer (2008:164). On guilt, Schwartz (1990:43) noted, *in asserting its control over the participant's guilt, the organisation asserts its right to end it and asserts that it, itself, is free of guilt*. This applies not only to the de-personalised term 'the organisation' but also to the equally de-personalised term 'management'. The managerial structure of every company depicts an Egyptian pyramid, designed to generate and secure authority. Ideologically, HRM's idea of promotions as a pathway to the top is no more than an illusion for the vast majority of those *who make things* (Aristotle). Numerically, the pyramidal structure of corporations acts against HRM's ideology of promotions. The idea of promotions is part of the arsenal of managerial weapons. The careerist orientation of others is very helpful because they want to appear *'promotable'*, co-operative, helpful, showing upward appeal, and signal competitiveness. Senior management needs to foster the illusion of success and promotion and loyalty, compliance, coalition-building, and collusion are virtually guaranteed (Schrijvers 2004).

204 Katz and Kahn (1966:352) emphasised that *most people don't get promoted at all. Most production workers remain production workers, and most typists remain typists*. In fact, those in managerial authority are numerically shielded against those in the lower ranks.

205 According to Magretta (2002) hierarchies and lines of authority are essential to management. *Self-organisation...sounds seductive but is wishful thinking because as a concept for management self-organisation is fundamentally flawed.*

206 Cf. Marcuse (1966); Foucault (1995); tenBos (1997); Leslie's *Walter Benjamin – Overpowering Conformism* (2000).

207 Bauman (1989:151ff.); cf. Baillargeon (2007:210ff.).

208 As much as Bauman's thesis that the Holocaust was an application of modern managerial means and not the work of evil and insane monsters is correct, it can in no way relieve Germans and German Nazis from their collective guilt. Bauman explains – he does not excuse.

209 According to Magretta (2002), management *must keep cost down* through *co-ordination and co-operation that come with hierarchy (that is, with ownership)* establishing clear *command-and-control structures.*

210 Magretta (2002) noted on authority, it is *the sometimes invisible, but always important, lines of authority* that make management possible. And, *having the authority to reward and punish – being in charge* is the essence of management...*people need clarity about roles, authority, and accountability...designing the organisation – drawing its boundaries and lines of authority.* And on obedience, Schrijvers (2004) noted, *all of this* [management] *is bountiful ground for authoritarian, totalitarian, anti-democratic, inhuman, and unethical conduct usually administered from managers above. It demands obedience and servility from those below.*

211 According to Magretta (2002), it is not so much the *de-layering* as there are *the sometimes invisible, but always important, lines of authority* that are relevant to management. While standard management textbooks focus on the myth of *de-layering*, the managerial reality focuses on *lines of authority* and there are plenty of lines.

212 *Impression management* enables managers to act towards *self-enhancement* that consists of *seeing oneself responsible for positive outcomes and others responsible for negative outcomes...so that the subordinate has to see the world in a way that enhances, not his or her own self-image, but the self-image of the leader* (Schwartz 1990:25; cf. Rosenfeld et al. 1995).

213 Schrijvers (2004) noted, *an important source of power can be found in all sorts of rules, regulations, procedures, statues, and laws. We call these formal sources. You can find tips about how to uphold your rights and how to evade your responsibilities.*

214 According to Magretta (2002), in management, *everyone is focused on the problem they have to solve. Too often, managers are forced by deadlines and other pressures to look at a problem and simply ask, 'how can I resolve this in the quickest way?'.*

215 Delaney (2005:2004) writes, *Friedman, in his classical book Capitalism and Freedom, noted that 'there is one and only one social responsibility of business – to use its resources and engage in activities designed to increase its profits'.*

216 Moral selfishness and ethical egoism represent the opposite of Kant, Hegel, and utilitarianism. Utilitarianism includes the *Greatest Happiness Principle* demanding the greatest amount of happiness for the greatest number of people. Ethical egoism denotes that people only do what they want to do. The only moral reason for doing something is that you want to do it. Moral egoism requests that I have a moral obligation to do what matters to me. Moral egoism demands that I am someone who is not moved by the predicament of others, of society, or of universal humanity (Kant). A moral egoist is *not distressed by the distress of others.*

217 Actors who subscribe to moral egoism are made to do what management wants them to in expectation of rewards. Magretta (2002) quoted *Peter Drucker* who *had the last word. One can never simply hire a hand, he wrote, the whole person always comes with it. And that is the problem. Workers had only to do exactly what they were told, and supervisors made sure they complied.* Management is about *having the authority to reward and punish – being in charge.*

218 This negates Greek virtue ethics, Kant, Hegel, Rawls, and utilitarianism.

219 Chomsky (1994:9) wrote *146 countries...ratified the international convention on the rights of children, but one had not: the US. That's a standard pattern of international conventions on human rights. However, just of fairness, it's only proper to add that...conservatism is catholic in its anti-child, anti-family spirit, so the World Health Organisation (WHO) voted to condemn the Nestle Corporation for aggressively marketing their infant formula which kills plenty of children. The vote was 118 to 1. I'll leave you to guess the one. However, this is quite minor compared with what the WHO calls the 'silent genocide' that's killing millions of children every year as a result of the free market policies for the poor and the refusal of the rich to give any aid. Again, the US has one of the worst and most miserly records among the rich societies.* While written in 1994, it appears that not much progress has been made since then (cf. Monbiot 2008).

220 According to Magretta (2002) *good managerial negotiators see the deal through the other party's eyes. Increasingly, our working relations – up, down, and lateral – have come to resemble negotiations.* Management deems some relationships as absolutely necessary. These are conducted through *give and take* negotiations in a *zero-sum game.*

221 For non-textbook writer Schrijvers (2004:16–18) management often *mouths phrases about 'openness and honesty', 'commitment', 'synergy', and yet they know that top management always keeps essential information to itself, that personnel says one thing in the canteen and another in meetings, and that everybody fences in their own little backyard.*

222 The ability to bargain for oneself reflects Gare's concept of *The Triumph of the Airheads and the Retreat from Commonsense* (2006). One does not need managerial and technical expertise but a Machiavellian character.

223 Cf. Nietzsche (1886); Marcuse (1972); Weber (1904–05); Beder (2000); Ward (2006).

224 It might have culminated in a maxim like this: *believe in God and obey the church, and no punishment will come to you.* Today's version is: *believe in management and Managerialism and obey the will of management and no demotion, dismissal, pay-cut, etc. will come to you.*

225 If one seeks to position HRM inside Kohlberg's morality, it reflects level three (3). It complies with management's wishes and is instrumental rather than ethical. According to Legge (2005:39) this *rules out a truly Kantian ethical position;* (cf. Simon and Barnard 1965).

226 The 'we...' ideology of HRM has been put into three perspectives by Stewart (2007:73): *knowledge = cognitive domain = we think; values = affective domain = we feel; skills = action domain = we do* (cf. Jacoby's *Conformist Psychology,* 1977:46–72; 1997).

227 According to Magretta (2002) *we all learn to think like managers.* As a consequence, now we *'Manage your Family';* instead of having relationships, now we *'Manage your Relationship';* and instead of having a sex life, now we *'Manage your Sex Life',* and so on.

228 In opposing *self-alienation, existentialism* argues that its quintessential maxim for humans is the idea of self-determination as the only possible response to *acting in good faith.* Self-determination represents the core of existentialism's radical freedom. When we say *'I can't do this because I*

must...' we often create false necessities. We justify something that operates on the '*I can*' or '*I can't*' level rather than on the level of necessity: 'I must'. Such forms are a delusion because there is no practical necessity for saying '*I must*'. We can always choose the affirmative or the negative, to accept or reject something. Humans have the ability to choose. Hence we must avoid affirmation to operate in accordance with our political masters, people in authority, and managers. The only thing of real substance is that we arrive at an ethical answer by a free and independent process of rational-ethical thought. On the downside rests the fact that individuals who claim radical freedom must also be able to accept the full responsibility for their action. They must be able to carry the consequences.

229 Cf. Marcuse's *A study on Authority [1936]*, in his: *Studies in Critical Philosophy* (1972:49–156).

230 In managerially guided books this conversion is portrayed as: *organisational socialisation represents the processes by which an individual makes the transition from 'outsider' to 'organisational member'* (Jex 2002:62). There are '*individuals*' (Unspeak: 'worker', Poole 2006) who work in '*organisations*' (Unspeak: profit-making companies) who do not '*make*' but are '*made to be*' *Organisation Men* (Whyte 1961; cf. Simon and Barnard 1965*)*. Obviously, they have been *outsiders* (outsider = negative and insider = positive). Who wants to be an outsider if one can be an insider? Now they can be *organisational members* like members in a sports club. Managerial language like that masks the reality of work. The conversion of humans into profit-maximising human resources/material makes it possible that *new members can learn the culture of an organisation* (Jex 2002:62). It is a deeply psychological process that relies heavily on behaviourist theories. It converts human beings into conforming *objects of power* (Bauman 1989) directed towards profits. This is cloaked as *given the opportunity to learn a culture*. In reality it is system integration into a one-dimensional managerial process of *productive behaviour* (Jex 2002:87). There is no *culture in corporations:* no arts, no music, no opera, no movies, no paintings, no sculptures, etc. (Adorno 1944; Alvesson 2002).

231 Most interestingly, the voice in advertising is almost always a male voice. Male voices sound authoritarian. They establish authority over a target audience enticing consumers into buying.

232 Bowles & Gintis' *Schooling in Capitalist America: Educational Reform and the Contradictions of Economic Life* (1976; cf. 1981 and 2001); *Bauman's Hurried Life, or Liquid-Modern Challenges to Education*, 2009:144ff.).

233 This has been supported by the French religious philosopher *Blaise Pascal* who thought that *the wise citizen would not seek political participation, but would live simply and quietly, away from the political arena* (Krailsheimer 1980:39). He also emphasised that *the sole cause of man's unhappiness is that he does not know how to stay quietly in his room* (Krailsheimer 1980:53).

234 A good example of labour-management relations at stage four is DeCeri and Kramer's (2005:629) chapter on *Fundamental Rights of Employees*.

235 Managerial rules and HRM policies operate implicitly/formal and explicitly/ informal. In the first case, rules are stated publicly (codified) while in the latter they are non-codified (dress codes); cf. *Adam Smith's On the Role of Positive Laws in Humankind's Evolution* (Evensky 2005:59–84).

236 The task is to close Hirschman's (1970) exit-option, lower the voice-option, and increase the loyalty-option.

237 In system theory, rules are established as neutral elements that establish system equilibriums (static). Simultaneously, they establish the managerial status quo, i.e. they asphyxiate power relationships between management and labour. System theory is a most welcome tool in the hands of *The Servants of Power* (Baritz 1960). It establishes domination by redirecting and confining emancipatory energies towards the self-balancing of the system.

238 Hesiod (700 BC) thought that *just man is above all a law-abiding one*. The association of justice and *nomos* runs deep in Greek thinking (Barney 2004).

239 *Utilitarianism* has the ethical goal of happiness that is achieved through the *Happiness Principle*. It denotes the moral demand to create *the greatest happiness for the greatest number of people* as outlined in the chapter on utilitarianism. Somewhat influenced by utilitarianism Kantian *formulism* and *universalism* denotes specific rules that govern morality (Chapter 4). Through a critique on Kant, Hegel developed the ethical concept of *Sittlichkeit*. It is based on social conditions (Chapter 5). Hegel also saw ethics related to the *master-slave dialectics* (Chapter 6). Rawls' (1921–2002) *Theory of Justice* (1971) and *Political Liberalism* (1993) and *A Theory of Justice* in: Shafer-Landau (2007); Nozick (1974); cf. Marx (1890); Goodrich (1920); Chandler (1962); Marglin (1974); Jacoby (1977); Ramsay (1977); Styron (1979); Offe and Wiesenthal (1980); Honneth (1995); Rosenfled et al. (1995); Bird (1996); Punch (1996 and 2008); Searle (1996); Unger (1996) in: Pogge and Horton (2008); Monbiot (2008); Gladwell's (2002) *The Talent Myth*, www.newyorker.com/printables/fact/0207222fa_fact; Whittington (2001); Bagley (2003:19); Bakan (2004); www.corporatewatch; Sample et al. (2004:445–455); Gautrey and Phipps (2006); Wiggins (2006: 198); Leap (2007); Minkes and Minkes (2008); Klikauer (2007: 128–142 and 149–159 and 208ff.); Klikauer (2008: 45f. and 96–108); Schaefer (2007: 166); Kinicki and Kreitner (2008:29); Boatright (2009:1, 25–26, 29, 55–56, 61, 82–83, 87, 105–106, 109, 133–134, 137, 160–162; 167, 197–198, 204, 242, 152, 259, 266, 305, 312, 336–341, 347, 370–373, 378, 408–410, 416, and 443–447); Kreitner (2009:42 and 121).

240 Cf. Budd and Scoville (2005:5) includes *fairness and justice*. Bowie's *Kantian Ethical Thought* (2005:61ff.); cf. Bauman (1989); Parker (1998); Singer (2000 and 2005).

241 According to Magretta (2002) management is about *creating value for shareholders* – not stakeholders – and to *maximise value for shareholders* [because already] *Milton Friedman has argued that the shareholder must always come first.*

242 Kant uses the ethical example of a shopkeeper who operates honestly because it is good for business and not because his morality motivates him to do so. This shopkeeper acts immoral because his motivation is not based on ethics but on business.

243 Watson (2003:48) has summed this up in the following way: when those who speak the managerial language *wish to demonstrate their concern for the less fortunate or the less profitable, or the community at large, they speak of*

addressing the triple bottom line through corporate social responsibility known as CSR...Principally...their language has been stripped of meaning. They don't have words like generous, charitable, kind, and share...welfare, wealth transfer, social service, social benefit, social policy, and social contract. Watson's look at the starved language of management makes visible that their focus is neither on *social* issues nor on *morality* and, above all, not on *social morality.*

244   Together with Marcuse, Fromm, Adorno, Horkheimer, and Honneth, Habermas is one of the latest representatives of the so-called *Frankfurt School* that became known as '*Critical Theory*' (Klikauer 2007:76–96). It is in the tradition of Kant's *Three Critiques* (1781, 1788, 1790), *Hegel*'s dialectical philosophy, and Marx' *Kritik der politische Ökonomie* or *Critique of the Political Economy – Das Kapital (1890)*. It advocates *immanent critique* (internal inconsistencies and contradictions) and *defetishising critique* (a procedure of showing that what appears as given is in fact not a '*natural fact*' but a historically and socially formed reality (Benhabib 1986:21); cf. Baillargeon (2007).

245   *In the established vocabulary, violence is a term which one does not apply to the action of the police, the National Guard, the Marshals, the Marines, the bombers. The bad words are a priori reserved for the enemy, and their meaning is defined and validated by the actions of the enemy regardless of their motivation and goal* (Marcuse 1966:75). Adorno (1944:5) commented on this: *by adapting to the weaknesses of the oppressed, one confirms in such weaknesses the prerequisite of domination, and develops in oneself the measure of barbarity, thickheadedness and capacity to inflict violence required to exercise domination.* He (1944:65) emphasised that *violence, on which civilization is based, means the persecution of all by all, and those with persecution manias miss the boat solely, by displacing what is brought by the whole onto their neighbours, in the helpless attempt to make incommensurability commensurable.*

246   Adorno (1944:22) noted *the decomposition of human beings into capabilities is a projection of the division of labour on its presumed subjects, inseparable from the interest in deploying them with ulterior motives, above all in order to be able to manipulate them.*

247   According to Heath (2003:4) *the key idea in Habermas' theory of communicative action is that speech acts cannot be planned or executed with entirely strategic intent.* Ideal speech, *communicative action, and communicative ethics* cannot be instrumentally guided towards strategic goals. They need to fulfil conditions that free communication from system interferences.

248   Management needs to *put the best people on the biggest opportunities and the best allocation of dollars in the right places* (Magretta (2002).

249   One of the key problems of management is that it is a male occupation (most CEOs and most Fortune-500s are men or run by men); most textbooks are written by men for men; and most teaching of management subjects at universities is done by men. This leads to a certain gender blindness that also exists in management ethics (Chanter 2006).

250   One of the most prominent voices in advanced animal rights is the philosopher Peter Singer's *Animal Liberation* (1975); *Practical Ethics* (1993); *Writings on an Ethical Life* (2000); cf. Singer (2005); cf. *Animal Rights & Environmental Ethics* in Olen et al. (2005:452ff.). This represents the exact opposite of what

Stoops (1913:462) detected: *it is said that the packing houses turn to profit every part of the pig but its squeal.*

251 *'Mono'*-culture reflects consumer society as a monopoly on culture in which *culture* has been reduced to saleability. It is the monopoly of the market that determines what culture is. The seemingly fast array of consumer choice provides no more than cosmetic alterations of the same thing. These ornamental choices of consumerism are paralleled by a significant reduction of life-choices creating a one-dimensional society of *birth→school→work→consumerism→death* (Marcuse 1966).

252 Bauman (2009:194ff.); Olen et al. (2005); Light and Ralston (2003); Chanter (2006); Desjardins (2006 and 2007).

253 The managerial process demands that nature is nothing more than a commodity to be used and – if needed – abused when shareholder values are at stake. Like no other life-form on earth, managerial corporations intervene in nature on a scale unseen in the history of planet earth. It started with gold, silver, and copper mining in South America, moved on to the slave trade through the triangle of death, to oil exploration (Middle East), and the attempted patent of an entire natural rainforest as the latest act. This has had a ravaging effect on nature and culminated in the distinction of entire species and global warming. Almost everything management does to nature indicates the total opposite of Kohlberg's ethics at level seven. For Mander (2001) it is *corporate misbehaviour*. For Magretta (2002) it is the essence of management that demands the treatment of nature in such a way.

254 If truth does not fulfil managerial demands, it is without value to management. What counts for management is saleability, not truth. Marcuse (1966:143) saw truth inside an existing order as problematic because *when truth cannot be realised within the established social order, it always appears to the latter as mere utopia.* Management is not a utopian enterprise. It deals with facts and figures, with here and now, and with *'what is'* rather than with *'what ought to be'* (Kant).

255 In life-centred morality it is *the good (well-being, welfare) of individual organisms* [that is] *considered as* entity. *It has inherent worth that determines our moral relations with the Earth's wild communities of life. From the perspective of a life-centred theory, we have prima facie moral obligations that are owed to wild plants and animals themselves as members of the Earth's biotic community* (Taylor 2004:505; cf. Olen et al. 2005:485ff.).

256 According to Magretta (2002), *operating measures and financial measures tell managers how well they're using resources, people, facilities, and capital. Good managers know they can't live without performance measures...resource allocation is one of those awful, technocratic phrases that make people's eyes glaze over* but management is essentially about allocating resources.

257 For Singer (1990) *the idea of equality is a moral idea, not an assertion of fact. The principle of the equality of human beings is not a description of an alleged actual equality among humans; it is a prescription of how we should treat human beings.*

258 Singer (1990:494–495) notes *the capacity for suffering and enjoyment is a prerequisite for having interests at all, a condition that must be satisfied before we can speak of interests in a meaningful way. A stone does not have interests*

because it cannot suffer. A mouse, for example, does have an interest in not being kicked along the road, because it will suffer if it is. If a being suffers there can be no moral justification for refusing to take that suffering into consideration. No matter what the nature of the being, the principle of equality requires that its suffering be counted equally with the like suffering – insofar as rough comparison can be made – of any other being; cf. Regan (2006).

259 Singer (1990:495) emphasises that *racists violate the principle of equality by giving greater weight to the interests of members of the own race when there is a clash between their interest and the interests of those of another race. Sexists violate the principle of equality by favouring the interests of their own sex. Similarly, speciesists allow the interests of their own species to override the greater interests of members of other species.*

260 German philosopher Herbert Marcuse (1898–1979) *called private profits a totalitarian logic* in his work The *One-Dimensional Man* (1966).

261 Arrington (1998:24); Klikauer (2008:108ff.).

262 Cf. Petrick & Quinn (1997:26). The infamous *prisoner dilemma* was first created by Flood and Dresher of the Rand Corporation and popularised by Neumann and Morgenstern (1944).

263 The idea of individualism has been highlighted by Danish philosopher Søren Kirkegaard (1813–1855) who emphasised that *only as the single individual is he the absolute, and this consciousness will save him from all revolutionary radicalism;* cf. Feinberg's *Psychological Egoism* (1978).

264 All ethics is subjective to each individual human being. It differs from individual to individual and there is no universal morality and no universal ethical standard. It is the extreme opposite of Kantian universalism. Therefore, *moral relativism* is highly suitable to management. Under moral relativism management can claim that everyone is different. We are not all the same and therefore morality is different too. Even every system of ethics is different and there have been many different forms of ethics – some of which are even contradictory to each other. Consequently, every company and every management can act differently, have different moral standards, and still be an ethical actor. It is also the complete opposite of the *Universal Declaration of Human Rights* which applies to anyone without exception.

265 Cf. G. E. Moore's *Pincipia Ehica* (*The Principles of Ethics*).

266 This is not to say that scepticism about moral values is the same as nihilism. Nihilism and Nietzsche are not widely read inside business ethicists (Jones et al. 2005:169; cf. Warren 1988:13ff.).

267 For Nietzsche (1880) *radical nihilism is the conviction of an absolute untenability of existence when it comes to the highest values one recognises; plus the realisation that we lack the least right to posit a beyond or an in-itself of things that might be divine or morality incarnate.*

268 Arrington (1998:367ff.); American ethicist *Henry Sedgwick* argued that there is no such thing as an objective moral truth.

269 Kojève (1947) noted that *man can appear on earth only within a herd...the human reality is a social reality.* The first part carries connotations to Nietzsche's herd morality in which there is a leader and followers. The second part reflects on the sociological character of human beings.

270 For Nietzsche, it was the priestly caste that was responsible for changing the notion of badness – initially denoting the plebeian.

271   On Nietzsche's understanding of values and the blindness thereof, the philosopher Gadamer (1900–2002) noted: *Nietzsche traces the value-blindness back to the conflict between the alienated historical world and the life-powers of the present.*

272   It testified to that as much as managerial capitalism's support for tyrannical regimes including Italian Fascism, Franco's Falange in Spain, Chile's Pinochet as well as virtually every single South American and Caribbean country during the 19th and 20th century, Indonesia, the Philippines, post-WWII South Korea, Iraq, Persia/Iran, Morocco, Tunisia, Egypt, Kenya, South African apartheid, and Blood Diamonds in other African countries to name a few. For management, tyranny, dictatorship, oppression, and autocracy have never been a hindrance but *industrial democracy* has. *Industry tyranny* would not, is not, and never has been a hindrance for management. More often than not, management operates with tyrannical methods but surely never with democratic ones. Aristotle was right: managers have always provided the *sort of man they want*. And these men are not *democratic men* but *Organization Man* (Whyte 1961). Management's men are *pleasant companions in the tyrants' favourite pursuit* (Aristotle).

273   Hesiod's '*Works and Days*' (ca. 700 BC) does not define justice, but the injustices he denounces include bribery, oath-breaking, perjury, theft, fraud (Barney 2004).

274   The Mother Theresas and Nelson Mandelas of this world are poor while top-management, CEOs, and business owners bathe in money and power.

275   Callicles (Greek: Καλλικλης) is a character in Plato's dialogue *Gorgias*. He is an Athenian citizen, who is a student of the Sophist Gorgias. In the dialogue, he argues that it is natural and just for the strong to dominate the weak and that it is unfair for the weak to resist such oppression by establishing laws to limit the power of the strong (approx. 483 BC). We know nothing about Callicles and he may even be Plato's literal or poetic invention. Callicles argued that the institutions and moral codes of his time were not established by Gods but by men who were looking after their own interests (Barney 2004).

276   This simply follows from the fact that *when two men desire the same thing which cannot be enjoyed by both, they become enemies.* For management *this is what strategists call 'a zero-sum game'* because what one gains, the other one loses. On strategies, Hobbes warns that defensive strategies – *the general-ship of deceiving an enemy* (Klikauer 2007:129ff.) – are not enough to protect ourselves. Hence, management has developed a raft of forward-looking and aggressive strategies, called *strategic management*. It is offensive rather than defensive. As Hobbes explains, management must *mistrust others* and hence *anticipate attacks*, called friendly or unfriendly corporate take-overs. Management must *seek to subdue* its business enemies before they subdue them. Cf. Magretta (2002); this is very much in line with the so-called *Pareto-Optimum* stating that *no one could do better without someone else doing worst;* cf. Buskirk (1974). These are the classical lessons taught at almost every management school. According to Magretta (2002), the essence of management is to *know the battleground* and to be *better prepared than* one's *opponents*.

277   According to Magretta (2002), in the managerial war game *the other side will be defeated*. In the *strategists zero-sum game any victory for 'A' is necessarily a defeat for 'B'*. Philosopher Hobbes supports this notion.

278   Magretta (2002) noted that to *sustain a competitive advantage* is paramount for management...*in a competitive world, doing a good job of creating value is a necessity*.

279   Cf. Bernays (1928); Chomsky's *Media Control – The Spectacular Achievements of Propaganda* (1991) and *Profit over People: Neoliberalism and Global Order* (1999); Beder's *Free Market Missionaries – The Corporate Manipulation of Community Values* (2006); Michael Wolff (2008) noted in his authorised biography of News Limited's CEO, Rupert Murdoch, *The Man Who Owns The News*, It's this company that acts in a hungry, animal fashion. That impulse is not modulated in any way. It's raw. It's real (Munro 2008:46).

280   Buchanan & Badham (2008:40ff.); cf. Buskirk (1974:7).

281   Nietzsche's idea of *strong vs. weak* carries strong connotations of the *survival of the fittest*. Despite the common myth, *survival of the fittest* has not been invented by Darwin but by *social-Darwinist* Herbert Spencer (1820–1903). Darwin assigned his idea of survival to adaptation to environmental changes. Spencer – without the empirical foundation of Darwin – claimed it is down to the fittest. The ideology of *the survival of the fittest* became popular during the rise of industrial capitalism in the 19th century. It is still carried through in management. Representing an ideology, social-Darwinism has been important to justify free-market capitalism. It is used as an ideology and as a weapon against the opponents of competition. It is directed against those who see human society not based on rivalry, opposition, and antagonism, but on solidarity, community, and mutual support. Management, managers, Managerialism, and corporate PR have linked competition and survival to the *survival of the fittest* and corporate mass media have successfully moored it in the mind of the public. Darwin's *The Decent of Man* (1871); cf. German philosopher Max Scheler's (1874–1928) *Man's Place in Nature*.

282   Management needs to follow Noble Prize Winner Milton Friedman's (1970) maxim: *it is the social responsibility of business to increase its profits*. Already on the first page of Sage's *Encyclopedia of Business Ethics and Society* (Sage 2007), Milton Friedman's famous statement is mentioned (cf. Jones et al. 2005:161).

283   According to Magretta (2002) *we all need management, managers can also control events, managers get organisations to perform*, and *managers will go about their business of making things work*. As Magretta (2002) says *management creates performance through others;* e.g. Bhopal, James Hardie Industries, Seveto, Enron, Ford Pinto, and simple downsizing and outsourcing activities.

284   Following one's instincts is something *we have inherited from our non-human ancestors* (Singer 1994:6).

285   Engels (1892); Webb and Webb (1894); Thompson (1963); Arnold (2005:250); Brown and Kelly's *You're History!* (2006).

286   Management tends to employ the rather nonsensical term of *pro-active*.

287   It appears that most of Nietzsche's ethics is nothing more than a reversal of traditional Greek ethics. He also seems to have misappropriated large

sections of Hegel and simply reversed it; Hegel's *Master-Slave* dialectics becomes the power of the strong to rule the weak in Nietzsche.

288   Schrijvers (2004:16–18) was correct when he stated that managers *feel...employees think only about themselves.*

289   On the uncritical belief in technology, German philosopher Herbert Marcuse (1966) commented: *technological rationality reveals its political character as it becomes the great vehicle of better domination, creating a truly totalitarian universe in which society and nature, mind and body are kept in a state of permanent mobilisation for the defence of this universe.*

290   Tellingly, Nazi-philosopher Heidegger (1889–1976) emphasised on interpretation: *the manner of access and interpretation must instead be chosen in such a way that this being can show itself to itself on its own terms.* In other words, the being of management must select interpretations that show management to management in management's terms. Hence, management is the centre, creates its own interpretations on its own terms, and thereby creates its own reality that only needs to be projected onto others.

291   Horkheimer and Adorno (1947:12) emphasised: *as immovably, they insist on the very ideology that enslaves them.*

292   This has been perfectly summed up by the former US president, George W. Bush who said: *we're an empire now, and when we act, we create our own reality. And while you're studying that reality – judiciously, as you will – we'll act again, creating other new realities, which you can study too, and that's how things will sort out. We're history's actors...and you, all of you, will be left to just study what we do.*

293   Cf. Wood (1990:195). Hegelian *Sittlichkeit* does not represent Kantian formalism or utilitarian happiness but has freedom as its goal.

294   In management, we already find similar institutions. These range from Ombudsmen to EEO-officers (equal employment opportunity) and affirmative action experts.

295   Given the proven failure of industry self-regulation (anti-trust laws, competition laws, contract laws, accounting regulations, shareholder regulations, corporations law, OHS laws, consumer protection laws, taxation laws, IR laws, working time laws, maternity laws, banking regulations, etc.), the introduction of *ethics councils* cannot be left to industry alone. It has to be legislated by governments. An *Ethics Council Act* needs to make them compulsory for all profit- and non-profit companies. It should state that whenever managerial decisions impact on *human beings, plant and animal life*, the *ethics council* has to approve such action. Failure of an ethics approval needs to incur civil and criminal sanction. All operating costs of such councils are to be covered by companies in full. Their operation, facilities, staffing, resources, finances, etc. have to be equal to top-management. An ethics council is elected in any company. If a company has between five and 20 employees, at least two employees should compose a council. With 21–50 employees, a council should have at least three members. 51–100 employees = 5 members, 101–500 = 9 members, 501–1,000 = 13, 1,001–2,000 = 17 members. After that for every 1,000 employees, two more ethics council members should be elected. In companies with more than 200 employees, at least one ethics council member should be fully relieved from all work commitments. In companies

between 200 and 500 employees, two members should be relieved. From 501–1,500 three, from 1,501–2,000 four, from 2,001–5,000 five, and thereafter all members should dedicate their time fully to council affairs.

296 Cf. McCarthy's *Kantian Constructivism and Reconstructivism: Rawls and Habermas in Dialogue* (1994).

297 *In the established vocabulary, violence is a term which one does not apply to the action of the police, the National Guard, the Marshals, the Marines, the bombers. The bad words are a priori reserved for the enemy, and their meaning is defined and validated by the actions of the enemy regardless of their motivation and goal* (Marcuse 1966:75). Adorno (1944:5) commented on this: *by adapting to the weaknesses of the oppressed, one confirms in such weaknesses the prerequisite of domination, and develops in oneself the measure of barbarity, thickheadedness and capacity to inflict violence required to exercise domination. Violence, on which civilization is based, means the persecution of all by all, and those with persecution manias miss the boat solely, by displacing what is brought by the whole onto their neighbours, in the helpless attempt to make incommensurability commensurable.*

298 Adorno (1944:22) noted *the decomposition of human beings into capabilities is a projection of the division of labour on its presumed subjects, inseparable from the interest in deploying them with ulterior motives, above all in order to be able to manipulate them.*

299 *In general, statements are attempts to describe issues or situations in the world which exist independent of the statement. The statement will be true or false depending on whether these things really are the way the statement says they are* (Searle 1996:200).

300 Eco (1977:159) noted that *Kant explicitly states in the first Kritik that the activity of our reason consists largely…in the analysis of ideas which we already have with regard to objects.* Kant saw that when we communicate or construct statements during a discourse, we reflect on the objective world through ideas that we – at least partially – have already been familiar with. The creation of such ideas, however, has to be done rationally. Only this process can advance discourses (cf. Cook 2004:71ff.; Baillargeon 2007).

301 Social-moral action must, in many parts, be able to overcome all forms of previously conditioned authoritarian and social control mechanisms that have colonised the human mind from early childhood onwards (Klikauer 2007:183–204).

302 Groupthink is a highly problematic mode of thinking. It occurs when group members intentionally conform to what they perceive to be the consensus of the group. The group tends to find solutions and common agreements that are, in fact, not based on objective assessments. Groups reach false conclusions and false agreements because of false internal assumptions. Groupthink causes groups to reach false conclusions. It can result in irrational decisions and actions. Groupthink is dysfunctional social group behaviour. The best known example of group thinking has been the US invasion of the Bay of Pigs in Cuba. The wrong decision is largely attributed to *groupthink*. *Group thinking* led a closed-off group of so-called governmental experts in the mistaken belief that an invasion was the right thing to do. It was a mutually reinforcing and escalating degree of a group-internal hysterical anti-communism.

303 Often this is reaffirmed through a raft of management texts, seminars, conferences, journals, newspapers, esteemed professors, reputable business schools, and honourable journals, etc. They are all trapped into a CCTV-like cybernetic system of a self-regulating network confined to endless circular motions in support of management. It isolates management and its *Servants of Power* (cf. Lynd 1939; Baillargeon 2007) from being challenged by discomforting reports and evidence, *critical management studies* (Grey and Willmott 2005), contradictory evidence, counter-arguments, the pure force of Kant's *Critique of Pure Reason*, and Hegelian negatives and contradictions. Instead, it strengthens and secures their circular self-invented and self-affirmative belief-system that is based on something closely resembling *group thinking* (Janis 1985; cf. Rosenfeld et al. 1995).

304 Neither *thought* nor *communication* can bring about social change unless they are transformed into moral action.

305 Chomsky (1966:26) noted that *if a man acts in a purely mechanical way, we may admire what he does, but we despise what he is.*

306 Many conservative models of human behaviour in social science assume that humans can be reasonably approximated or described as rational. This is especially the case in system theory, behaviourism, and rational choice theory. Many neo-liberal economic models assume that people are hyper-rational, and would never do anything to violate their preferences. In reality, however, most people are only partly rational because subjectivity often prevails. They are emotional and sometimes even irrational. Hence many of their actions are not rational actions (e.g. emotional marketing). Agents trapped in bounded rationality experience limits in formulating and solving complex problems. The processing, receiving, storing, retrieving, and transmitting of information and meanings is not thoroughly rational.

307 *Communicative ethics* as much as natural or managerial science can fail when products remain unsold, commodities are unwanted, bridges collapse, satellites crash into planets, space rockets explode, computers break down, software deletes itself, atomic power stations release deadly radioactive gases, etc.

308 A dilemma can be seen as a situation that requires a choice between options that are – or seem to be – equally unfavourable or mutually exclusive. This is a problem that seems to defy a satisfactory solution. It also creates an argument that presents two alternatives both of which have the same consequence.

309 Managerialism and advanced capitalism had to deal with system integration and the social integration of workers. System integration mobilised counteractive forces.

310 The SWOT analysis is a managerial tool used for instrumental planning. It is used to evaluate the strengths, weaknesses, opportunities, and threats of a managerial project or business venture. It is a form of instrumental decision-making that confines thinking and communication into four boxes directed towards highly functional forms of communication. In extreme cases, this can be a form of TINA. It pretends that there are no alternatives to SWOT, it delivers infallible outcomes, it is overtly rational, and delivers the right decisions at the right time.

311 Social philosophers (not Charles Darwin) have created the idea of *the survival of the fittest* and the *fight of all against all* to survive. This idea supports capitalism's idea of competition. Corporate mass-media have successfully – but wrongly – assigned it to Charles Darwin. But the vast majority of animal life relies on co-operation – not competition – for survival. Darwin's real idea has been the *survival of those who can adapt* themselves to natural changes. Overall, animals, early humans, and humans in advanced societies rely more on co-operation than on competition to survive. We all depend on others. The survival-of-the-fittest ideology presents a somewhat alien idea to human life and economic affairs. It is an ideology that supports competition. In reality large parts of our economy are based on co-operation, oligopolies, and monopolies.

312 On the social character of language, Chomsky (1966:26) noted *for Humboldt, a language is not to be regarded as a mass of isolated phenomena – words, sounds, individual speech production, etc. – but rather as an 'organism' in which all parts are interconnected and the role of each element is determined by its relation to the generative process that constitutes the underlying form.* For that reason, workers' language was developed in the workers' domain during the 19th century. Historically, it was connected to the *workers' milieu*. This proletarian milieu has been comprehensively defeated by corporate mass-media and petty-bourgeois lifestyles. And as such the language used by corporate mass media has influenced people's language use. What has been seen during the last 200 years is a gradual replacement of workers' language by the language of corporate mass media and Managerialism. For example, there are no more talks on workers' co-operatives, industrial democracy, syndicalism, and so on. Today it is all about *key performance indicators*.

313 Increasingly labour has to overcome Managerialism's and corporate mass-media guided de-solidarisation (cf. mechanical vs. organic solidarity, in http://durkheim.itgo.com/solidarity.html).

Bibliography

Adorno, T. W. 1944. *Minima Moralia – Reflections from the Damaged Life*, Dennis Redmond (2005) translation: http://www.efn.org/~dredmond/MinimaMoralia. html

Adorno, T. W. 1959. *Kant's Critique of Pure Reason*, Stanford: Stanford University Press.

Adorno, T. W. 1971. *Erziehung zur Mündigkeit*, Frankfurt: Suhrkamp Publishing.

Adorno, T. W. 1973. *Negative Dialectics*, London: Routledge.

Adorno, T. 1993. *Hegel – Three Studies*, Cambridge: MIT Press.

Adorno, T. W. 2005. *Critical Models – Interventions and Catchwords*, New York: Columbia University Press.

Adorno, T. W. 2006. *The Cultural Industry* (reprint), London: Routledge.

Adorno, T. W. & Horkheimer, M. 1944. *The Culture Industry: Enlightenment as Mass Deception*, Transcribed by Andy Blunden 1998; proofed and corrected Feb. 2005, web-download, November 2005.

Adorno, T. W., Frenkel-Brunswick, E., Levinson, D. J. & Nevitt, R. 1964. *The Authoritarian Personality*, New York: John Wiley.

Ackroyd, S. & Thompson, P. 1999. *Organisational Misbehaviour*, London: Sage.

Ahlers, R. 1975. How Critical is Critical Theory? Reflections on Jurgen Habermas, *Philosophy and Social Criticism*, vol. 3.

Albert, M 2006. *Realizing Hope – Life beyond Capitalism*, London: Zed Books.

Allee, W. C. 1931. *Animal Aggregations: A Study in General Sociology*, Chicago: The University of Chicago Press.

Allee, W. C. 1938. *The Social Life of Animals* (1st ed.), New York: Norton.

Althusser, L. 1997. *The Spectre of Hegel – Early Writings*, London: Verso.

Althusser, L. 2001. *Lenin and Philosophy and Other Essays*, New York: Monthly Review Press.

Alvesson, M. 2002. *Understanding Organisational Culture*, London: Sage.

Apel, K-O. 1980. *Towards a Transformation of Philosophy*, London: Routledge.

Arendt, H. 1951. *The Origins of Totalitarianism*, Orlando: A Harvest/HBJ Book.

Arendt, H. 1958. *The Human Condition*, Chicago: Chicago University Press.

Arendt, H. 1994. *Eichmann in Jerusalem: A Report on the Banality of Evil*, New York: Penguin.

Arnold, J. 2005. *Work Psychology – Understanding Human Behaviour in the Workplace* (4th ed.), London: Prentice-Hall.

Arrington, R. L. 1998. *Western Ethics – An Historical Introduction*, Oxford: Blackwell Press.

Bagley, C. E. 2003. The Ethical Leader's Decision Tree, *Harvard Business Review*, February, p. 19.

Baillargeon, N. 2007. *A Short Course in Intellectual Self-Defense – Find your inner Chomsky*, Toronto: Seven Stories Press.

Bakan, J. 2004. *The Corporation – The Pathological Pursuit of Profit and Power*, London: Free Press.

Bales, K. & Trodd, Z. 2008. *To Plead Your Own Cause: Personal Stories by Today's Slaves*, Cornell: Cornell University Press.

Baritz, L. 1960. *The Servants of Power: A History of the Use of Social Science in American Industry*, Middletown: Wesleyan University Press.

Barney, R. 2004. Callicles and Thrasymachus, *Stanford Encyclopaedia of Philosophy* (internet: first published: Wed Aug. 11, 2004).

Barthes, R. 1987. *Criticism and Truth*, London: Athlone Press.

Baudrillard, J. 1993. *Symbolic Exchange and Death*, London: Sage.

Baudrillard, J. 1994. *Simulacra and Simulation*, Ann Arbor: University of Michigan Press.

Baum, W. 2005. *Understanding Behaviorism – Behavior, Culture, and Evolution*, Oxford: Blackwell.

Bauman, Z. 1990. Effacing the Face: On the Social Management of Moral Proximity, *Theory, Culture & Society*, vol. 7.

Bauman, Z. 1993. *Postmodern Ethics*, Oxford: Blackwell.

Bauman, Z. 1994. Morality without Ethics, *Theory, Culture & Society*, vol. 11.

Bauman, Z. 1989. *Modernity and the Holocaust*, Oxford: Blackwell.

Bauman, Z. 2005. *Work, Consumerism, and New Poor* (2nd ed.), Maidenhead: Open University Press.

Bauman, Z. 2009. *Does Ethics have a Chance in a World of Consumerism?*, Cambridge: Harvard University Press.

Baxter, G. D. & Rarick, C. A. 1987. Education for the Moral Development of Managers: Kohlberg's Stages of Moral Development and Integrative Education, *Journal of Business Ethics*, vol. 6, no. 3, pp. 243–248.

Baynes, K. 2002. Freedom and Recognition in Hegel and Habermas, *Philosophy and Social Criticism*, vol. 28.

Beder, S. 2000. *Selling Work Ethics – From Puritan Pulpit to Corporate PR*, London: Zed Books.

Beder, S. 2006. *Free Market Missionaries – The Corporate Manipulation of Community Values*, London: Earthscan Press.

Bell, D. 1960. *The End of Ideology*, Glencoe: Free Press.

Belmonte, N. 2002. Evolving Negativity: From Hegel to Derrida, *Philosophy and Social Criticism*, vol. 28.

Benhabib, S. 1986. *Critique, Norm and Utopia – A Study of the Foundations of Critical Theory*, New York: Columbia Press.

Berger, P. & Luckmann, T. 1967. *The Social Construction of Reality*, New York: Garden City.

Bernays, E. 1928. *Propaganda* (2005 edition), New York: IG Publishing.

Bernstein, R. J. 1992. *The New Constellation*, Cambridge: MIT Press.

Bernstein, J. M. 2001. *Adorno – Disenchantment and Ethics*, Cambridge: Cambridge University Press.

Bird, F. B. 1996. *The Muted Conscience – Moral Silence and the Practice of Ethics in Business*, Westport: Quorum Books.

Bleicher, J. 1980. *Contemporary Hermeneutics*, London: Routledge.

Blum, L. 1988. Gilligan and Kohlberg: Implications for Moral Theory, *Ethics*, vol. 98, no. 3.

Blumenberg, H. 1990. *Work on Myth*, Cambridge: MIT Press.

Boatright, J. R. 2009. *Ethics and the Conduct of Business* (6th ed.), London: Pearson.

Bordum, A. 2005. Immanuel Kant, Jurgen Habermas and the Categorical Imperative, *Philosophy and Social Criticism*, vol. 13, no. 7.

Bowie, N. E. 1999. *Business Ethics – A Kantian Perspective*, Oxford: Blackwell.

Bowie, N. E. 2005. Kantian Ethical Thought, in: Budd, J. & Scoville, J. (eds), *The Ethics of Human Resources and Industrial Relations*, Champaign: Labor and Employment Relations Association.

Bowie, N. E. & Werhane, P. 2005. *Management Ethics*, Oxford: Blackwell.

Bowles, S. & Gintis, H. 1976. *Schooling in Capitalist America: Educational Reform and the Contradictions of Economic Life*, New York: Basic Books.

Bowles, S. & Gintis, H. 1981. Contradictions and Reproduction in Educational Theory, in: Barton, L. (eds), *Schooling, Ideology, and Curriculum*, Sussex: Falmer Press.

Bowles, S. & Gintis, H. 2001. *Schooling in Capitalist America Revisited*, http://www-unix.oit.umass.edu/~bowles.

Brecht, B. 1960. *The Caucasian Chalk Circle*, London: Methuen Press.

Brown, H. C. 1935. The Ethical Evaluation of a Social Order, *International Journal of Ethics*, vol. 45, no. 4.

Brown, M. & Kelly, R. (eds) 2006. *You're History!*, London: Continuum.

Brunsson, N. 2002. *The Organisation of Hypocrisy – Talk, Decisions and Actions in Organisations* (2nd ed.), Abingdon: Marston Books.

Buchanan, D. & Badham, R. 2008. *Power, Politics, and Organisational Change* (2nd ed.), London: Sage.

Budd, J. & Scoville, J. 2005. Moral Philosophy, Business Ethics, and the Employment Relationship, in: Budd, S. & Scoville, J. (eds), *The Ethics of Human Resources and Industrial Relations*, Champaign: Labor and Employment Relations Association.

Burawoy, M. 1979. *Manufacturing Consent*, Chicago: Chicago University Press.

Buskirk, R. H. 1974. *Modern Management and Machiavelli*, New York: Meridian Books.

Calaco, M. & Atterton, P. (eds) 2003. *The Continental Ethics Reader*, London: Routledge.

Campbell, J., Parker, M. & ten Bos, R. 2005. *For Business Ethics*, London: Routledge.

Canfora, L. 2006. *Democracy in Europe – A History of an Ideology*, London: Blackwell.

Caputo, J. D. 1993. *Against Ethics – Contributions to a Poetics of Obligation and Constant Reference to Deconstruction*, Bloomington: Indiana University Press.

Chandler, A. 1962. *Strategy and Structure*, Cambridge: MIT Press.

Chanter, T. 2006. *Gender – Key Concepts in Philosophy*, New York: Continuum.

Chomsky, N. 1959. *Review of Skinner's Verbal Behavior, Language*, vol. 35, no. 1.

Chomsky, N. 1966. *Cartesian Linguistics – A Chapter in the History of Rationalist Thought*, London: Harper & Row.

Chomsky, N. 1971. The Case against B. F. Skinner, *The New York Review of Books*, December 30th (internet download).

Chomsky, N. 1991. *Media Control – The Spectacular Achievements of Propaganda* (2nd ed.), New York: Seven Stories Press.

Chomsky, N. 1994. *Democracy and Education, Mellon Lecture*, Loyola University, Chicago, October 19th, download: www.zmag.org/chomsky/talks/.

Chomsky, N. 1999. *Profit Over People: Neoliberalism and Global Order*, New York: Seven Stories Press.

Ciulla, J. B. (eds) 2004. *Ethics, the Heart of Leadership* (2nd ed.), Westport: Praeger.
Clegg, S. & Rhodes, C. (eds) 2006. *Management Ethics – Contemporary Contexts*, London: Routledge.
Collins, D. 2000. The Quest to Improve the Human Condition: The First 1,500 Articles Published in Journal of Business Ethics, *Journal of Business Ethics*, vol. 26, no. 1.
Connerton, P. 1980. *The Tragedy of Enlightenment: An Essay on the Frankfurt School*, Cambridge: Cambridge University Press.
Cook, D. 1984. Hegel, Marx and Wittgenstein, *Philosophy and Social Criticism*, vol. 10.
Cook, D. 2004. *Adorno, Habermas, and the Search for a Rational Society*, London: Routledge.
Cottingham, J. 1995. *Descartes*, Oxford: Blackwell.
Craig, G., Gaus, A., Wilkinson, M., Skrivankova, K. & McQuade, A. 2007. *Contemporary Slavery in the UK*, London: Rowntree Foundation.
Dahl, R. A. 1957. The Concept of Power, *Behavioural Science*, vol. 2, pp. 210–215.
Damasio, A. R. 1994. *Descartes's Error – Emotion, Reason, and the Human Brain*, New York: Avon Books.
Darwin, C. 1871. *The Decent of Man, and Selection in Relation to Sex* (2nd ed.), London: John Murray.
D'Augusto, F. 1986. *Chomsky's System of Ideas*, Oxford: Clarendon Press.
DeCieri, H. & Kramer, R. 2005. *Human Resource Management in Australia* (2nd ed.), Sydney: McGrath-Hill.
Deetz, S. 1992. *Democracy in an Age of Corporate Colonization*, Albany: State University of New York Press.
Deetz, S. 2001. Conceptual Foundations, in: Jablin, F. & Putnam, L. (eds), *The New Handbook of Organizational Communication – Advances in Theory, Research, and Methods*, London: Sage.
Delaney, J. 2005. Ethical Challenges to Labor Relations, in: Budd, S. & Scoville, J. (eds), *The Ethics of Human Resources and Industrial Relations*, Champaign: Labor and Employment Relations Association.
Deleuze, G. & Guattari, F. 1994. *What is Philosophy?*, New York: Columbia University Press.
Deranty, J. P. 2005. Hegel's Social Theory of Values, *Philosophical Forum*, vol. xxvi, no. 3.
Deranty, J. P. & Renault, E. 2007. Politicizing Honneth's Thesis of Recognition, Thesis Eleven, no. 88.
Descartes, R. 1628. Rules for the Direction of our Native Intelligence, in: Descartes, R. 1988 edition of *Descartes Selected Philosophical Writings*, Cambridge: Cambridge University Press.
Desjardins, J. E. 2006. *Environmental Ethics – An Introduction to Environmental Philosophy*, Belmont: Thomson – Wadsworth.
Desjardins, J. E. 2007. *Business, Ethics, and the Environment*, London: Pearson.
Devas, C. S. 1899. The Moral Aspect of Consumption, *International Journal of Ethics*, vol. 10, no. 1.
Dewitt, M. & Hanley, R. 2006. *The Blackwell Guide to the Philosophy of Language*, Oxford: Oxford University Press.
Dreier, J. (eds) 2006. *Contemporary Debates in Moral Theory*, Oxford: Blackwell.
Driver, J. 2007. *Ethics – The Fundamentals*, Oxford: Blackwell.

Dryzek, J. 1996. *Democracy in Capitalist Times – Ideals, Limits, and Struggles*, Oxford: Oxford University Press.

Dugatkin, L. A. 1997. *Cooperation Among Animals – An Evolutionary Perspective*, Oxford: Oxford University Press.

Eagleton, T. 1990. *The Significance of Theory*, Oxford: Blackwell.

Eagleton, T. 1994. *Ideology*, London: Longman Press.

Eagleton, T. 2003. *After Theory*, New York: Basic Books.

Ecke, V. W. 1982. Ethics and Economics: From Classical Economics to neo-Liberalism, *Philosophy and Social Criticism*, vol. 9.

Eco, U. 1977. *A Theory of Semiotics*, London: Macmillan.

Edwards, R. 1979. *Contested Terrain*, London: Heinemann.

Engels, F. 1892. *The Condition of the Working Class in Britain in 1844*, London: Allen & Unwin (reprint 1952).

Enzensberger, H. G. 1974. *The Consciousness Industry – On Literature, Politics, and the Media*, New York: Continuum Book, The Seabury Press.

Evensky, J. 2005. *Adam Smith's Moral Philosophy – A Historical and Contemporary Perspective on Markets, Law, Ethics, and Culture*, Cambridge: Cambridge University Press.

Feinberg, J. 1978. Psychological Egoism, in: Cahn, S. & Markie, P. (eds), 2006. *Ethics – History, Theory, and Contemporary Issues* (3rd ed.), Oxford: Oxford University Press.

Feldman, F. 1978. *Introductory Ethics*, Englewood Cliffs: Prentice Hall.

Feldman, S. 1998. Playing with the Pieces: Deconstruction and the Loss of Moral Culture, *Journal of Management Studies*, vol. 35. no. 1.

Feyerabend, P. 1981. *Realism, Rationality, and Scientific Method*, Cambridge: Cambridge University Press.

Feyerabend, P. 1987. *Farewell To Reason*, London: Verso.

Finlayson, J. G. 2002. Adorno on The Ethical and The Ineffable, *European Journal of Philosophy*, vol. 10, no. 1.

Fodor, J. A. & Katz, J. J. 1964. *The Structure of Language*, Englewood: Prentice-Hall.

Foucault, M. 1995. *Discipline and Punish: The Birth of the Prison*, New York: Vintage Books.

Fox, A. 1966: Managerial Ideology and Labour Relations, *British Journal of Industrial Relations*, vol. 4, no. 3, pp. 366–378.

Fraser, G. 2006. Suffer, the Little Children, *The Guardian Weekly*, vol. 174, no. 26, p. 16.

Friedman, M. 1970. The Social Responsibility of Business is to Increase its Profits, *The New York Magazine*, 13th September 1970.

Fromm, E. 1957. Man is not a Thing, *Saturday Review*, vol. 40.

Fromm, E. 1960. *The Fear of Freedom*, London: Routledge.

Fromm, E. 1995. *To Have or To Be?*, London: Abacus.

Gadamer, H-G. 1985. *Philosophical Apprenticeships*, Cambridge: MIT Press.

Gadamer, H-G. 1998. *Reason in the Age of Science*, Cambridge: MIT Press.

Gare, S. 2006. *The Triumph of the Airheads and the Retreat from Common-sense*, Ch. 8: Management for Airheads, Double Bay (Sydney): Media21 Publishing.

Gautrey, C. & Phipps, M. 2006. *21 Dirty Tricks at Work*, New York: MJF Books/Fine Communications.

Gibbs, J. 2003. *Moral Development and Reality – Beyond the Theories of Kohlberg and Hoffman*, London: Sage.

Gilligan, C. 1982. *In a Different Voice: Psychological Theory and Women's Development*, Cambridge: Harvard University Press.

Gladwell, M. 2002. *The Talent Myth*, www.newyorker.com/printables/fact/0207222fa_fact.

Goldman, A. I. 1993. Ethics and Cognitive Science, *Ethics*, vol. 103, no. 2.

Goodchild, P. 1997. Deleuzean Ethics, *Theory, Culture & Society*, vol. 14.

Goodpaster, K. 1982. Kohlbergian Theory: A Philosophical Counterinvitation, *Ethics*, vol. 92, no. 3.

Goodrich, C. L. 1920. *The Frontier of Control*, London: Pluto Press.

Gore, A. 2007. *The Assault on Reason*, London: Bloomsbury.

Graham, G. 2004. *Eight Theories of Ethics*, London: Routledge.

Graves, H. B. 1924. Codes of Ethics for Business and Commercial Organisations, *International Journal of Ethics*, vol. 35, no. 1.

Greco, J. & Sosa, E. (eds) 1999. *The Blackwell Guide to Epistemology*, Oxford: Blackwell.

Green, A. 1999. *The Work of the Negative*, London: Free Association Books.

Green, R. M. 2001. What does it Means to Use Someone as 'A Means Only': Rereading Kant, *Kennedy Institute of Ethics Journal*, vol. 11, no. 3.

Grey, C. & Willmott, H. (eds) 2005. *Critical Management Studies – A Reader*, Oxford: Oxford University Press.

Gross, R. 1976. Speculation and History: Political Economy from Hobbes to Hegel, *Philosophy and Social Criticism*, vol. 4.

Grumley, J. 2005. Hegel, Habermas, and the Spirit of Critical Theory, *Critical Horizons*, vol. 6, no. 1.

Gurciullo, S. 2001. Making Modern Indentity: Charles Taylor's Retrieval of Moral Sources, *Critical Horizons*, vol. 2, no. 1.

Habermas, J. 1986. *Autonomy & Solidarity – Interviews with Jürgen Habermas* (ed. By Peter Dews), London: Verso.

Habermas, J. 1987. *Knowledge and Human Interests*, Cambridge: Polity Press.

Habermas, J. 1988. *Structural Transformation of the Public Sphere*, Cambridge: MIT Press (reprint 2006).

Habermas, J. 1990. *Moral Consciousness and Communicative Action*, Cambridge: Polity Press.

Habermas, J. 1997. *The Theory of Communicative Action: Reason and the Rationalisation of Society*, Volume I & II, reprint, Oxford: Polity Press.

Haigh, G. 2006. *Asbestos House: The Secret History of James Hardie Industries*, Melbourne: Scribe.

Hamilton, C. & Dennis, R. 2005. *Affluenza – When Too Much is Never Enough*, Sydney: Allen & Unwin.

Harding, N. 2003. *The Social Construction of Management – Texts and Identities*, London: Routledge.

Hare, R. M. 1989. *Essays in Moral Theory*, Oxford: Oxford University Press.

Harris, A. 1953. Veblen as Social Philosopher – A Reappraisal, *Ethics*, vol. 63, no. 3, part 2.

Harris, L. 2002. Achieving a Balance in Human Resourcing between Employee Rights and Care for the Individual, *Business and Professional Ethics Journal*, vol. 21, no. 2.

Harrison, M. R. 2005. *An Introduction to Business and Management Ethics*, Houndmills: Palgrave.

Hartman, E. 1996. *Organisational Ethics and the Good Life*, Oxford: Oxford University Press.

Haspels, N. & Jankanish, M. 2000. *Action Against Child Labour*, Geneva: International Labour Organisation.

Hatcher, T. 2002. *Ethics and HRD*, Cambridge: Perseus Press.

Heath, J. 2003. *Communicative Action and Rational Choice*, Cambridge: MIT Press.

Hegel, G. W. F. 1803/4. *System of Ethical Life*, edited and translated by T. M. Knox (1979), Albany: State University of New York Press. marxist.org/reference/hegel

Hegel, G. W. F. 1807. *The Phenomenology of Mind*, Mineola: Dover Publications (2003); see also: Phenomenology of Spirit, in: McNeill, W. & Feldman, K. (eds), 1998. *Continental Philosophy – An Anthology*, Oxford: Blackwell.

Hegel, G. W. F. 1811. *Encyclopedia of the Philosophical Science* (ed. Behler E., 1990), New York: Continuum.

Hegel, G. W. F. 1816. *The Science of Logic* (trans. by Miller A. V., 1969), London: Allen & Unwin.

Hegel, G. W. F. 1820. *Elements of the Philosophy of Right* (edited by Wood, A. W.; transl. by Nisbet, H. B.), Cambridge: Cambridge University Press (1991), see also: The Philosophy of Right, in: McNeill, W. & Feldman, K. (eds), 1998. *Continental Philosophy – An Anthology*, Oxford: Blackwell.

Hegel, G. W. F. 1830. *The Philosophy of History*, Mineola: Dover Publications.

Hinman, L. M. 2008. *Ethics – A Pluralistic Approach to Moral Theory* (4th ed.), Belmont: Thomson.

Hirschman, A. 1970. *Exit, Voice, and Loyalty: Responses to Decline in Firms, Organizations, and States*, Cambridge: Harvard University Press.

Hobbes, T. 1651. *Leviathan*, London: Dent.

Honneth, A. 1995. *The Struggle for Recognition – The Moral Grammar of Social Conflict*, Cambridge: Polity Press.

Honneth, A. & Gaines, J. 1988. Atomism and Ethical Life: On Hegel's Critique of the French Revolution, *Philosophy and Social Criticism*, vol. 14.

Horin, A. 2009. The recession that doesn't have to hurt if we share the pain, *Sydney Morning Herald*, 3rd to 4th January 2009, p. 19.

Horkheimer, M. 1937. Traditional and Critical Theory, in: Horkheimer, M. *Critical Theory – Selected Essays*, translated by O'Connell, M. J. et al., 1972, New York: Herder.

Horkheimer, M. 1947. *The Eclipse of Reason*, New York: Oxford University Press.

Horkheimer, M. 1974. *Critique of Instrumental Reason*, New York: Continuum Books.

Horkheimer, M. & Adorno, T. 1947. *Dialectic of Enlightenment*, London: Verso (1989).

Hosmer, L. T. 2008. *The Ethics of Management* (6th ed.), New York: McGraw-Hill.

Husserl, E. 1993. *Cartesian Meditations – An Introduction to Phenomenology*, London: Kluwer Publishers.

Hyman, R. 1987. Strategy or Structure, *Work, Employment & Society*, vol. 1, no. 1.

Jackall, R. 1988. *Moral Mazes – The World of Corporate Managers*, Oxford: Oxford University Press.

Jackson, F. & Smith, M. (eds) 2005. *The Oxford Handbook of Contemporary Philosophy*, Oxford: Oxford University Press.

Jacoby, R. 1977. *Social Amnesia: A Critique of Conformist Psychology from Adler to Laing*, Hassocks: Harvester Press.

Jacoby, R. 1997. *Social Amnesia – A Critique of Contemporary Psychology*, London: Transaction Publishers.

James, D. 2007. *Hegel – A Guide for the Perplexed*, London: Continuum.

Jameson, F. 1992. *Late Marxism – Adorno, or, The Persistence of the Dialectic*, London: Verso.

Janis, I. L. 1982. *Victims of Groupthinking*, Boston: Houghton Mifflin Press.

Jex, S. 2002. *Organisational Psychology – A Science-Practitioner Approach*, New York: Wiley.

Johnson, A. 2008. *Žižek's Ontology – Transcendental Materialist Theory of Subjectivity*, Evanston: Northwestern University Press.

Johnson, C. E. 2007. *Ethics in the Workplace – Tools and Tactics of Organizational Transformation*, Thousand Oaks: Sage.

Jones, C., Parker, M. & ten Bos, R. 2005. *For Business Ethics*, London: Routledge.

Kain, P. J. 1988. *Marx and Ethics*, Oxford: Clarendon Press.

Kagan, S. 1989. *The Limits of Morality*, Oxford: Clarendon Press.

Kant, I. 1781. Critique of Pure Reason, in: McNeill, W. & Feldman, K. (eds), 1998. *Continental Philosophy – An Anthology*, Oxford: Blackwell.

Kant, I. 1788. *The Critique of Practical Reason*, eBooks, Project Gutenberg.

Kant, I. 1790. *Critique of Moral Judgement*, Indianapolis (1987): Hackett Publishing Co.

Kaplan, R. S. & Norton, D. P. 1992. The Balanced Scorecard: Measures that Drive Performance, *Harvard Business Review*, Jan.–Feb., pp. 71–80.

Kaplan, R. S. & Norton, D. P. 1993. Putting the Balanced Scorecard to Work, *Harvard Business Review*, Sep.–Oct., pp. 2–16.

Kaplan, R. S. & Norton, D. P. 2004. The Strategy Map: Guide to Aligning Intangible Assets, *Strategy & Leadership*, vol. 32, no. 5, pp. 10–17.

Katz, D. & Kahn, R. 1966. *The Social Psychology of Organizations*, New York: Wiley.

Katz, J. J. 1980, Chomsky on Meaning, *Language*, vol. 51, no. 1.

Kedourie, E. 1995. *Hegel and Marx – Introductory Lectures*, Oxford: Blackwell.

Kelemen, M. & Peltonen, T. 2001. Ethics and Morality in the Subject: The Contribution of Zygmunt Bauman and Michael Foucault to 'Postmodern' Business Ethics, *Scandinavian Journal of Management*, vol. 17, pp. 151–166.

Kellner, D. 1989. *Jean Baudrillard – From Marxism to Postmodernity and Beyond*, Cambridge: Polity Press.

Kelly, M. (eds) 1994. *Critique and Power – Recasting the Foucault/Habermas Debate*, Cambridge: MIT Press.

Kemple, T. M. 2007. Spirits of Late Capitalism, *Theory, Culture & Society*, vol. 24.

Kinicki, A. & Kreitner, R. 2008. *Organizational Behavior – Key Concepts, Skills & Best Practices*, New York: McGraw-Hill.

Klikauer, T. 2007. *Communication and Management at Work*, Basingstoke: Palgrave.

Klikauer, T. 2008. *Management Communication – Communicative Ethics and Action*, Basingstoke: Palgrave.

Kohlberg, L. 1958. *The Development of Modes of Thinking and Choices in Years 10 to 16*, PhD Thesis at the University of Chicago (San Francisco: Harper & Row, 1981).

Kohlberg, L. 1971. From is to ought, in: Mishel, T. (eds), *Cognitive Development and Epistemology*, New York: Academic Press.

Kohlberg, L. 1973. The Claim to Moral Adequacy of a Highest Stage of Moral Judgement, *The Journal of Philosophy*, vol. 70, no. 18.

Kohlberg, L. 1981 and 1984. *Essays on Moral Development* (vols 1 and 2), San Francisco: Harper & Row.

Kohlberg, L. & Kramer, R. 1969. Continuities and Discontinuities in Child and Adult Moral Development, *Human Development*, vol. 12, pp. 93–120.

Kojève, A. 1947. *Introduction to the Reading of Hegel*, Ithaca (1969): New York: Basic Books and Cornell University Press (1986).

Korsgaard, C. M. 1996. *Creating the Kingdom of Ends*, Cambridge: Cambridge University Press.

Krailsheimer, A. 1980. *Pascal*, Oxford: Oxford University Press.

Krantz, S. 2002. *Refuting Peter Singer's Ethical Theory – The Importance of Human Dignity*, Westport: Praeger.

Kreitner, R. 2009. *Management* (11th ed.), Boston: Houghton Mifflin Harcourt Publishing.

Kropotkin, P. A. 1902. *Mutual Aid: A Factor of Evolution*, New York: Knopf Press [1916 & 1925].

Lachs, J. 1981. *Responsibility and the Individual in Modern Society*, Brighton: Harvester Press.

Laclau, E. 1977. *Politics and Ideology in Marxist Theory – Capitalism, Fascism, Populism*, London: Verso.

LaFollette, H. (eds) 2000. *The Blackwell Guide to Ethical Theory*, Oxford: Blackwell.

Layard, T. 2005. *Happiness – Lessons From A New Science*, London: Allan Lane.

Leap, T. 2007. *Dishonest Dollars: The Dynamics of White-Collar Crime*, Cornell: Cornell University Press.

Legge, K. 2005. *Human Resource Management – Rhetoric and Reality – Anniversary Edition*, London: MacMillan.

Lemov, R. 2006. *World as Laboratory – Experiments with Mice, Mazes and Men*, New York: Hill and Wang.

Leonard, R. 2010. *Von Neumann, Morgenstern, and the Creation of Game Theory: From Chess to Social Science, 1900–1960*, New York: Cambridge University Press.

Leslie, E. 2000. *Walter Benjamin – Overpowering Conformism*, London: Pluto.

Levi, A. W. 1941. Language and Social Action, *Ethics*, vol. 51, no. 3.

Levi-Strauss, C. 1962. *The Savage Mind*, London: Weidenfeld and Nicholson.

Levinas, E. 1961. *Totality and Infinity*, Pittsburgh: Duquesne University Press.

Levy, N. 2002. *Moral Relativism – A Short Introduction*, Oxford: Oneworld Press.

Lewin, K. 1951. *Field Theory in Social Science*, Westport: Greenwood Press.

Lieten, G. K. 2004. *Working Children around the World*, New Delhi: Institute for Human Development.

Light, A. & Roston, H. 2003. *Environmental Ethics – An Anthology*, Oxford: Blackwell.

Linstead, S., Fulop, L., Lilley, S., Banerjee, B. 2004. *Management and Organization – A Critical Text*, Basingstoke: Palgrave (see also 2009 edition).

Locke, J. 1690. *Second Treatise of Government*, New York (2004): Barnes & Noble Books.

Lockwood, D. 1964. *Social Integration and System Integration*, in G. K. Zollschau & W. Hirsch (eds), *Explanations in Social Change*, London: Routledge & Kegan Paul.

Lodziak, C. & Tatman, J. 1997. *Andre Gorz – A Critical Introduction*, London: Pluto.

Luhmann, N. 1991. Paradise Lost: On the Ethical Reflections of Morality: Speech on the Occasion of the Award of the Hegel Price 1988, *Thesis Eleven*, no. 29.

Lukács, G. 1922. *History and Class Consciousness*, London (1971): Merlin Press.

Lukács, G. 1980. *The Destruction of Reason*, London: Merlin Press.

Lukes, S. 1985. *Marxism and Morality*, Oxford: Oxford University Press.

Luxemburg, R. 1919. *The Russian Revolution, and Leninism or Marxism?* (new introduction by Wolfe, B. D.), Westport: Greenwood Press (1981 & 1961).

Lynd, R. S. 1939. *Knowledge For What? – The Place of Social Science in American Culture*, Princeton: Princeton University Press.

MacIntyre, A. 1989. *A Short History of Ethics*, London: Routledge.

Macklin, R. 2007. The Morally Decent HR Manager, in: Pinnington, A. et al., *Human Resource Management – Ethics and Employment* (eds), Oxford: Oxford University Press.

Magretta, J. 2002. *What Management is – How It Works and Why It's Everyone's Business*, New York: Free Press.

Mandell, B. 2002. The Privatisation of Everything, *New Politics*, vol. 9, no. 1.

Mander, J. 2001. The Rules of Corporate Behaviour, in: Goldsmith, E. & Mander, J. (eds), *The Case Against the Global Economy – And for a Turn Towards Localisation*, London: Earthscan Press.

Marcuse, H. 1941. *Reason and Revolution – Hegel and the Rise of Social Theory*, Boston (1961): Beacon.

Marcuse, H. 1964. *Industrialization and Capitalism in the Work of Max Weber*, republished in Negations, 1968.

Marcuse, H. 1966. *One-Dimensional Man: Studies in the Ideology of Advanced Industrial Societies*, Boston: Beacon Press.

Marcuse, H. 1972. *Studies in Critical Philosophy*, London: New Left Review Press.

Marglin, S. 1974. What do Bosses do? – The Origins and Functions of Hierarchy in Capitalist Production, *Review of Radical Political Economy*, vol. 6, no. 2.

Margolis, J. & Rockmore, T. (eds) 1999. *The Philosophy of Interpretation*, Oxford: Blackwell.

Martin, G. & Pear, J. 2007. *Behavior Modification – What It Is and How to Do It*, Upper Saddle River: Prentice Hall.

Marsden, R. & Townley, B. 1996. The Owl of Minerva: Reflections on Theory and Practice, in: Clegg, S., Hardy, C. & Nord, W. R. (eds), *Handbook of Organisation Studies*, London: Sage.

Marshall, L. 1976. *The !Kung of Nyae Nyae*, Cambridge: Harvard University Press.

Martin, M. W. 2007. *Everyday Morality – An Introduction to Applied Ethics* (4th ed.), Belmont: Thompson Press.

Marx, K. 1844. Economic and Philosophical Manuscripts, in: McLellan, D. (eds), *Karl Marx: Selected Writings*, Oxford: Oxford University Press.

Marx, K. 1847. *The Poverty of Philosophy*, Internet: Maxists.org.
Marx, K. 1890. *Das Kapital – Kritik der politischen Ökonomie (Capital – A Critique of Political Economy)*, Hamburg: 4th edited version by F. Engels, reprinted 1986: Berlin: Dietz-Press.
Mason, H. E. (eds) 1996. *Moral Dilemmas and Moral Theory*, Oxford: Oxford University Press.
McAlpine, A. 1998. *The New Machiavelli – The Art of Politics in Business*, New York: John Wiley.
McCarty, G. 1985. Marx's Social Ethics and Critique of Traditional Morality, *Studies in Soviet Thought*, vol. 29, pp. 177–199.
McCarthy, T. 1994. Kantian Constructivism and Reconstructivism: Rawls and Habermas in Dialogue, *Ethics*, vol. 105, no. 1.
Mead, G. H. 1930. The Philosophies of Royes, James, and Dewey in their American Setting, *International Journal of Ethics*, vol. 40, no. 2.
Melé, D. 2009. *Business Ethics in Action – Seeking Human Excellence in Organizations*, Houndmills: Palgrave.
Midgley, M. 1983. Duties Concerning Islands, *Encounter*, vol. 60, no. 2; reprinted in: Singer, P. 1994. *The Oxford Reader on Ethics*, Oxford: Oxford University Press.
Milgram, S. 1974. *Obedience to Authority*, New York: Harper and Row.
Mill, J. S. 1861. *Utilitarianism*, London [1861] (1985): Routledge & oll.livberty-fund.org/title/241.
Min, A. 1986. Hegel on Capitalism and the Common Good, *Philosophy and Social Criticism*, vol. 11.
Minkes, J. & Minkes, L. (eds) 2008. *Corporate and White-Collar Crime*, London: Sage.
Mintzberg, H. 1973. *The Nature of Managerial Work*, London: Harper & Row.
Monbiot, G. 2008. *Bring on the Apocalypse – Six Arguments for Global Justice*, London: Atlantic Books.
Monk, R. 1997. *Just Managing*, Sydney: McGraw-Hill.
Moore, E. G. 1903. *Pincipia Ehica*, Cambridge: Cambridge University Press.
Moore, M. 1989. *Roger & Me*, Warner Brothers (documentary), December 20, 1989 (USA), 91 min. English.
Moser, P. & Carson, T. (eds) 2001. *Moral Relativism – A Reader*, Oxford: Oxford University Press.
Mumby, D. 2001. Power and Politics, in: Jablin, F. & Putnam, L. (eds), *The New Handbook of Organisational Communication – Advances in Theory, Research, and Methods*, London: Sage.
Munro, I. 2008. Murdoch's World of Opportunity, *Sydney Morning Herald*, 6th December, Weekend Edition, p. 46.
Myerson, G. 1995. Hypothetical Dialogue and Intellectual History: Frege, Freud, and the Disarming of Negation, *History of Human Science*, vol. 8, no. 4.
Nazer, M. (2005), *Slave – My True Story*, New York: Public Affairs.
Negri, A. 1970. *The Political Descartes – Reason, Ideology, and the Bourgeois Project*, London: Verso.
Neumann, J. & Morgenstern, O. 1944. *Theory of Games and Economic Behaviour*, Princeton: Princeton University Press.
Nietzsche, F. 1880. *The Will to Power* (translated by Walter Kaufmann and R. J. Hollingsdale, 1968), New York: Random House.

Nozick, R. 1974. *Anarchy, State, and Utopia*, New York: Basic Books.

O'Connell Davidson, J. (2005), *Children in the Global Sex Trade*, Oxford: Polity Press.

Offe, C. & Wiesenthal, H. 1980. *Two Logics of Collective Action: Theoretical Notes on Social Class and Organisational Form*, in: Zeitlin, M. (eds), *Political Power and Social Theory – A Research Annual*, vol. 1, Greenwich: JAI Press.

Olen, J., van Camp, J. C. & Barry, V. E. 2005. *Applied Ethics – A Text with Readings* (9ᵗʰ ed.), Belmont: Thomson.

Orwell, G. 1949. *Nineteen Eighty-four*, London: Secker & Warburg.

Parker, I. 2004. *Slavoj Zizek – A Critical Introduction*, London: Pluto Press.

Parker, M. 1998. Business Ethics and Social Theory: Postmodernizing the Ethical, *British Journal of Management*, vol. 9 (September).

Parker, M. 2002. *Against Management – Organisation in the Age of Managerialism*, Cambridge: Polity Press.

Passer, M. & Smith, R. 2007: *Psychology – The Science of Mind and Behavior*, Boston: McGraw-Hill.

Perlmutter, D. D. 1997. Manufacturing Visions of Society and History in Textbooks, *Journal of Communication*, vol. 47, no. 3.

Petrick, J. A. & Quinn, J. F. 1997. *Management Ethics – Integrity at Work*, London: Sage.

Pinkard, T. 2000. *Hegel – A Biography*, Cambridge: Cambridge University Press.

Plesch, D. & Blankenburg, S. 2008. *How to Make Corporations Accountable*, London: Institute of Employment Rights.

Pogge, T. & Horton, K. 2008. *Global Ethics – Seminal Essays*, St Paul: Paragon House Press.

Poole, S. 2006. *Unspeak*, London: Little Brown.

Postone, M. 1993. *Time, Labor, and Social Domination*, Cambridge: Cambridge University Press.

Punch, M. 1996. *Dirty Business – Exploring Corporate Misconduct: Analysis and Cases*, London: Sage.

Punch, M. 2008. The Organisation, Did It – Individuals, Corporations and Crime, in: Minkes, J. & Minkes, L. (eds), *Corporate and White-Collar Crime*, London: Sage.

Rachels, J. 2003. *The Elements of Moral Philosophy* (4ᵗʰ ed.), Boston: McGraw-Hill.

Ramsay, H. 1977. Cycle of Control: Worker Participation in Sociological and Historical Perspective, in: *Sociology*, vol. 11, pp. 441–506.

Rawls, J. 1971. *A Theory of Justice*, Cambridge: Belknap Press of Harvard University Press.

Rawls, J. 1993. *Political Liberalism*, New York: Columbia University Press.

Reed, T. 1987. Review: Developmental Moral Theory, *Ethics*, vol. 97, no. 2.

Rees, S. & Rodley, G. (eds) 1995. *The High Cost of Managerialism*, Sydney: Pluto Press.

Regan, T. 2006. The Case for Animal Rights, in: Cahn, S. & Markie, P. (eds) 2006. *Ethics – History, Theory, and Contemporary Issues* (3ʳᵈ ed.), Oxford: Oxford University Press.

Reich, W. 1946. *The Mass Psychology of Fascism* (transl. by Wolfe, T. P.), New York: Orgone Institute Press; also: New York (1970): Farrar, Straus & Giroux.

Rest, J., Narvaez, D., Bebeau, M. J. & Thoma, S. J. 1999. *Postconventional Moral Thinking – A Neo-Kohlbergian Approach*, London: Lawrence Erlbaum.

Ricoeur, P. 1978. *The Rule of Metaphor*, London: Routledge.

Riezler, K. 1954. Political Decisions in Modern Society, *Ethics*, vol. 64, no. 2.

Ritter, J. 1982. *Hegel and the French Revolution*, Cambridge: MIT Press.

Rockmore, T. 1981. Human Nature and Hegel's Critique of Kantian Ethics, *Philosophy and Social Criticism*, vol. 8.

Rockmore, T. 1992. *Before and After Hegel – A Historical Introduction to Hegel's Thought*, Berkeley: University of California Press.

Rockmore, T. 2002. *Marx after Marxism – The Philosophy of Karl Marx*, Oxford: Blackwell.

Roper, C. 1983. Taming the Universal Machine, in: Aubrey, C. (eds), *The Making of 1984*, in: Aubrey, C. & Chilton, P. (eds), *Nineteen Eighty-Four in 1984 – Autonomy, Control & Communication*, London: Comedia Publishing Group.

Rosenfeld, P., Giacalone, R. A. & Riordan, C. 1995. *Impression Management in Organisations – Theory, Measures, Practice*, London: Routledge.

Ross, D. 1954. *Kant's Ethical Theory*, Oxford: Clarendon Press.

Rousseau, J. J. 1750. *A Discourse on the Moral Effects of the Arts and Science*, Dijon: Academy of Dijon.

Rousseau J. J. 1755. *Discourse on the Origins of Inequality*, http://oll.libertyfund.org & www.libertarian-alliance.org.uk.

Russell, J. M. 2007. *Philosophical Classics – The Thinking Person's Guide to Great Philosophical Books*, Wingfield: Cameron House.

Sage 2007. Management Ethics, in: *Encyclopedia of Business Ethics and Society*, London: Sage.

Sahlins, M. 1976. *Culture and Practical Reason*, Chicago: Chicago University Press.

Sample, R. J., Wills, C. W. & Sterba, J. P. 2004. *Philosophy – The Big Question*, Oxford: Blackwell.

Samson, D. & Daft, R. 2009. *Management* (3rd Asia Pacific Edition), Melbourne: Cengage Learning.

Sartre, J. P. 1992. *Being and Nothingness*, New York: Washington Square Press.

Schaefer, D. L. 2007. Procedural versus Substantive Justice: Rawls and Nozick, Social *Philosophy and Policy Foundations*, vol. 24, no. 1.

Scheler, M. 1928. *Man's Place in Nature* (transl. by Meyerhoff, H.), Boston: Beacon Press (1961).

Scherer, A. G. & Palazzo, G. 2007. Toward a Political Conception of Corporate Responsibility: Business and Society seen from a Habermasian Perspective, *Academy of Management Review*, vol. 32, no. 4.

Schrijvers, J. 2004. *The Way of the Rat – A Survival Guide to Office Politics*, London: Cyan Books.

Schrijvers, J. 2005. *The Monday Morning Feeling – A Book of Comfort for Sufferers*, London: Marshall Cavendish.

Schwartz, H. S. 1990. *Narcissistic Process and Corporate Decay – The Theory of the Organisational Ideal*, New York: New York University Press.

Searle, J. R. 1969. *Speech Acts – An Essay in the Philosophy of Language*, Cambridge: Cambridge University Press.

Searle, J. R. 1996. *The Construction of Social Reality*, London: Penguin Press.

Sedgwick, S. 2000. *The Reception of Kant's Critical Philosophy: Fichte, Schelling, and Hegel*, Cambridge: Cambridge University Press.

Sen, A. 1987. *On Ethics and Economics*, Oxford: Blackwell.

Shafer-Landau, R. 2007. *Ethical Theory: An Anthology*, Oxford: Blackwell.

Shafer-Landau, R. & Cueno, T. 2007. *Foundations of Ethics: An Anthology*, Oxford: Blackwell.

Sidgwick, H. 1874. *The Methods of Ethics*, London: Macmillan.

Sidgwick, H. 1889. Some Fundamental Ethical Controversies, *Mind*, vol. 14, no. 56.

Sikula, A. 1996. *Applied Management Ethics*, Chicago: Irwin.

Simon, H. 1951. A Formal Theory of the Employment Relationship, *Econometrica*, vol. 19, no. 3.

Simon, H. & Barnard, C. 1965. *Administrative Behavior – A Study of Decision-Making Process in Administrative Organization*, New York: The Free Press.

Simon, R. (eds) 2002. *The Blackwell Guide to Social and Political Philosophy*, Oxford: Blackwell.

Sinnerbrink, R. 2007. *Understanding Hegelianism*, London: Acumen Press.

Singer, P. 1972. Famine, Affluence, and Morality, *Philosophy and Public Affairs*, vol. 1, no. 3.

Singer, P. 1975. *Animal Liberation: A New Ethics for our Treatment of Animals*, New York: New York Review; Distributed by Random House

Singer, P. 1978. The Fable of the Fox and the Unliberated Animals, *Ethics*, vol. 88, no. 2.

Singer, P. 1980. *Marx*, Oxford: Oxford University Press.

Singer, P. 1983. *Hegel*, Oxford: Oxford University Press.

Singer, P. 1993. *Practical Ethics*, Cambridge: Cambridge University Press.

Singer, P. 1994. *The Oxford Reader on Ethics*, Oxford: Oxford University Press.

Singer, P. 2000. *Writings on an Ethical Life*, New York: Ecco Press.

Singer, P. 2005. *In Defense of Animals – The Second Wave*, Oxford: Blackwell.

Singer, P. 2007. All Animals are Equal, in: Shafer-Landau (eds), *Ethical Theory*, Oxford: Blackwell.

Smith, J. 1982. *Persuasion and Human Action – A Review and Critique of Social Influence Theories*, Belmond: Wadsworth Press.

Smith, S. B. 1987. Hegel's Idea of a Critical Theory, *Political Theory*, vol. 15, no. 1.

Speight, A. 2008. *The Philosophy of Hegel*, Stocksfield: Acumen Publishing.

Sterrett, J. M. 1892. The Ethics of Hegel, *International Journal of Ethics*, vol. 2, no. 2.

Steuerman, E. 2000. *The Bounds of Reason – Habermas, Lyotard, and Melanie Klein on Rationality*, London: Routledge.

Stewart, J. 2007. The Ethics of HRD, in: Rigg et al. (eds) *Critical Human Resource Development*, London: Prentice Hall.

Stoops, D. 1913. The Ethics of Industry, *International Journal of Ethics*, vol. 23, no. 4.

Styron, W. 1979. *Sophie's Choice – A Novel*, New York: Random House.

Subhabrata, B. B. 2007. *Corporate Social Responsibility – The Good, the Bad and the Ugly*, Cheltenham: Edward Elgar.

Taylor, C. 1975. *Hegel*, Cambridge: Cambridge University Press.

Taylor, C. 1991. *The Ethics of Authenticity*, Cambridge: Harvard University Press.

Taylor, F. W. 1911. *The Principles of Scientific Management*, New York: Norton Press (reprinted in Handel, M. (eds) 2003. *The Sociology of Organizations – Classic, Contemporary and Critical Readings*, London: Sage).

Taylor, P. W. 1981. *The Ethics of Respect of Nature*, in: Sample, R. et al. 2004. *Philosophy – the Big Question*, Oxford: Blackwell.

Taylor, P. W. 2004. The Ethics of Respect for Nature, in: Sample, R. et al. (eds), *Philosophy – The Big Question*, Oxford: Blackwell.

tenBos, R. 1997. Business Ethics and Bauman Ethics, *Organisation Studies*, vol. 18, no. 6.

tenBos, R. 2006. The Ethics of Business Communities, in: Clegg & Rhodes (eds), *Management Ethics – Contemporary Contexts*, London: Routledge.

Thompson, E. P. 1963. *The Making of the English Working Class*, London: Victor Gollancz.

Townley, B. 2005. Performance Appraisals and the Emergence of Management, in: Grey, C. & Willmott, H. (eds), *Critical Management Studies*, Oxford: University of Oxford Press.

Triado, J. 1984. Corporatism, Democracy, and Modernity, *Thesis Eleven*, no. 9.

Waldron, V., Cegala, D. J., Sharkey, W. F. & Teboul, B. 1990. Cognitive and Tactical Dimensions of Conversational Goal *Management, Journal of Language and Social Psychology*, vol. 9, no. 1–2.

Walsh, A. & Lynch, T. 2008. *The Morality of Money – An Exploration in Analytical Philosophy*, London: Macmillan.

Ward, A. 2006. *Kant – The Three Critiques*, Cambridge: Polity Press.

Warren, M. 1988. *Nietzsche and Political Thought*, Cambridge: MIT Press.

Watson, D. 2003. *Death Sentence – The Decay of Public Language*, Sydney: Knopf.

Watson, D. 2009. *Bendable Learnings: The Wisdom of Modern Management*, Sydney: Knopf.

Watson, J. 1894. The Problem of Hegel, *Philosophical Review*, vol. 3, no. 5.

Webb, B. & Webb, S. 1894. *The History of Trade Unionism*, London: Longmans.

Weber, M. 1904–05. *The Protestant Ethics and the Spirit of Capitalism*, London: Harper Collins (1930).

Weber, M. 1924. *Economy and Society*, Berkeley: University of California Press (reprint in: Handel, M. (eds) 2003. *The Sociology of Organizations – Classic, Contemporary and Critical Readings*, London: Sage).

Weber, M. 1947. *The Theory of Social and Economic Organization*, Oxford: Oxford University Press.

Whittington, R. 2001. *What is Strategy – And Does it Matter?* (2nd ed.), London: Routledge.

Whyte, W. H. 1961, *The Organisation Man*, Harmondsworth: Penguin.

Wiggins, D. 2006. *Ethics – Twelve Lectures on the Philosophy of Morality*, London: Penguin.

Williams, B. 1985. *Ethics and the Limits of Philosophy*, London: Fontana Press.

Williams, B. 2006. A Critique of Utilitarianism, in: Cahn, S. & Markie, P. (eds) 2006. *Ethics – History, Theory, and Contemporary Issues* (3rd ed.), Oxford: Oxford University Press.

Williams, R. 2002. *Managing Employee Performance*, London: Thomson.

Wilson, D. S. & Sober, E. (1994). Reintroducing Group Selection to the Human Behavioral Sciences, *Behavioral and Brain Sciences*, vol. 17, no. 4, pp. 585–654.

Windsor, D. 2006. Corporate Social Responsibility: Three Key Approaches, *Journal of Management Studies*, vol. 43, no. 1.

Wolff, M. 2008. *The Man Who Owns the News: Inside the Secret World of Rupert Murdoch*, New York: Broadway Books.

Wood, A. 1990. *Hegel's Ethical Thought*, Cambridge: Cambridge University Press.
Wren, D. A. 2005. *The History of Management Thought* (5th ed.), Hoboken: Wiley.
Young, S. 2003. *Moral Capitalism – Reconciling Private Interest with the Public Good*, San Francisco: Berrett-Koehler.
Zengotita, T. 2005. *Mediated – How the Media Shapes Your World and the Way You Live in it*, New York: Bloomsbury.
Žižek, S. 1989. *The Sublime Object of Ideology*, London: Verso Press.
Žižek, S. 1993. *Tarrying with the Negative – Kant, Hegel, and the Critique of Ideology*, Durham: Duke University Press.

Index